SERMONS

AUGUSTINIAN HERITAGE INSTITUTE

THE WORKS OF SAINT AUGUSTINE
A Translation for the 21st Century

Part III — Sermons
Volume 5: Sermons 148-183

The English translation of the works of Saint Augustine has been made possible with contributions from the following:

Order of Saint Augustine

    Province of Saint Thomas of Villanova (East)
    Province of Our Mother of Good Counsel (Midwest)
    Province of Saint Augustine (California)
    Province of Saint Joseph (Canada)
    Vice Province of Our Mother of Good Counsel
    Province of Our Mother of Good Counsel (Ireland)
    Province of Saint John Stone (England and Scotland)
    Province of Our Mother of Good Counsel (Australia)

    The Augustinians of the Assumption (North America)
    The Sisters of Saint Thomas of Villanova

Order of Augustinian Recollects

    Province of Saint Augustine

Mr. and Mrs. James C. Crouse
Mr. and Mrs. Paul Henkels
Mr. and Mrs. Francis E. McGill, Jr.
Mr. and Mrs. Mariano J. Rotelle

THE WORKS OF SAINT AUGUSTINE
A Translation for the 21st Century

SERMONS

III/5
(148-183)
on the New Testament

translation and notes
Edmund Hill, O.P.

editor
John E. Rotelle, O.S.A.

New City Press
New Rochelle, New York

Published in the United States by New City Press
86 Mayflower Avenue, New Rochelle, New York 10801
©1992 Augustinian Heritage Institute

Cover design by Ben D'Angio

Library of Congress Cataloging-in-Publication Data:

Augustine, Saint, Bishop of Hippo.
    The works of Saint Augustine.

    "Augustinian Heritage Institute"
    Includes bibliographical references and indexes.
    Contents: — pt. 3. Sermons.   v. 1. 1-19.
Introduction   /   Michele Pellegrino   —   pt. 3. Sermons on the Old
Testament.   v. 2   20-50 — [etc.] — pt. 3.   Sermons on the
New Testament.   v. 3. 51-94. v. 4.   94A-147A. v. 5. 148-183.
    1.   Theology — Early Church, ca. 30-600.   I. Hill,
Edmund.   II. Rotelle, John E.   III. Augustinian
Heritage Institute.   IV. Title.
BR65.A5E53   1990   270.2   89-28878
ISBN 0-911782-75-3 (pt. 3, v. 1)
ISBN 0-911782-78-8 (pt. 3, v. 2)
ISBN 0-911782-85-0 (pt. 3, v. 3)
ISBN 1-56548-000-7 (pt. 3, v. 4)
ISBN 1-56548-007-4 (pt. 3, v. 5)

Nihil Obstat: John E. Rotelle, O.S.A., S.T.L.
Delegated Censor
Imprimatur: Thomas V. Daily, D.D.
Bishop of Brooklyn
Brooklyn, New York: October 6, 1992

Printed in the United States

CONTENTS

and healed — 91; How "in the flesh" — 91; How "in the Spirit" — 92; Death—and life—now — 92; Death—and life—to come — 93 loved the stately home on high, but have been ignorant of the humble way there — 131; You are aiming at Christ exalted on high; come back to him crucified on the cross — 131; Circumcision is the sign of the Old Testament; the cross is the sign of the New Testament — 132; Do not be ungrateful for grace — 133

Lying — 208; If you put aside lying, take off Adam; if you speak the truth, put on Christ — 208; Put on Christ, and you will be truthful — 209; God wants to make you a god, by his gift and by adoption — 209

Sermons

SERMON 148

ON THE WORDS OF THE ACTS OF THE APOSTLES 5:4: *WHILE IT REMAINED WITH YOU, DID IT NOT REMAIN*, ETC. PREACHED AT THE SHRINE OF THE TWENTY HOLY MARTYRS ON THE SUNDAY AFTER EASTER

Date: after 409[1]

Temporal death is not a severe punishment

1. When the reading from the book entitled the Acts of the Apostles was read, you will have noticed what happened to those who sold a property, kept back some of the price of the property, and laid the rest at the feet of the apostles as though it were the whole price. Straightaway, on being rebuked, they both expired, the man and his wife. Some people think this punishment was too severe, that people should die just for withholding money from their assets. The Holy Spirit, though, didn't do this out of avarice, but the Holy Spirit in this way punished a lie. I mean, you heard the words of the blessed Peter, who said, *While it remained with you, did it not remain, and on being sold, was it not in your power?* If you didn't want to sell, who was forcing you to? If you wanted to offer half the price, who was exacting the whole of it? I mean if half was what you intended to offer, half is what you should have called it. To offer half as though it were the whole, that's the lie that had to be punished.

In any case, brothers and sisters, we shouldn't think of temporal death as being a severe punishment. If only, indeed, punishment stopped there![2] After all, did anything very dreadful happen to mortal creatures who were going to die anyway, some time or other? But God wished by their temporal punishment to leave us in no doubt about his discipline. In any case, we may well believe that after this life God spared them, for great is his mercy.[3]

About deaths which occur as a punishment the apostle Paul has something to say somewhere, when he is rebuking those who were going wrong in their treatment of Christ's body and blood; he says, *That is why there are many who are weak and sick among you, and a sufficient number are asleep*; as many, that is, as are sufficient to impose discipline. Many among you are falling asleep, that is, are dying. You see, they were being disciplined by the scourge of the Lord, they were falling sick and dying. And he went on, after these words, to say, *For if we judged ourselves, we would not be judged by the Lord. But when*

17

we are judged, we are being rebuked by the Lord, in order not to be condemned with the world (1 Cor 11:30-32). So what if something like that happened to this man and his wife? They were corrected with the scourge of death, in order not to be punished with eternal torment.

The fulfillment of vows

2. Would your graces please consider this one point, that if God was displeased by people keeping back some of the money they had vowed (and that money of course was needed for human use), how angry God must be when chastity is vowed and not kept; when virginity is vowed and not kept! This, you see, is vowed for God's use, not that of human beings. What's this I've said, for God's use? It's because God makes himself a house out of the saints, makes himself a temple in which he is pleased to dwell; and of course he wants his temple to remain holy. So to a virgin nun who marries, one can say what Peter said about money: "While your virginity remained with you, did it not remain? And before you vowed it, was it not in your power?" But any women who have done this, have made such vows and not kept them, should not imagine they will just be corrected with a temporal death; they must realize they will be condemned to eternal fire.[4]

NOTES

1. One scholar dates this sermon after 409, another after 412. It is rather an odd sermon to be preached on the Sunday after Easter. Normally Augustine would have been addressing his remarks on this Sunday to the newly baptized in his cathedral church. It seems unlikely that on this occasion, at a local shrine dedicated to the twenty holy martyrs, whoever they were, there were any of these newly baptized Christians present. Presumably a number of nuns were. After being surprisingly lenient (for a preacher of those times) on Ananias and Sapphira, Augustine becomes excessively harsh, to our modern way of thinking, on nuns who after taking the vow of chastity later decide to marry. He makes no mention of religious men who do the same thing, though presumably his strictures would apply equally to them. There was presumably some particular occasion for his remarks; but there is just a whiff here of the pagan Roman savagery (a juster word, I think, than severity) toward any of the Vestal Virgins who were found to have been unchaste.

2. He is clearly only thinking of death as a punishment from God, as in this case, and the others at Corinth which he goes on to mention. He is saying nothing one way or the other about capital punishment in criminal law.

3. See Ps 51:1.

4. Without even the possibility of repentance? This is hardly the note on which one expects the great pastor to end his sermon.

SERMON 149

ON FOUR QUESTIONS: FIRST ON PETER'S VISION: ACTS 10;
THEN ON THREE QUESTIONS ARISING FROM THE SERMON ON THE MOUNT:
MATTHEW 5:16 AND 6:1; 6:3; 5:44

Date: 412[1]

Peter's vision

1. I remember that the day before last Sunday I became a debtor to your holinesses on the subject of some questions propounded from the scriptures.[2] The time has come to pay, if the Lord is good enough to enable me to do so. I don't like being in debt too long, except for the one debt of charity, which is always being paid and always being owed.

I said then that we would have to inquire about Peter's vision, what the meaning could be of that *receptacle, like a linen sheet let down from heaven by four lines, and in it were all the four-footed beasts of the earth, and creeping things, and birds of the sky*; and of what Peter was told by the divine voice, *Kill and eat* (Acts 10:11-13); and of its being done three times, and then taken up.

Immoderate use of God's gifts is a sin

2. Against those who choose to think that Peter was being ordered by the Lord God to be a glutton, it is easy to argue. First of all, because even if we were to choose to take literally the command, *Kill and eat*, killing and eating is not a sin; what is a sin is immoderate use of God's gifts, which he has allotted to human use.

Eating certain meat—symbolic sign of future realities

3. The Jews, you see, had accepted that there were certain animals which they could eat, and others from which they must abstain. The apostle Paul makes it clear that they received this law as a symbolic sign of future realities, when he says, *Therefore let no one judge you over food or over drink, or over the matter of a festival day or new moon or sabbath, which is all a shadow of things to come* (Col 2:16-17). And so now, in the time of the Church, he says some-

19

where else, *All things are clean for the clean; but it is bad for the person who eats so as to give cause for offense* (Tit 1:15; Rom 14:20).

At the time the apostle wrote this, you see, there were people who used to eat meat in such a way as to make the weak stumble. You see, the sacrificial flesh of animals the diviners used to sacrifice[3] was then sold in the butchers' shops, and many of the brethren used to abstain from eating any meat at all, in case even in ignorance they should come upon cuts from animals from which sacrifice had been made to idols. That's why the same apostle says elsewhere, in case consciences should be worried stiff with fear, *Anything up for sale at the butcher's, eat without asking any questions for the sake of conscience, for the earth is the Lord's and its fullness* (Ps 24:1). And again, *But if any unbeliever invites you, and you want to go, eat everything that is set before you without making any distinctions because of conscience. But if someone tells you that it is sacrificial meat, do not eat it, for the sake of the one who has pointed it out, and for the sake of conscience* (1 Cor 10:25-28). So in these matters everything is established as being clean or unclean, not in virtue of physical contact, but in virtue of purity of conscience.

The meaning of the forbidden animals

4. That's why a freedom has been granted to Christians that was not granted to Jews. It's because all the animals which the Jews were forbidden to eat are signs of things, and, as it says, *shadows of things to come*. As for example, what was prescribed for them that any animals which chew the cud and have cloven hoofs they could eat; but any which lack one or other of these conditions, or both of them, they should not eat; certain kinds of people are here signified who do not belong to the company of the saints.

The cloven hoof, you see, refers to morals,[4] the chewing of the cud to wisdom. Why does the cloven hoof signify good morals? Because it doesn't slip easily; slipping up, you see, is the sign of sin. And how does chewing the cud refer to the teaching of wisdom? Because scripture says, *A desirable treasure rests in the mouth of the wise man, while the foolish man swallows it* (Prv 21:20 LXX). So those who hear, and out of carelessness forget, so to say swallow what they have heard, so that they no longer have a taste of it in the mouth, but just bury what they hear under forgetfulness.[5] But those who meditate on *the law of the Lord day and night* (Ps 1:2) are chewing the cud, as it were, and enjoying the flavor of the word with a kind of palate of the heart. So the commandment given to the Jews signifies what sort of people do not belong to the Church, that is to the body of Christ, to the grace and company of the saints; those, namely, who are either heedless listeners, or have bad morals, or who are to be censured for both kinds of vice.

Christians not bound by Jewish observances

5. So too all the rest of the commandments given to the Jews in this way are shadowy signs of things to come. After the light of the world, our Lord Jesus

Christ, has come, they are read only in order to be understood, not also in order to be observed.[6] So Christians have been given the freedom not to observe this idle custom, but to eat what they like, in moderation, with a blessing, with thanksgiving. So perhaps Peter too was told *Kill and eat* in this sense, that he need no longer be bound to Jewish observances; he was not, however, being ordered to satisfy an insatiable maw or become a disgusting glutton.

Symbolic meaning of Peter's vision

6. But all the same, to prove to you that all this was a symbolic showing, that vessel contained creeping things; could he possibly eat creeping things? So what does all this symbolism mean? That receptacle signifies the Church; the four lines it was hanging from are the four quarters of the earth, through which the Catholic Church stretches, being spread out everywhere. So all those who wish to go apart into a party,[7] and to cut themselves off from the whole, do not belong to the sacred reality signified[8] by the four lines. But if they don't belong to Peter's vision, neither do they do so to the keys which were given to Peter. You see, God says his holy ones are to be gathered together at the end from the four winds,[9] because now the gospel faith is being spread abroad through all those four cardinal points of the compass. So those animals are the nations. All the Gentile nations, after all, were unclean in their errors and superstitions and lusts before Christ came; but at his coming their sins were forgiven them and they were made clean. Therefore now, after the forgiveness of sins,[10] why should they not be received into the body of Christ, which is the Church of God, which Peter was standing for?

Peter represents the Church

7. It's clear, you see, from many places in scripture that Peter can stand for, or represent, the Church; above all from that place where it says, *To you will I hand over the keys of the kingdom of heaven. Whatever you bind on earth shall also be bound in heaven; and whatever you loose on earth shall also be loosed in heaven* (Mt 16:19). Did Peter receive these keys, and Paul not receive them? Did Peter receive them, and John and James and the other apostles not receive them? Or are these keys not to be found in the Church, where sins are being forgiven every day? But because Peter symbolically stood for the Church, what was given to him alone was given to the whole Church.

So Peter represented the Church; the Church is the body of Christ. Let him then receive the Gentiles now made clean, their sins having been forgiven; that's why the Gentile Cornelius had sent for him, and the Gentiles who were with him. This man's charities had been accepted and had cleansed him after a fashion;[11] it only remained for him, like clean food, to be incorporated into the Church, that is, into the Lord's body. Peter, though, was worried about handing the gospel over to the Gentiles, because those of the circumcision who believed were not allowing the apostles to hand on the Christian faith to the uncircumcised; and they were saying they ought not to be admitted to share in the gospel unless they accepted circumcision, which had been the tradition of their ancestors.[12]

The receptacle

8. So that receptacle removed this hesitation of his; and that's why after that vision he was given the nod by the Holy Spirit to go down and go with the men who had come from Cornelius; and off he went. Cornelius, you see, and the people with him were to be regarded as being among those animals which had been shown him in that receptacle; God, however, had already made them clean, because he had accepted the charitable acts they had performed from there.[13] So now they had to be killed and eaten; that is, the old life in which they had not known Christ was to be slain in them, and they were to pass over into his body, as into the new life of the fellowship of the Church.

Peter too, I mean, when he came to them, briefly told them what he had been shown in that vision. He said, you see, *And you people know how unlawful it is for a man who is a Jew to associate with or visit a foreigner;*[14] *but God showed me not to call any person common or unclean* (Acts 10:28). God showed him this, of course, when those words were heard, *What God has cleansed, do not you call unclean* (Acts 11:9). And afterward on coming to the brethren in Jerusalem, when some of them kicked up a fuss because he had handed on the gospel to Gentiles, he calmed their agitation by telling them too of the same vision; which there would have been no point in telling them about unless it referred precisely to this question.

The linen sheet

9. Some perhaps may also want to know why the thing in which those animals were seen was made of linen.[15] Of course there must be some reason. You see, we know that linen is resistant to moths, which spoil other fabrics. Let us all shut out from our hearts the moths of bad desires, and thus keep ourselves strong and unspoiled in the faith, with no depraved thoughts eating into it like moths, if we wish to belong to the sacred reality signified by that linen sheet, in which the Church is represented.

The triple letting down

10. Why was it let down three times from heaven? Because all these nations, who belong to the four quarters of the globe, where the Church signified by the four lines to which that receptacle was connected is being sown like seed, are baptized in the name of the Trinity. They are being renewed by believing in the name of the Father and of the Son and of the Holy Spirit, in order to belong to the company and communion of the saints. So the four lines and the triple letting down also yields the number twelve of the apostles; as though three each were allotted to the four quarters. Four threes, you see, make twelve. I think that's enough, don't you, about this vision.[16]

11. Another question we put off dealing with was why the Lord, in the sermon which he preached on the mountain, said *Let your works shine before men, so that they may see your good deeds, and glorify your Father in heaven* (Mt 5:16); and a little later in the same sermon said, *Beware of performing your justice before men, to be seen by them*; and also, *Let your giving of alms be in secret, and your Father who sees in secret will pay you back* (Mt 6:1.4).

Very often when doing good, people wobble between these two admonitions, not knowing which one to comply with, when of course they want to comply with the advice of the Lord, who gave them both. How will our works shine before men, so that they may see our good deeds; and again, how will our giving of alms be in secret? If I want to observe this one, I offend against that one; if I observe that one, I sin on this side. So each place of scripture has to be treated and tempered in such a way as to show that the divine precepts and admonitions cannot contradict each other. What I mean is, that what seems to be a conflict here in words calls for a peaceful understanding. Only let each of us be in harmony with God's word in our hearts, and there will be no disharmony in scripture.

12. So imagine a person giving alms in such a way, that if it's at all possible absolutely nobody knows about it, not even the one it's being given to; so that to avoid even his seeing it, she prefers to put out something for him to find rather than to offer him something to receive. What more could she do to conceal her almsgiving? She of course runs foul of that other saying, and does not do what the Lord tells us: *Let your works shine before men, so that they may see your good deeds* (Mt 5:16). Nobody sees her good deeds, she is not inviting imitation. As far as she is concerned, the rest of them will remain sterile, thinking that nobody does what God commanded, if people so act that their good works cannot be seen; though someone who is shown a good example to imitate is being done a greater kindness, than someone who is offered food to nourish the body.

Now imagine another person, advertising his almsgiving among the people and boasting about it all, and only wanting to be admired for it all; let his works shine before men. Notice that he is not offending against that admonition; but he is offending against the other one, where the Lord says, *Let your giving of alms be in secret* (Mt 6:4). Anyone of this sort even grows slack if some godless people turn up to object perhaps to what he is doing. He depends totally on the tongues of admirers; he is like the virgins who don't take any oil with them.

You know, of course, about the five foolish virgins who didn't take any oil with them, and the other wise ones who did take oil with them. The lamps of all of them were shining; but some didn't have anything with them to feed that light on, and they were distinguished from the others who did, by being called foolish, while the others were called wise.[17] So what's the meaning of bringing oil with you, if not having the conscious intention of pleasing God with your good works, and not just doing it for the ultimate pleasure of being admired by men who cannot see your intentions? That you do it, I mean, any man can see; but with what kind of intention you do it only God can see.

13. So now let's imagine some people who follow both admonitions, obey each of them. They offer bread to the hungry, and offer it in the presence of others whom they wish to encourage to imitate them. In this they themselves also imitate the apostle, where he says, *Be imitators of me, as I too am of Christ* (1 Cor 11:1). So they offer their bread to the poor, openly for all to see in their work, devoted to God in their hearts. Whether they are thereby seeking admiration for themselves or glory for God, no human being can see, no human being can judge. Yet any who are prepared to imitate them with an eager good will, can believe that the good they see being done is done with a devout and religious intention; and they praise God, at whose command and by whose grace they see such things being done.

So their works are open and public, so that people may see, and glorify the Father who is in heaven; but their motives[18] are in the heart, so that their giving of alms may be in secret, and the Father who sees in secret may pay them back. These people have kept the due proportion, ignoring neither admonition, carrying out each one. They take care, you see, that their justice is not performed before men; that is, that they don't make it their object to be admired by men, seeing that they wished the praise for their good works to go to God, not themselves. But because this will or intention is inside in their consciences, it follows that their giving of alms was done hiddenly in secret, to be rewarded by the one from whom nothing is hidden. Is there anybody, after all, who can reveal his heart to people when he does something, to show with what conscious intention he does it?[19]

14. As a matter of fact, brothers and sisters, the Lord weighed the very words he used carefully enough. Notice how he puts it: *Beware of performing your justice before men, to be seen*, he says, *by them* (Mt 6:1). Thus[20] he stated the aim when he said *to be seen by them*; this aim is wrong and reprehensible, to wish to do good just to win people's admiration, and not to look for anything further. So anyone who just does it in order to be seen by men is faulted by the Lord in this judgment of his.

In the place, though, where he bids us have our deeds seen by men, he didn't state that as the aim, so that it would simply be a matter of people seeing us and admiring us; but he went on from there to God's glory, to direct our intention in doing good as far as that. *Let your works*, he said, *shine before men, so that they may see your good deeds*; but that is not what you should be looking for.

For what, then? He adds something else, and says, *and may glorify your Father who is in heaven* (Mt 5:16). If that's what you are looking for, that God may be glorified, don't be afraid of being seen by men. Even when you are, your giving of alms is in secret, where he alone whose glory you seek can see that that is what you are seeking.

So it is that the apostle Paul, after the persecutor of the gospel has been laid low and the preacher of it lifted up to his feet, can say, *But I was not known personally to the churches of Judaea which were in Christ. But they had only been hearing that the one who used to persecute us once, now preaches the good news of the faith which he once used to ravage; and in me*, he says, *they glorified God* (Gal 1:22-24). He wasn't rejoicing because the man who had received the grace was getting well known, but because God who had given it was being praised.

He himself said, after all, *If I were still pleasing men, I would not be Christ's servant* (Gal 1:10). And yet in another place he says, *Just as I too try to please everyone in everything.* Here too we have the same problem. But what does he add? *Not seeking*, he says, *my own interests, but those of the many, that they may be saved* (1 Cor 10:33). That's the same as what he says in the other place, *and in me they glorified God*; also as what the Lord says, *that they may glorify your Father who is in heaven.* That, you see, is when they are saved, when in the works which they see done by men they glorify the one from whom men received the grace to do these things.

The left and right hands

15. There are two questions left; but I'm afraid of being a burden to those of you who are easily bored, while again I'm afraid of cheating those of you who are still hungry. Still, I remember what I have answered, and what I am owing. It remains to see what the meaning is of, *Do not let your left hand know what your right hand is doing* (Mt 6:3); and also on the subject of loving one's enemy, why the people of old were apparently authorized to hate the enemies whom we are commanded to love. But what am I to do? If I explain these points briefly, perhaps I won't be understood in the right way; if I take a bit longer, I'm afraid I may weigh you down with the load of my words, rather than lift you up with the results of my explanations. But certainly, if you grasp less than is satisfactory to you, hold me in your debt to talk about these things more fully some other time. All the same we ought not to leave them now with absolutely nothing said about them.

The left hand of the spirit is material greed, the right hand of the spirit is spiritual love. So if, when you give alms, you mix in some greed for temporal advantages, hoping to gain some such thing from that good work, you are mixing the left hand's knowledge with the right hand's works. But if you come to a person's help out of simple charity and with a pure conscience before God, with an eye on nothing else but to please the one who enjoins such acts, then your left hand does not know what your right hand is doing.

16. The question, though, about loving one's enemy is more difficult, and cannot be answered so shortly. But while you are listening, pray for me; and perhaps God will quickly give us what we imagine to be difficult. We all live, after all, from one and the same storeroom, because we are all in one and the same household. So what you and I imagine to be hidden away somewhere in the furthest corner cupboard, perhaps the one who is dealing out[21] the rations is placing on the doorstep, so that it can be most easily given to those who ask for it.

The Lord Christ himself loved his enemies; didn't he say, hanging on the cross, *Father, forgive them, because they do not know what they are doing* (Lk 23:34)? Stephen followed his example, when stones were being hurled at him, and said, *Lord, do not hold this crime against them* (Acts 7:59). The servant imitated his Lord, so that none of the other servants might be reluctant, and imagine that doing this was something only the Lord could do. So if it's too hard for us to imitate the Lord, let us imitate our fellow servant. After all, we have all been called to the same grace.

So why were the ancients told, *You shall love your neighbor and hate your enemy* (Mt 5:43)?[22] Because, perhaps they were also told the truth; but it has been told us more openly, thanks to the succession of the ages, through the presence in our New Testament age of the one who could see what needed to be concealed and what plainly revealed and for whom. Thus,[23] you see, we do have an enemy whom we are never ordered to love; but it's the devil. *You shall love your neighbor*, a human being; *and hate your enemy*, the devil. But while enmities often arise among men toward us, in the minds of those who by their disbelief give the devil a foothold[24] and become his instruments, enabling him to operate through the children of unbelief;[25] still it can happen that a person relinquishes his ill-will and is converted to the Lord. So even while he is still ranting and roaring, and persecuting, he is to be loved, and prayed for, and done good to. In this way you will both fulfill the old commandment to love your neighbor, a man, and hate your enemy, the devil; and also fulfill the new one to love your enemies, men, and to pray for those who persecute you.

17. Unless of course you assume that Christians at that time didn't pray for Saul the persecutor of Christians. Perhaps his conversion was due to those words of the martyr Stephen being heard. After all, he was among the number of his persecutors, and watched over the clothes of those who stoned him.[26] Furthermore, the same man writing to Timothy said, *I beg you above all to have prayers, supplications, intercessions and thanksgivings made for all men, for kings and all who are in high places, that we may lead a quiet and tranquil life* (1 Tm 2:1-2). So he was giving instructions for kings to be prayed for; and at that time the kings were persecuting the Churches. Yes, they were then persecuting the Churches that were praying for them; they are now protecting the Churches that were heard for them.

18. So do you also want to keep that command given to the people of old? Love your neighbor, that is, every human being. After all, we all derive from the first two parents, so we are of course all neighbors. In any case, there is no doubt that the same Lord Jesus Christ who commands enemies to be loved, testified that the whole law and the prophets depend on those two command- ments: *You shall love the Lord your God with your whole heart, and your whole soul, and your whole mind*; and, *You shall love your neighbor as yourself* (Mt 22:37-40). He said nothing there about loving one's enemy. So does that mean these two commandments don't contain the whole? What an idea! Because when he says, *You shall love your neighbor*, that includes all human beings, even though they are enemies; because even in terms of spiritual relationship,[27] you don't know what the person, who for the moment seems to be your enemy, really means to you in God's foreknowledge. Since God's patience, you see, is leading him to repentance,[28] perhaps he will come to acknowledge and follow your lead.

God, after all, though he knows who are going to persist in their sins, who are going to forsake justice and lapse irrevocably into iniquity, still makes his sun rise on the good and the bad, and sends rain on the just and the unjust,[29] inviting them of course to repentance by his patience, so that those who are indifferent to his goodness may experience at the last his severity. How ready, then, should we be at all times to be easily placated, in case perhaps by concen- trating only on someone's present hostility toward us, and not knowing how he is going to turn out in the future, we end up by hating someone with whom we are going to share a reign of eternal bliss.

So then, carry out the old commandment: love your neighbor, every human being; and hate your enemy, the devil. Also carry out the new one: love your enemies, but your human ones; pray for those who persecute you, for human beings; do good to those who hate you, to human beings.[30]

19. *If your enemy is hungry, feed him; if he is thirsty, give him a drink; for by so doing you will heap coals of fire upon his head* (Rom 12:20). Here too there is a question. I mean, how can you love someone you wish to burn up with coals? But if it's properly understood, there is no argument. It's said about those devastating coals which are to be given people against their deceitful tongues.[31] You see, when you do your enemy a kindness, and are not overcome by the evil in him, you will have overcome evil with good;[32] often enough he will repent of his hostility and be angry with himself, because he has harmed such a good person. That burning, then, is repentance, which like coals of fire consumes his hostility and ill-will.

NOTES

1. Two scholars give this date; one dates the sermon to 400. I have very considerably abbreviated the title as given by the Maurists, which runs: "In which questions are solved from the Acts of the Apostles (ch. 10) and from the gospel; or on four questions: the first on Peter's vision; the second on the words of the gospel, *Let your light shine before men, so that they may see your good deeds*, and shortly afterward, *Beware of performing your justice before men, in order to be seen by them*, etc.; the third on the words of the gospel, *Do not let your left hand know what your right hand is doing*; the fourth on loving one's enemy (Mt 5:16; 6:1-4; 5:43-46)." This, I take it, was the composition of an over-conscientious copyist.

2. I cannot trace which sermon he is referring to.

3. Not necessarily soothsayers (*haruspices*). But Augustine, with his Latin, Roman background, would naturally think of animals slaughtered in order to divine by examining their entrails, usually the liver. The rest of the carcass would then be sold to the butchers. But he goes on to widen the scope of the matter to include any idolatrous sacrifice.

4. For us the cloven hoof has become the sign of the devil, along with horns and tail, because of the medieval representation of him as a goat. Augustine, it seems, knew nothing of that; as it is part of being a clean animal, its significance must be positive, not negative.

5. Memory, at every level of consciousness—or even of the unconscious—played a prominent part in Augustine's spiritual psychology, as can be seen from the last three books of the *Confessions* and books IX - XIV of *The Trinity*. Forgetfulness, negligence, heedlessness, carelessness—they are all much the same thing, and the mark of the fool. See Jas 1:23-24, which he may have had at the back of his mind. He never made Luther's mistake of dismissing this letter as an epistle of straw.

6. This is an important practical principle for a specifically Christian interpretation of the Old Testament. We still receive it as the word of God, as inspired scripture, unlike the Manichees and other ancient dualists like Marcion. But we receive it in the framework of the history of salvation, in a context of promise, of foreshadowing and preparation, leading to fulfillment. This is pre-eminently the view of Paul: 1 Cor 13:11; Gal 3-4.

7. He is referring specifically to the Donatists.

8. *Sacramentum.*

9. See Mk 13:27.

10. By this he seems here to mean the great act of redemption that secured the forgiveness of all sins, Christ's death and resurrection.

11. See Acts 10:1-5.

12. Augustine is getting the sequence of events slightly mixed up. It was not until some years after the baptism of Cornelius that the party of the circumcision sent people to Antioch to insist that Gentile converts must be circumcised (Acts 15:1).

13. That is, from the receptacle; from their pagan situation, not yet "killed and eaten" by the Church.

14. *Alienigenam*, translating the equivalent Greek word, which is regularly employed by the Septuagint, not for all and any Gentiles, but specifically for the Philistines. It is an interesting point that Caesarea, where Cornelius was stationed, was in the old Philistine territory.

15. One reason that has been suggested, which would never have occurred to Augustine, and which he would have regarded as totally insignificant if he had been told about it, was that Peter in Joppa was by the sea, and from the roof of the house on which he was resting he could see all the sails of the boats on the water. so the "receptacle" he saw in his vision would have been a sail. Perhaps ancient sails were made of linen before canvas was invented—or perhaps canvas is a very strong, coarse linen.

16. He probably felt he was running out of numerological steam. For Augustine's fascination with the "mystique" of numbers see Sermon 51, note 1.

17. See Mt 25:23.

18. Reading *affectus* instead of the *effectus* of the printed text, which may well be a misprint.

19. Most of us, I suppose, would be inclined to answer "Yes." Our actions can and do reveal our motives and intentions. To which Augustine would reply that they do not do so demonstratively. Other people can never see our motives or intentions as they can see, and judge, our actions; they can only infer them, from probable (or improbable) opinions about them, believe that they are what we say they are, or what our actions seem to betray them to be. In this he is warmly supported by Newman, who throughout his public life campaigned against the habit of attributing bad motives to opponents, whose actions and expressed opinions were, perhaps rightly, disapproved of.

20. Reading *Sic* instead of the *Si*, If, of the text.

21. *Qui promittit*; this would normally mean "the one who promises." But here I think the basic meaning of the word, of "putting or bringing forward," must be intended. God is being pictured as the storeman issuing stores.

22. The second part, "and hate your enemy," is not to be found in the Law of Moses; so one could say that it was not a command given to the ancients. But as Jesus says it was, Augustine could not possibly get out of the problem that way! The extra phrase would seem to be a gloss put on the law (Lv 19:18) by what he elsewhere calls the tradition of the elders.

23. Again reading *Sic* instead of *Si*.

24. See Eph 4:27.

25. See Eph 5:6.

26. See Acts 7:58.

27. This is nowadays the official term for the relationship between godparents and godchildren. It could have been so in Augustine's day, and he may have been saying, "You may one day find yourself sponsor at the baptism of the person who is now your enemy." But he probably meant it in a much wider sense, and considered Paul, for example, to be the spiritual son of Stephen.

28. See Rom 2:4.

29. See Mt 5:45.

30. See Mt 5:44.

31. See Ps 120:3-4.

32. See Rom 12:21.

SERMON 150

ON THE WORDS OF THE ACTS OF THE APOSTLES 17:18-34: *BUT SOME EPICUREAN AND STOIC PHILOSOPHERS BEGAN DEBATING WITH HIM*, ETC.

Date: 413-414[1]

The preaching of Paul in Athens

1. Your graces will have noticed, together with me, when the book of the Acts of the Apostles was being read, that Paul spoke to the Athenians, and that those of them who were contemptuous of the preaching of the truth called him *a sower of words* (Acts 17:18).[2] It was said, certainly, by scoffers, but it should not be rejected by believers. After all, that man was indeed a sower of words, but also a harvester of good deeds. I too, midget though I am and in no way to be compared to his pre-eminence, am sowing the words of God in God's field, which is your hearts, and am looking for a bumper harvest of good habits from you.

However, I would urge your graces to pay particular attention to what is contained in this reading, which requires me to talk to you about it, if somehow or other, with the help of the Lord our God, I manage to say something which cannot be easily understood by everyone even if[3] it is said; and which ought not to be shrugged aside by anyone even when it is understood.

Speaking to the learned

2. He was talking at Athens. The Athenians enjoyed a great reputation among other peoples for every kind of learning and doctrine. The city was the native home of great philosophers. From it had spread through the rest of Greece and other countries of the world a complex variety of philosophies. That's where the apostle was talking, that's where he was proclaiming *Christ crucified, to the Jews indeed a stumbling block, to the nations folly; but to those who are called, Jews and Greeks alike, Christ the power of God and the wisdom of God* (1 Cor 1:23-24).

How risky it was to proclaim this among proud and learned people I leave you to imagine. Anyway, when he finished his address and they heard mention[4] of the resurrection of the dead, which is the most distinctive point of the faith

30

of Christians, some of them scoffed, while others said, *We will hear you again on this matter* (Acts 17:32). And among them were some who believed, and we are told the name of one of them, Dionysius the Areopagite, which means he was a leading Athenian (Areopagos, you see, was what the Athenian senate was called); and there was a noble lady,[5] and some others.

So when the apostle spoke, the crowd listening to him was divided into three parts, arranged in a wonderfully graded order, into scoffers, doubters, believers. *Some*, you see, as we heard it is written in the text, *started scoffing, others were saying, we will hear you again on this matter*; these were the doubters. Others believed. Between the scoffers and the believers were the doubters in the middle. If you scoff, you fall; if you believe, you stand; if you doubt, you wobble. *We will hear you again on this matter*, they say. We can't tell whether they were going to fall with the scoffers or stand with the believers.

All the same, did that sower of words labor to no purpose? Well, if he had been afraid of scoffers, he would never have got through to believers; just as that sower in the gospel whom the Lord tells us of (because of course that was Paul[6]), if he had hesitated to broadcast the seed in case some should fall on the road, some among the thorns, some on rocky places, the seed could never have reached the best soil either.[7] I too must sow, must scatter seed; get your hearts ready, bear a good crop.

Epicurean and Stoic philosophers

3. Another thing too, if your graces remember, we heard when the passage was read that some of the Epicurean and Stoic philosophers began debating with the apostle.[8] Who are or were the Epicurean and Stoic philosophers, that is what their ideas were, what they thought to be true, what goal they pursued in their philosophizing, many of you undoubtedly don't know; but because I am speaking in Carthage, many do.[9] So they must now help me in what I am going to say to you. What I think has to be said is very much to the point. Please listen to me, both those of you who don't know and those who do; those who don't know, to be instructed, those who do, to be reminded; the former can get to know something, the latter can recognize what they know.

The urge for the happy life is common to philosophers and Christians

4. First let me tell you in general that there is one overriding concern common to all philosophers, and that in this common concern they divided up into five different sets of special opinions. In common, all philosophers strove by dedication, investigation, discussion, by their way of life, to lay hold of the blessed life.[10] This was their one reason for philosophizing; but I rather think the philosophers also have this in common with us. I mean, if I were to ask you why you believe in Christ, why you became Christians, every single one of you answers me truthfully: "For the sake of the blessed life." Therefore the urge for the blessed life is common to philosophers and Christians.

But where can such an unanimously agreed upon object be found, that's what the question's about, that's where the differences begin. After all, to strive for the blessed life, to want the blessed life, to yearn for, long for, pursue the blessed life, I reckon that's the case with the whole human race. So I see that I understated it when I said that this appetite for the blessed life is common to philosophers and Christians; I ought to have said that it is characteristic of everybody, absolutely everybody, good and bad alike. People who are good, after all, are good in order to be happy, and those who are bad would not be bad unless they hoped they could thereby be made happy.[11]

About the good it is easy to answer that it is because they seek the happy life, that's what makes them good. About the bad, some people perhaps have their doubts, whether they too are seeking the happy life. But if I could separate the bad, and question them apart from the good, and say: "Do you want to be happy?" none of them would say, "I don't." For example, bring me a thief; I ask him, "Why do you steal?" "To have something," he says, "which I didn't have." "Why do you want to have something you didn't have?" "Because it's wretched not to have it." So if it's wretched not to have it, he thinks it's blessed to have it. But what makes him both shameless and mistaken is that he wants to become happy by being bad.

Being happy, of course, is good for everybody. So where does he go wrong? By seeking something good and doing something bad. What's he looking for, then? Why does the greed of the bad aspire to the reward of the good? The happy life is the reward of the good; goodness is the work, happiness the reward. God orders the work, offers the reward. He says, "Do this, and you will get that." This bad man, though, answers us, "Unless I do something bad, I won't be happy." As if someone were to say, "I won't arrive at the good unless I'm bad." Can't you see that good and bad are opposites? You are looking for what's good, and doing what's bad? You're running in the opposite direction; when are you ever going to arrive?

The opinion of the Epicureans and the Stoics on the happy life

5. So let's leave these for the time being; there will be an opportunity to come back to them, perhaps, when we have completed what we set out to say about the philosophers. Personally, you see, I don't think it is without point or significance that something important was done by people who were quite unaware of it; I think it was arranged by divine providence that, while there were several schools of philosophers in the city of Athens, only the Stoics and Epicureans should have debated with the apostle Paul. When you hear what their opinions are in their respective schools, you will see how it was not for nothing that of all the philosophers these alone should debate with Paul. After all, he couldn't choose for himself who would be arguing with him and whom he would have to answer. But the divine wisdom which governs all things[12] set before him precisely those with whom practically the entire nub of disagreements between philosophers is to be found.[13]

So I shall state it briefly; the unlearned must believe me, the learned must make their own judgment about me. I don't think I will have the nerve to lie to the unlearned, with the learned sitting there to judge; especially as I am going to say something about which both learned and unlearned alike can correctly judge for themselves. So I begin by saying that man consists of soul and body. Here I am not asking you to believe, but I am asking you too to judge. I'm not afraid, you see, that over this statement any will pass an adverse judgment on me who can recognize themselves. Man, then, which nobody questions, consists of soul and body.[14] This substance, this thing, this person which is called a human being, seeks the happy life. This too you know; I'm not insisting you should believe it, but I am reminding you to recognize it.

Human beings, I am saying, these by no means trifling objects, of greater worth than all cattle, than everything that flies and everything that swims, and anything at all that has flesh and is not human; human beings, then, consisting of soul and body; but not any kind of soul, because beasts also consist of soul and body; so human beings, consisting of rational soul and mortal flesh, seek the happy, or blessed life. When they know what thing it is that makes a life happy, then unless they hold onto it, pursue it, claim it for themselves, take possession of it if that's a possibility, ask for it if there's a difficulty, they simply cannot be happy. The whole question therefore is: what makes life happy?

Now set before your eyes Epicureans, Stoics, the apostle; which I could also have said like this: Epicureans, Stoics, Christians. Let's first question the Epicureans on what thing it is that makes life happy. They answer, "Bodily pleasure."[15] Here I am now asking you to believe, because I have got judges. I mean, you don't know whether the Epicureans say this and think this, because you haven't read those books; but there are people here who have read them. So let's get back to the interrogation.

"What do you say, Epicureans, what thing is it that makes life happy?"

"Bodily pleasure," they reply.

"Stoics, what thing is it that makes life happy?"

"A virtuous mind," they reply.

Would your graces please concentrate with me; we are Christians, we are deciding between philosophers. Notice why those two schools alone were brought on to debate with the apostle. There's nothing else in human beings, as regards their substance and nature, besides body and soul. Of these two, the Epicureans placed the happy life in one of them, that is in the body; the Stoics placed the happy life in the other, that is in the soul. As far as we human beings are concerned, if the happy life just comes to us from ourselves, then there is no other source or place for it besides body and soul. Either the body is the cause of the happy life, or else the soul is the cause of the happy life. If you look for any other cause, you are departing from the limits of the human. So those who have placed the blessed life of man in man have been unable to locate it anywhere else but either in the body or in the soul. Of those who have placed it in the body, the Epicureans have held the chief place; of those who have placed it in the soul, the Stoics have held the chief place.

The apostle's opinion

6. There they are; they are debating with the apostle. Could the apostle have anything more, or would he necessarily have to agree with one of these two schools, and in his turn also locate the cause of the blessed life either in the body or in the soul? Paul would never locate it in the body; after all, it's of no great importance, seeing that those people who have the more correct ideas about the body,[16] don't place the cause of blessedness in the body. The Epicureans, you see, have the same view of both the body and the soul, that each is mortal. And what's even more serious and abhorrent, is that they say that after death the soul disintegrates before the body. While the corpse still remains, they say, after the last breath has been drawn, and its parts retain their shape for some time, the soul disintegrates as soon as it departs, whisked away in all directions like smoke by the wind. So don't let's be surprised that they placed the supreme good, that is to say the cause of blessedness, in the body, which they opined was the better part of them, rather than the soul.

Would the apostle ever do that? Away with the idea that he would ever place the supreme good in the body. The supreme good, after all, is the cause of blessedness; indeed though, the apostle was grieved that some from among the Christians had opted for the opinion of the Epicureans, pigs rather than men. Of their number, you see, were those who were corrupting good habits with bad conversation, and saying, *Let us eat and drink, for tomorrow we shall die* (1 Cor 15:32). This amounts to saying, "There will be nothing after death, for our life is a passing shadow" (Wis 2:2.5). *For they said to one another*, among other things, *not thinking straight, let us crown ourselves with roses, before they fade; let there be no meadow where our revelry does not pass through; let us everywhere leave the signs of our merriment, because this is our portion, this our lot* (Wis 2:1.8-9).

Let us fast and pray, for tomorrow we shall die

7. If we fiercely rebuke such talk, if we vehemently oppose such lusts, they will even say what comes next: *Let us oppress the just man who is poor* (Wis 2:10). And yet for all that, I'm not afraid to say, even though I find myself in this position, "Do not be Epicureans."[17] Think indeed about what was said by these people, not talking straight: *For tomorrow we shall die.* But we shan't die totally; you see, there remains after death what follows death. As you die, you will have as your companion either life or punishment. Don't let anyone say, *"Who has ever come back here from there?"* (Wis 2:1). That rich man in his purple wanted too late to return, and could not get permission. He begged for a drop of water in his thirst, though he had disdained the poor man in his hunger.[18]

So don't any of you say, *Let us eat and drink, for tomorrow we shall die* (1 Cor 15:32). If you want to say, *Tomorrow we shall die*, I won't try to stop you; but say something different first. Yes, the Epicureans, as though they are not going to live after death, as though they have nothing else but what delights the flesh, yes they can say, *Let us eat and drink, for tomorrow we shall die.* Keep the bit, though, *Tomorrow we shall die*, and say, "Let us fast and pray, for tomorrow we shall die." I will definitely add something else, add a third point, and not pass over what has to be observed above all else, so that the hunger of the poor may be relieved by your fasting, or if you can't fast you should rather feed someone whose full belly can get you granted a pardon. So let Christians say, "Let us fast and pray and give, for tomorrow we shall die." Or if they want to say two things only, I would prefer them to say "Let us give and pray" rather than "Let us fast and not give."

Away with the idea, then, that the apostle would ever place in the body man's supreme good, that is to say, the cause of blessedness.

The opinions of the Stoics are not approved by the apostle

8. But with the Stoics there is, perhaps, a not ignoble contest. Here they are, you see, when questioned about where they place the efficient cause of the happy life, that is the thing in man that makes life happy; they answer that it's not bodily pleasure but a virtuous mind. What says the apostle? Does he agree? If he agrees, let us agree too. But he doesn't agree; because scripture checks those who trust in their own virtue.[19] And so the Epicurean who places man's supreme good in the body is placing his hopes in himself. But after all, the Stoic who places man's supreme good in the mind has indeed placed it in man's better part; but even he has placed it in himself. Now the Stoic is a man just as much as the Epicurean. *Cursed therefore is every one who places his hope in man* (Jer 17:5).

So what now? Here we have three people set before our eyes, an Epicurean, a Stoic, a Christian. Let us question them one by one.

"Tell us, Epicurean, what thing makes one blessed."

"Bodily pleasure," he replies.

"Tell us, Stoic."

"A virtuous mind."

"Tell us, Christian."

"The gift of God."

The rejection of the Epicureans and the Stoics

9. And so, brothers and sisters, in front of our very eyes, you might say, Epicureans and Stoics have been debating with the apostle, and teaching us by their debate what we should reject and what we ought to choose. A virtuous mind is something very praiseworthy; sagacity, telling the difference between bad things and good, justice, distributing to all what is theirs by right, moderation, curbing lusts, courage, imperturbably enduring trials.[20] A great thing, an admirable thing; admire it, Stoic, as much as ever you can. But tell me: where do you get it from? It is not precisely your virtuous mind that makes you happy, but the one who has given you virtue, who has inspired you to desire it, and granted you the capacity for it.[21]

I know you are probably going to make fun of me, and you will be joining those of whom it says that they made fun of Paul.[22] If you are the path,[23] I am sowing seed; I'm a sower of words, you see,[24] in my small measure. What was a sneer for you is a duty for me. I am sowing the seed; what I sow falls on you, as on hard ground. I'm not being idle, and I'm finding good ground. What am I to do for you?[25]

You have been reprimanded, and reprimanded by the very oracle of God. You are among those who trust in their own virtue; among those who place their hopes in man.[26] Virtue delights you; it's a good thing that delights you. I know, you are thirsty for it; but you can't pour yourself a drink of virtue. You're dry; if I show you the *fountain of life* (Ps 36:9), you will probably mock. You're saying to yourself, you see, "Am I going to drink from this crag?" The rod was brought, and water poured out.[27] *For Jews seek a sign*; but you're not a Jew, Stoic, I know; you're a Greek: *and Greeks seek wisdom. But we preach Christ crucified*; the Jew is shocked, the Greek sneers; *to the Jews indeed a stumbling block, and to the nations folly; but to those who have been called, Jews and Greeks*; that is, to Paul himself, once Saul, and to Dionysius the Areopagite, and such as these and such as those, *Christ the power of God and the wisdom of God* (1 Cor 1:22-24).

Now you are not mocking the crag; recognize the cross in the rod, Christ as the gushing torrent; and if you are thirsty, drink your fill of virtue. Take your fill from the fount, and perhaps you belch out your gratitude. What you get from him you won't now be giving yourself, and you will exclaim with your belching, *I will love you, Lord, my virtue* (Ps 18:1).[28] You won't say anymore, "My own virtuous mind makes me happy." You won't be among those who, while they know God, *have not glorified him as God, or given thanks; but they have become futile in their thoughts, and their insensate hearts have been darkened; for, calling themselves wise, they have become fools* (Rom 1:21-24). What does *calling themselves wise* mean, after all, but saying they get it from themselves, they are self-sufficient? *They have become fools*; quite rightly fools; true foolishness is false wisdom.

But you will be among those of whom it is said, *Lord, they shall walk in the light of your countenance, and in your name they shall exult all day long, and in your justice shall they be exalted; since you are the glory of their virtue* [29] (Ps 89:15-17). You were seeking virtue; say, *Lord, my virtue* (Ps 18:1). You were looking for the blessed life; say, *Blessed is the man whom you instruct, Lord* (Ps 94:12). Blessed, you see, is the people, not for whom the pleasure of the flesh, not for whom their own virtue; but, *Blessed is the people for whom the Lord is their God* (Ps 144:15). This is the blessed home country which all desire, but not all seek in the right way. As for us, let us not try to work out a way to such a home country as though by our own ingenuity, and attempt devious, misleading byways; the way too comes to us from there.[30]

We all want truth and life

10. What, after all, does the happy person want, but not to be duped, not to die, not to suffer pain? And what's he looking for? To be hungrier still, and to eat still more? What if it would be better not to be hungry at all? Nobody is really happy,

really blessed, except the one who lives for ever, without anything to fear, without anything to be deceived by; because the soul hates being deceived.

You can tell just how much the soul naturally hates being deceived from this, that people who laugh when they have lost their wits are wept for by the sane; and a person, of course, would much rather laugh than cry. If you were given the choice of these two things: "Do you want to laugh or cry?" is there anyone who would give any other answer but "laugh"? Again, if you were given the choice of these two: "Do you want to be deceived, or have the truth?", everybody answers, "Have the truth." You prefer both to laugh and to have the truth; but of this pair, laughing and crying, laughing; and of that pair, false information and the truth, having the truth. And yet such is the overwhelming power of unconquerable truth, that one would rather keep one's wits and cry than lose one's wits and laugh.

So there in that home country there will be truth, and nowhere at all falsehood and error. But as well as there being truth, there will also not be any weeping. Because there will be both true laughter and joy in the truth, since there will be life there. Because if there is any pain, there won't be any life there; I mean, everlasting and undying torment is not to be called life. That's why the Lord doesn't call it life, what the wicked are going to have,[31] even though they are going to live in the fire; their life won't end, so that their punishment won't end, because *their worm will not die, and their fire will not be quenched* (Is 66:24). Still, he refused to call it life, but he called life the sort that is both eternal and blessed. So when that rich man asked the Lord, *What good must I do, to obtain eternal life?*—and he too, of course, by eternal life meant only the blessed life. Because the wicked will have an eternal, but not a blessed, life, since it will be filled with torment. So he said, *Lord, what good must I do, to obtain eternal life?* The Lord answered him about the commandments. He said, "I've done all that." But when he gave his answer about the commandments, what did he say? *If you want to come to life* (Mt 19:16-17). He didn't say "blessed life," because a wretched one isn't really to be called life. He didn't say "eternal life," because where there is fear of death, it isn't really to be called life.[32]

So there is no life that deserves the name, to be called life, but a blessed life; and there can be no blessed life that is not eternal. This is what everybody wants, this is what we all want: truth and life. But how is one to get to such a great possession, such a grand fortune? The philosophers have worked out for themselves ways that go wrong; some have said, "This way," others, "Not that way, but this one." They have missed the true way, because God opposes the proud.[33] We would also miss it, unless it had come to us. That's why the Lord says, *I am the way* (Jn 14:6). Lazy traveler, you didn't want to come to the way; the way came to you. You were inquiring how you should go: *I am the way*; you were asking where you should go: *I am the truth and the life.* You won't go wrong when you go to him, by him. This is the doctrine of Christians; certainly not something to be set beside the doctrines of the philosophers, but to be set incomparably above them, whether the sordid one of the Epicureans, or the arrogant one of the Stoics.

NOTES

1. The sermon was preached in Carthage.

2. See Acts 17:18. The Latin translation, *verborum seminator*, gets the Greek word, *spermologos*, the wrong way round; it really means "picker of seeds," like birds that eat seeds. So it came to mean someone who picks up and trots out all the clichés, the latest "in" words; ultimately in fact much the same as the Latin translation!

3. Reading *etsi dicatur* instead of the *nisi dicatur* of the text. This, "unless it is said," seems to rob the sentence of all point, since unless it was said, there would be nothing for anyone to understand. He is in fact going on to draw attention to the distinction within his congregation between the educated few and the uneducated, even illiterate many, to whom he is going to explain the difference between Epicureans and Stoics, and between Christian doctrine and either of them. So he is not very confident of "everybody" understanding.

4. He appears to take a very odd liberty with Latin grammar here, inserting a nominative pronoun in the middle of an ablative absolute clause: *audita illi resurrectione mortuorum*. He would certainly have been beaten as a schoolboy for perpetrating such a howler. The likelihood is, however, that he was simply echoing the bad grammar of a very literal Latin translation.

5. Luke does not say she was noble, but does give her name, Damaris. Augustine got his wires crossed with 17:4, which tells us that among those who believed were "noble ladies not a few."

6. A very bold statement, that in the parable of the sower Jesus had Paul specifically in mind. But that is what Augustine says: *hoc erat Paulus*; not *tale erat Paulus*, that is what Paul was like.

7. See Mk 4:3-9.

8. See Acts 17:18.

9. Carthage being a very large city indeed, and in modern terms also a university city.

10. Could this be said to be the common concern of modern philosophers? I doubt it. But it was true of the ancient world, where philosophy really was concerned with ultimate causes, meanings and values, and was much closer to religion, or to theology, than it appears to be nowadays. Besides the Epicureans and the Stoics, the other three schools were the Academics (Platonists of a rather debased sort), Peripatetics (Aristotelians), and Cynics. He discusses them at length in book XIX of *The City of God*. He discusses the universal desire for the blessed (or happy) life in book XIII, 6-12, of *The Trinity*. One of his earliest works, composed in Italy between his conversion and his baptism, was *On The Happy Life*.

11. I am treating "happy" and "blessed" as synonyms, both rendering *beatus*. Neither is really satisfactory, "happy" because it has become so flat and banal, and "blessed" because it is either a religious word, or at least implies someone who blesses, which *beatus* does not do; that is more the connotation of *benedictus*.

12. See Wis 8:1.

13. A pardonable preacher's oversimplification, I suppose; you are either essentially an Epicurean or essentially a Stoic—except that he will himself contradict this by insisting that a Christian is neither. One is reminded, rather, of the statement in Gilbert & Sullivan's *Iolanthe*, making a universal absolute out of nineteenth century British politics:

> Every boy and every gal
>
> That's born into this world alive,
>
> Is either a little Liberal,
>
> Or else a little Conservative.

14. It should be borne in mind that *anima* was a less loaded word in Latin than "soul" has become in English. It obviously signified that which "animates" a body; so if a body is alive, is animated, it clearly has an *anima*, a principle of life. The English word "soul" has come to be loaded with a particular, religious idea about the immortal, and immaterial nature of this life-principle; which is why English-speaking people can, without being *prima facie* irrational, disagree that man consists of soul and body, whereas Latin speakers could not. To do so would in effect have been to deny that living beings have life.

15. *Voluptas corporis*. The very word in Latin, and its English derivatives, suggest the voluptuary, the glutton, winebibber, and lecher. Augustine is simply echoing the gross caricature of Epicurus' teaching that became stock form in the ancient world, where for several centuries Stoicism had carried all before it among the educated classes, only to yield in the third and fourth centuries to the rather more sophisticated philosophy of Neoplatonism.

Epicurus' genuine doctrine is best set out, perhaps, in the great Latin poem of his disciple Lucretius, *De Rerum Natura*. They were both, to be sure, materialists and atheists, and saw religion as one of the greatest causes of human unhappiness, because it instills fear, and prompts to dreadful acts; as Lucretius puts it, *Tantis religio potuit suadere malorum*, "To such great evils has religion been able to persuade man."

But then the Stoics too, though superficially more high-minded than the Epicureans, were also materialists, and if not atheists, then pantheists, which is not much better from a Christian point of view. Had the openly secular ideas of the Epicureans been the dominant philosophy that early Christianity encountered and partially absorbed, it would have distorted authentic gospel values far less than Stoicism did; just as in a parallel way the down-to-earth secular philosophy of Aristotle has been less damaging to the expression of Christian doctrine and ethics than the more religious and spiritual philosophy of Plato.

16. He was probably thinking of the Neoplatonists.

17. It is hard to see why he should have been afraid to say it, especially from his position as a visiting bishop. It may possibly be an allusion to the situation in Carthage at the time, when Augustine's friend, the imperial tribune Marcellinus, and his brother Apringius had just been done to death by Count Marinus, whom Augustine may have considered to be a libertine.

18. See Lk 16:24.27. No doubt the rich man would have liked to return himself; but in the actual parable he asks Abraham to send Lazarus back to his five brothers—as of course Augustine knew perfectly well. He is, in fact, being a little inconsequential in this passage. He tells us not to imitate the skepticism of the wicked by asking, "Who has ever returned from there?" Then he introduces the rich man, to prove apparently that no one has ever returned from there, thus in a sense making the point of the wicked for them. But of course he has really introduced him to illustrate punishment as the possible companion of the dying. As so often, his teeming imagination and intelligence is providing him with too many things to say at once.

19. In the texts he is going to quote or allude to, and in the whole armory of texts, especially from Romans and Galatians, which he employed against the Pelagians, who were, I suppose, the prime instance of Christian Stoics.

20. The four cardinal virtues of classical ethics, more conventionally and perhaps slightly misleadingly known as prudence, justice, temperance, and fortitude.

21. See, for example, Phil 2:13.

22. See Acts 17:32.

23. See Mk 4:4.

24. See Acts 17:18.

25. It is really the Pelagians here on whom through the Stoics Augustine is putting down his barrage.

26. See Jer 17:5.

27. See Nm 20:11.

28. Ps 18:1. It should be "my strength," of course; but in this context one has to keep "my virtue" for *virtus mea*.

29. See note 28.

30. See Jn 14:6.

31. See Mt 25:46.

32. What, one asks, one's head in a whirl at this unpardonably involved argument, has the fear of death got to do with anything we have been talking about? Only this, that life in this world, which is inevitably overshadowed by the fear of death, doesn't really deserve to be called life. So Christ did not need to say either "blessed life" or "eternal" life, because the only life worthy of the name is necessarily both blessed and eternal.

33. See Jas 4:6; 1 Pt 5:5; Prv 3:34.

SERMON 151

ON THE WORDS OF THE APOSTLE, ROMANS 7:15-25: *FOR IT IS NOT THE GOOD I WANT TO THAT I DO, BUT THE EVIL I DO NOT WANT TO, THAT IS WHAT I DO*, ETC.

Date: 419[1]

Words of warfare; words of triumph

1. The divinely inspired reading from the letter of the apostle Paul which has just been chanted—every time it's read I am afraid of its being taken in the wrong way to give a plausible excuse to people who are on the lookout for plausible excuses. People, I mean to say, are only too prone to sin, and are scarcely able to restrain themselves. So when they hear the apostle saying, *It is not the good I want to that I do, but the evil I hate, that is what I do* (Rom 7:15), they proceed to do evil, and then being apparently displeased with themselves for doing evil, they think they are like the apostle, who said, *For it is not the good I want to that I do, but the evil I do not want to, that is what I do.*

So this passage is read from time to time, and then it imposes on us[2] the duty of explaining it, in case people should take it in the wrong way and turn wholesome food into poison. So would your graces please pay close attention, until I manage to say to you what the Lord may grant to me; so that where you may see me, perhaps, struggling with some difficult obscurity, you will be able to help me with your sympathetic solidarity.

Warfare before triumph

2. So then, first remind yourselves of something which, thank God, you are quite used to hearing, that the life of the just in this body is still a warfare, not a triumphal celebration.[3] One day, though, this warfare will have its triumphal celebration. That's why the apostle spoke both words of warfare and words of triumph. Words of warfare we heard a moment ago: *For it is not what I want to that I do; but what I hate, that is what I do;*[4] *but if what I hate is what I do, I agree with the law, that it is good. To want to do good is available to me, but to carry out the good I do not find in my power. But I see another law in my members, fighting against the law of my mind, and taking me prisoner to the law of sin, which is in my members* (Rom 7:15-16.18.23). When you hear

"fighting against," when you hear "taking prisoner," you surely recognize the language of warfare, don't you?

So it's not yet time for the language of triumph; but that it's going to come the same apostle tells you, when he says, *It is necessary for this perishable thing to put on imperishability, and this mortal thing to put on immortality. But when this perishable thing has put on imperishability, and this mortal thing has put on immortality*—here's the language of triumph—*then will come to pass the word that is written: Death has been swallowed up in victory.* Let those celebrating their triumph say, *Where, death, is your strife?* (1 Cor 15:53-55; Is 25:8; Hos 13:14).

So we shall say that; some time or other we shall say it, and that some time or other will not be long. There is not as much left, you see, of this world's time as has already been spent, so we shall say this then;[5] but now, in this time of warfare, we mustn't let this reading be wrongly understood, and so become a clarion call for the enemy instead of for us, one by which he will be encouraged instead of one by which he will be defeated. So be on your guard against this, I beg you, brothers and sisters, and those of you who are battling, battle on. You see, those of you who are not yet battling are not going to understand what I have to say; while those of you who are already engaged in the battle are going to understand. My words will be uttered openly, yours in silence.

First let me remind you of what he wrote to the Galatians; from that we can come to a good and proper explanation of this text. He says, you see, speaking to the faithful, speaking to the baptized, all of whose sins had of course been forgiven in the holy bath;[6] while speaking to these, he is also speaking to people who are fighting, and he says, *But I say: Walk by the Spirit, and do not carry through with the lust of the flesh.* He didn't say "Do not carry them," but "Do not carry through with them."[7] Why so? He goes on to say, *For the flesh lusts against the Spirit, the Spirit against the flesh. For these are opposed to each other, so that you do not do the things that you wish to. But if you are led by the Spirit, you are not still under the law* (Gal 5:16-18); of course not, but under grace. *If you are led by the Spirit.* What does being led by the Spirit mean? Agreeing with the commands of the Spirit of God, not with the lusts of the flesh. All the same, the flesh lusts, and you resist it;[8] it wants something, and you don't want it. Persevere, so that you go on not wanting it.

Do not go after your lusts

3. And yet your desire ought to be so totally directed toward God, that there isn't even any lust for you to resist. Notice what I've said: Your desire, I repeat, ought to be so totally directed toward God, that there is absolutely no lust at all which you have to resist. Yes, you are resisting, and by not agreeing to it, you are overcoming it; but it's better not to have an enemy than to overcome one. Sooner or later this enemy will be no more. Turn your mind to that shout of triumph, and see if it will still be there: *Where, death, is your strife? Where, death, is your sting?* (1 Cor 15:55; Hos 13:14). You will look for its place, and you won't find it.

This lust is not, you see—and this is a point you really must listen to above all else: you see, this lust is not some kind of alien nature, as the ravings of the Manichees would have it. It's our debility, it's our vice. It won't be detached from us and exist somewhere else, but it will be cured and not exist anywhere at all.

So *Do not carry through with the lusts of the flesh* (Gal 5:16). It would be better, clearly, to fulfill what the law said: *Do not lust* (Rom 7:7). That is the fullness of virtue, the perfection of justice, the palm of victory: *Do not lust.*[9] But because that cannot be achieved here, at least let us achieve what holy scripture says yet again: *Do not go after your lusts* (Sir 18:30). It would be better not to have any; but because they are there, do not go after them. They aren't keen to go after you; don't you be keen to go after them. If they did want to go after you, they would cease to be, because they would not be rebelling against your mind.[10] They are rebels, be a rebel yourself against them; they are fighting, fight them back; they are fighting to the finish, fight to the finish yourself;[11] make sure of one thing alone: don't let them win.

Opposing concupiscence and bad habits

4. Here you are, I'll posit one instance, from which you can work out all the rest. You know there are such things as sober people; few enough of them, but they exist. You know there are also drunkards; they are two a penny. A sober man is baptized; as regards drunkenness, he has no lust to fight against; he has other lusts to fight with. But to help you understand about the rest, let us organize a bout in the ring with only one enemy. A drunkard also is baptized. He has heard, and heard with dread, that among other evils which bar evil-living people from entry into the kingdom of God, drunkenness is also mentioned; because where it says, *Neither fornicators, nor worshippers of idols, nor adulterers, nor the effeminate, nor those who lie with men, nor thieves*, it goes on to add, *nor drunkards . . . will take possession of the kingdom of God* (1 Cor 6:9-10).

He has heard this, and been filled with dread. He has been baptized, all his sins of drunkenness have been forgiven him; there remains as his adversary the habit. So he has something to fight with once he has been born again. His past vicious behavior has all been forgiven him; he must be alert, keep awake, fight, in order not to get drunk again some time. So the lust for a tipple wells up in him, tickles his fancy, parches his throat, lays siege to his senses; it would like, if it possibly could, to penetrate the very walls, to get at him sheltering behind them, to drag him away prisoner.

It's fighting, fight back. Oh, if only it didn't exist at all! If with bad habits it has increased in strength, with good habits it will die; all you have to do is not give it satisfaction, not give in and so gorge it, but resist and so kill it. Still, as long as it's there, it's your enemy. If you don't consent to it, and never get drunk, it will grow less and less every day; because it gets its strength from your submission to it. I mean, if you do give in to it, and get drunk, you are giving it strength.

Strength against me, do you suppose, and not against yourself? All I'm doing is warning you from this pulpit, telling you, preaching; announcing beforehand what evil lies in store for drunkards. You've no occasion to say, "I never heard about it." You've no occasion to say, "God requires my life from the hand of that man who kept quiet to me about it."[12]

But you're in trouble, because with your bad habits you've made for yourself a doughty opponent. You haven't taken any trouble previously, and so you have fattened him up; take some trouble now, in order to defeat him. And if you are less than a match for him, ask God for help. Still, if he doesn't defeat you, although it's your own bad habit that has been wrestling with you, but if it doesn't defeat you, you have done what the apostle Paul says: *Do not carry through with the lusts of the flesh* (Gal 5:16). The lust has been carried by tickling your fancy; but it hasn't been carried through by boozing.

The origin of lust

5. What I have said about drunkenness can be said about all vices, all greedy desires. Some, you see, we are born with, others we have acquired by habit. It's because of those we are born with that babies are baptized, to be released from the guilt of the race, not from that of any bad habits, which they haven't yet got. So we always have a fight on our hands, because the very covetousness we are born with can never be finished off as long as we live; it can be lessened day by day, it can't be finished off completely. Because of it this body of ours is called a body of death.[13] About it the apostle says, *For I take delight in the law of God according to the inner self. But I see another law in my members fighting against the law of my mind, and taking me prisoner to the law of sin which is in my members* (Rom 7:22-23).

This law was born when the first law was broken. Then, I repeat, was this law born when the first law was ignored and broken. What is the first law? The one the man was given in paradise?[14] Why were they naked, and unashamed, if not because there was as yet no law in their members fighting against the law of the mind? Man committed a deed which deserved to be punished, and discovered in himself a motion of which he must blush. They ate in spite of the prohibition, and their eyes were opened. Well, what does that mean? Had they previously been wandering round paradise with their eyes shut, or blind? Absurd idea. After all, how had Adam managed to give names to the birds and the beasts, when all the animals were brought to him?[15] How could he give them names if he couldn't see them? Later on it says, *The woman saw the tree, that it was pleasing for the eyes to see* (Gn 3:6). So they had their eyes open, and they were naked and were not ashamed.

But their eyes were opened to something they had never perceived, something they had never been shocked by in the movement of their bodies. Their eyes were opened to notice, not just to see; and because they perceived it as something to blush for, they took care to cover it up. *They sewed fig-leaves together*, it says, *and made themselves aprons* (Gn 3:7). What they covered up is where they felt shame.[16]

There you have what original sin is derived from, there you have the reason why nobody is born without sin. There you have the reason why the Lord did not wish to be so conceived, the Lord whom the virgin conceived. He broke the hold of sin, because he came without it; he broke its hold because he did not come from it.[17] Thus we have one single man and another single man; one for death, the other for life. The first man for death, the second man for life. But why was that man for death? Because he was only man.[18] Why is this man for life? Because he is God and man.

Observe the apostle engaged in combat, and don't let yourself grow desperate

6. So it is not what he wants to that the apostle does; because he wants not to lust or covet, and yet he does so; that's why he does what he doesn't want to. Did that evil covetousness or lust subdue the apostle and drag him into fornication and adulteries? Perish the thought. Such ideas must never enter our heads. He was struggling, he was not subdued. But because he did not want even to have this thing to struggle with, that's why he said *It is not what I want to, that I do* (Rom 7:15). I don't want to covet, but yet I do. So I do something I don't want to; but all the same, I don't consent to this lust.

After all, he would not otherwise have said, *Do not carry through with the lusts of the flesh* (Gal 5:16), if he had carried through with them himself. But he set out his own struggle before your eyes, so that you wouldn't be afraid of yours. After all, if the blessed apostle hadn't said this, then when you saw lust stirring in your members, without yourself consenting to it; nonetheless, when you saw it stirring, you would perhaps despair of yourself, and say, "If I belonged to God, I wouldn't be stirred like this." Observe the apostle engaged in combat, and don't let yourself grow desperate. *I see another law*, he says, *in my members, fighting against the law of my mind*; and because I don't want it to fight back, since after all it's my flesh, it's what I am, it's part of me, *it is not what I want to that I do; but the evil I hate is what I do* (Rom 7:23.15); I covet, I feel lust.

"Doing" does not mean "accomplishing"

7. So what is the good that I do? That I don't consent to a bad desire. I do good, and I don't carry the good through; and my enemy, lust, does evil and doesn't carry the evil through. How do I do good and not carry through with the good? I do good when I do not consent to the evil lust; but I do not carry through with the good, so as not to covet or have any lust at all. So again, how does my enemy too do evil and not carry through with the evil? It does evil, because it stirs up an evil desire; it does not carry the evil through, because it does not drag me into committing the evil.

And in this warfare consists the whole life of holy people. Now what am I to say about the impure, who don't even put up a fight? They are subjugated and dragged around; no, they are not even dragged around, because they follow willingly of their own accord. This, I repeat, is the battle of the saints; and in this warfare you are always at risk, until you die. But at the end, in the triumphant celebration of that victory, what is being said? Or rather, what does the apostle say, as he already anticipates his triumph? *Then will come to pass the word that is written: Death has been swallowed up in victory. Where, death, is your strife? Where, death, is your sting?* It's the language of people celebrating their triumph. *Where, death, is your sting? Now the sting of death is sin*, because it was sin pricking us that brought about death. Sin is a kind of scorpion; it pricked us with its sting, and we died.

But when it says, *Where, death, is your sting?*, the sting you were made by, not one you made; so when it says, *Where, death, is your sting?*, of course it won't be anywhere, because there won't be any sin anywhere. *Now the sting of death is sin*. It was against sin that the law was given; *but the power of sin is the law* (1 Cor 15:54-56). How is the law the power of sin? *It was introduced so that the transgression might multiply* (Rom 5:20). How is that? Because before the law man was a sinner; once the law was given and broken, he also became a transgressor. People were already guilty of sin; once the law was given they became even more guilty of transgression.

Hope is only through grace

8. Where is there any hope, except in what follows: *Where sin has multiplied, grace has multiplied over and above* (Rom 5:20)? That's why this soldier, somehow or other so experienced in this warfare, so experienced indeed that he was also a captain, when he was in trouble in this war against the enemy and saying, *I see another law in my members fighting back against the law of my mind, and taking me prisoner to the law of sin which is in my members*, a foul law, a wretched law, a wound, an infection, a sickness—that's why he added, *Wretched man that I am, who will deliver me from the body of this death?* And help came to him in his groans. How did help come? *The grace of God through Jesus Christ our Lord* (Rom 7:23-25) will deliver you from the law of this death, that is from the body of this death; *the grace of God through Jesus Christ our Lord.*

When will you have a body in which no lust or covetousness remains? *When this mortal thing has put on immortality, and this perishable thing has put on imperishability*, and you will say to death, *Where, death, is your strife?* (1 Cor 15:54-55), and it won't be anywhere at all. But now, at this moment, what? Listen: *I myself, therefore, serve the law of God in my mind, but in the flesh the law of sin* (Rom 7:25). *In the mind I serve the law of God* by not consenting; *but in the flesh the law of sin* by feeling lust. Both the law of God in the mind, and the law of sin in the flesh. I both take delight in this one, and at the same time I feel lust there. But I am not overpowered; it tickles the fancy, it lays siege to me, it hammers at the door, it tries to drag me away. *Wretched man that I am, who will deliver me from the body of this death?* I don't want to have to win all the time; but I want some time or other to reach the haven of peace.

So now, brothers and sisters, hold fast to this rule: serve the law of God in the mind, but in the flesh the law of sin; but out of stern necessity, because you have lustful desires, not because you consent to them. Sometimes this lust presses so hard on holy people that it does to them when they are asleep what it cannot do when they are awake. Why did you all shout, if not because you all took the point?[19] Modesty forbids me to dwell on the subject, but don't let it put you off praying to God about it.

Turning to the Lord, etc.

NOTES

1. O. Perler, *Les Voyages de Saint Augustin* (Paris, 1969) pages 357-358, demonstrates beyond question that Sermons 151-156 (not including 154A) were all preached in Carthage in October of 419; this Sermon 151 at the beginning of the month.

2. Not just Augustine, but any bishop or preacher. But Augustine must have felt the responsibility much more keenly than most, because this whole passage would have been one of his most useful texts against the Pelagians. See, for example, Sermon 30.

3. See Job 7:1. What precisely he is alluding to in saying that they are used to hearing this statement it is impossible to say. Perhaps it was known to be a favorite theme of Augustine's friend and host, Aurelius the bishop of Carthage.

4. He now quotes the text more accurately, in words that are closer to the Greek original. The earlier quotations, putting in the words "good" and "evil," represent the Vulgate and presumably earlier Latin versions.

5. The final "then" of 1 Cor 13:12. 13.

6. See Eph 5:26; Tit 3:5.

7. The contrast he makes is between *ne feceritis* and *ne perfeceritis*, a neater one, but really no less artificial than the one I manage to make in the translation. *Ne feceritis* means "Do not act, do not do them," which would naturally mean "Do not act on them, or carry them out"—in fact the same as *Ne perfeceritis*. But as will become clear, he really means by it "Do not have or feel them," "Do not covet, lust, or desire."

8. Reading *et resistis* as suggested by the editors, instead of *et resistit* of the text; this would mean that the flesh lusts and resists the Spirit.

9. The law, in fact, does not make such a general—and unreasonable—prohibition, but specifies that you must not lust after, or covet, your neighbor's wife or any of his possessions (Ex 20:19). Paul, however, is generalizing it to mean any "inordinate desire," which is the sense that at least in Church usage is conveyed by the Latin *concupiscere* and *concupiscentia*.

10. And it is in the nature of your lusts to rebel against your mind; that is what makes them what they are.

11. *Expugnare* normally means to take by storm or to overpower. But it cannot mean that here, so I am translating it simply as an intensive form of *pugnare*.

12. See Ez 3:16-21; 33:1-9. Why this sudden intrusion of his own person into the subject? Perhaps someone in the congregation, well known as a hard drinker, made a kind of hostile gesture at him, half in jest, half in earnest.

13. See Rom 7:24.

14. See Gn 2:25.

15. See Gn 2:19-20.

16. For Augustine it is primarily, if not solely, the sexual appetite that is disordered as a result of the first sin, and is the carrier, and as it were concrete embodiment of original sin in all Adam's descendants. The appetite itself, as an element of divine creation, is good, and on this point Augustine was much clearer and more definite than many of his contemporaries, for instance Jerome. But it is never, now, without its disorderliness, and it is this disorder that he calls *concupiscentia*, and he regards as a sign of this disorder what the moral textbooks call, or used to call, "the inordinate motion of the flesh," that can and does occur without deliberate intention—and sometimes doesn't even when deliberately intended. In other words, it illustrates the disobedience, or rebellion of the flesh against the mind.

17. Sin, original sin, and concupiscence, in the sense just defined, are here all being treated as identical with each other.

18. He was Adam, which means man. Christ is the last Adam, thus also "the Man," but man plus.

19. For a personal treatment of this matter, see *Confessions* X, 30, 41-42.

SERMON 152

ON THE FURTHER WORDS OF THE APOSTLE, ROMANS 7:25—8:3, AS FAR AS *GOD SENT HIS SON IN THE LIKENESS OF THE FLESH OF SIN*, ETC.

Date: 419[1]

The work of the workers and of the Creator

1. Your graces should remember that I discussed with you the very difficult question raised by the apostle Paul's letter, where he says, *For it is not what I want to that I do; but what I hate, that is what I do* (Rom 7:15). So those of you who were here will remember; continue to be present with your minds, and so add to what you have already learned. The reading which was chanted today, you see, follows on that one, though the reader in fact began with the words, *God sent his Son in the likeness of the flesh of sin, and from sin condemned sin in the flesh; so that the justice of the law might be fulfilled in us, who walk not according to the flesh but according to the Spirit* (Rom 8:3-4). But the words which were read on that occasion and not commented on, go as follows: *Therefore I myself with the mind serve the law of God, but with the flesh the law of sin. There is therefore no condemnation to those now who are in Christ Jesus. For the law of the Spirit of life in Christ Jesus has delivered you from the law of sin and death. For what was impossible for the law, in that it was weakened through the flesh*—and then follows what was read today—*God sent his Son in the likeness of the flesh of sin* (Rom 7:25—8:3).[2]

There is no difficulty with obscure meanings when the Spirit is helping us. May he help us then through your prayers; because the very desire with which you want to understand is itself a prayer to God. So it's from him that you ought to look for assistance. I, you see, like a countryman in his orchard, am working from the outside. But if there was nobody working from the inside, the seed wouldn't take root in the earth, nor would the treetop rise in the orchard, nor the sapling grow stout and hard and become a treetrunk, nor branches nor fruit nor leaves ever be produced. That's why the apostle himself said, to distinguish between the work of the workers and of the Creator, *I myself planted, Apollo watered; but it was God who gave the growth.* And he added, *Neither the one who plants nor the one who waters is anything, but only God who gives the growth* (1 Cor 3:6-7). If God is not giving any growth from within, then this

48

sound reaching your ears is just worthless. But if he is giving it, then what I am planting and watering has some value, and my efforts are not worthless.

Do not consent to the desires of the flesh

2. I have already told you how to take what the apostle says: *With the mind I serve the law of God, but with the flesh the law of sin* (Rom 7:25);[3] it means you must allow the flesh nothing more but its desires, without which it cannot exist. But if you consent to evil desires and haven't struggled against them, you will have to bewail your defeat; and I hope you do bewail it, or you may lose all sense of sorrow. So as far as our wishes go, our will, our prayer when we say, *Do not bring us into temptation, but deliver us from evil* (Mt 6:13), what we long for, of course, is that these evil desires should not even well up from our flesh. But as long as we are living here, we are unable to bring this about.

That's why he says, *But to carry through with the good I do not find in my power* (Rom 7:18). What do I find it in my power to carry out?[4] Not to consent to the evil desire. To carry through with it I do not find in my power: not to have any evil desire. So it remains for you in this battle to serve the law of God by not consenting in your mind to evil lusts; but in your lustful flesh, without your consenting to it however, to serve the law of sin. So the flesh carries out its desires; mind you carry out yours too. Its desires are not suppressed, not extinguished by you; don't let it extinguish yours; in this way you will find the contest hard going, but you won't be defeated and dragged away a prisoner.

Fight as a true citizen

3. So the apostle goes on to say, *So there is no condemnation now for those who are in Christ Jesus* (Rom 8:1). Even if they have desires of the flesh which they don't consent to; even if the law in their members is fighting back against the law of their minds, and trying to take their minds prisoner; still, by the grace of baptism and the bath of regeneration not only has the guilt with which you were born been canceled, but also any consent you have previously given to any evil lust, whether by committing any crime or misdeed, or by any evil thought or any evil speech, they have all been blotted out in that font, into which you stepped a slave, and from which you came out a free person;[5] therefore, because this is so, *There is now no condemnation for those who are in Christ Jesus.*

There is none now; there was before. From one man all were brought to condemnation.[6] This evil was the effect of being born; that good was the effect of being born again. *For the law of the Spirit of life in Christ Jesus has delivered you from the law of sin and death* (Rom 8:2). It is present in your members, but it doesn't make you guilty. You have been set free from it; fight as a free citizen. But see to it you are not defeated, and again made a slave. You have a hard time of it, fighting; but you will have a joyful time of it celebrating your triumph.

Avoid the error of the Manichees

4. Now there is one thing I have told you, something you really must remember, in case you should think that because of this battle, without which a person cannot exist, even one who lives a just life; indeed that's the one who is in the thick of it, the one who lives justly; because the one who doesn't live a just life doesn't even put up a fight, but is just dragged off; so you mustn't think, because of all this, that there are two natures, so to say, coming from different sources, as the ravings of the Manichees would have it, as though the flesh didn't come from God. That's quite false; each part comes from God. But human nature deserved to have this warfare[7] in itself as a result of sin. So it's a sickness, and when it's cured it just ceases to exist.

The discord now experienced between spirit and flesh is really a struggle for concord; the reason the spirit struggles is to bring the flesh into peace and concord with itself. Just as if in one home a man and his wife are quarreling, what the man ought to strive for is to tame his wife; his wife once tamed, to subject her to her husband; his wife once subjected to her husband, to establish peace in the home.[8]

The law of sin, the law of faith, the law of deeds

5. But after saying, *The law of the Spirit of life in Christ Jesus has delivered you from the law of sin and death,* he set us the task of understanding these laws. Observe, and distinguish them; you certainly need to be able to distinguish them. *The law,* he says, *of the Spirit of life*—there's one law—*has delivered you from the law of sin and death*—there's another law, and he goes on: *For what was impossible for the law—in that it was weakened through the flesh* (Rom 8:2-3)—there's the third law. Or perhaps this is one of those two? Let's look and, with the Lord's help, see.

What did he say about that good law? *The law of the Spirit of life has delivered you from the law of sin and death.* He didn't say this law wasn't strong enough to achieve anything. *It has delivered you,* he says, *this law of the Spirit of life, from the law of sin and death.* That good law delivered you from this bad law. What, after all, is the bad law? *I see another law in my members fighting back against the law of my mind, and taking me prisoner to the law of sin, which is in my members* (Rom 7:23).

Why is this also called a law? It's absolutely right. It was perfectly fair, after all, and legitimate that man who refused to be obedient to God should be denied obedient service by his own flesh. Your Lord is above you, your flesh beneath you. Serve your betters, if you want to be served by your inferior. You despised your superior, you are tormented by your inferior. So that then is the law of sin, the law also of death. *Death,* after all, *through sin* (Rom 5:12). *The day you eat, you shall die the death* (Gn 2:17).

So this law of sin is a drag on the spirit, and strives to subjugate it. *But I take delight in the law of God according to the inner self* (Rom 7:22). And thus that battle occurs, and in the course of the contest it can be said, *With the mind I serve the law of God, but with the flesh the law of sin. The law of the Spirit of life has delivered you from the law of sin and death* (Rom 7:25; 8:2). Well, how has this law of the Spirit of life delivered you? First of all, it has given you pardon for all your sins. This is the law, you see, about which one says to God in the psalm, *And from your law have mercy on me* (Ps 119:29). The law of mercy, the law of faith, not of deeds.

So what is this law of deeds? You have already heard about the good law of faith: *The law of the Spirit of life has delivered you from the law of sin and death.* You have also heard of this other law of sin and death. *For what was impossible for the law, in that it was weakened through the flesh* (Rom 8:3). So this law, mentioned in the third place, somehow or other fails to achieve I don't know what; but that law of the Spirit of life did achieve it; because it delivered you from the law of sin and death. And so this law, mentioned third, is that law which was given to the people through Moses on Mount Sinai, and is called the law of deeds. It is able to threaten, not to help; able to command, not to assist. It's the law that said, *You shall not covet* (Ex 20:17). Which is why the apostle says, *I would not know covetousness, unless the law said, You shall not covet.* And what good did it do me, that the law said, *You shall not covet? Sin, seizing its opportunity through the commandment, deceived me, and through it slew me* (Rom 7:7.11). I was forbidden to covet, and I didn't observe the order, but was defeated. Before the law I was a sinner; after receiving the law, I became a transgressor. *For sin, seizing its opportunity, through the commandment deceived me, and through it slew me.*

The law of Moses is defended against the Manichees

6. *And so,* he goes on, *the law is indeed holy.* So this law too is good (because the Manichees condemn it, just as they do the flesh). The apostle says about it, *And so the law indeed is holy, and the commandment is holy, and just, and good. So did something that is good become death for me? Perish the thought! But sin, in order to be seen as sin, through the good wrought death for me* (Rom 7:12-13). They are the apostle's words; take note and pay attention to them. *And so the law indeed is holy.* What could be holier than *You shall not covet?* Transgression of the law wouldn't be bad, unless the law itself were good. After all, if it wasn't good, it wouldn't be bad to transgress a bad thing. But because it is bad to transgress it, therefore it is itself good. What could be so good as, *You shall not covet?*

The law indeed is holy, and the commandment is holy, and just, and good. How he does plug it, how he does drum it into us! It's as if he is shouting against its detractors. What have you got to say, Manichee? Is the law that was given through Moses bad? "Yes, it's bad," they say. How monstrous, how absolutely brazen! You have said just one word, "Bad"; listen to the apostle saying, *The law indeed is holy, and the commandment is holy, and just, and good.* Will you shut up at last, then? *So did something that is good,* he says, *become death for me? Perish the thought! But sin, in order to be seen as sin, through the good wrought death for me.* Here again, *through the good*; he so accuses the guilty party, that he does not cease to praise the law. *Through the good*, he says, *it wrought death for me.* Through what good? The commandment. Through what good? The law.

In what measure did it bring about death? *In order to be seen as sin; in order that it might become sin above measure, as one offends through the commandment* (Rom 7:13).[9] When he offended without a commandment, it was a lesser matter; when he offends through the commandment, it goes beyond measure. After all, when someone is not actually forbidden to do something, he thinks it's all right to do it. When he's forbidden, he starts by being unwilling to comply; he's defeated, dragged off, enslaved; now all that remains to him is to call out for grace, because he couldn't keep the law.

Two divine laws, two testaments

7. And thus the law of which it is said, *For the law of the Spirit of life has delivered you from the law of sin and death* (Rom 8:2), is the law of faith, the law of the Spirit, the law of grace, the law of mercy. The law of sin and death, on the other hand, is not the law of God, but of sin and death. That other one, though, of which the apostle says *The law is holy, and the commandment is holy, and just, and good* (Rom 7:12), is the law of God, but a law of deeds, a law of works; a law of works which commands and does not help; a law which shows you sin, and doesn't take it away. By one law sin is shown to you, by another it is taken away.

They are the two testaments or covenants, the old and the new. Listen to what the apostle says about them: *Tell me, you that wish to be under the law, have you not read the law? For it is written that Abraham had two sons, one by the slavegirl, one by the free woman. But the one by the slavegirl was born according to the flesh, while the one by the free woman was born through the promise. All this is said in an allegory. For these are the two covenants, one indeed on Mount Sinai bringing forth into slavery, which is Hagar,* Sarah's maid, who was given to Abraham, and bore Ishmael as a slave. So it is the old covenant that belongs to Hagar, *bringing forth into slavery. But the Jerusalem which is above is free, and that is our mother* (Gal 4:21-24.26). So the sons of grace are the sons of the free woman; the sons of the letter are the sons of the slavegirl.

Look for the slavegirl's children: *The letter kills*; look for the free woman's children: *But the Spirit gives life* (2 Cor 3:6). *The law of the Spirit of life in Christ Jesus has delivered you from the law of sin and death*, from which the law of the letter could not deliver you. *For what was impossible for the law, in that it was weakened through the flesh*—your flesh, you see, was rebelling, your flesh was enslaving you; it heard the law, and stirred up your covetousness, your lust, more than ever. So the law of the letter was weakened through the flesh; and thus it was impossible for the law of the letter to deliver you from the law of sin and death.[10]

Christ came by grace

8. *God sent his Son in the likeness of the flesh of sin*; not in the flesh of sin. In the flesh, certainly, but not in the flesh of sin. The flesh of all other human beings is the flesh of sin; only his is not the flesh of sin, because his mother conceived him not by lust but by grace. Nonetheless, his has the likeness of the flesh of sin, which is why he could be suckled, and feel hunger and thirst, and sleep and grow tired, and die. *In the likeness of the flesh of sin God sent his Son, and from sin condemned sin in the flesh* (Rom 8:2-3).

Christ had no sin

9. Which sin? From which sin? *From sin he condemned sin in the flesh, that the justice of the law might be fulfilled in us.* Now let that justice of the law be fulfilled in us; now let that justice which is commanded be fulfilled in us through the Spirit who assists; that is, let the law of the letter be fulfilled in us through the Spirit of life; *in us, who walk, not according to the flesh, but according to the Spirit* (Rom 8:3-4). So what sin did the Lord condemn, and from what sin?

I can see, yes certainly I can see what sin he condemned; I can see it straightaway: *Behold the Lamb of God, behold the one who takes away the sin of the world* (Jn 1:29). What sin? Every sin, he condemned every single sin of ours. But *from* what sin? He himself had no sin; of him it is said, *Who committed no sin, nor was deceit found in his mouth* (1 Pt 2:22; Is 53:9). Absolutely none at all, neither by contracting any, nor by adding any; he had no sin whatever, neither of origin nor of his own wickedness. The virgin declares his origin;[11] while his own holy way of life indicates clearly enough that he did nothing for which he deserved to die.

That's why he said, *Behold, the prince of this world* (he means the devil) *is coming, and in me he will find nothing.* The prince of death will find no reason to justify his killing me. And why then do you die? *But that all may know that I do my Father's will, let us go from here* (Jn 14:30-31). And he went off to meet his death, a voluntary death, one not of necessity but of free choice. *I have power to lay down my life, and I have power to take it up again. No one takes it from me, but I lay it down myself, and again I take it up* (Jn 10:17-18). If you are amazed at this power, recognize the majesty. Christ is speaking in the way that God speaks.

God made Christ into sin for us . . .

10. So from what sin did he condemn sin? Some people, trying to understand, have arrived at a sense that is certainly not to be rejected out of hand. And yet, as far as I can see, they have not really been able to fathom what the apostle has said. However, they have said something that is not bad in itself. I'll tell you this first, and then what I think myself, and what the divine scripture itself shows to be the truest explanation.

When they were pestered with the question, "From what sin did he condemn sin? Did he have any sin?"—this is what they said: *"From sin he condemned sin*, from sin that was not his own; all the same, *from sin he condemned sin."*

"So if not from his own, from whose?"

"From the sin of Judas, from the sin of the Jews. After all, how did he come to shed his blood for the forgiveness of sins? Because he was crucified. Who was he crucified by? The Jews. Who betrayed him to them? Judas. When the Jews killed him, Judas betrayed him, did they do good, or did they sin? They sinned. There you have the sin from which he condemned sin."

It's a good answer, and it's quite true that from, or by means of, the sin of the Jews Christ condemned every sin, because it was in consequence of their persecution that he shed his blood, with which he canceled all sin. Nonetheless, notice what the apostle says somewhere else: *On Christ's behalf*, he says, *we are acting as ambassadors, as though God were exhorting you through us; we beg you on behalf of Christ*, that is, as though Christ were begging you, we beg you on his behalf, *be reconciled to God*. And he continues, *Him who knew no sin*, God to whom we are begging you to be reconciled *made into sin for us*, made him who knew no sin, made him *into sin for us, that we might be the justice of God in him* (2 Cor 5:20-21). Can sin here be understood as the sin of Judas, the sin of the Jews, the sin of any other human being, when you hear *Him who knew no sin, he made into sin for us*? Who made whom? God made Christ, God made Christ into sin for us. He didn't say "made him a sinner for us," but *made him into sin*. If it's abominable, impious, to say Christ sinned, who can tolerate Christ's being sin? And yet we can't contradict the apostle. We can't say to him, "What on earth are you saying?" I mean, if we say this to the apostle, we are saying it to Christ. You see, he says somewhere else, *Or do you want proof of Christ speaking in me?* (2 Cor 13:3).

. . . That we may be the justice of God in him

11. So what's the solution? Would your graces please pay close attention to a great and profound mystery. You will be truly blessed if you cherish it once you have understood it, and attain to it once you cherish it.[12] Certainly, certainly, Christ our Lord, Jesus our savior, our redeemer, was made into sin for us, that we might be the justice of God in him. How? Listen to the law. Those who are familiar with it know what I am saying; and those who are not can read it, or listen to it. In the law, those sacrifices which were offered for sins, were also called sins. You have this instance: when the victim to be offered for sin was led up, the law says, *Let the priests lay their hands upon the sin* (Lev 4:4), that is, upon the victim for sin. And what else is Christ, but the sacrifice for sin? *As Christ too*, he says, *loved you and gave himself up for you as an offering and sacrifice to God for an odor of sweetness* (Eph 5:2).

There you have the sin from which he condemned sin; from the sacrifice he became for sins, that's the vantage point from which he condemned sin.[13] That is *the law of the Spirit of life*, which *delivered you from the law of sin and death*

(Rom 8:2). Because that other law, the law of the letter, the law that commands, is indeed good; *the commandment is holy, and just, and good* (Rom 7:12); but it *was weakened through the flesh* (Rom 8:3), and was unable to achieve in us what it commanded. So let one law, as I was saying earlier on, show you what sin is, let the other take it away; let the law of the letter show you sin, let the law of grace take sin away.

NOTES

1. The sermon was preached in Carthage shortly after Sermon 151, perhaps the following Sunday; probably not, to judge from the way it begins, on the very next day.

2. Either Augustine is covering up for the reader's mistake in beginning the reading too far down the page, by assuming that the sentence and a half he had left out was read on the previous occasion; or else the readings were divided in a distinctly arbitrary fashion. In either case the earlier reading can scarcely have stopped halfway through the sentence of 8:3.

3. Sermon 151, 8.

4. The same contrast between *perficere* and *facere* as he was making in Sermon 151, 2, note 7.

5. The font in churches of those times was a shallow pool into which candidates stepped to be baptized.

6. See Rom 5:16.

7. Augustine just says *istam*, "this" in the feminine singular. It could just as well be "this lust." One thing it cannot be is "this flesh," because he has just firmly rejected the Manichee idea that the flesh, like everything material only more so, is intrinsically, substantively, evil; and has also just said that God created each part of human nature; that is, in this context, flesh and mind or spirit.

8. Well, Shakespeare too wrote a play called *The Taming of the Shrew*! Without wishing to excuse this endorsement by Augustine of the conventional masculine ethos of his society, I think it is worth noting that he develops a similar theme at length in Book XII of *The Trinity*, most of which was probably written a short time before he preached this sermon. And there, in elaborating the analogy between the relations of husband and wife (Adam and Eve) and the structure of the human psyche, he explicitly rejects what was in fact a conventional assimilation of the mind to Adam and the flesh to Eve. Instead he introduces a distinction into the mind itself, or rather into its functioning, and has Adam, the husband, represent its contemplative activity (wisdom), and Eve, the wife, its practical activity (knowledge). The role of the flesh is played by the serpent.

9. The Greek of the last clause means "in order that sin might become sinful above measure through the commandment." But Latin has no adjective, "sinful," and so the translator of Augustine's text used the participle *delinquens*, "offending"; and the sentence ought to be translated "in order that sin might become offending above measure." But Augustine, I think, took the participle *delinquens* as a masculine noun, "the offender," not as a neuter, qualifying *peccatum*.

10. The Latin text, introducing Section 8 here, really does obscure the progress of his thought. Section 8 should belong to the previous paragraph.

11. That is, by conceiving him as a virgin she shows he was not conceived by sexual concupiscence, which in Augustine's view is the means by which the defect of original sin is transmitted down the generations.

12. The great and profound mystery grows in this sentence from being the meaning of Christ's being in any sense sin, into the mystery of Christ himself in his fullness: the Word incarnate, crucified, risen, glorified.

13. Saint Augustine is to be congratulated (if that doesn't sound too patronizing) on achieving the right interpretation of Rom 8:3 in spite of the misleading translation and punctuation his Latin

version provided him with. What the Greek text has is, very literally, "God, having sent his Son in the likeness of the flesh of sin and about sin, condemned sin in the flesh." The Latin of Augustine's text (not the later Vulgate) changed the participle "having sent" into the main verb, "God sent"; so it naturally implied a comma after "flesh of sin," and continued with another parallel sentence, "and about sin condemned," etc. But it translated the Greek word for "about" quite correctly if literally with the Latin *de*. This preposition *de*, however, in the new structure of the Latin sentence inevitably changed its meaning from "about" to "from."

Now Paul's peculiar phrase "and about sin" is a piece of biblical Hebrew shorthand for "and a sacrifice about (for) sin." Augustine is stuck with the incorrect punctuation of the sentence, but correctly divines the meaning of "sin" in this expression.

SERMON 153

ON THE WORDS OF THE APOSTLE, ROMANS 7:5-13: *WHEN WE WERE IN THE FLESH, THE PASSIONS OF SINS WHICH COME THROUGH THE LAW WERE WORKING IN OUR MEMBERS, TO BEAR FRUIT FOR DEATH*, ETC. OPENLY AGAINST THE MANICHEES, AND TACITLY AGAINST THE PELAGIANS

Date: 419[1]

Troublesome passages of the apostle's letter

1. We heard, and in harmony we made the response, and sang to God with harmonious voices, *Blessed is the man whom you instruct, O Lord, and teach him from your law* (Ps 94:12). If you keep quiet, you will be able to hear. Wisdom can find no place, unless patience is there to prepare it.[2] I'm talking, but it's God who's instructing; I'm talking, but it's God who's teaching. After all, it doesn't say blessed is the man whom man teaches, but *whom you instruct, O Lord*. I can plant and water, but it belongs to God to give the growth.[3] The one who plants and waters is working from the outside; the one who gives the growth is supplying strength from within.

The reading from the holy apostle's letter which has been prescribed for us to talk about, and how difficult it is, how complicated, how dangerous indeed if it is not understood or understood wrongly, I think you realize, brothers and sisters; indeed I know you do, because you heard it when it was chanted to us just now. And if you noticed this, you were left in doubt and suspense; or if some of you did understand what he is saying, you undoubtedly saw how hard this is. So this is the reading that I have undertaken to explain, with the help of God's mercy, by going through it in detail, through this whole obscure and troublesome passage of the apostle's letter, which is however very helpful and wholesome to those who understand it rightly. I know I am in debt to your graces, and I have a feeling you are demanding payment. Just as I, then, am praying that you may grasp it all, so you too must pray that I may have the ability to explain it to you. If our prayers, you see, are in tune with each other, then God will make both you proper hearers, and me a truly reliable repayer of this debt.

2. *For when we were in the flesh*, says the apostle, *the passions of sins which come through the law were working in our members, to bear fruit for death* (Rom 7:5). Here it seems—and this is the first and great danger for those who don't understand it properly—that the apostle is blaming and finding fault with the law of God. Someone will say, "The very idea of such a thought crossing the mind of any kind of Christian! Could even a lunatic have the nerve to suspect the apostle of such a thing?" And yet, my dear brothers and sisters, these words, wrongly understood, have contributed a kind of lunatic fuel to the ravings of the Manichees. The Manichees, you see, say that the law of God which was given through Moses was not in fact given by God, and they maintain that it is contrary to the gospel.

And when you deal with them, they try to use these texts of the apostle Paul, which they don't understand, to convince—what shall I say?—Catholics who don't understand, or rather Catholics who won't take any trouble? It's not asking very much, after all, if you are prepared to take a little trouble, to suggest that after you have heard the heretic's misrepresentations, you should at least look up the whole context of the reading in the book.[4] If you do that, you will soon find the means of refuting the arguments of your talkative opponent, and of laying low the rebellious enemies of the law. Even if you are a bit slow to understand what the apostle says, the praises of God's law are expressed there quite openly.

3. First of all, though, see for yourselves that that's the case, and take note of it. *For when we were in the flesh*, he says, *the passions of sins which come through the law were working*. Here's the Manichee already squaring his shoulders, raising his horns, charging down on you, making a charge: "There you are," he says; "*the passions of sins which come through the law.* How can the law be good, through which the passions of sins are found in us, and are working in our members to bear fruit for death?"

Read on, go a little further, listen to the whole passage with patience, even if not with understanding. I agree, what he says here, *the passions of sins which come through the law are working in our members*, is hard for you to understand; but first join me in praising the law, and then you will deserve also to understand it. You've got a closed mind, and are you blaming the key?[5] Come then, let us set aside for the time being what we don't understand, and come to the plain, straightforward praise of the law.

The passions of sins, he says, *which come through the law, were working in our members to bear fruit for death. Now therefore we have been rid of the law of death by which we were being held down, in such a way that we may serve in the freshness of the spirit, and not in the staleness of the letter* (Rom 7:5-6). He still seems to be impeaching the law, blaming, rejecting, disavowing it—but only to those who don't understand does he seem so. I agree, when he says,

When we were in the flesh, the passions of sins which come through the law, were working in our members to bear fruit for sin. Now therefore we have been rid of the law of death by which we were being held down, in such a way that we may serve in the freshness of the spirit and not in the staleness of the letter, it seems as if with every word[6] he is accusing and blaming the law. He saw this himself, he saw it, he had a feeling he was not being understood, and people's thoughts were stirring against the obscurity of his words; he had a feeling about what you may say, he had a feeling about the objection you may be able to bring; and he wanted to say it first, so that you would be unable to find anything to say yourself.

The law is not sin

4. *What then are we to say?* he says. That's how he continues: *What therefore are we to say? That the law is sin? Perish the thought!* (Rom 7:7). At a stroke he acquitted the law, condemned its accuser. You were bringing the apostle's authority against me, you Manichee, and you were saying to me when you were damning the law, "Look, listen to the apostle, read the apostle: *The passions of sins which come through the law were working in our members to bear fruit for death. Now therefore we have been rid of the law of death, by which we were being held down, in such a way that we may serve in the freshness of the spirit and not in the staleness of the letter.*" You were preening yourself, crying yourself up, saying, "Listen, read, see." That's what you were saying, and now you're very keen to turn your back on me and go away.

Wait, though; I listened to you, now you listen to me. Or rather, neither I to you nor you to me, but let's both listen together to the apostle, who unties himself and ties you up. *What then are we to say?* he says. *That the law is sin?* That's what you were saying: "The law is sin"; that's just exactly what you were saying. There you are, you've heard what you were saying; now hear what you ought to say. You were saying God's law is sin, when you were blindly and thoughtlessly damning it. You were mistaken. Paul saw your mistake; what you were saying, he said himself. *What then are we to say? That the law is sin?* What you were saying, is that what we say, *that the law is sin? Perish the thought!* If you were following the apostle's authority, weigh his words, and get some good advice from them. Listen: *That the law is sin? Perish the thought!* Listen: *Perish the thought!* If you follow the apostle, and attach great weight to his authority, listen: *Perish the thought!*, and may the thought you were thinking perish from you.

What then are we to say? Well, what are we to say? Because I said, *The passions of sins which come through the law were working in our members to bear fruit for death*; because I said, *We have been rid of the law of death, by which we were being held down*; because I said, *that we may serve in the freshness of the spirit, and not in the staleness of the letter*, does that mean *that the law is sin? Perish the thought!* Why, in that case, my dear apostle, did you say all that?

5. Perish the thought that the law may be sin. *But I would never have known about sin*, he goes on, *except through the law. For I would not know about lust, unless the law said: You shall not lust* (Rom 7:7). Right now I'm going to question you, Manichee; now I'm questioning you, answer me please. Is the law bad which says, *You shall not lust*? Not even the most shameless of lechers will give me that answer. After all, even the most dissolute rakes blush when they are rebuked for their behavior; and when they are in the company of clean-living people, they don't dare to indulge in loose behavior. So if you say that the law is bad which says, *You shall not lust*, it means you want to lust with impunity; you bring a charge against the law, because it lashes out at lustfulness.

My dear brothers and sisters, even if we never heard the apostle saying, *That the law is sin? Perish the thought!*, but only heard him reminding us of the words of the law where it says, *You shall not lust*; even if he wasn't praising the law, we would have to praise it ourselves; praise the law, accuse ourselves. Here's the law, here's the divine clarion call crying out to mankind from above, *You shall not lust*. You shall not lust; damn it if you can; if you can't damn it, do it. You heard, *You shall not lust*; you daren't damn it, because what it said is good: *You shall not lust*. It's bad to lust. The law is blaming something bad, it is restraining you from your badness. So the law brands lust as bad, it restrains you from your badness. So do what the law commands, don't do what the law forbids, don't lust.

6. But what does the apostle say? *I would not know about lust, unless the law said, You shall not lust.* You see, I was following my own lust, and running off wherever it drew me, and regarding its charming allurements, so enjoyable with the delights of the flesh, as great happiness. *The sinner*, you see, *is praised*, says the law, *in the desires of his soul; and the one who commits wicked deeds is blessed* (Ps 10:3).

You can find a man pursuing his carnal lusts, giving himself over to them totally as their slave, chasing pleasures in every direction, fornicating, getting drunk; I won't add any more; fornicating, I say, getting drunk. I've mentioned things which can be committed legally, but not according to God's laws. I mean, who was ever taken before a judge, because he went to a whorehouse? Who was ever charged in open court because he let himself go in dirty little games with his lyre girls? What married man ever found himself branded a criminal because he violated his maidservant? But in the law courts, not in heaven; according to the law of the world, not the law of the world's Creator. On the contrary, the lewd, licentious man, the lecher, is called happy for having such a good time, enjoying such pleasures.

And now, if he drowns himself in wine, if he drinks measures without measure, that he doesn't find himself facing a criminal charge is nothing; he gets a name for being a tough guy; all the more wicked for being unconquered in his drinking. When this sort of thing is praised, and people say, "Lucky man, he's a great fellow, he's all right"; and this is not only not considered to be a sin, but is even thought to be either a gift from God, or at least a good that is pleasant, attractive and legitimate; the law of God steps in and says, *You shall not lust.*

The man who thought it was a really good thing, and reckoned it a great piece of luck not to deny his lust whatever lay in his power, but to follow wherever it drew him, now hears *You shall not lust,* and recognizes that it's a sin. God has spoken, man has heard. He has believed God, he has seen his sin; he has realized that what he thought was good is bad; he has wanted to bridle his lust, not to follow it, he has pulled himself together, or at least he has tried hard to do so—and he has been defeated. Previously unaware of his badness, he has now been both educated and more badly than ever defeated; he has begun to be not only a sinner but also a transgressor. He was a sinner, after all, even previously; but before he heard the law, he didn't know he was a sinner. He heard the law, he saw the sin, he made an effort to conquer it, he was overcome and laid low; having previously been a sinner without knowing it, he has become in addition a transgressor of the law. That's what the apostle says: *The law is sin? Perish the thought! But I would never have known about sin, except through the law. For I would not know about lust, unless the law said, You shall not lust* (Rom 7:7).

How the law strengthens lust

7. *But seizing its opportunity, sin through the commandment worked in me every kind of lust* (Rom 7:8). There was less of lust when you were sinning before the law without a care in the world; but now that the law's barricades have been set in place against you, the stream of lust has been checked a little as by a dam, but not dried up. When there were no barriers, it used to carry you along; now its pressure builds up, it bursts the barriers and overwhelms you. Your lust was less strong when it needed only to sway your fancy; but it's a swollen flood[7] when it also overflows the law. Would you like to see how huge it is? Look at what it has burst through: *You shall not lust.* It's not man that said this, God said it, the Creator said it, the eternal judge said it, it wasn't just anybody who said it. So do what he said. You don't do it? Take note of him judging you, the one who said it. But what are you to do, man? The reason you haven't been victorious is that you have been presumptuously self-reliant.

How the law makes transgressors

8. Now look back at the earlier words, which seemed so obscure: *For when we were in the flesh.* Think back to what I said are the earlier words, with which the reading began that seemed so obscure: *For when we were in the flesh, the passions of sins which come through the law* (Rom 7:5). Why do they come through the law? Because we were in the flesh. What does that mean: because

we were in the flesh? We were presumptuously relying on the flesh.[8] I mean, the apostle talking here hadn't already departed from this flesh, had he? He surely wasn't talking to people who had departed from this flesh, was he? Of course not, but according to the manner of this present life, both he that was talking and the ones he was talking to were in the flesh.

So what's the meaning of *When we were in the flesh*, if not "When we were presumptuously relying on the flesh," that is, only taking ourselves into consideration? You see, a human being was told, and he was told it about human beings, *All flesh will see the salvation of God* (Lk 3:6). What does *All flesh will see* mean, but "All human beings will see"? And what does *The Word became flesh* mean, but "The Word became man" (Jn 1:14)? It isn't the case, I mean, that the Word was flesh, without there being a soul there;[9] but the word "flesh" signifies "man" in the text *The Word became flesh*.

So, *when we were in the flesh*, that is were taken up with the lusts of the flesh, and placing all our hope there as in ourselves, *the passions of sins which come through the law* were increased through the law, because by being forbidden they created a transgressor of the law; because the one who became a transgressor did not have God as a helper. So *they were working in our members to bear fruit*, for what, if not *for death*? If the sinner deserved condemnation, what hope was there for the transgressor?

Place your hopes in God

9. So then, man and woman,[10] your lust has conquered you, because it found you in a bad place; it found you in the flesh, that's why it conquered you; emigrate from there. Why panic? I haven't told you to die. Don't panic because I said, "Emigrate from the flesh." I haven't told you to die—or rather I've the nerve to say, yes I have told you to die. If you have died with Christ, seek the things that are above.[11] While living in the flesh, don't go on being in the flesh. *All flesh is grass, but the Word of the Lord abides for ever* (Is 40:6.8). Make the Lord your refuge. lust is pressing its attack, it's pushing you hard, it has received powerful reinforcements against you, it has grown stronger by the very fact of the law forbidding it, you have a greater enemy than ever to put up with. Make the Lord your refuge, a tower of strength in the face of the foe.[12]

So don't go on being in the flesh, start being in the spirit instead. What's being in the spirit? Place your hopes in God. Because if you place your hopes just in the spirit which makes you a human being, your spirit is again slipping back into the flesh, because you haven't surrendered to the one on whom it should depend. It won't keep a hold on itself, unless it is held together by him. Don't stay in yourself, rise above even yourself; place yourself in the one who made you and your true self. Because if you have hoped in yourself, once you have received the law you will be a transgressor. The enemy finds you bereft of a refuge, he invades you; look out he doesn't perhaps grab you like a lion, and there's nobody to rescue you.[13]

Pay attention to the words of the apostle, praising the law, accusing himself, pleading guilty under the law, and perhaps making himself your representative, as he says to you, *I would never have known about sin, except through the law. For I would not know about lust, unless the law said, You shall not lust. But seizing its opportunity, sin through the commandment worked in me every kind of lust. For without the law sin is dead.* What's the meaning of *sin is dead*? It's hidden, it doesn't show at all, it's as unknown as if it were dead and buried. *But when the commandment came, sin revived* (Rom 7:7-9). What's the meaning of *revived*? It began to show, it began to be felt, it began to rebel against me.

Do what you praise

10. *But I died.* What's the meaning of *I died*? I became a transgressor, *and the commandment which was directed toward life* (Rom 7:10). Notice that the law is being praised; *the commandment which was directed toward life.* I mean, what sort of life must it be, not to feel lust? Oh what an agreeable life! Pleasure, of course, is agreeable to lust; it's true, and people wouldn't pursue it unless it was agreeable. The theater, the circus, the sexy harlot, filthy songs,[14] all these things are agreeable to lust; obviously agreeable, pleasant, delightful. But, *The unjust described delights to me, but not like your law, O Lord* (Ps 119:85). Happy is the soul which is entertained by delights of this sort, in which it is not sullied by anything vile, and is purified by the serenity of truth. But any of you whose delight is *in the law of God* (Ps 1:2), and who are delighted by it in such a way that it beats all the delights of loose living,[15] must not claim credit for this delight for yourselves; *it is the Lord who will give delight* (Ps 85:12).

What shall I say? "Lord, give me this delight, or that one"? *You are delightful, Lord, and in your delightfulness teach me your just judgments* (Ps 119:68). Teach me in your delightfulness, and then you really do teach me. Then I really learn to do it, if you teach me in your delightfulness. But when iniquity beckons alluringly and iniquity is sweet, then truth is bitter. *In your delightfulness teach me*, so that truth may be sweet, and iniquity be put in the shade by your delightfulness. Truth is much, much better and more delicious; but it's to the hale and hearty that bread is tasty.[16] What could be better and more excellent than the bread of heaven?[17] But provided iniquity doesn't set your teeth on edge. Scripture says, you see: *As sour grapes are painful to the teeth, and smoke to the eyes, so is iniquity to those who make use of it* (Prv 10:26).

What's the use of praising this bread, if you live bad lives? It means you don't eat what you praise. So when you hear a word, when you hear a word of justice and truth, and praise it, it would be much more praiseworthy if you did it. So then, do what you praise. Or are you going to say, "I have the will, but not the wit or the way"? Why haven't you got the wit or the way? Because there is no health in you. How did you lose your health? Because you offended your Creator by sinning. So then, in order to eat his bread, which you praise, with delight, which means with good health, say to him, *I said, Lord, have mercy on me; heal my soul, since I have sinned against you* (Ps 41:4).

Therefore, Paul says, *The commandment which was directed toward life, was found for me to be the occasion of death* (Rom 7:10). Previously, you see, he was a sinner without realizing it himself; now he has become an unmistakable transgressor. So that's it; what was directed toward life was found to be for him the occasion of death.

Don't trust in your own strength

11. *But seizing its opportunity*, he says, *sin through the commandment deceived me, and through it slew me* (Rom 7:11). That's what happened first of all in paradise. *It deceived me*, he says, *seizing its opportunity through the commandment.* Notice the serpent whispering to that woman. It inquired of her what God had said; she answered, *God said to us: Of every tree that is in paradise you shall eat; but of the tree of the knowledge of good and evil you shall not eat. If you eat of it, you will die the death.*[18] That's God's command. Against it the serpent says, *You will not die the death. For God knew that on the day you eat of it your eyes will be opened, and you will be like gods* (Gn 3:4-5).

So, *seizing its opportunity, sin through the commandment deceived me, and through it slew me.* With the very sword you were carrying the enemy slew you; he defeated you with your own weapons, destroyed you with your own weapons. Receive the commandment; understand it's a weapon which is not meant for the enemy to kill you with, but with which you are meant to kill him. But don't rely presumptuously on your own strength. Look at little David against Goliath, look at the little lad against the giant; but he's relying on the name of the Lord. *You come against me*, he says, *with shield and lance; I, though, in the name of the Lord almighty* (1 Sam 17:45). Yes, that's the way, that's the way; no other way; in absolutely no other way at all is the enemy to be laid low. Anybody who trusts in his own strength is laid low himself before the fight even begins.

Paul praises the divine law

12. Notice though, dear friends, notice how again and again the apostle Paul praises the divine law as openly as you could wish against the ravings of the Manichees; notice what he adds: *And so the law indeed is holy, and the commandment holy, and just, and good* (Rom 7:12). Could it be more highly praised than that? A little earlier, with his words *Perish the thought!* (Rom 7:7) he had been defending it against an accusation, not praising it. It's one thing to defend against an accusation that has been leveled, another to proclaim the worth of something with proper commendation. The accusation leveled was: *So what are we to say? That the law is sin?* The defense was, *Perish the thought!* The truth is defended with a single phrase, because the apostle defending it has great authority. Why spend a lot of time defending? *Perish the thought!* is quite enough. *Or do you wish to be given proof*, he says, *of Christ speaking in me?* (2 Cor 13:3). But now: *And so the law is holy, and the commandment holy, and just, and good.*

13. *Did what is good, therefore, become death for me? Perish the thought!* Because death is not good. *But sin, that it might be seen to be sin, through the good worked death for me* (Rom 7:13). The law isn't death, but sin is. But he had already said, *Without the law sin was dead* (Rom 7:8); where I reminded you that by *is dead* he meant is hidden and unnoticed, is not seen. Now you can see how right that explanation was: *Sin,* he says, *that it might be seen to be sin.* He didn't say "that it might be sin," because it was already there even when it wasn't seen as such.

Sin, that it might be seen to be sin. What's the meaning of *that it might be seen to be sin?* The same as, *I would not know about lust, unless the law said, You shall not lust* (Rom 7:7). He didn't say, "I wouldn't have lust," but *I would not know about lust.* So too here, he doesn't say, "that it might be sin," but *that it might be seen to be sin, through the good it worked death for me.* What death? *That it might become above measure sinner* (or sin)[19] *through the commandment* (Rom 7:13). Notice, *above measure sinner.* Why *above measure?* Because now it's also transgression. *For where there is no law, neither is there any transgression* (Rom 4:15).

14. So then observe, brothers and sisters, observe how the human race has flowed from the death of that first man. Thus: *Sin entered* from the first man *into this world, and through sin death, and thus it passed through into all men* (Rom 5:12). *Passed through*; take note of these words you heard; reflect, and see what is meant by *passed through.* It passed through; as a result, even the baby is guilty; it hasn't yet committed sin, but it has contracted it. You see, that sin didn't remain in its source, but *passed through,*[20] not into this person or that, but *into all men.* The first sinner, the first transgressor, begot sinners liable to death.

To heal them, the savior came from the virgin; because he didn't come to you the way you came, seeing that he did not originate from the sexual appetite of male and female, not from that chain of lust.[21] *The Holy Spirit,* it says, *will come upon you.* That was said to the virgin glowing with faith, not seething with carnal lust. *The Holy Spirit will come upon you, and the power of the Most High will overshadow you* (Lk 1:35). Being overshadowed like that, how could she be seething with the heat of sexual desire?

So, because he didn't come to you the way you came, he sets you free. Where did he find you? Sold under sin,[22] lying in the death of the first man, deriving sin from the first man, having guilt before you could have any free choice. That's where he found you, when he found you as a baby. But you have got beyond your infant years; why look, you've grown up, to the first sin you have added many more, you have received the law, you have turned out a transgressor. But don't worry: *Where sin abounded, grace has abounded even more* (Rom 5:20).

Turning to the Lord, etc.

NOTES

1. Thanks to the information that Sermon 156 was preached on the feast day of the Bolitan Martyrs, that and the three preceding sermons can be dated very precisely, because that feast day in the Carthaginian calendar was 17 October. Sermon 156 was preached two days after 155, while 153-155 were preached on three consecutive days. So we have for this sermon the date (and day of the week, Perler page 359, note 1), Monday 13 October.

2. *Non invenit locum sapientia ubi non est patientia.* I suppose there was some jostling and pushing to get to a place where they could hear easily. His voice did not always carry very well.

3. See 1 Cor 3:7.

4. Could Augustine really assume that most of his audience would have copies of Paul's letters, or easy access to them, or even that most of them could read? But then if the Manichee quotes Paul at them, they can at least, he is saying, insist on the whole passage being read.

5. A nice turn of phrase, but one mustn't press the comparison too hard. What his interlocutor is blaming is the law, and Augustine is not really suggesting that the law is the key to understanding either the law or Paul. The key is reading the whole passage carefully and objectively.

6. Reading *ubique* with several manuscripts instead of *utique*, certainly, with the text.

7. Reading *amnis* instead of the *omnis*, all, of the text—which may well, indeed, be a misprint.

8. That is to say, on ourselves. He is here just repeating, as an interpretation of Paul's "flesh" language, what he has just said in his own words at the end of the previous paragraph.

9. This was a view put forward by Bishop Apollinaris, a staunch supporter of Athanasius of Alexandria, about 360. It was vehemently and rightly opposed by the theological school of Antioch, which insisted on the complete and integral humanity of Jesus, even to the point (so their Alexandrian rivals would say) of maintaining that he was a distinct person from the divine Word who assumed him. While the issue was to be dogmatically resolved by the Council of Chalcedon, 451, defining that Jesus Christ, the Word incarnate, is one person in two natures, true God and true man, in historical fact it brought about the first great breach in Catholic unity that has remained permanently unhealed to this day.

10. This is either Everyman, as represented by Paul in Romans 7, or Adam. The switch from first person plural to third singular is characteristic of his *ex tempore* style.

11. See Col 3:1-3.

12. See Ps 61:3.

13. See Ps 10:9, combined slightly incongruously with Ps 50:22.

14. That he makes no distinction between theater and circus (*spectaculum*—I use "circus" in the modern sense of a show with clowns, acrobats, etc.) on the one hand, and harlots and indecent songs on the other, simply reflects the conventional moral stance of the Church at the time: straitlaced and puritanical.

15. Perhaps in his mind he gave a backward glance at his account of his own conversion in the garden in Milan, *Confessions* VIII, 16-30.

16. An Augustinian "rhyme to remember": *sed sanis suavis est panis.*

17. He is not thinking here of the eucharist; rather of the divine Word, as fed to us through the divine words, law and gospel.

18. Gn 3:2-3, mixed up with 2:16-17.

19. In the previous sermon, 152, 6, he quoted this text differently; see Sermon 152, note 8. In the interval between that sermon and this one—and this may indicate that this one was preached later—he had perhaps consulted the Greek text again; or else he had a more accurate Latin version. In any case here he, or his version, renders the Greek *hamartōlos*, which is primarily an adjective meaning "sinful," and secondarily a noun meaning "sinner," by the Latin *peccator*, which is only a noun meaning "sinner." Well, to call sin sinner is very odd, Just as odd in Latin as in English; so he adds his own brief explanation, "or sin" in brackets. Thus he does not seem here to construe the phrase in the way I suggested he did in Sermon 152 (note 8). See also Sermon 155, note 9.

20. According to the most reliable Greek manuscripts, and the Latin Vulgate, Paul is saying that death, not sin, passed through to all men. So this text can only be taken as a very indirect authority

for the doctrine of original sin, and not be read as an actual statement of the doctrine, as Augustine supposed.

21. The chain going right back to Adam is what he means.

22. See Rom 7:14.

SERMON 154

ON THE WORDS OF THE APOSTLE, ROMANS 7:14-25: *WE KNOW THAT THE LAW IS SPIRITUAL; BUT I AM OF THE FLESH*, ETC.; AGAINST THE PELAGIANS WHO SAY THAT ONE CAN BE WITHOUT SIN IN THIS LIFE: PREACHED AT THE SHRINE OF THE HOLY MARTYR CYPRIAN

Date: 419[1]

Why was the law given?

1. Those of you who were present for the sermon, heard what was read yesterday from the letter of the holy apostle Paul; the reading that has been chanted today follows on that one. We are still dealing with that difficult and perilous passage, which with the help of our Lord, and the assistance of your religious supplications to him, I have undertaken to explain and unravel for you, with whatever powers he is pleased to grant me. Would your graces please be patient with me, so that even if I have some difficulty, because of the obscurity of the subject, in marshaling my arguments, I may at least find it easy to make my voice heard.[2] I mean to say, if the business is difficult on both counts, then it's really hard labor—and I only hope it won't be labor wasted. But for my labors to be any use, you please must listen patiently.

That the apostle finds no fault with the law, I rather think I proved to the satisfaction of those who heard me yesterday. Thus he said then, *What then are we to say? That the law is sin? Perish the thought! But I would never have known about sin except through the law. For I would not know about lust, unless the law said, You shall not lust. But seizing its opportunity, sin through the commandment worked in me every kind of lust. For without the law sin is dead*; that is, it's hidden, it isn't seen as such. *But I was alive once without the law; but with the coming of the commandment, sin revived. I, though, died, and the commandment which was directed toward life*—what, after all, is so relevant to life as "You shall not lust"?—*was found to be for me the occasion of death. For sin seizing its opportunity through the commandment deceived me, and through it slew me.* It[3] terrified lust, it didn't extinguish it; terrified it, without suppressing it; induced fear of punishment, not love of justice. *And so*, he says, *the law indeed is holy, and the commandment holy, and just, and good. Did what is good, therefore, become death for me? Perish the thought!* Because the law isn't death,

68

but sin is death. So what did it use the commandment as an opportunity for? *But sin, in order that it might be seen to be sin*; it was hidden, you see, when it was said to be dead; *through the good worked death for me; so that*, with transgression now added, *it might become above measure sinner* (or sin) *through the commandment* (Rom 7:7-13); because transgression wouldn't be added to sin if there were no commandment. Somewhere else, you see, the same apostle says plainly, *For where there is no law, neither is there transgression* (Rom 4:15).

So what now? Need we doubt that the law was given for this reason, so that we might discover ourselves? When God didn't actually forbid us to do evil, you see, we were hidden from ourselves; we only discovered how feeble our powers were, when we received the prohibitions of the law. So we find ourselves, we find ourselves immersed in evils. Where can we escape to from ourselves? After all, wherever we run away to from ourselves, we follow ourselves. And what use is the knowledge we have when we have found ourselves, when in our consciences we continue to wound ourselves?

Perhaps Paul speaks of himself

2. So in this reading too, which was chanted today, the person is speaking who has found himself. *For we know*, he says, *that the law is spiritual; I, though, am of the flesh, sold under sin. For I do not understand how I am behaving; for it is not what I want to that I do; but what I hate, that is what I carry out* (Rom 7:14-15). Here people inquire with great persistence who is to be understood here; whether it's the apostle himself who was talking, or whether he has transposed someone else onto himself, whom he was getting at in his own person, in the way he mentioned somewhere or other: *But all this I have transposed onto myself and Apollo for your sakes, so that you may learn a lesson from us* (1 Cor 4:6).

So if it's the apostle speaking (and nobody questions that), and if when he says, *It is not what I want to that I do; but what I hate, that is what I carry out*, he is not saying it about someone else, but about himself; how are we going to understand this, my dear brothers and sisters? Does it mean that the apostle Paul did not want, for example, to commit adultery, and did commit adultery? That he didn't want to be a miser, and was a miser? Is there any of us who would have the nerve to take responsibility for such a slander, as to have that sort of opinion of the apostle? So perhaps it's someone else; perhaps it's you, or it's you, or it's him, or it's me. So if it's one of us, let us hear about ourselves as though we were him, and correct ourselves without getting angry about it.

But if it's himself, and perhaps after all it is also himself, we shouldn't take what he said, *It is not what I want to that I do, but what I hate, that is what I carry out*, as meaning that he wanted to be chaste, and was in fact an adulterer; that he wanted to be kind, and was in fact cruel; that he wanted to be religious, and was in fact irreligious. That's not the sense in which we should understand, *For it is not what I want to that I do, but what I hate, that is what I carry out*.

Paul was not without lust in his flesh

3. But in what sense? "I want not to lust, and yet I do lust." What did the law say? *You shall not lust* (Rom 7:7). Man heard the law, recognized his vice, declared war on it, found himself its prisoner. But perhaps some other man, not the apostle. So what are we saying, my dear brothers and sisters? That the apostle had no lust in his flesh, which he would much rather not have, but which he didn't consent to, though it arose, tickled his fancy, gave him ideas, drew him on, boiled up, tempted him? I'm telling your graces, if we believe the apostle had absolutely no weakness of lust he had to struggle against, then we are believing something splendid about him; and if only it were so! It's not for us, after all, to be jealous of the apostles, but to imitate them.

However, my very dear friends, I can hear the apostle himself confessing that he had not yet arrived at such a perfection of justice as we believe the angels enjoy; the angels whom we are looking forward to being the equals of, if we finally reach what we desire. What else, after all, is the Lord promising us in the resurrection, when he says, *In the resurrection of the dead they do not marry either husbands or wives; for they are not going to die any more, but will be equal to the angels of God* (Lk 20:35-36).

Paul speaks of his own imperfections

4. So someone will say to me, "And how do *you* know that Paul the apostle did not yet have the justice and perfection of an angel?" I'm not doing the apostle an injustice, I'm only believing the apostle himself, I'm not calling any other witness; I don't listen to suspicions, I don't care about excessive praise. Tell me, holy apostle, about yourself, where nobody can doubt that you are talking about yourself. Because where you said, *It is not what I want to that I do; but what I hate, that is what I carry out*, people come forward to say that you were transposing to yourself, the case of goodness knows who else, struggling, failing, beaten, taken prisoner. You please tell me about yourself, where no one can doubt that you are talking about yourself.

Brothers, says the apostle, *I, certainly, do not reckon that I have attained the goal.* And what are you achieving? *One thing, however, forgetting what lies behind, stretching out to what lies ahead, according to intention*, he says, not according to perfection; *according to intention I follow after to the palm of God's calling from above in Christ Jesus.* He had just said already, *Not that I have already obtained it, or am already perfect* (Phil 3:13-14.12).

Still the objection comes, and someone says, "The apostle was saying this because he had not yet attained to immortality, not because he had not yet attained to the perfection of justice. So he was already as just as the angels are, but not yet as immortal as the angels are. Yes," they say, "yes, that's certainly how it is." So what you have just said is this: "He was as just as the angels are, but not yet as immortal as the angels are. So he already possessed the perfection of justice, but by following after to the palm up above, he was seeking immortality."

Listen to Paul's confessions in order to profit from his instruction

5. Tell us, holy apostle, about some other clearer place, where you are not seeking immortality, but where you are confessing infirmity. Even here there is already whispering going on, already objections being made. I seem to hear what some people are thinking; even here they are saying to me: "It's true, I know what you're going to say; he confesses infirmity, but of the flesh, not of the mind; he confesses to infirmity, but of the body, not of the spirit. But it's in the spirit that perfect justice is to be found, not in the body. Everybody knows, of course, that the apostle was frail of body, was mortal in his body, as he says himself: *We have this treasure in earthen vessels* (2 Cor 4:7). So what business of yours is the earthen vessel? Say something about the treasure. If he was lacking anything, if there was anything that could be added to the gold of his justice, let's find out what it was."

Well, let's listen to him, if we don't want to be regarded as being unjust to him. *And lest by the magnitude of my revelations*, the apostle says; *lest I should grow proud in the magnitude of my revelations* (2 Cor 12:7). Here, surely, you can recognize the apostle enjoying the greatness of the revelations, and fearing the precipice of pride. So to show you that the apostle too, who was eager to save others, was still in need of care; to show you that he himself was still needing treatment, if you set such store by his honor, listen to what the doctor prescribed for his tumor; don't listen to me, listen to him. Listen to his confession, in order to profit from his instruction. Listen: *And lest by the magnitude of my revelations I should grow proud.* There you are, I can now say, can I, to the apostle Paul, "Lest you should grow proud, holy apostle? *You*, you still have to beware of growing proud? To prevent *you* growing proud, some medicine still has to be found for this weakness?"

Paul was humbled

6. "What do you think you are saying to me?" he says. "You too, listen to what I am, and *don't be high-minded, but fear* (Rom 11:20). Listen to how carefully the little lamb should step, where the ram is in such grave danger." *Lest by the magnitude*, he says, *of my revelations I should grow proud, there was given me a goad in my flesh, a messenger of Satan to knock me about* (2 Cor 12:7-9). What sort of tumor must he have feared, if he could accept such a smarting, stinging poultice as that? So now then, now say that there was as much justice in him as there is in the holy angels. Or perhaps a holy angel in heaven, in order not to grow proud, receives as a goad a messenger of Satan, to be knocked about by? Far be it from us to suspect such a thing about the holy angels.

We are human, we acknowledge that the holy apostles were human; chosen vessels, certainly, but still fragile; still wanderers abroad in this flesh, not yet triumphantly victorious in the heavenly home country. So since he asked the Lord three times for this goad to be taken away from him, and his wishes were ignored, because his welfare was being considered and restored; perhaps in that case he is not improperly speaking about himself, when he says, *But we know that the law is spiritual; I, however, am of the flesh* (Rom 7:14).

7. So the apostle is of the flesh, is he, though he said to others, *You that are spiritual, instruct such a one in a spirit of gentleness* (Gal 6:1)? He addresses others as spiritual, and is himself of the flesh, is he? But what did he say even to these spiritual people, precisely because they were not yet in a state of heavenly and angelic perfection, not yet in the safe haven of that home country, but still situated amid the anxieties of this earthly journey? What did he say to them? Certainly, he called them spiritual: *You*, he said, *who are spiritual, instruct such a one in the spirit of gentleness, looking to yourself, lest you too should be tempted.* There you are, he has already called him spiritual, but he's afraid for him about temptation, and the frailty through which a spiritual person could be tempted, not through the mind, but certainly through the flesh. He's spiritual, you see, because he lives according to the spirit; but still, as regards his mortal part, of the flesh; the same person, at once spiritual and carnal, or of the flesh. Here you have him spiritual: *With the mind I serve the law of God*; here he is, of the flesh: *but with the flesh the law of sin* (Rom 7:25). So is he too at once both spiritual and carnal? Yes certainly, he too, as long as he is living here, is like that.

8. Don't be surprised, whoever you are, whoever gives in and consents to the lusts of the flesh, and either regard them as good, for satisfying your instincts to the full, or else while already seeing that they are bad, nonetheless consent to them by giving in, and follow where they lead, and commit whatever evil deeds they suggest; you are totally flesh-bound, carnal. You, yes you, whichever of you is like that, are totally carnal. But if you lust indeed, which the law forbids when it says *You shall not lust* (Rom 7:7); but all the same keep the other commandment of the same law, *Do not go after your lusts* (Sir 18:30); then you are spiritual in the mind, flesh-bound in the flesh. It's one thing, after all, not to lust; another not to go after one's lusts. Not to lust is the mark of the altogether perfect person; not to go after one's lusts marks the person who is fighting, struggling, toiling.

While the battle rages, why despair of victory? When will victory come? When death is swallowed up in victory. Then will be the time for the victor's triumphant shout, now is the time for the fighter's sweat. What will that shout of triumph be, when this perishable thing has put on imperishability, and this mortal thing has put on immortality? You see the winner, you hear him boasting; wait for his moment of triumph.[4] *Then the word will come to pass which is written: Death has been swallowed up in victory. Where, death, is your strife? Where, death, is your sting?* (1 Cor 15:53-55). Where is it? There you are, it was, and it isn't.

Where, death, is your strife? Here's the striving of death: *It is not what I want to that I do.* Here's the striving of death: *We know that the law is spiritual, but I am of the flesh* (Rom 7:15.14). So if the apostle is saying this about himself (I say "if"; I'm not asserting it); if the apostle says, *We know that the law is spiritual, but I am of the flesh*; spiritual in mind, of the flesh in body;[5] when will he be entirely spiritual? When: *it is sown embodying the soul; it will rise again embodying the spirit* (1 Cor 15:44). So now, while death is striving furiously, *it is not what I want to that I do*. I'm partly spiritual, partly flesh-bound; spiritual in the better part, flesh-bound in the lower. I'm still locked in combat, I haven't yet conquered; it's a great thing for me not to have been conquered. *It is not what I want to that I do; what I hate, that is what I carry out* (Rom 7:15). What do you carry out? I lust. Even if I don't consent to lust, even if I don't go after my lusts; all the same, I still lust; and of course I am myself in that part too.

One person, divided

9. You see, it's not a case of it's being me in the mind, someone else in the flesh. But what is the case? *I myself, therefore*; because it's I myself in the mind, I myself in the flesh. It's not a case, you see, of two opposed natures, but of one human being made from each nature; because it is one God by whom humanity was made.[6] *I myself, therefore*, I myself, *with the mind serve the law of God, but with the flesh the law of sin* (Rom 7:25). With the mind I do not consent to the law of sin; but for all that, I would much rather there wasn't any law of sin in my members. So because I would much rather not, and yet all the same there is: *it is not what I want to that I do*; because I lust, and don't want to, *it is not what I want to that I do; but what I hate, that is what I carry out*. What do I hate? Lusting. I hate lusting, and yet I do it, with the flesh, not the mind. *What I hate, that is what I carry out*.

"Doing" may be desiring, consenting, or accomplishing

10. *But if what I carry out is what I do not want to, I give my consent to the law, that it is good* (Rom 7:16). Now what's this: *if what I carry out is what I do not want to, I give my consent to the law that it is good*? You would give your consent to the law if you did what it wanted; you carry out what the law hates, how are you giving your consent to it?

"No, certainly: *if what I carry out is what I do not want to, I give my consent to the law that it is good*."

"How?"

"What does the law command?"

"*You shall not lust* (Rom 7:7)."

"What do I want? Not to lust. By wanting what the law wants, *I give my consent to the law that it is good*. If the law said, *You shall not lust*, and I wanted to lust, I would not be giving my consent to the law, but would stand out as moving in an entirely different direction owing to that perversity of will. Clearly, if the law says, *You shall not lust* and I would like to lust, I am not giving my consent to the law of God. But what's the actual case? What do you say, law? *You shall not lust*. I too don't want to lust; I too don't want to. What you don't want, I don't want; that's why I am giving you my consent, because I don't want what you don't want. My weakness isn't fulfilling the law; but my will is praising the law. So if it's what I don't want to that I do, that is precisely why I am giving my consent to the law, because I don't want what it doesn't want; not because I do what I don't want to."

The doing here, you see, is the lusting, it isn't the consenting to the lust; in case anyone should now look to the apostle to get himself an example of sinning, and should himself set a bad example. *It is not what I want to that I do.* After all, what does the law say? *You shall not lust.* I too don't want to lust, and yet I do lust; although I don't yield consent to my lust, although I don't go after it. I stand up to it, you see, I turn my mind away from it, I refuse it any weapons, I restrain my members. And yet what I don't want occurs in me. What the law doesn't want, I join the law in not wanting; what it doesn't want, I don't want either; so I give my consent to the law.

"I do not acknowledge what I do"

11. But because it is I that am in the mind, I that am in the flesh—but I am more in the mind than in the flesh. You see, because it is I that am in the mind, I am in the ruler; the mind, after all, rules, the flesh is ruled; and I am more in that by which I rule than in that in which I am ruled. So because I am more in the mind, *But now it is no longer I that perform it. But now*—what does that mean? *But now,* now that I am already redeemed, previously having been sold under sin (Rom 7:14), now that I have received the grace of the savior so as to take delight in the law of God with my mind,[22] *it is no longer I that perform it, but sin that is living in me. For I know that there does not live in me*—so once again, "in me"; listen to what follows—*that is in my flesh, any good. For to will it is available to me* (Rom 7:17-18).

"*I know.* What do you know?"

"That there does not live in me, that is in my flesh, any good."

"You had already said earlier on, *How I am behaving, I do not understand.* If you don't understand, how do you know? One moment you say *I don't understand,* the next you say *I know.* How *I* am to understand, I really do not know."

Or is this how I should understand it? I mean, where he said *How I am behaving, I do not understand,* by *I do not understand* he meant "I don't approve, I don't accept, it doesn't please me, I don't consent, I don't admire." It's hardly the case, you see, that Christ won't understand those to whom he is going to say *I never knew you* (Mt 7:23). And of course, this is also how I can understand it: *What I am carrying out I do not understand,* because *I* do not know what *I* am not doing; *for it is not I that perform it, but the sin that is living in me* (Rom 7:17). That's why I do not know it, do not understand it; because it's not I that am doing it. It's like what was said about the Lord: *Him who did not know sin* (2 Cor 5:21). What does it mean, he did not know it? So didn't he know what he was censuring, didn't he know what he was punishing? So if he didn't know what he was punishing, he was punishing unjustly. And yet it's true he didn't know sin, because he hadn't committed sin.

For how I am behaving, I do not understand; For it is not what I want to that I do; but what I hate, that is what I carry out. But if what I don't want to is what I carry out, I give my consent to the law that it is good. But now, having already received grace, *it is not I that perform it*—for the mind is free, the flesh a prisoner. *It is not I that perform it, but the sin that lives in me. For I know that there does not live in me, that is in my flesh, anything good* (Rom 7:15-18).

Willing is not accomplishing

12. *For to will it is available to me, but to carry through with the good is not available* (Rom 7:18). To will is available, to carry through is not available. He didn't say to carry out, but to carry through with it.[7] It isn't the case, after all, that you don't carry out anything. Lust rebels, and you don't consent; you take a fancy to another man's wife, but you don't give your approval, you turn your mind away, you enter the inner sanctum of your mind. You see lust kicking up a rumpus outside, you issue a decree against it, to cleanse your conscience. "I don't want to," you say, "I won't do it. Granted it would be delightful, I won't do it, I have something else to delight in. *For I delight in the law of God according to the inner self.* Why are you rowdily proposing foolish, temporal, transient, vain and harmful delights, and telling me about them like a boring old chatterbox?

"The wicked have told me of delights. Among them also this lust; it tells me of delights, *but not like your law, O Lord* (Ps 119:85). *For I delight in the law of God*, not by myself all on my own, but by the grace of God. You, lust, are making a row in the flesh, you are not subduing the mind to yourself. *In God I will hope; I will not fear what flesh may do to me* (Ps 56:4). While I, I myself, that is the mind, do not consent, the flesh is making a row. *In God*, it says, *will I hope, I will not fear what flesh may do to me.* Neither what anybody else's flesh may do, nor likewise what mine either."

So people who act like that in themselves, are they carrying out nothing? They are carrying out a great deal; it's great, what they are carrying out; but all the same, they are not carrying it through. What would it mean, after all, to carry through with it? *Where, death, is your strife?* (1 Cor 15:53). So, *to will is available to me, but to carry through with the good, not* (Rom 7:18).

The conflict is one's own

13. *For it is not the good I wish to that I carry out; but the evil I do not wish, that is what I do.* And he repeats it: *But if what I do not wish is what I carry out,* that is to say, I lust; *it is now not I performing it, but the sin that lives in me. Therefore I find for me wishing to carry out the law as a good thing.*[8] I find the law is a good thing; the law is a good thing, the law is something good. How do I prove it? Because I want to fulfill it. *Therefore I find for me wishing to carry out the law as a good thing, that evil is at hand for me* (Rom 7:10-21).

This too "for me." Because it's not the case that the flesh isn't mine, or that the flesh is from another substance, or that the flesh is from another principle, or that the soul is from God, and the flesh from the race of darkness.[9] Perish the thought! Disease is fighting against health. He's lying half dead on the road, he is still being cared for, all his diseases are being cured.[10] *It is not what I wish to that I do; but what I hate, that is what I carry out* (Rom 7:15). *But if what I myself do not wish is what I carry out . . . I find therefore for me wishing to carry out the law as a good thing, that evil is at hand for me* (Rom 7:20-21). What evil?

A conflict of delight

14. *For I delight in the law of God according to the inner self. I see another law in my members, fighting back against the law of my mind, and taking me prisoner to the law of sin, which is in my members* (Rom 7:22-23); prisoner, but as regards the flesh; prisoner, but only partly so. Because the mind is fighting back, and delighting in the law of God. That, anyway, is how we ought to understand it, if the apostle is talking about himself. So now if the mind doesn't consent to sin tickling its fancy, making suggestions, beckoning it on; if the mind doesn't consent, because it has other inner delights of its own, in no way to be compared with the delights of the flesh; so if it doesn't consent, and there is in me something dead and something alive, death is still striving, but the mind's alive and not consenting. Does that mean that death itself is not in you? That the something dead doesn't belong to you? The strife is still your business. What can you also hope to get from it?

A conflict from which to be freed

15. *Wretched man that I am*; even if not in the mind, still in the flesh, wretched man. It's not the case, you see, that I'm man in the mind, and not man in the flesh. After all, who ever hated his own flesh?[11] *Wretched man that I am, who will deliver me from the body of this death?* (Rom 7:24). What's all this, brothers and sisters? As though he wants to be rid of the body. Why all the hurry? If that's what you're intent upon, to be rid of the body, death is going to come some time or other, and when your last day arrives it will without a shadow of doubt deliver you from this body of death.

Why all the urgency in the moaning and groaning? What's this you're saying, *Who will deliver me?* It's as a mortal you're speaking, as one who is going to die that you're speaking. The separation of mind from flesh is going to happen some time or other; because life is short, it can't be far off; because of daily accidents, you don't know when it will be. So whether you're in a hurry or whether you're dragging your feet, every human life is short. Why this urgent groaning, and saying *Who will deliver me from the body of this death?*

16. And he adds: *The grace of God through Jesus Christ our Lord* (Rom 7:25). Well, won't the pagans, who don't have the grace of God through Jesus Christ our Lord, won't they die? Won't they some time or other on their last day be released from the flesh? Won't they be delivered on that day from the body of this death? What's so important about the grace of God through Jesus Christ our Lord, that you want to attribute to it your deliverance from the body of this death?

The apostle answers you, if I have caught his meaning; indeed, because with the Lord's help I undoubtedly have caught his meaning, the apostle answers you and says: "I know what I'm talking about. You say the pagans are delivered from the body of this death, because the last day of this life is coming, and they will be released in due time from the body of this death. The day is also coming, *when all who are in the tombs will hear his voice; and those who have done good will come forth to the resurrection of life*; there you have the ones delivered from the body of this death. *Those who have done evil to the resurrection of judgment* (Jn 5:28-29); see, they will return to the body of this death. The body of this death is coming back to the wicked, nor will they ever be released from it. Then it will not be eternal life, but eternal death, because eternal punishment."

17. You, though, Christians, beg as insistently as you can, cry out and say, *Wretched man that I am, who will deliver me from the body of this death?* You will be given the answer, "You will reach safety, no thanks to you, but thanks to your Lord; you will reach safety, thanks to your pledge. Hope with Christ for the kingdom of Christ; you already hold as a pledge the blood of Christ." Say, yes say it: *Who will deliver me from the body of this death?*, so that you may receive the reply, *The grace of God through Jesus Christ our Lord* (Rom 7:24-25).

After all, you won't be delivered from the body of this death in such a way as no longer to have this body. You will have it, but no longer now "of this death." It will be the same one, but it won't be the same one. It will be the very same one, because it will be this flesh; it won't be the same one, because it won't be mortal. That, yes that is how you will be delivered from the body of this death, so that this mortal thing may put on immortality, and this perishable thing put on imperishability (1 Cor 15:53). By what, through whom will it be done? *The grace of God, through Jesus Christ our Lord* (Rom 7:25). *Because through one man death, and through one man the resurrection of the dead. Just as in Adam all die*—that's what you are groaning about, that's why you are locked in combat with death, that's where the body of this death comes from—*so too in Christ shall all be made alive* (1 Cor 15:21-22). You will be made alive by receiving an immortal body, when you can say, *Where, death, is your strife?* (1 Cor 15:55); you will be delivered from the body of this death; not, however, by your own virtue, but by *the grace of God through Jesus Christ our Lord*.

Turning to the Lord, etc.

NOTES

1. Preached on Tuesday, 14 October; see Sermon 153, note 1.

2. See Sermon 153, note 2.

3. He must mean the commandment; but he just says "it," which would naturally refer to sin, the subject of the last sentence.

4. The picture he brings to his audience's mind is now not that of a battle between armies, but of victory in athletic competition—perhaps in gladiatorial combat; even though this was no longer permitted, when he preached this sermon, such fights would still be fresh at least in older people's memories. In terms of modern sporting occasions, the moment of triumph would be the "lap of honor" that winners run, or their being carried shoulder high from the field.

The Latin text has the first verb in the indicative, the next two in the imperative. I emend the second verb, *audi exsultantem*, hear him boasting, to the indicative *audis exsultantem*; presumably the seeing and the hearing go together.

5. His reasoning here is very elliptical; a middle stage is simply assumed without being stated. He jumps from the law being spiritual to Paul being spiritual in mind, over the middle stage of "I delight in the law of God according to the inner self (the mind)" (Rom 7:22).

6. Again the reasoning is a little elliptical. The point is that he is here attacking the Manichee doctrine that I am my spirit or mind, and my flesh or body is not me, but an opposing nature, made by a deity opposed to the God who made me, my spirit. I am really two beings because created by two gods, one good and of the light, the other bad and of the dark. Not so, says Augustine (and he says it in the teeth of his inbuilt Platonism, of which Manicheeism was a kind of crude and extreme mythical extension); not so, because there is only one God who made the whole of me; therefore I am one being of two parts; he would even say, speaking rather loosely and by later standards misleadingly, of two natures; but still one being, one self, one me.

7. The distinction again between *facere* and *perficere*. See Sermon 151, note 7, and 152, note 4.

8. It is clear from what follows that Augustine construes this sentence in this very odd and frankly wrong-headed way. It should of course, even in his Latin text, be construed thus: "Therefore I find a law for myself, wishing to carry out the good, that the bad is at hand for me."

9. This is the Manichee doctrine.

10. The allusion is to the story of the good Samaritan, Lk 10:30-35, and Ps 103:3. What he is saying is that the war between the spirit and the flesh is not, as the Manichees would have it, a war between two opposing substances, but a disease, like malaria or any fever, in the one person—in Paul and every other descendant of Adam, represented by the man who fell among thieves and was left half dead in the road. And in this life this disease—or wound—is being cared for and treated by the good Samaritan (Christ) in the inn (the Church). But the cure won't be complete until he returns (Lk 10:35).

11. See Eph 5:29, where "his own flesh" in fact refers to a man's wife.

SERMON 154A

DISCOURSE OF SAINT AUGUSTINE ON WHAT THE APOSTLE SAYS, ROMANS 7:15: *IT IS NOT WHAT I WANT TO THAT I DO, BUT WHAT I HATE, THAT IS WHAT I CARRY OUT*

Date: 417[1]

The plight of the human person

1. When the apostle Paul was read, we heard what goes on in any human being; and everybody, if he took a look at himself, discovered that the apostle was telling the truth. He said, you see, that it is not what he wants to that he does, but what he hates, that is what he carries out. And he said, *If what I do not want is what I carry out, I give my consent to the law that it is good* (Rom 7:16); because what I don't want, the law doesn't want either; what the law forbids me to carry out, I myself don't want to carry out either. But what I don't want to, that . . .[2] there is in me something else which fights against my will. And he said, *For I delight in the law of God according to the inner self; but I see another law fighting back against the law of my mind, and taking me prisoner to the law of sin, which is in my members.* There you are, that's what's going on in each and every human being. But notice what he said next: *Unhappy man that I am, who will deliver me from the body of this death? The grace of God through Jesus Christ our Lord* (Rom 7:22-25).

In the human person a quarrel takes place

2. So let every single person take a good look at himself, because in his letter Paul has placed a mirror, in which everybody can see himself. What the law commands delights our minds, and what the law forbids delights our flesh; and our minds and our flesh struggle together; mind struggles for the law, flesh against the law, and every single individual goes about with this quarrel going on inside him. The quarrel is taking place within the individual person; the tongue is silent, and inside there's uproar. Let me give you an example, where you can see better what I'm saying. A man sees someone else's wife, and lusts after her. He thinks of the law, which says, "Do not fornicate," and what does the mind of the man say inside? "The law has spoken well, it's a great thing the law has said, it loves chastity." And the flesh delights in iniquity. A quarrel has

broken out in the man; well, let two win against one; let two, the law and the mind, win against the flesh opposing them.

But notice what the mind actually said: *I see another law in my members fighting back against the law of my mind, and taking me prisoner to the law of sin, which is in my members.* So the mind is being beaten by the flesh. Let it call on the Savior for help, and avoid the deceiver's trap. I mean, just notice what the apostle has said. What a man the apostle was, what a great and mighty athlete of God! And yet he would be taken away as a prisoner, if the man who was crucified didn't come to his aid. Therefore, when he was in deadly peril, what did he say? *Wretched man that I am, who will deliver me from the body of this death,* so that I do not commit the iniquity that delights my flesh? *The grace of God through Jesus Christ our Lord* (Rom 7:23-25).

Christ is watching you fighting

3. So Christ is watching you fighting. The ring is your conscience, where two contestants are matched, mind and flesh. The mind supports the law, the flesh opposes the law, and it wants to curb the flesh.[3] A hard struggle; but the one who is watching you fighting can help you when you are in danger of losing. Now if you were boxing against another man, he would hit you, and you would hit him, and another man would be watching you, to see which of you would win. Whichever succeeded in winning would get the prize. What the man watching was entitled to say to you was, "Whichever of you wins will get this." He was quite prepared to award you the prize if you won; was he able to help you if you looked as if you were losing?

But now the one who's watching you is Christ; yell to him when you are losing, so that you may win; because your flesh too is striving to win, to its own hurt.[4] I mean, if you were just two men facing each other in a boxing match, whichever of you won would get the prize. But in this bout, if the mind wins it sets free both the soul and the flesh; if the flesh wins, both are thrown into hell. That's why the flesh is striving to its own hurt, and to its own hurt wants to win. It is to the advantage of the flesh to be beaten, to save it from being punished in everlasting fire.

Winning means not consenting to evil desires

4. So the psalm we have just sung also agrees about this; as we said, *Out of the depths I have cried to you, O Lord; Lord, hear my voice* (Ps 130:1-2). This is the depth, where flesh is striving against mind. If mind wins, you see, both are lifted up by it to the surface; the defeated flesh is lifted up there as well, because it has been defeated for its own good. It's like a house, when a bad wife is fighting a good husband; she wins to her own hurt, she loses for her own good. I mean, if the bad wife wins, the house is all back to front, with the bearded male serving the bad woman.[5] But if the bad wife loses, she starts serving the good husband; and the woman becomes good herself, because she is serving the good husband.

So it's the same with our flesh too, as it is with the bad wife when she's beaten, because it's beaten for its own good. To summon to our aid the one who can join the two together[6] and give them both the prize, that's why we cry out of this depth to our Lord, as we said in the psalm. Because if we conquer and do not consent to the evil desires of our flesh, later on the flesh will rise again; and there you won't find any evil desires to contend with.

Now, of course, you do find evil desires, which you have got to fight against; and you are told, "Win, and you get the prize." And what does winning now mean for you? Not consenting to evil desires. Because you can't help having those evil desires, can you? But winning means not consenting to them.[7] When, however, we get the flesh back again on the day of resurrection, the flesh is itself converted, it becomes immortal; and now you no longer find any desire you have to struggle with, but a fullness with which to be rewarded.[8] And now that you are up above with your flesh, you are not crying from the depth, are you, where you were once wrangling with your flesh?

The Canaanite woman finds herself seated at the table

5. And that woman who was crying out after the Lord; that Canaanite woman, how she did cry out! Her daughter was suffering from a demon; because the flesh wouldn't agree with the mind, it was possessed by the devil.[9] If she cried out so much for her daughter, how much ought we to be crying out for our flesh and soul? You can see, after all, what she won by crying out. Because first of all she was ignored; she was, after all, a Canaanite, from a bad race, in which idols were worshipped. But the Lord Jesus Christ was going around in Judaea,[10] from where came the patriarchs, from where came the virgin Mary who gave birth to Christ; and that was the only nation that worshipped the true God, and didn't worship idols. So when some Canaanite woman or other started begging him for a favor, he refused to listen to her. The reason he ignored her was that he knew what he was keeping for her; it wasn't in order that he should deny her a favor, but that she should obtain it by her perseverance.

So his disciples said to him, "Lord, *send her away now*, give her an answer; you can see that *she is crying out after us*, and she's making herself a nuisance to us." And he said to his disciples, *I have only been sent to the lost sheep of the house of Israel* (Mt 15:23-24). I was sent to the Jewish people, where I was to look for the sheep that had got lost. There were other sheep in other nations, but Christ had not come to them, because they didn't believe in Christ when he was present, but they believed, later on, in the gospel of Christ. That's why he said, *I was only sent to the sheep of the house of Israel*;[11] that's why he chose the apostles during his presence on earth. And one of these sheep was Nathanael, of whom he said, *Behold an Israelite, in whom there is no guile* (Jn 1:47). To those sheep belonged that huge crowd which carried branches before the Lord's donkey and said, *Blessed is he who comes in the name of the Lord* (Mk 11:9). Those sheep of the house of Israel had got lost, and they recognized their shepherd when he was present among them, and they believed in Christ when he was present.

So when that woman was left in suspense, she was being put off with the Gentile sheep. When she heard what the Lord said to his disciples, she went on crying out, and didn't give over. And the Lord said to her, *It is not a good thing to take the children's bread and throw it to the dogs.* He made her a dog; why? Because she was a Gentile, and they worshipped idols; dogs, you see, lick stones.[12] *It is not a good thing to take the children's bread and give it to the dogs.* And she didn't say, "Lord, don't make me out to be a dog, because I'm not a dog"; instead she said, "You're right, Lord, I am a dog." For accepting the insult, she deserved the favorable result; because while iniquity is left bewildered, humility is rewarded.[13] *Yes, Lord,* you're right; *but even the dogs eat from the scraps that fall from the table of their masters.* And then the Lord said, *O woman, great is your faith; be it done for you as you wish* (Mt 15:26-28). A moment ago a dog, now a woman, transformed by your barking. She only asked for the scraps falling from the table; suddenly she finds herself seated at the table. You see, when he says to her, *Great is your faith*, it means he has already counted her among those whose bread he refused to throw to the dogs.

We should persevere in praying

6. What does all this teach us, but that when what we ask God for is something good, we should persevere in praying for it until, panting with desire, we receive it. You see, that's why God puts off our requests, to stimulate our desires. But eternal life is what we ought to ask for with deep sighs and groans; here a good life, and afterward eternal life. Because you ought also to ask God for a good life, asking him to assist your will. If he doesn't come to your help, you remain defeated. You will be on the point of being taken prisoner, if you are not helped by what is mentioned here: *Wretched man that I am, who will deliver me from the body of this death? The grace of God through Jesus Christ our Lord* (Rom 7:24-25).

So there are two things we should ask for with calm assurance: in this world a good life, in the world to come eternal life. About everything else, we don't know whether it will be good for us. A man asks God to help him find a wife; how does he know if getting married will be for his good? A man prays to God to help him get rich; how does he know whether, sleeping soundly as a poor man, once he's rich he won't dream of robbers? So he doesn't know which out of all the things to be found in this world will be good for him. But he can beg without the slightest hesitation for a good life, and for eternal life; a good life here, to deserve well of God, eternal life there as the reward from God.

And what is a good life? To love God with all your heart and all your soul and all your mind, and to love your brother and sister as yourself. So let us love our God, let us love each other in his unity; let us have peace in him, charity among ourselves; so that when Christ our Lord comes himself, we can say,[14] "Lord, with your help we have done what you ordered; by your gracious favor, may we receive what you promised."

NOTES

1. There is no obvious indication of where this sermon was preached. It clearly does not belong to the same series as the previous four sermons. It is as likely to have been preached in Hippo Regius as anywhere else. One gets the impression that Augustine did not think he had quite such a sophisticated audience in front of him.

2. There is a short gap in the text here. Presumably the missing words were something like, "I do carry out, because."

3. That is what the text says; as it seems to be in rather a poor state, it is not at all certain that it is what Augustine said. He could, I suppose, have so phrased it that he made the middle clause sound like a parenthesis, thus leaving it clear that "mind" was the subject of the third one; or else the middle phrase is a marginal comment by some reader that crept into the text; or the word *mens*, as subject of the third clause, has been omitted by mistake.

4. Perhaps a ripple of shocked surprise ran through the congregation at the gross unfairness of the referee, or judge, joining in to help one of the contestants. So Augustine explains why his doing so will in fact benefit both of them.

5. See Sermon 152, 4, note 8 for this whole slightly regrettable comparison. It is not immediately obvious what idea Augustine would have suggested to his audience by calling the husband *barbatus*. From classical times through to the collapse of the empire in Augustine's own day, Romans at least of the upper classes were usually clean shaven. They sometimes referred to the ancient Romans, always with respect as models of civic and manly virtue, as *barbati*, because they had worn full beards; and apparently also philosophers, so Lewis & Short inform us, were sometimes referred to as *barbati* by the classical poets. So Augustine's picture is not so much of the he-man, as of the virtuous and dignified sage, whom everybody recognized as a somewhat mythical stereotype, and whom no mere woman, of course, could hope to equal (at least on the mythical stage).

6. See Mk 10:9.

7. Another gap in the Latin text, which runs, *Sed vincere est . . . consentire.* I have supplied *non eis*.

8. And yet another gap in the text: *jam non invenis desiderium quo lucteris . . . in qua coroneris.* It calls for a feminine noun contrasting with *desiderium*. I supply *sed plenitudinem*.

9. Augustine is not here explaining why the girl was possessed; he is treating her case as representative of the general condition of "the flesh" in fallen humanity.

10. Augustine was being careless about his geography, because the gospel states that at this point Jesus was going through the Gentile territory of Tyre and Sidon—and anyhow he spent most of his time in Galilee, not Judaea. But he is here to be taken as meaning "among the Jews" by "in Judaea."

11. The Latin omits "of the house of Israel." Augustine must surely have said it. My guess is that the stenographer did not bother to write it down, having indicated the quotation. Perhaps this is a clue to why there are so many little gaps in the text; it derives from a stenographer who was a little too slow at his job, either because he was a novice, or because he was getting old and arthritic.

Augustine's argument here is characteristically elliptic—or rather he keeps on using the word "because" in a very loose sense. What he is saying is that Christ was only sent in person to Israel; but that did not exclude the sheep from other nations, who were to be catered for by the preaching of his gospel after his ascension. To make provision for that he chose his apostles during his earthly ministry.

12. Equivalent to Gentiles worshipping stones—licking the boots of stone idols! A farfetched reason for calling Gentiles dogs; it was in fact just a straightforward piece of conventional racial abuse.

13. The implication is that the woman had first acted iniquitously when she was left in suspense by being ignored. What he seems to mean is that she represented the iniquity of idolatry, by being a Canaanite.

14. A final little gap in the text, which I have filled with the word "say": *dicere*.

SERMON 155

ON THE WORDS OF THE APOSTLE, ROMANS 8:1-11: *THERE IS THEREFORE NO CONDEMNATION NOW FOR THOSE WHO ARE IN CHRIST JESUS*, ETC. AGAINST THE PELAGIANS, PREACHED IN THE BASILICA OF THE HOLY SCILLITAN MARTYRS

Date: 419[1]

Sin has to lose its power to reign

1. Yesterday the reading from the holy apostle ended where it says, *I myself therefore with the mind serve the law of God, but with the flesh the law of sin* (Rom 7:25). In concluding like that, the apostle showed why he said what he had said above: *Now it is no longer I that perform it, but the sin that lives in me* (Rom 7:20); it was because he wasn't performing it by consenting with the mind, but by lusting with the flesh. He gives the name of sin, you see, to that from which all sins spring, namely to the lust of the flesh.

Whatever kinds of sin there are, in words, in deeds, in thoughts, they spring from nothing else but evil desire, they spring from nothing else but unlawful pleasure. So if we stand up to this unlawful pleasure, if we don't consent to it, if we don't provide it with our members to be its weapons, then sin doesn't reign in our mortal bodies.[2] Sin, after all, first has to lose its power to reign, and that is how it fades away. So in this life, where holy people are concerned, it loses its power to reign, in the other life it fades away. Here, you see, it loses its power to reign when we *don't go after our lusts* (Sir 18:30); while there it fades away, when they will say, *Where, death, is your striving?* (1 Cor 15:55)

"Now" and "then"

2. So when the apostle said, *With the mind I serve the law of God, but with the flesh the law of sin*, not by giving my members over to committing iniquities, but only by feeling lust, without however giving a hand to unlawful lust; so when he said *with the mind I serve the law of God, but with the flesh the law of sin*, he went on to add, *There is therefore no condemnation now for those who are in Christ Jesus* (Rom 8:1). For those who are in the flesh there is condemnation; for those who are in Christ Jesus no condemnation. In case you should assume this is going to be the case afterward,[3] that's why he added "now."

84

What you must look forward to afterward is not even to have any lust in you which you have to contend with, which you have to combat, which you mustn't consent to, which you have to curb and tame; look forward to its simply not being there afterward. I mean to say, if what is now contending with us from its base in this mortal body is going to be there afterward, the taunt *Where, death, is your striving?* will be untrue. So let us be quite clear about what it's going to be like afterward. *Then,* you see, *will come about the word that is written: Death has been swallowed up in victory* (Is 25:8). *Where, death, is your striving? Where, death, is your sting?* (Hos 13:14) *For the sting of death is sin; but the power of sin, the law* (1 Cor 15:54-56). Because desire was increased, not extinguished, by being forbidden. The law gave sin power, by just commanding through the letter, without assisting through the spirit.

So all this won't exist then, but what about now? Are you wanting to know what's the case now? What he also said a little earlier on: *But now it is no longer I that perform it* (Rom 7:17); there too there is a "now."[4] So what's the meaning of *It is not I that perform it?* I don't consent, I don't give the go-ahead, I don't decide to do it, it always displeases me; I keep my members in check. And that's certainly something. Since lust comes from the flesh, and the members of the body belong to the flesh, it means that when sin, that is the lust of the flesh, doesn't reign, the mind has more right to restrain the members of the flesh from being given over as weapons of iniquity, than the lust of the flesh has to move the members of the flesh.

And so lust is of the flesh, and the members are of the flesh; and yet because the mind has the mastery—provided it gets help from above, or else when we concede it too much against the grace of God, we may make it into a tyrant instead of a king—so the mind has so much authority, it rules (when it is ruled) so effectively, that over the members of its own flesh it can act against the lust of its own flesh, and do what the apostle says: *Do not let sin, therefore, reign in your mortal bodies, to obey their desires; and do not present your members to sin as weapons of iniquity* (Rom 6:12-13).

The law of the Spirit of life in Christ Jesus

3. *There is therefore no condemnation now for those who are in Christ Jesus.* They mustn't worry if their fancy is tickled by unlawful lusts; they mustn't worry because there still seems to be a law in their members fighting back against the law of the mind. Because *there is no condemnation.* But for whom? Even *now,* for whom? *Those who are in Christ Jesus.* And where does that leave the conviction of which he said a short while before: *I see another law in my members fighting back against the law of my mind, and taking me prisoner to the law of sin which is in my members* (Rom 7:23)? But he was talking about "me" with respect to the flesh, not to the mind. So, where is that law,[5] if there is no condemnation for those who are in Christ Jesus? *For the law of the Spirit of life in Christ Jesus*—for the law, not that one on Mount Sinai given in the letter; for the law, not that one in the staleness of the letter[6]—but *the law of the*

Spirit of life in Christ Jesus has delivered you from the law of sin and death (Rom 8:1-2).

After all, how would you have it in you to delight in the law of God according to the inner self,[7] unless the law of the Spirit of life in Christ Jesus delivered you from the law of sin and death? So don't claim the credit for yourself, human mind, just because you don't consent to the desires of the flesh, just because the law of sin hasn't pushed you out of the command post: *The law of the Spirit of life in Christ Jesus has delivered you from the law of sin and death.* You have not been delivered by that other law of which it was said above, *That we may serve in newness of spirit, and not in the staleness of the letter* (Rom 7:6). Why did that one not deliver you? Was it not also written by the finger of God? Isn't the finger of God to be understood as being the Holy Spirit? Read the gospel, and see that where one evangelist has the Lord saying, *If I with the Spirit of God cast out demons* (Mt 12:28), another says, *If I with the finger of God cast out demons* (Lk 11:20). So if that law too was written by the finger of God, that is by the Spirit of God, the Spirit by which Pharaoh's magicians were defeated, so they said, *This is the finger of God* (Ex 8:19); so if that law too, indeed because that law too was composed by the Spirit of God, that is, by the finger of God, why can it not be said of it, *For the law of the Spirit of life in Christ Jesus has delivered you from the law of sin and death?*[8]

The law of the letter and the law of sin and death

4. I mean, the law that was given on Mount Sinai is not called the law of death, it isn't called the law of sin and death. What is called the law of sin and death is the one about which he groans as he says, *I see another law in my members fighting back against the law of my mind* (Rom 7:23). But the other law is the one of which it is said, *And so the law indeed is holy, and the commandment holy, and just, and good.* And he added, *Did what is good, therefore, become death for me? Perish the thought! But sin, in order that it might be seen to be sin, through the good worked death for me; so that it might become above measure sinner or sin through the commandment* (Rom 7:12-13).[9]

What does *above measure* mean? The adding of transgression. So that law was given in order to bring the infirmity to light. That's saying nothing; not only to bring it to light, but also to make it worse, and so at least in that way to get the doctor sent for. If it was only a slight malady, I mean, it would be ignored; if it was ignored, the doctor would not be sent for; if the doctor wasn't sent for, the malady would never end. That's why, where sin abounded, grace abounded all the more, blotting out all the sins it discovered, and bringing aid to our wills not to sin; so that our very own wills might find their praise not in themselves but in God. *In God*, you see, *shall we find praise all day long* (Ps 44:8); and *In the Lord shall my soul find praise; let the meek hear and rejoice* (Ps 34:2). Let the meek hear, because the proud and quarrelsome don't hear.

So then, why is this law, written by the finger of God, not the one which brings this support of grace we are talking about? Why not? Because it was written on tablets of stone, not on the fleshly tablets of the heart.[10]

5. Finally, my dear brothers and sisters, in a profound mystery[11] observe the harmony, observe the difference: harmony of the law, difference of the people. Passover, as you know, is celebrated among the ancient people by the slaying of the lamb and unleavened bread; where the slaying of the sheep signifies Christ, while the unleavened bread stands for the new life, one that is without the yeast of staleness. That's why the apostle says to us, *Purge out the old yeast, that you may be a new dough, just as you are unleavened. For Christ has been sacrificed as our Passover* (1 Cor 5:7). So the Passover was celebrated by that ancient people, not yet in the brightness of broad daylight but in the symbolism of a shadow; and fifty days after the celebration of Passover, as anybody who wants to can find out by just counting, the law was given on Mount Sinai, written by the finger of God.

Came the true Passover, Christ was sacrificed; he made the passage from death to life; the Hebrew Pascha,[12] you see, means passage or passing over; the evangelist made this point when he said, *When the hour had come for Jesus to pass over from this world to the Father* (Jn 13:1). So the Passover is celebrated, the Lord rises again, he makes the passage from death to life, which is *the* Passover; and fifty days are counted, and the Holy Spirit comes, the finger of God.[13]

6. But notice how it happened there, and how it happened here. There, the people stood a long way off, there was an atmosphere of dread, not of love. I mean, they were so terrified that they said to Moses, *Speak to us yourself, and do not let the Lord speak to us, lest we die* (Ex 20:19). So God came down, as it is written, on Sinai in fire; but he was terrifying the people who stood a long way off, and *writing with his finger on stone* (Ex 31:18), not on the heart.

Here, however, when the Holy Spirit came, the faithful were gathered together as one; and he didn't terrify them on a mountain, but came in to them in a house. There came a sudden sound, indeed, from heaven, as of a fierce squall rushing upon them; it made a noise, but nobody panicked. You have heard the sound, now see the fire too, because each was there on the mountain also, both fire and sound; but there, there was smoke as well, here though the fire was clear. *There appeared to them*, scripture says, you see, *divided tongues, as of fire*. Terrifying them from a long way off? Far from it. Because, *it settled upon each one of them and they began to talk in languages, as the Spirit gave them utterance* (Acts 2:1-4). Hear a person talking a language, and understand the Spirit writing not on stone, but on the heart.

So, *the law of the Spirit of life*, written on the heart, not on stone, *in Christ Jesus*, in whose person was celebrated the ultimately real and genuine Passover, *has delivered you from the law of sin and death* (Rom 8:2). I mean, to show you that here we have the clearest statement of the enormous difference between the old and the new covenants or testaments, which leads the apostle too to say, *not on tablets of stone, but on the fleshly tablets of the heart* (2 Cor 3:3), the Lord himself says in the prophet, *Behold, the days are coming, says the Lord, and I will conclude over the house of Jacob a new covenant, not like the covenant which I made with their fathers, on the day when I took them by the hand and led them out of the land of Egypt.* Then to make the difference absolutely clear, he says, *Putting my laws in their hearts; on their hearts,* he says, *I will inscribe them* (Jer 31:31-33). So if the law of God is written on your heart, it shouldn't be terrifying you from the outside, but soothing you inside; then, *the law of the Spirit of life in Christ Jesus will deliver*[14] you from the law of sin and death.

God sent flesh on behalf of flesh

7. *For what was impossible for the law.* That's how it goes on in the reading from the apostle: *What was impossible for the law* (Rom 8:3). And in case the law itself should be blamed, what did he add? *In that it was weakened through the flesh.* The law, you see, commanded, and did not implement, because the flesh, where there was no grace, put up an unconquerable resistance. And the law was weakened through the flesh, because *the law is spiritual, but I am of the flesh* (Rom 7:14). So how could the law bring me relief, when it commanded through the letter and didn't give grace? What did God do, when this was impossible for the law, and it was weakened through the flesh? *God sent his Son.*

Now what was the law weakened through, and what made this impossible for the law? *It was weakened through the flesh.* So what did God do? He sent flesh against flesh; or rather he also sent flesh on behalf of flesh. You see, he slew the sin of the flesh, delivered the substance of the flesh. *God sent his Son in the likeness of the flesh of sin* (Rom 8:3). In real flesh, certainly, but not in the flesh of sin. Well, how? *In the likeness of the flesh of sin.* That is, to be flesh, real flesh. And where does the likeness of the flesh of sin come from? Because death comes from sin; death, of course, is in all the flesh of sin, about which the apostle says, *that the body of sin might be brought to nothing* (Rom 6:6). So because there was death in all the flesh of sin—as a matter of fact they were each there, both death and sin, in all other flesh. In the flesh of sin there is both death and sin; in the likeness of the flesh of sin there was death, there was no sin.

If it had really been the flesh of sin, and he had paid the penalty of death as the proper deserts of sin, the Lord would not have said himself, *Behold, the prince of the world is coming, and in me he will find nothing* (Jn 14:30). So why did he slay me? Because *for robbery I did not commit I then paid the price* (Ps 69:4). Certainly, he dealt with death in the same way as he dealt with the tax. The tax was demanded, the double-drachma. *Why,* said the man, *do you and your disciples not pay the tax?* He called Peter to himself, and said, *From whom do the kings of the world exact taxes? From their children, or from strangers? The answer came, From strangers. Therefore, he said, the children are free. Nonetheless, in order not to shock them, go to the sea, throw in a hook, and the one that first rises*, that is, the first-born from the dead, *open its mouth, and you will find there a stater*, that is, two double-drachmas, four drachmas; because a double-drachma, that is two drachmas a head, was being demanded. *You will find there a stater*, that is four drachmas; *give it to them for me and for you* (Mt 17:24-27). What does it mean, *for me and for you?* Christ himself, Peter, the Church of Christ, the four gospels of the Church; a mystery was hidden there;[15] Christ, however, paid a tax he did not owe. In the same way, he paid the price of death; he didn't owe it, and he paid it. If he hadn't paid what he didn't owe, he would never have delivered us from the debt we did.

Christ had no sin, but he was sin

8. So, *what was impossible for the law*, which was making us into transgressors because the mind, though convicted of sin, had not yet started seeking a savior, *in that it was weakened through the flesh, God sent his Son in the likeness of the flesh of sin, and from sin condemned sin in the flesh* (Rom 8:3). So how can it be true that he had no sin, if it was from sin that he condemned sin? I have already explained this to you a short while ago;[16] still, let those of you who remember recognize what I say, those of you who didn't hear it, hear it now, those of you who have forgotten, recall it to mind.

In the law a sacrifice for sin was called sin; the law regularly reminds us of this; not once, not just twice, but ever so often sacrifices for sins were called sins. That's the kind of sin Christ was. I mean, what are we to say? That he had sin? Perish the thought! He had no sin, and he was sin. I said he was sin, according to that meaning of the word, because he was the sacrifice for sin. Listen to this, showing that he was sin in that way, listen to the apostle himself. Speaking about him, he says, *him who knew no sin*—that's the statement I was explaining to you when I was talking about this[17]—*him*, he says, *who knew no sin* God the Father *made into sin for us; him*, Christ himself, *who knew no sin* God the Father *made into sin for us, that we, in him, might be the justice of God* (2 Cor 5:21).

Two points to notice: God's justice, not ours; in him, not in ourselves. That's where we get those great saints from, about whom the psalm says, *Your justice like the mountains of God* (Ps 36:6). And as though it said in this very psalm, after saying *Your justice*—not their justice, you see, but—*Your justice like the mountains of God*—because *I lifted up my eyes to the mountains; from where shall help come to me?* Not from the mountains, though, because *My help comes from the Lord, who made heaven and earth* (Ps 121:1-2).[18] So after saying *Your justice like the mountains of God*, as though someone asked, "Why then are other people born who do not belong to the justice of God?", it added, *Your judgments like the great abyss*. It's deep, unfathomable, inaccessible to the human gaze. The riches of God, you see, are inscrutable; *inscrutable his judgments, unsearchable his ways* (Rom 11:33). So here too, *God sent his Son* for the sake of those who are foreknown and predestined, who are to be called, justified, glorified; as mountains of God let them say, *If God is for us, who is against us?* (Rom 8:29-31). *God sent his Son in the likeness of the flesh of sin, and from sin condemned sin in the flesh, that the justice of the law might be fulfilled in us* (Rom 8:3-4). It wasn't being fulfilled by itself; it was fulfilled through Christ. He did not come, after all, to undo the law but to fulfill it (Mt 5:17).

Walking according to the Spirit

9. But how may the justice of the law be fulfilled in us, or how is it fulfilled by us, or by which of us? Do you want to hear in which of us? *Who walk not according to the flesh, but according to the Spirit* (Rom 8:4). What does walking according to the flesh mean? Consenting to the lusts of the flesh. What does walking according to the Spirit mean? Being helped by the Spirit in the mind, and not obeying the lusts of the flesh. So that's how the law is fulfilled in us, how the justice of God is fulfilled in us. What is being fulfilled now, for the time being, is, *Do not go after your lusts* (Sir 18:30). When you hear "your lusts," you must take it as meaning the unlawful ones.[19] *Do not go after your lusts* must be fulfilled by our wills, assisted by the grace of God. Yes, this has to be fulfilled, *Do not go after your lusts.*

You see, whatever past sins were brought about in us by that lust of the flesh, whether in deed or in word or in thought, they have all been rubbed out by holy baptism; one pardon has canceled all debts. So conflict with the flesh remains, because while iniquity has been rubbed out, infirmity is left. It's built in, the delight of unlawful lust tickles your fancy. Fight, stand up to it, don't consent, and then you fulfill this law, *Do not go after your lusts*; because even if they worm their way in sometimes, and take over an eye, an ear, a tongue, a fleeting thought, not even so should we despair of our salvation. That's why we say every day, *Forgive us our debts* (Mt 6:12). *That the justice of the law,* he says, *might be fulfilled in us.*

From disability to ability

10. But in which of us? *Who do not walk according to the flesh, but according to the Spirit. For those who are according to the flesh, savor the things of the flesh; those, however, who are according to the Spirit, the things of the Spirit. For the thinking of the flesh is death; the thinking of the Spirit, however, life and peace. For the thinking of the flesh is at enmity with God. For it is not subject to the law of God; nor indeed can it be* (Rom 8:4-7). What's the meaning of *nor indeed can it be?* Not that the person cannot be, not that the soul cannot be, not, finally, that the flesh, being God's creation, cannot be; but that the thinking of the flesh cannot be, the vice, not the nature, cannot be.

It's as if you were to say, "Lameness is not subject to walking straight; nor indeed can it be." The foot can be, but lameness cannot be. Remove the lameness, and you will see straight walking. But as long as the lameness is there, it cannot be; in the same way, as long as the thinking of the flesh is there, it cannot be subject to the law of God. Let there be no thinking of the flesh, and the person can be. *The thinking of the Spirit, life and peace.*

So as for his saying *The thinking of the flesh is at enmity with God*, don't take it as implying that this enemy could hurt God at all. Its enmity consists in opposing, not in killing, God. The one it does harm, though, is the one in whom the thinking of the flesh is to be found, because the vice harms the nature in which it occurs. The reason, however, why medicine was invented was to get rid of the vice and heal the nature. So the savior healer came to the human race, found none of it healthy, and therefore came as a great doctor.

The same nature, wounded and healed

11. The reason why I have said this, is that the Manichees want to introduce another substantive nature of evil against God, and they reckon their error is supported to some extent by the apostle's testimony here, and they think the words "it cannot be" refer somehow to nature being *at enmity with God; for it is not subject to the law of God, nor indeed can it be* (Rom 8:7). And they haven't noticed that "it cannot be" is not said about the flesh; "it cannot be" is not said about the person; "it cannot be" is not said about the soul, but about the thinking of the flesh. This kind of thinking is a vice.

Do you want to know what being *wise*[20] *according to the flesh means? It means death* (Rom 8:6). But one and the same person, one and the same nature created by the Lord, the true and good God, was wise yesterday according to the flesh, is wise today according to the Spirit; the vice has been got rid of, the nature healed. Because as long as that thinking of the flesh was going on, it could not be subject in any way at all to the law of God. As long as lameness, you see, is there as a kind of vice, in no way can there be straight walking. Cure the vice, though, and the nature is mended. *You were once darkness, but now light in the Lord* (Eph 5:8).

How "in the flesh"

12. So notice what follows: *But those who are in the flesh*—that is, who trust in the flesh, who follow their lusts, who settle down in them, who are entertained by the pleasures they provide, who place the blessed and happy life in the enjoyment of them, they are the ones "in the flesh"—*cannot please God* (Rom 8:8). Now it doesn't say *But those who are in the flesh cannot please God*, as though it meant that while they are people in this life they cannot please God. So didn't the holy patriarchs please God? So didn't the holy prophets please him? So didn't the holy apostles please him? Wasn't he pleased with the holy martyrs, who before laying aside the body by suffering death, by confessing Christ, not only scorned pleasure, but also endured pain with the utmost patience? They certainly pleased him, but they weren't in the flesh. They were carrying flesh, but they weren't being carried by the flesh. The paralytic had already been told, *Pick up your pallet* (Mk 2:11).[21] So *those who are in the flesh,*

not, as I've said, as I've just explained, by living in this world, but by consenting to the desires of the flesh, *cannot please God.*

How "in the Spirit'

13. Finally, listen to him solving the problem beyond a shadow of doubt. He was speaking, of course, to people alive[22] in this body; and yet he added, *But you are not in the flesh.* I wonder if, perhaps, there is anyone here among us to whom this was said? Look, he said it to the people of God, he said it to the Church. He was writing to the Romans, certainly, but he meant it for the universal Church of Christ; but he meant it for the wheat, not the chaff, he meant it for the hidden pile, not for the visible straw. I hope you will all, each one of you, acknowledge what he says in your hearts. I am speaking to ears, I can't see consciences; and yet in view of what I have said earlier on, I consider in Christ's name that there are among Christ's people those to whom it is said, *But you are not in the flesh but in the spirit; if, that is, the Spirit of God is dwelling in you* (Rom 8:9).

You are not in the flesh, because you are not carrying out the works of the flesh by consenting to the lusts of the flesh. But you are in the Spirit, because according to the inner self you are *delighting in the law of God* (Rom 7:22); with this proviso: *if, that is, the Spirit of God is dwelling in you.* Because if you are relying presumptuously on your own spirit, you are still in the flesh. So you are not in the flesh in such a way[23] that you are in the Spirit of God; it's only then, you see, that you are not in the flesh. Because if the Spirit of God withdraws, the human spirit rolls back under its own weight into the flesh, returns to the deeds of the flesh, returns to worldly lusts; and *the last state of such a person will be worse than was the first* (Lk 11:26). So then, hold on to free will in such a way that you implore God's help. *You are not in the flesh;* and is this because of your own powers? Perish the thought! Because of what, then?

If, that is, the Spirit of God is dwelling in you. But if anybody does not have the Spirit of Christ, that person does not belong to him (Rom 8:9). So it mustn't spread itself, mustn't vaunt itself, mustn't claim for itself its own proper virtue and power, this needy and spoilt nature. O human nature! O Adam, when you were healthy you couldn't stand on your own feet, and have you got up again by your own strength? *If anybody does not have the Spirit of Christ*—the Spirit of God is the same as the Spirit of Christ, being the Spirit, after all, of both the Father and the Son—*If anybody does not have the Spirit of Christ,* let him not deceive himself, *that person does not belong to him.*

Death—and life—now

14. But look, with the help of his mercy we do have the Spirit of Christ; from our delight in justice, our complete faith, our Catholic peace,[24] we know that the Spirit of God is within us. But what about that mortal flesh? What about the law in our members fighting back against *the law of the mind* (Rom 7:23)? What

about that groan, *Wretched man that I am* (Rom 7:24)? Listen: *But if Christ is in you, the body indeed is dead because of sin, but the spirit is life because of justice* (Rom 8:10). So must we now despair about the body which is dead because of sin? Is there no hope? Does it so sleep that it may not ever rise again?[25] Perish the thought!

The body indeed is dead because of sin, but the spirit is life because of justice. We are left with sadness about our bodies. But nobody ever hated his own flesh.[26] We can see what care is taken over the burial of the dead. *The body indeed is dead because of sin, but the spirit is life because of justice.* You were already consoling yourself with the reflection, "I would indeed like my body too to be in life; but because it can't be, at least let my spirit be, at least let my soul be." Wait, though, don't worry.

Death—and life—to come

15. *For if the Spirit of him who raised Jesus from the dead dwells in you, he that raised Christ Jesus from the dead will bring to life your mortal bodies also* (Rom 8:11). What are you afraid of? Why are you anxious even for the flesh itself? *Not a hair of your head shall perish* (Lk 21:18). By his sin, Adam condemned your bodies to death; but Jesus, if his Spirit is in you, *will bring to life your mortal bodies also*, because he gave his blood for your health and salvation. You hold a pledge like that, and can you have any doubt about the promise being kept? So that, man, is how *the strife of death* (1 Cor 15:54) will be no more, how this that he says will be fulfilled: *Wretched man that I am, who shall deliver me from the body of this death?* (Rom 7:24); because it is Christ Jesus, if his Spirit dwells in you, who *will bring to life our mortal bodies also.*

In this way you will be delivered from the body of this death (Rom 7:24), not by not having a body, or by having another one, but by not dying any more. You see, if he hadn't added *of this death,* and had just said *Who will deliver me from the body,* an error would perhaps have suggested itself to human reflections, and they would say, "You see, don't you, that God doesn't want us to be with the body?" *From the body,* he said, *of this death.* Take away death, and the body is good. Let death, the last enemy,[27] be removed, and my flesh will be for ever my friend. Nobody, after all, ever hated his own flesh.

Even if the spirit lusts against the flesh, and the flesh lusts against the spirit;[28] even if now there is dissension in the house, the husband in pursuing the quarrel is not seeking the ruin of his wife, but her agreement. Perish the thought, my brothers and sisters, perish the thought that in lusting against the flesh the spirit hates the flesh. It hates the vices of the flesh, hates the thinking of the flesh, hates the striving of death.[29] Only let this perishable thing put on imperishability, and this mortal thing put on immortality; let it be sown embodying the soul, and rise embodying the spirit;[30] and you will see full and perfect agreement, you will see the creature praising the creator.

So *if the Spirit of him who raised Jesus from the dead dwells in you; he that raised Christ from the dead will bring to life your mortal bodies also, because of his indwelling Spirit who dwells in you* (Rom 8:11); not because of your merits, but because of his gifts.

Turning to the Lord, etc.

NOTES

1. Preached on Wednesday, 15 October, also in Carthage; see Sermon 153, note 1.

2. See Rom 6:12.

3. That is, in the kingdom, in the life of the world to come.

4. As well as in the opening sentence of today's reading, "There is therefore no condemnation now for those who are in Christ Jesus," Rom 8:1.

5. Presumably the law of sin, to which I have been taken prisoner.

6. See Rom 7:6; also 2 Cor 3:6.

7. See Rom 7:22.

8. The text ends with the words "Christ Jesus." But I feel certain Augustine completed the quotation, since he is precisely asking why that law cannot be said to have delivered us. We have to do here with a stenographer's abbreviation, which was not filled out in the fair copy.

9. Eugene Teselle has shown that the curious reading "has become sinner or sin" is due to a misreading of the Greek feminine article *he* as the conjunction *e*, meaning "or." The sentence should read, "so that sin might become above measure sinful." Latin, having no real adjective "sinful," has to use the noun "sinner," or as in the Vulgate the participle "sinning."

10. See 2 Cor 3:3.

11. By mystery here he means what he often also calls sacrament; namely a piece of biblical symbolism—one that is indeed built into the Christian calendar.

12. *Pascha*, of course, is the Greek and Latin transliteration of the Hebrew *pesach*. As it has been traditionally translated in English into "passover," his explanation sounds a little redundant. It should also be noted that *Pascha* in Latin refers both to Passover and to Easter.

13. So far he has just explained the harmony in the great mystery between the old and new Passovers, the old and new Pentecosts. The difference is to be explained in the next section.

14. Some manuscripts here have the future *liberabit* instead of the perfect *liberavit* of the text; I think they are more likely to be right.

15. He leaves us to work out precisely what this mystery was! He has already identified the risen Christ with the fish Peter was to catch—a very traditional symbolism, of course, Christ the fish, ICHTHUS, *Iesous Christos Theou Uios Soter*, Jesus Christ God's Son Savior. Does he mean here that the tax is paid for Christ, representing his Church, and for Peter, representing the gospels of the Church? But then the careful reduction of the "stater" to four drachmas implies that that is what represents the four gospels. He was clearly wise not to elaborate on his sudden bright idea!

16. See Sermon 152, 10-12, to which he is almost certainly referring here. But he also dealt with the point more briefly, also in Carthage but on a different occasion, in Sermon 134, 4-6.

17. This aside just seems to be a space filler; I cannot remember Augustine ever having felt it necessary to *explain* that Christ knew no sin; this is a basic datum of faith which he and his congregation shared without question. Though it's true, he has explained how Christ escaped the damning inheritance of original sin, by being conceived and born of the virgin. See Sermon 152, 9.

18. Augustine at his most tortuously rambling. Just leave out the parenthesis, which is little more than a stream of biblical consciousness, and you will get his drift more easily.

19. "Lust" in English means in itself something sinful, or at least rather bad, unless the context explicitly rules out that connotation. The Latin *concupiscentia* is in itself more neutral; though

Augustine's theological use of it would make it in theological Latin almost what "lust" has become in English.

20. The same word as was translated in the first paragraph of section 10 "*savor* the things of the flesh"; in Latin *sapere*. But there it governed a direct object, here he paraphrases the direct object away; and one can hardly say "savoring according to the flesh." In fact he is talking about "the thinking (*prudentia*) of the flesh."

21. His congregation evidently didn't require (or he didn't think they did) any unpacking of the allusion. The paralytic carried on his pallet represented the human soul or mind just carried along by the flesh (giving in to its lusts). But when he is cured, revived, like the Christian cured and revived by baptism, the roles are reversed.

22. Reading *vivis* with some manuscripts instead of the *vivens* of the text: he was speaking while still living in the body.

23. Reading *Sic* at the beginning of the sentence, instead of *Si*. This, if accepted as the correct reading, results not only in a non-sentence, but in one without much sense anyway: "So if you are not in the flesh, so that you are in the Spirit of God, only then, you see, are you not in the flesh."

24. Reading *delectatione justitiae* instead of *dilectione justitiae*, our love of justice; and *catholica pace* instead of *catholica fide*, our Catholic faith, with some manuscripts. "Catholic peace" is a common expression of his, meaning the unity of the Catholic, worldwide, universal Church.

25. See Ps 45:8.

26. See Eph 5:29.

27. See 1 Cor 15:26.

28. See Gal 5:17.

29. See 1 Cor 15:55.

30. See 1 Cor 15:53. 44.

SERMON 156

ON THE WORDS OF THE APOSTLE, ROMANS 8:12-17: *THEREFORE, BROTHERS, WE ARE DEBTORS, NOT TO THE FLESH TO LIVE ACCORDING TO THE FLESH*, ETC. AGAINST THE PELAGIANS, PREACHED IN THE BASILICA OF GRATIAN ON THE BIRTHDAY OF THE BOLITAN MARTYRS

Date: 419[1]

The law was given to help us

1. The depths of meaning in the word of God are there to excite our eagerness to study, not to prevent us from understanding. If everything was locked up in riddles, there would be no clue to the opening up of obscure passages. Again, if everything was hidden, there would be nothing for the soul to derive nourishment from, and so gain the strength which would enable it to knock at the closed doors.[2] In the previous readings from the apostle, which I have been explaining to your graces, as far as the Lord has been pleased to assist me, I have experienced considerable difficulties and anxieties. I was sharing your difficulties, and I was also anxious both for myself and for you.[3]

But as far as I can tell, the Lord helped both me and you; and he was pleased through me so to disentangle what seemed impossibly difficult, that no problem remained to trouble the religious mind. The irreligious mind, of course, hates even the truth when rightly understood; and sometimes people's minds are so twisted, that they are afraid of understanding, in case they should be obliged to carry out what they have understood. It is of such people that the psalm says, *They refused to understand, so as to act well* (Ps 36:3). You though, my dear friends—because it is only right I should think well of you—insist on understanding, and God insists on the fruits of your so doing. *Understanding*, you see, as it says, *is good for all who carry it out* (Ps 111:10).[4]

The part that remains, however, which was chanted today, does not have such difficulties in it as did the earlier passages, which with the Lord's help we have found our way through as best we could; still, it requires your close attention. It comes, you see, as a kind of conclusion to what was said in the previous readings, where we found the going hard, to save the apostle from being judged guilty somehow of all possible sins, because he said, *For it is not what I want to that I do* (Rom 7:15). Next, in case it should seem that the law could be all that people need who have free will, even if no divine help is extended to them over and above the law, or else in case you should think it was given to no purpose, we were also told the reason why the law was given, because it too was given to help us, though not in the way grace does.

The law cannot give life;
the law is part of the promise

2. It was given, you see, as I have already explained, and as you must hold onto firmly, and as I must ever more insistently and tirelessly urge upon you; it was given so that we human beings might discover ourselves; it wasn't given to cure the disease, but to aggravate it with transgression, so that the doctor would be asked for.[5] And who can this doctor be, but the one who said, *It is not the healthy who need the doctor, but those who are ill* (Mk 2:17)? So those who won't acknowledge the Creator are proudly denying their maker, while those who deny their sickness don't acknowledge the necessity of a savior. So let us both praise the Creator for our nature, and for the flaw in it which we have inflicted on ourselves, let us seek a savior.[6]

And what do we seek a savior for? To give us a law? That's too little: *For if a law had been given which could bring to life, justice would really come from the law.* So if a law wasn't given which could bring to life, why was it given? He goes on to show why it was given; because even in this case it was given to help you, to stop you imagining you were healthy. So *if a law had been given which could bring to life, justice would really come from the law.* And as though we asked, "So why was it given?", *But scripture,* he says, *locked all things up under sin, so that Jesus Christ's promise out of faith[7]* might be given to those who believe (Gal 3:21-22). When you hear of a promiser, wait for a doer.

Human nature was capable by free will of wounding itself; but once wounded and sickly, it is not capable by free will of healing itself. After all, if you want to live so intemperately that you get ill, you don't require a doctor to help you; you yourself are all you need for falling down. But when by your intemperate behavior you have begun to get ill, you cannot deliver yourself from sickness in the same way as you were able by your excesses to ruin your health. And yet even when you are in good health, the doctor prescribes moderation. That's what a good doctor does; he doesn't want to be needed when you are ill.

So too the Lord God created man without a flaw, and was good enough to prescribe moderation to him;[8] and if he had followed the prescription, he would not later on be desiring a doctor for his disease. But because he didn't follow it, he grew feeble, he fell; in his infirmity he created infirm descendants; that is to say, in his infirmity he begot infirm descendants. And yet in all his infirm descendants as they are born, God provides what is good, by forming the body, giving life to the body, providing nourishment, sending his rain and his sunlight on *the good and the bad* (Mt 5:45); not even the bad have any cause to find fault with his goodness.

Furthermore, even though the human race stood condemned by his just judgment, he was unwilling to leave it to its fate of everlasting ruin; instead he also sent a doctor, he sent the savior, he sent the one who would cure them for nothing; not content with curing them free, gratis and for nothing, once they were cured he would give them a reward. Nothing can be added to such good will. I ask you, who would ever say, "Let me cure you, and I will give you a reward"? What he did was the absolute best. You see, he knew he had come as a rich man to poor people; he both cures the sick, and once they are cured gives them a present, and the present he gives is none other than himself. The Savior is the help of the ailing, the same Savior is the reward of those he has cured.

The law leads to Christ

3. *Therefore, brothers,* as you have been reminded today, *we are debtors, not to the flesh to live according to the flesh* (Rom 8:12). This is what we have been helped for, what we have received the Spirit of God for, this is why we also beg for help every day in our difficulties. The law subjects to itself those whom it threatens for not fulfilling its commands; they are under the law, not under grace. *The law is good, if one uses it lawfully* (1 Tm 1:8). So what does it mean, lawfully to use the law? To recognize through the law one's disease, and to desire divine assistance in getting better. Because, as I have said, and it can't be said too often, *If the law could bring to life, justice would really come from the law,* and a savior wouldn't be required, nor would Christ come, nor would he seek the lost sheep with his blood. The apostle indeed says as much in another place: *For if justice came through the law, then Christ died for nothing* (Gal 2:21).

What's the use of the law, then, and how does it help? Because *scripture locked all things up under sin, so that Jesus Christ's promise out of faith might be given to those who believe. And so the law,* he says, *was our pedagogue*[9] in Christ Jesus (Gal 3:22.24). See if you can get the point I'm making from this comparison. The pedagogue doesn't take the boy to himself, but to the schoolmaster; but once the boy has been well educated and grown older, he won't continue to be under the pedagogue.

The Physician comes

4. The apostle also deals with this subject somewhere else; he is very persistent, you see, in driving the point home—I only hope it isn't into deaf ears. He persistently urges the point, impressing on the Gentiles the necessity of faith; because it is by faith they obtain the help needed to fulfill the law, obtaining the strength to fulfill it through faith, not through the law itself. In particular it's because of the Jews that the apostle is so persistent in saying all this and urging it on us; they were always boasting about the law, and claiming that the law was enough to direct their freedom of choice. And thus, because they claimed the law was enough to direct their freedom of choice, *being ignorant of the justice of God,* that is, of the justice given by God as a result of faith, *and wishing to establish their own,* as though it were achieved by their own powers, not obtained by the cries of faith for help, *they are not subject,* as he says, *to the*

justice of God. For the end of the law is Christ, to be justice for everyone who believes (Rom 10:3-4).

So when he's discussing this point, he has made this objection to himself: *So why the law?*, as though to say, "What use is the law?" He answers, *It was laid down for the sake of transgression* (Gal 3:19).[10] This is the same as what he says elsewhere: *The law was introduced so that the offense might abound.* And what did he add there? *But where the offense has abounded, grace has abounded all the more* (Rom 5:20). Because with a milder kind of sickness the help of medicine was ignored, the disease grew worse, and the doctor was asked for. *So why the law? It was laid down for the sake of transgression*; as a means to humble the stiff necks of the proud who attribute too much to themselves, and claim credit for their wills alone, imagining that their freedom of choice is all they need for being just. Well, when this freedom was unimpaired, that is in paradise, it demonstrated what its powers were, it showed how much they could do—collapse into ruin, not rise up again. So *the law was laid down for the sake of transgression, until the seed should come to whom the promise had been made, being disposed through angels in the hand of the mediator.*[11]

Grace is a medicine

5. *But a mediator is not of one; but God is one* (Gal 3:19-20). What does it mean, *a mediator is not of one*? Well of course, a mediator is between two parties. If God is one, and a mediator is not of one, between what and God are we looking for a mediator? Because *a mediator is not of one, but God is one.* We can discover between what and what the mediator is from what the same apostle says: *For there is one God, and one mediator of God and men, the man Christ Jesus* (1 Tm 2:5). If you weren't lying there,[12] half dead, you would have no need of a mediator; but because you are lying there, and cannot get up, God has somehow stretched out his arm to you as a mediator. *And the arm of the Lord, to whom has it been revealed?* (Is 53:1).

So don't let anybody say, "Because we are not under the law but under grace, let us therefore sin, let us therefore do what we like." If you say this, it means you love sickness, not health. Grace is a medicine; if you want to be sick all the time, it means you are ungrateful for the medicine. *Therefore, brothers,* having received this help, this divine help, the arm of the Lord reaching down to us from above, and the help of the Holy Spirit extended to us by this very arm of the Lord, *we are debtors, not to the flesh to walk according to the flesh.* Because faith cannot work well, except through love. Such, you see, is the faith of the faithful; it mustn't be the same as the faith of demons, because the demons too believe, and tremble.[13] So the faith to be admired, the true faith of grace, is the sort that works through love.[14]

Now to have love, and to be able to have good works as a result of it, is that something we can give ourselves, seeing that it is written, *The love of God has been poured out in our hearts through the Holy Spirit which has been given to us* (Rom 5:5)? So entirely is love or charity the gift of God that it is even called

God, as the apostle John says: *Charity is God*,[15] and whoever remains in charity remains in God, and God in him (1 Jn 4:16).

"By what"—and "according to what"—do we live?

6. *Therefore, brothers, we are debtors, not to the flesh to live according to the flesh. For if you live according to the flesh, you shall die* (Rom 8:12). He had already said earlier on, *The thinking of the flesh is death* (Rom 8:6).[16] Not that the flesh is something bad; I mean, it too is a creation of God's made by the very one who made the soul; neither the one nor the other is a part of God;[17] both the one and the other are creations of God. So the flesh is not something bad; but living according to the flesh is bad. God is supremely good, because he is supremely the one who can say *I am who I am* (Ex 3:14).[18] So God is supremely good; the soul is a great good, but not the supreme good.

When you hear, though, "God is supremely good," you mustn't suppose it's said only of God the Father, but of the Father and the Son and the Holy Spirit. These three, you see, are one, and are one God, who is supremely good. God certainly is one in such a way, that when you are questioned about the Trinity, this is how you should answer; in case perhaps, when you hear that God is one, you should suppose the same one is the Father, the same one the Son, the same one the Holy Spirit.[19] That's not how it is; but the one who is the Father in that Trinity is not the Son; the one who is the Son in that Trinity is not the Father; the one who is the Holy Spirit in that Trinity is neither the Son nor the Father, but the Spirit of the Father, and equally the Spirit of the Son. You see, he is the one Holy Spirit of both Father and Son, coeternal with Father and Son, consubstantial, equal. This whole Trinity, these three, are one God, supremely good.

The soul, however, as I said, created by the supreme good, is all the same not the supreme good, but a great good. Again the flesh is neither the supreme good nor a great good; but still it's a small good. So the soul is a great good, but not the supreme good; it's living between the supreme good and a small good, that is, between God and the flesh, below God, above the flesh; why then does it not live according to the supreme good, but instead live according to the small good? To put it more plainly: why does it not live according to God, but live instead according to the flesh? It is a debtor, not to the flesh to live according to the flesh. The flesh ought to live according to it, not it according to the flesh. Let the flesh, which gets its life from the soul, live according to the soul. Certainly, each of them should live according to that from which it gets its life. What does your flesh get its life from? Your soul. What does your soul get its life from? Your God.

Let each of them live according to its own life. The flesh, you see, is not its own life, but it's the soul which is the life of the flesh. The soul is not its own life, but it's God who is the life of the soul. So the soul which ought to live according to God (it is not a debtor to the flesh, remember, to live according to the flesh); so if the soul, which ought to live according to God, lives according to itself, it falls short; can it live according to the flesh and make progress? The flesh, though, will be living rightly according to the soul, if the soul is living according to God. Because if the soul wants to live, I don't say according to the flesh, but according to itself, as I said just now—I'm going to tell you what it means for the soul to live according to itself; it's good, after all, that you should know this, and extremely beneficial.

Living according to the flesh, the soul, and God

7. There have been philosophers of this world; some of them have thought that the only happiness is to live according to the flesh, and they have placed man's good in the pleasures of the body. These philosophers were called Epicureans, from a certain Epicurus, their founder and teacher, and any others like them.[20] However, others came along, proud men claiming to distance themselves from the flesh, and setting all their hopes of happiness on their souls, by placing their supreme good in their own virtue.[21] Your religious feelings, clearly, have recognized in yourself the words of the psalm; you know, you realize, you recognize how the holy psalm mocks *those who trust in their own virtue* (Ps 49:6). Such were the philosophers who were called Stoics. You have the first lot living according to the flesh, this second lot living according to the soul, neither the one nor the other living according to God.

That's why, when the apostle Paul came to the city of the Athenians, where these philosophical schools engaged in feverish study and wrangling, as you can read in the Acts of the Apostles—and I'm glad to see you have run ahead of what I'm saying, with your quick and lively memories—as it's written there, *Certain philosophers of the Epicureans and Stoics conferred with him* (Acts 17:18); those who were living according to the flesh conferred with him, those who were living according to the soul conferred with him, he, living according to God, conferred with them. The Epicurean said, "For me to enjoy the flesh is good"; the Stoic said, "For me to enjoy my mind is good"; the apostle said, *For me, though, to cling to God is good* (Ps 73:28). The Epicurean said, "Blessed is the man who has the enjoyment of the pleasures of his flesh"; the Stoic said, "Blessed, rather, is the man who has the enjoyment of the virtue of his mind"; the apostle said, *Blessed is the man whose hope is the name of the Lord.*

The Epicurean has got it all wrong; I mean, it's simply untrue that a person who has the enjoyment of the pleasures of his flesh is blessed. The Stoic too is quite mistaken; I mean it's simply untrue, it's absolutely incorrect that a person who has the enjoyment of the virtue of his mind is blessed. So, *Blessed is the man whose hope is the name of the Lord*; and because those others are vain windbags and liars, *and who has not paid attention to vanities and lying follies* (Ps 40:4).

The way to death

8. *Therefore, brothers, we are debtors, not to the flesh to live according to the flesh*, like the Epicureans. But even if the soul wished to live according to itself, it will be of the flesh, or carnal; it is savoring the flesh, not rising above

the flesh. There is no way, you see, you can rise above it, if you don't hold on to the arm reaching down to you as you lie there. *For if you live according to the flesh*—in the same place as it says *What can man do for me*, it also says *What can flesh do for me* (Ps 56:11.4)—*For if you live according to the flesh, you shall die* (Rom 8:13). Not the death when you depart from the body, because you will die that death even if you live according to the Spirit; but that death about which the Lord says so terrifyingly in the gospel, *Fear him who has the power to destroy both soul and body in the gehenna of fire* (Mt 10:28). So, *if you live according to the flesh, you shall die.*

The way to life

9. *But if with the spirit you put to death the doings of the flesh, you shall live* (Rom 8:13). That is our work in this life, with the spirit to put to death the doings of the flesh; every day to afflict them, diminish them, rein them in, do away with them. How many things, I ask you, no longer delight those who are making progress, which previously used to delight them? So when something used to give delight, and was not consented to, it was being put to death. Trample on the one that's dead, go on next to the one that's alive; trample on the one that's fallen, wrestle with the one that is still resisting. You see, one pleasurable habit may be dead, but another is very much alive; this one too, as long as you don't consent to it, you are putting to death; when it begins not to be pleasurable at all, you have put it to death. This is our action, this our warfare. While we are wrestling in this contest, we have God as a spectator; when we are in trouble in this contest, we can ask for God as a helper. Because if he doesn't help us himself, we won't be able, I don't say to win, but even to fight.

Led by the Spirit of God

10. So after the apostle said, *But if with the spirit you put to death the doings of the flesh, you shall live*; that is, those lusts of the flesh which it is most admirable not to consent to, perfection not to have; if you put to death these unwholesome doings of the flesh which have their striving from death,[22] you shall live. Here it is already to be feared that some people may again presumptuously rely on their own spirit to put to death the doings of the flesh. You see, it isn't only God who is spirit; your soul too is spirit, and your mind is spirit. And when you say, *With the mind I serve the law of God, but with the flesh the law of sin* (Rom 7:25); because *the spirit lusts against the flesh, and the flesh against the spirit* (Gal 5:17); so it is to be feared you may presumptuously rely on your own spirit to mortify the doings of the flesh, and so perish for pride, and find yourself withstood for being proud, not granted grace for being humble; because *God withstands the proud, but gives grace to the humble* (Jas 4:6; 1 Pt 5:5).[23]

So to prevent this kind of pride creeping up on you, notice what follows. After saying, *If with the spirit you put to death the doings of the flesh, you shall live*; to stop the human spirit swaggering and boasting that it is fit and strong for this work, he went on to add, *For as many as are led by the Spirit of God, these are God's sons* (Rom 8:14).

So why were you ready straightaway to start swaggering, when you heard *If with the spirit you put to death the doings of the flesh, you shall live?* Yes, I know, you were going to say, "This is what my will can do, this is what my freedom of choice can do." What will? What freedom of choice? Unless he's in control of you, you fall; unless he picks you up, you lie there. So how can it be with your spirit, when you hear the apostle saying *For as many as are led by the Spirit of God, these are God's sons?* Do you want to lead yourself, do you want to be led by yourself to the putting to death of the doings of the flesh? What good will it do you, not being an Epicurean, and being a Stoic instead? Whether you are an Epicurean or a Stoic, you won't be among God's sons. Not those who live according to the flesh, not those who live according to their own spirit; not those who are drawn by the pleasures of the flesh, not those who are led by their own spirit, but *as many as are led by the Spirit of God, these are God's sons.*

Acted on—and active

11. Someone will say to me, "So we are led, acted on, we don't act."[24] I answer: Rather, you both act and are acted on; and it is precisely then that you act well, when you are acted on by one who is good. The Spirit of God, you see, who is leading you or acting on you, is your helper in your own action. He gave you this very word "helper," because you too have to do something. You must realize what you are asking for, realize what you are admitting, when you say, *Be my helper, do not forsake me* (Ps 27:9). You are, of course, calling on God as your helper. None are helped if they don't do anything themselves. *For as many*, he says, *as are led by the Spirit of God, these are God's sons*; not led by the letter, but by the Spirit, not by the law commanding, threatening, promising, but by the Spirit urging, enlightening, helping. *We know*, says the same apostle, *that for those who love God all things work together for the good* (Rom 8:28). If you weren't working, he wouldn't be working together with you.

Active only if acted on

12. But you must be very determined to keep wide awake, in case perhaps your spirit starts saying, "If God's cooperation and God's help is withdrawn, my spirit can still do this; even though with trouble, even though it can only do it with considerable difficulty, still it can fulfill the task." It's as if somebody said, "We can of course get there by rowing, though with considerable trouble; oh, if only we had some wind, we would get there so much more easily!"

That's not what God's help is like, that's not what Christ's help is like, that's not what the help of the Holy Spirit is like. If it's completely lacking, you won't be able to do anything good whatsoever. You can indeed act by your free will without him helping; but only badly. That's what your will, which is called free, is fit for; and by acting badly it becomes a slave deserving to be condemned. When I tell you, "Without God's help you can do nothing," I mean nothing good.[25] Because without God's help you have free will to act badly; although it isn't in fact free. *For whoever anyone is defeated by, to that person he is allotted as a slave* (2 Pt 2:19); and *Everyone who commits sin is the slave of sin*; and *If the Son sets you free, then you will be truly free* (Jn 8:34.36).

The error of Pelagius:
The grace of God is help for doing things more easily

13. You simply must believe this, that this is how you act with a good will. Of course, because you are alive, you act. After all, he isn't helping you if you are doing nothing; he isn't working together with you, if you aren't doing any work yourself. Understand, however, that you do good things in such a way that the Spirit is your director and helper; if he isn't with you, you are incapable of doing anything good whatsoever. It's not like what some people have started saying, constrained at last to admit the reality of grace; and we bless God because eventually they have at least said this much; by coming so far, they will be able to make progress, and come to what is really the right understanding. So they now say that the grace of God is help for doing things more easily. Here are their very words: "The reason," they say, "why God has given his grace to people, is to enable them to fulfill more easily by grace what they are commanded to do by free will."[26] It's easier sailing, harder rowing; and yet even just by rowing you can get there. It's easier riding, harder walking; yet even on foot you can arrive.

That's not what it's like. I mean, what does the true master say, who flatters no one, deceives no one, the honest and reliable teacher who is also the savior, to whom we have been brought by that tiresome, nagging pedagogue? When he was speaking about good works, that is about the fruit carried by the twigs and branches, he didn't say, "Without me you can indeed do something, but it will be easier through me," he didn't say, "You can bear your fruit without me, but a better crop through me." That's not what he said. Read what he said; it's the holy gospel, treading on the proud necks of one and all. This isn't what Augustine says, it's what the Lord says. What does the Lord say? *Without me you can do nothing* (Jn 15:5).

Right now, though, when you hear, *As many as are led by the Spirit of God, these are God's sons*, don't slacken off and give up. After all, God is not building his temple out of you as out of stones which can't move themselves; they are picked up, placed in position by the mason. That's not what living stones are like: *And you like living stones are being built together into the temple of God* (1 Pt 2:5). You are being led, but you too must run; you're being led, but you must follow; because when you do follow, that will still be true, that without him you can do nothing. Because *it does not depend on the one who wills or the one who runs, but on God who has mercy* (Rom 9:16).

14. Perhaps you were going to say, "All we need is the law."²⁷ The law handed out fear; and just notice what the apostle went on to add on this point, after saying, *For as many as are led by the Spirit of God, these are the sons of God*; because when they are led by the Spirit of God, they are being led by charity; for *the charity of God has been poured out in our hearts through the Holy Spirit who has been given to us* (Rom 5:5); he went on to add, *For you have not received the Spirit of slavery again in fear* (Rom 8:15). What does he mean by "again"? As with that tiresome, nagging pedagogue frightening you. What does he mean by "again"? As on Mount Sinai you received the Spirit of slavery.

Somebody says, "The spirit of slavery is one thing, the spirit of freedom another." If it was a different Spirit,²⁸ the apostle wouldn't have said, "again." So it's the same Spirit, but in fear on the tablets of stone, in love on the tablets of the heart.²⁹ Those of you who were here the day before yesterday, heard how the people standing a long way off were terrified by voices, fire, smoke on the mountain;³⁰ but how when the Holy Spirit came, himself being the finger of God, how he came on the fiftieth day after the shadow Passover,³¹ and in tongues of fire settled on each one of them.³² So no longer now in fear, but in love; that we might be, not slaves, but sons.

Those, you see, who only do good still because they are afraid of punishment, don't love God, are not yet counted among his sons; at least it's something, though, that they are afraid of punishment. Fear is a slave, charity a free lady; and let us say that fear is the slave of charity. To prevent the devil from taking possession of your heart, let the slave come ahead first into your heart, and keep a place for his lady who is coming. Do it, do good at least out of fear of punishment, if you can't yet do it out of love of justice. The lady will come, and the slave withdraw, because *perfected charity casts out fear* (1 Jn 4:18). *For you have not received the Spirit of slavery again in fear* (Rom 8:15). It's the new covenant, not the old. *The old things have passed away, and behold all things have been made new; but all things are from God* (2 Cor 5:17-18).

15. Finally, what comes next? As though you were to say, "So what have we received?" *But you have received the Spirit of sonship by adoption, in which we cry out, Abba, Father* (Rom 8:15). A lord and master is feared, a father is loved. *You have received the Spirit of sonship by adoption, in which we cry out, Abba, Father.* This is a cry of the heart, not of the mouth, not of the lips; it makes itself heard inside, it makes itself heard in God's ears. Her mouth closed, her lips not moving, Susanna cried out with these words (Dn 13:35). *But you have received the Spirit of sonship by adoption, in which we cry out, Abba, Father.* Let the heart cry out, *Our Father, who art in heaven* (Mt 6:9).

So why not just "Father"? What's the meaning of *Abba, Father*? I mean, if you ask what "Abba" means, you will be told, "Father." "Abba" is the Hebrew for "Father." Why did the apostle want to put them both? Because he could see that the cornerstone, which the builders rejected and which became the head of the corner,[33] was called the cornerstone with good reason; it was because it receives in a kiss of peace each wall coming from a different direction. From one direction the circumcision, from the other the uncircumcision; as distant from each other and between each other as they are from the corner; the nearer they are to the corner, the less of course the gap between them; and right in the corner actually joined together. *For he is our peace, who has made the two one* (Eph 2:14.20-22). So from one direction the circumcised, from the other the uncircumcised, the walls harmonized, the corner glorified. *You have received the Spirit of sonship by adoption, in which we cry out, Abba, Father.*

An earnest rather than a pledge

16. What must the actual thing be like, if that is what the pledge is like?[34] And it should be called an earnest rather than a pledge. When a pledge is put down, you see, it is taken back when the thing pledged is given back. But an earnest is given as part of the thing which is being promised; so when the whole thing is handed over, what has already been given is completed, not exchanged.

So let us look, each of us, to our own hearts, whether from the bottom of our hearts and with a sincere love we can say *Father*. The question at the moment is not how much that love is, whether great or small or middling; what I'm asking is whether it's there at all. If it has come to birth, it grows by keeping quiet, it will reach maturity by growing, once matured it will remain forever. You see, it doesn't decline from maturity into old age, and from old age go on to death; it will mature precisely in such a way as to remain everlasting. I mean, just notice what comes next: *We cry out Abba, Father. The Spirit itself bears witness to our spirit that we are children of God* (Rom 8:16).

We are God's heirs in such a way that God is our inheritance

17. *But if children, then heirs also.* After all, we aren't sons for nothing. This is the reward: *heirs also.* It's what I was saying earlier on, that our doctor both restores us to health and is pleased over and above that to lavish a reward on us. What is this reward? An inheritance. But it's not like an inheritance from a human father. He, you see, leaves it to his children, he doesn't possess it with his children; and yet he makes a big thing of it, and expects to be thanked profusely, because he has been willing to give what he can't take away. I mean, could he take it away with him when he dies? I guess that if he could, he wouldn't leave his children here anything. We are God's heirs in such a way that God himself is our inheritance, to whom the psalm says, *O Lord, my share of the inheritance* (Ps 16:5). *Heirs indeed of God;* if that's not enough for you, listen to what more there is for you to enjoy: *Heirs indeed of God, and co-heirs of Christ* (Rom 8:17).

Turning to the Lord, etc.

NOTES

1. As we can gather from section 14, the second paragraph, the sermon was preached two days after Sermon 155. It is rambling, almost incoherent at times, giving the impression that the preacher was by this time a very tired man. It is as much a sermon on Gal 3:19-26 as on the text of Romans.

It is thanks to the information about the Bolitan martyrs that we can date the whole series, Sermons 151-156, so precisely. This sermon was preached on Friday, 17 October. O. Perler (see Sermon 151, note 1) adds for good measure that Sermon 26 was preached on Saturday, 18 October, in the same year 419. It was clearly a marathon preaching session that Augustine undertook in that month.

2. Here, if he was writing expressly on the subject, or preaching a carefully prepared sermon, he would go on to put the other extreme possibility: if everything in scripture were plain sailing, we would take it all for granted, get bored with it, find it superficial, and so on. The fact that he doesn't do so here is already an indication of a mind less than usually alert; especially as throughout these sermons on Romans 7 & 8 he has been stressing the difficulties of the text. So it would have suited him better to begin by stating this other conditional case.

3. Anxious they shouldn't misunderstand Paul like either the Pelagians or the Manichees; anxious he himself should not fail to give them the true doctrine.

4. In fact the verse, as I am sure Augustine would agree, is to be taken the other way round, since it is the complement of the line, "The fear of the Lord is the beginning of wisdom, and *for those who practice it there is good understanding.*"

5. Sermon 155, 4.

6. In the first of these two sentences he seems to be referring both to the Manichees (not acknowledging the Creator) and the Pelagians (denying their sickness); but so succinctly as to involve himself, in the first part at least, in a rather glaring tautology; after all, what else is denying one's maker but not acknowledging the Creator?

It was not only the Manichees who thus proudly denied their maker, but also most contemporary philosophers who, both Stoics and Neoplatonists, were more or less pantheist in their world-views.

7. It seems clear that this is how Augustine construed this sentence—and I think he may have been right. Literally, in both Greek and Latin, it runs "so that the promise out of faith of Jesus Christ might be given," etc.; and this is customarily taken to mean "what was promised through faith in Jesus Christ" etc. This interprets "faith of Jesus Christ" as "faith in Jesus Christ," which is no doubt possible, but always strikes me as a very odd use of the genitive. What I, and I am sure Augustine, do is take "promise-out-of-faith" as a kind of enlarged noun, and so make it the promise of Jesus Christ.

8. Referring, presumably, to the command not to eat of the tree of knowledge of good and evil, Gn 2:17.

9. The Latin keeps the Greek word *paedagogus*; and so do I, because there is no real English equivalent, except possibly, changing the sex, "nanny." The pedagogue was the slave put in charge of the small boys of the family, responsible, as Augustine goes on to say, for taking them to school and delivering them to the schoolmaster.

10. In a rather bewildering selection of texts, it is worthwhile realizing that this whole section is a commentary on this passage in Galatians 3:10-24.

11. In the Greek it is quite clear that what was disposed through angels in the hand of a mediator was the law; and therefore the mediator was Moses. (This is clear enough, certainly; but what Paul means by his remark about the mediator is another matter.) Augustine's Latin text, however, makes it either the seed or the promise that was disposed in the hand of a mediator; and in this way the mediator is clearly Christ, so I feel justified in translating "the mediator" instead of "a mediator." At least in this way he makes more lucid sense of the apostle than the apostle manages to make of himself.

12. He simply says "lying there"; but I sense a slight allusion to the story of the good Samaritan, and the man who fell among thieves, Lk 10:30.

13. See Jas 2:19.

14. See Gal 5:6.

15. Augustine often takes this saying this way round, as well as in the more familiar way, "God is love." The Latin word order permits this ambiguity.

16. This sentence is only found in two manuscripts. But as introducing one more little complication of associated texts, it seems to me entirely authentic, and characteristic of this unusually and excessively convoluted sermon.

17. The Manichees, and to some extent the Stoics, considered the soul to be part of God; or so at least Augustine would construe their teaching.

18. Goodness goes with being; so it is graded according to the scale of being; that which supremely is, is supremely good. Evil on the other hand goes with "not being"; it is the deprivation of the good, the lack of a kind of being that ought to be.

19. He is describing, not very clearly it must be said, the Sabellian or Modalist error, which asserted that Father, Son, and Holy Spirit are just three names for one and the same being or person, thus denying any real distinction between the divine persons. This whole digression on the Trinity is again typical of this very rambling sermon; another indication of a very tired preacher.

20. For a longer discussion of Epicureans and Stoics see Sermon 150 and its notes.

21. Here, no doubt, a murmur of disapproval (cries of "Shame," as Hansard would put it) ran through the congregation.

22. An allusion to 1 Cor 15:55.

23. No less than two incomplete sentences in one paragraph; another sign of Augustine's weariness.

24. He is playing on the two meanings of *agere*, to do or act, and to lead or drive, as in Lk 4:1.

25. He is only enlarging, as he will soon make explicit, on the text of Jn 15:5, "Without me you can do nothing." By nothing good he is to be taken to mean nothing meritoriously good, nothing deserving of a heavenly reward, nothing proceeding from a motive of genuine charity or from the "justice which comes from God." He doesn't mean you won't be able to cook well, or do your job well or anything like that.

26. See his book, *The Grace of Christ and Original Sin* I, 26, 30.

27. Implying, it seems, that while it is true we cannot do anything without Christ, he is with us by giving the law.

28. Because Augustine is maintaining that it is the same Spirit, he must be thinking of it as the Holy Spirit; which is why I have been giving it a capital S.

29. See 2 Cor 3:3.

30. See Ex 20:18.

31. *Post umbram Paschae*; meaning, presumably, the Jewish passover which was the shadow or prefiguration of the true, real passover of Christ. For the Holy Spirit being called the finger of God, and being the same Spirit on Mount Sinai and at the New Testament Pentecost, see Sermon 155, 3-6.

32. See Acts 2:1-4

33. See Ps 118:22.

34. The pledge, which he says should really be called an earnest, is the Spirit of sonship by adoption. The pledge is the security, or the thing placed in pawn, which is taken back when the loan is repaid. The earnest is the first installment of a payment, which is then completed, and not taken back.

SERMON 157

ON THE WORDS OF THE APOSTLE, ROMANS 8:24-25: *IT IS BY HOPE THAT WE HAVE BEEN SAVED: BUT HOPE THAT CAN BE SEEN IS NOT HOPE*

Date: uncertain[1]

The promises of the world are deceptive; but God's promises never deceive

1. As your holinesses will remember the apostle said, my dearest brothers and sisters, *It is by hope that we have been saved. But hope,* he says, *that can be seen is not hope; for why should anyone hope for what he can see? But if we are hoping for what we cannot see, we wait for it in patience* (Rom 8:24). On this point I am reminded I must offer you words of encouragement and consolation by the Lord our God himself, to whom it says in the psalm, *My hope are you, my portion in the land of the living* (Ps 142:5). He himself, I am telling you, who is our hope in the land of the living, is bidding me address you in this land of the dying; to urge you not to be too concerned about the things that can be seen, but about the things that cannot be seen. *For the things that can be seen are temporal; but the things that cannot be seen are eternal* (2 Cor 4:18).

So because we are hoping for what we cannot see, and waiting for it in patience, we are very properly told in the psalm, *Bear patiently with the Lord, do manfully, and let your heart take courage, and bear patiently with the Lord* (Ps 27:14). The promises of the world, you see, are deceptive; but God's promises never deceive. But what the world promises, it is going to give us here, it seems, in this land of the dying; while what God promises, he is going to give us in the land of the living; with the result that many people grow tired of waiting for the truthful promiser, and are shameless enough to love the deceitful one. It is of such people that scripture says, *Woe to those who have lost patient endurance, and have turned aside into crooked ways* (Sir 2:16).

While the sons of everlasting death never stop taunting even those who are doing manfully and with courageous hearts are bearing patiently with the Lord, they flaunt their temporal delights, which for a time taste sweet to their palates, but afterward they will find them more bitter than gall. Well, they say to us, "Where is all this you have been promised after this life? Who ever came back here from there to show that what you believe is true? Look at us, enjoying our pleasures to the full, because we hope for what we can see; you, on the other hand, are tormenting yourselves with the hard grind of self-control, because you believe what you cannot see." Then they add what the apostle mentioned: *Let us eat and drink; for tomorrow we shall die.* But notice what he himself warned us to beware of: *Bad talk,* he goes on to say, *corrupts good habits. Be properly sober-minded, and do not sin* (1 Cor 15:32-34).[2]

By being meek and mild keep to the straight ways
which the Lord teaches you

2. So take care, brothers and sisters, that your habits aren't corrupted by that kind of talk, your hope undermined, your patience discouraged, and you yourselves turned aside into crooked ways. On the contrary, by being meek and mild keep to the straight ways which the Lord teaches you; about which the psalm says, *He will direct the meek in judgment, he will teach the mild his ways* (Ps 25:9). The truth is, without patience amid the troubles and trials of this life hope in the future life cannot be kept alive; and you cannot maintain unflagging patience unless you are meek and mild, never resisting God's will, because his *yoke is easy and* his *burden light* (Mt 11:30)—but for those who believe in God, and hope in him, and love him. Indeed, by being meek and mild like that, you will not only love his consolations, but also like good children put up with his thrashings; thus, since you are hoping for what you cannot see, you will be waiting for it in patience.

That's how you must act, that's how you must walk. You are, after all, walking in Christ, who said *I am the way* (Jn 14:6). Learn how you should walk in him not only from his words but also from his example. The Father, you see, did not spare this, his own Son, *but handed him over for us all* (Rom 8:32). Not that he himself was unwilling or reluctant; he was equally willing, because Father and Son have one and the same will according to their equality in the form of God, the form in which he did not think it robbery to be equal to God; and *he himself loved us and handed himself over for us as an offering and sacrifice to God for an odor of sweetness* (Eph 5:2). So the Father did not spare his own Son, but handed him over for us all, in such a way that the Son too handed himself over for us.

We are the body of that head in whom what we are hoping for
has already been fully achieved

3. So he was handed over, the Most High through whom all things were made, handed over thanks to the form of a servant, to be abused by men, cast aside by the people, to be ridiculed, to be scourged, to die on the cross; in this way he taught us by the example of his sufferings with what patience we must walk in him; and by the example of his resurrection he assured us of what we should be patiently hoping for from him. *For if we are hoping for what we cannot see, we wait for it in patience.* Yes, we are hoping for what we cannot see; but we are the body of

that head in whom what we are hoping for has already been fully achieved. About him, after all, it is said that *he is the head of the body of the Church, the firstborn, himself holding the first place* (Col 1:18); and about us it is written, *But you are the body and members of Christ* (1 Cor 12:27). But if we are hoping for what we cannot see, we wait for it in patience, with nothing to worry about; because the one who has risen is our head, he is keeping our hope warm for us.

And because our head was scourged before he rose again, he gave us a greater power of endurance. It's written, after all, *The Lord disciplines the one he loves, and scourges every son whom he receives* (Heb 12:6; Prv 3:12). Let us not fall away, then, under the lash, so that we may rejoice in the resurrection. So true is it, after all, that he scourges every son whom he receives, that he did not spare his only Son, but handed him over for us all. So fixing our gaze on him, who was scourged without any sin to deserve it, and who died for our offenses and *rose again for our justification* (Rom 4:25), let us not be afraid of being cast aside when we are scourged, but rather be confident that we will be received when we are justified.

We have been saved by hope

4. And as a matter of fact, even though we haven't yet reached the fullness of our joy, still even now we haven't been left without some joy; because we have been saved by hope. That's why this very apostle who says, *If we are hoping for what we cannot see, we wait for it in patience*, says somewhere else, *Rejoicing in hope, patient in tribulation* (Rom 12:12). *Having therefore such a hope, let us show boldness* (2 Cor 3:12); and let our words be steeped in grace, seasoned with salt, that we may know how we should answer everybody.[3]

Because, you see, when people who have lost their capacity for endurance, or never shown any, have the nerve even to revile us for waiting patiently for the Lord (because since we are hoping for what we cannot see, we wait for it in patience), when they ought to be imitating us, then we have to say to them, "Where are your delights, for the sake of which you are walking along crooked ways? We aren't saying, where will they be, when this life is over; but now, where are they? Since today has eliminated yesterday, and tomorrow is going to eliminate today, which of the things you love isn't running and flying past you all the time? Which of them isn't slipping through your fingers almost before you've caught it, seeing that of this very day today you can't keep hold of even a single hour? I mean, the second one is being pushed out of the door by the third, just as the first was pushed out by the second. Of that one hour which seems to be present now, nothing in fact is present; all its parts are fleeting, all its moments on the run.[4]

We make use of the world as though we are not using it

5. "What do people sin for? If they are not quite blinded while they are sinning, at least they could consider the matter when they have sinned.[5] They

ought to be able to see that a pleasure that's going to pass is desired without any forethought; at least when it has passed, it is thought of with regret. You laugh at us, because we are hoping for eternal things which we cannot see; though you yourselves, hooked on temporal things that can be seen, don't know what sort of day may dawn for you tomorrow; often, while hoping it will be a good day, you find it to be a bad one; and even if it turns out a good one, you won't be able to stop it running out on you. You laugh at us because we are hoping for eternal things; but they won't pass away when they come; because in fact they don't even come, but are always abiding, always there; we, though, will come to them, when along the Lord's way we have passed through these things that are passing away.

"You, on the other hand, never stop hoping for temporal things, and yet are frequently disappointed in your hopes. You never stop being excited by them before they come, being corrupted by them when they come, being tormented by them when they've gone. Aren't these the sort of things that glow brightly when coveted, grow dull when acquired, fade away when lost? We too make use of them according to the needs of our journey; but we don't set our heart's joy on them, in case when they collapse we should be buried in the ruins. You see, we make use of this world as though we were not using it,[6] in order to reach the one who made this world, and remain in him, enjoying his eternity.

Wait patiently for what you do not yet possess

6. "But what's this you say, who has ever come back here from there, and who has shown people what goes on among the denizens of the underworld? On this point too your mouths have been stopped by the one who brought a dead man back to life on the fourth day,[7] and himself rose again on the third day to die no more, and before he died, as being the one from whom nothing is hidden, described what sort of life awaits the dying, in the case of the poor man at rest and the rich man on fire.''[8]

But the people who say, "Who has ever come back here from there?" don't believe all this. They want it to look as if they would believe, if only any of their ancestors were to come back to life. But accursed be everyone who places his hope in man.[9] So that's why God became man, and wanted to die and rise again, so that what the future held in store for humanity might be revealed in human flesh, and yet that we might believe God, not man. And certainly the Church of the faithful, spread throughout the world, is there now before their very eyes. Let them read how it was promised so many centuries ago to one man, who believed in hope against hope, to become the father of many nations.[10] So we now see fulfilled what was promised to the single man Abraham as he believed; and are we to despair of what is promised to the whole world as it believes ever coming about?

Let them go off now and say, *Let us eat and drink, for tomorrow we shall die* (1 Cor 15:32). They still say they are going to die tomorrow, but Truth has found them, while they are saying it, to be already dead.[11] You though, brothers and sisters, children of the resurrection, fellow citizens of the holy angels, heirs of God and co-heirs of Christ, beware of imitating them; they die tomorrow as they expire, they are buried today as they drink. But, as the same apostle says, to avoid bad talk corrupting your good habits, *be properly sober-minded, and do not sin* (1 Cor 15:33-34). Walk along the narrow but sure way that leads to the wide open spaces of the heavenly Jerusalem, which is our eternal mother; hope with unshakable conviction for what you cannot yet see, wait patiently for what you do not yet possess; because you can be assured with absolute confidence that in Christ you have one whose promises are true.

NOTES

1. The sermon was preached in Carthage. Though no certain date can be assigned to it, I give reasons in note 3 below for surmising that it was preached fairly early in Augustine's career, about 400 to 405.

2. Paul first quotes Is 22:13 for the words of the worldly (the theme is developed at some length in Wis 2); and then the poet Manander's play *Thais* for his own piece of advice.

3. See Col 4:6.

4. Augustine devoted the last three books of *The Confessions* to an extended meditation on time, combining it there with reflections on memory. It is a theme he frequently comes back to; but his treatment of it here, together with the generally more polished style of this sermon, inclines me to guess a rather early date for it, say between 400 and 405.

This part of his reply to the worldly voluptuary is not, of course, specifically Christian; it is very much in the tone of the Preacher, Ecclesiastes.

5. The text here is difficult to make good sense of, and seems to be doubtful; there are alternative readings and punctuation. The printed text runs: *Propter quid peccat homo, si non excaecatus est cum peccat, vel cum peccaret attendat.* I punctuate differently, and emend one word, thus: *Propter quid peccat homo? Si non excaecatus est cum peccat, vel cum peccaverit attendat.*

6. See 1 Cor 7:31.

7. See Jn 11:39-44.

8. See Lk 16:22-23.

9. See Jer 17:5.

10. See Rom 4:18; Gn 15:5-6; 17:5.

11. Possibly an allusion to Lk 9:60.

SERMON 158

ON THE WORDS OF THE APOSTLE, ROMANS 8:30-31: *WHILE THOSE WHOM HE PREDESTINED HE ALSO CALLED; AND THOSE WHOM HE CALLED HE ALSO JUSTIFIED*, ETC.: *IF GOD IS FOR US, WHO IS AGAINST US?*: AGAINST THE PELAGIANS

Date: 417[1]

Nobody can harm us unless he first defeats God

1. We heard the blessed apostle urging us on and encouraging us, when he said, *If God is for us, who is against us?* He showed a moment before for whom God is, when he said: *While those whom he predestined, he also called; and those whom he called he also justified; and those whom he justified he also glorified. What therefore shall we say to this? If God is for us, who is against us?* (Rom 8:30-31). God is for us, so he predestined us; God is for us, so he called us; God is for us, so he justified us; God is for us, so he glorified us. *If God is for us, who can be against us?* He predestined us before we existed; he called us when we had turned away from him; he justified us when we were sinners; he glorified us when we were mortal. *If God is for us, who can be against us?*

Anybody who wishes to attack those who have been predestined, called, justified, glorified by God, must be prepared, if possible, to make war on God. I mean, when we heard, *If God is for us, who is against us*—well, nobody can harm us unless he first defeats God. And who can possibly defeat the Almighty? Whoever they may be who wish to fight back at him, they can only hurt themselves. That's just what Christ called out from heaven to Paul, while he was still Saul: *It is not good for you to kick against the goad* (Acts 26:14). Let him rage, rage as much as he can; if he kicks his heels against the goad, isn't he just raging against himself?

Christ became our debtor not by receiving anything from us, but by promising us what he pleased

2. Now as regards these four things, which the apostle has presented as being of particular significance in connection with those for whom God is, namely predestination, calling, justification, glorification; so as regards these four

114

things, we ought to consider what we already have, and what we are still waiting for. As regards those, you see, which we already have, we must praise God our generous benefactor; as regards those we don't yet have, we must hold him as our debtor. He became our debtor, you see, not by receiving anything from us, but by promising us what he pleased. It is not, after all, the same thing to say to someone, "You owe it to me, because I have given you something," as to say, "You owe it to me, because you promised it to me." When you say, "You owe it to me, because I have given you something," the benefit has come from you, but as a loan, not a gift. When, however, you say, "You owe it to me, because you promised it to me," you yourself have given nothing, and yet you are demanding something. And the goodness of the one who made you the promise will give it to you, or else trust would turn into spite. To cheat on a promise, after all, is spiteful.

Now can we say to God, "Pay me back, because I have given you something"? What have we given to God, seeing that everything we are, and everything good that we have, we have from him? So we have given him precisely nothing. There is no way we can use that tone of voice in making demands on God as our debtor, especially as the apostle tells us, *For who has known the mind of the Lord? Or who has been his adviser? Or who ever first gave to him, and will be repaid?* (Rom 11:34-35). So the only way we can make demands on our Lord, is by saying, "Give us what you have promised, because we have done what you told us to; and it's you that have done even this, because you helped us when we found it difficult."[2]

Predestined and justified, let us give thanks to God

3. So nobody should start saying, "The reason God called me is that I worshipped God." How could you have worshipped him, if you hadn't been called? If the reason God called you is that you worshipped God, that means you first gave him something, and he paid you back for it. Doesn't the apostle rule out these words of yours, when he says, *Or whoever first gave to him, and will be repaid?* (Rom 11:35)? But look here, when you were called, at least you already existed. You didn't when you were predestined.[3] What could you have given to God, when there was no "you" to give anything? So what did God do, when he predestined one who did not yet exist? What the apostle says: *Who calls things that are not like things that are* (Rom 4:17).

If you had already existed, you wouldn't have been predestined; if you hadn't turned away, you wouldn't have been called; if you hadn't been godless, you wouldn't have been justified; if you weren't earthly and a reject, you wouldn't be glorified. So *whoever first gave to him, and will be repaid? Since from him, and through him, and in him are all things.* So what can we pay back? *To him be the glory* (Rom 11:36). Because we didn't yet exist when we were predestined; because we had turned away when we were called; because we were sinners when we were justified, let us give thanks to God, in order not to remain ungrateful.

4. But I had suggested considering which of these four things we have already gained, which we are still waiting to acquire. Obviously, we have already been predestined, even before we existed. We were called, when we became Christians. So we have already got that. What about being justified? What does it mean, being justified? Have we got the nerve to say we already have this third thing? And will there be any of us bold enough to say, "I am just"? I assume, after all that "I am just" amounts to the same thing as "I am not a sinner." If you make so bold as to say that, John confronts you: *If we say that we have no sin, we deceive ourselves, and the truth is not in us* (Jn 1:8).

So what then? Have we no justice at all? Or do we have some, but not the whole of it? So this is what we have got to find out. So if there's something we have, and something we haven't got, we must let what we have grow, and what we haven't got will be completed. I mean, here we are with people who have been baptized, all their sins have been forgiven, they have been justified from their sins. We can't deny it.

There remains, however, the struggle with the flesh, there remains the struggle with the world, there remains the struggle with the devil. When you are struggling, you sometimes hit, sometimes you get hit; sometimes you win, sometimes you're done for; it remains to be seen how you leave the stadium.[4] Because *if we say that we have no sin, we deceive ourselves, and the truth is not in us*.

Again, if we say we have no justice at all, we are telling a lie about God's gifts. You see, if we have no justice at all, we haven't got faith either; and if we haven't got faith, we aren't Christians. But if we do have faith, we already have at least some justice. Do you want to know how much that some of it is? *The just live by faith* (Hab 2:4; Rom 1:17; Heb 10:38); *The just*, I repeat, *live by faith*, because they believe what they cannot see.

5. Our fathers, the holy rams,[5] our leaders the apostles, when they proclaimed the good news, had not only seen with their eyes, but also touched with their hands.[6] And yet the Lord, keeping the gift of faith for us, said to one of his disciples who was touching, feeling, seeking the truth with his fingers and finding it, exclaiming *My Lord and my God*; this very Lord and God said to him, *Because you have seen, you have believed*. And looking ahead to us in the future, *Blessed are those*, he said, *who have not seen and have believed* (Jn 20:27-29).

We haven't seen, we have heard, and believed. We were called blessed in advance, and have we no justice at all? The Lord came in the flesh to the Jews and was killed; he didn't come to us, and was accepted: *A people which I have not known has served me, has obeyed me by the obedient listening of the ear* (Ps 18:43-44). That's us, and have we no justice at all? We certainly do have some. Let us be grateful for what we have, so that what we don't have may be added to it, and we don't lose what we do have.

So this third thing is already happening in us. We have been justified; but this justice can grow, as we make progress. And how it can grow I will tell you, and after a fashion compare notes with you, so that you may all, each and every one of you, already established in the condition of justification, namely by receiving the forgiveness of sins in the washing of regeneration,[7] by receiving the Holy Spirit, by making progress day by day; so that you may all see where you are, put your best foot forward, make progress and grow, until you are finalized, in the sense not of being finished off, but of being perfected.

Pursue love single-mindedly

6. A person begins with faith; what's faith all about? Believing. But this faith still has to be distinguished from that of the unclean spirits. What's faith all about? Believing. But the apostle James says, *Even the demons believe, and tremble* (Jas 2:19). If you only believe, and live without hope, or don't have love—*even the demons believe, and tremble*. What's so great about it, if you say that Christ is the Son of God? Peter said that, and he was told, *Blessed are you, Simon Bar Jona* (Mt 16:16-17). The demons said it, and were told *Be quiet* (Mk 1:25). He was blessed, he was told, *Because flesh and blood did not reveal it to you, but my Father who is in heaven* (Mt 16:17). What they hear, though, is *Be quiet*; they say the same thing, and they are repulsed. They are the same words in either case; but the Lord interrogates the root, not the flower. Which is why it says in the letter to the Hebrews, *Lest any root of bitterness should sprout up and cause trouble, and many should be contaminated by it* (Heb 12:15).

So the first thing to do is to distinguish your faith from the faith of a demon. How are you to distinguish it? The demons said this out of fear, Peter out of love. So add hope to faith. And what is hope but the sign of at least some goodness of conscience? And to hope itself add love. From then on we have the eminent way, with the apostle telling us, *I will show you a more eminent way still: If I speak with the tongues of men and of angels, but do not have love, I have become like booming bronze, or a jangling cymbal* (1 Cor 12:31—13:1); and he lists other good things, and confirms that without love they are worthless. So let these remain, faith, hope, love; but the greatest of these is love;[8] pursue love single-mindedly.

So now distinguish your faith. You are already among the predestined, the called, the justified. The apostle Paul says, *Neither circumcision is of any avail, nor uncircumcision, but faith*—carry on, apostle, add something, make the distinction, because *the demons too believe and tremble* (Jas 2:19); so add some more, and make the distinction, since the demons believe, and tremble at what they hate. Make the distinction, apostle, and circumcise my faith, and distinguish my case from an unholy nation (Ps 43:1). He very clearly distinguishes, shows the difference, circumcises: and *faith*, he says, *which works through love* (Gal 5:6).[9]

The reward is God

7. Let all of us then, my brothers and sisters, take a look at ourselves inside, weigh ourselves up, test ourselves in all our deeds, our good works, to see which ones we do with love and for love, not expecting any temporal reward, but only God's promise, the sight of God's face.[10] After all, whatever God promises you, none of it is worth anything apart from God himself. Most certainly, God would never satisfy *me*, unless he promised me God himself. What's the whole earth, what's the whole sea, what's the whole sky worth? What are all the stars, the sun, the moon? What's the host of angels worth? It's the Creator of all these that I am thirsting for; I'm hungry for him, thirsty for him, it's to him I say, *Since with you is the fountain of life* (Ps 36:9). And he says to me, *I am the bread who came down from heaven* (Jn 6:41). May I hunger and thirst for this in my exile, on my journey, so that I may take my fill of it when I arrive in his presence. The world smiles on us with many things, things of beauty, power, variety; more beautiful is the one who made them, mightier and more brilliant the one who made them, more delightful, more delicious the one who made them. *I will be satisfied, when your glory is revealed* (Ps 17:15).

So if the faith which works through love is in you, you already belong to the predestined, the called, the justified; so see that it grows in you. The faith, after all, which works through love cannot exist without hope. But when we finally arrive, will there still be faith? Will we be told, "Believe"? Of course not. We shall see him, we shall contemplate him directly. *Beloved, we are God's children, and it has not yet appeared what we shall be.* Because it has not yet appeared, that's the reason for faith. *We are God's children*, predestined, called, justified; *we are God's children, and it has not yet appeared what we shall be.* So now faith, before it appears what we shall be. *We know that when he appears, we shall be like him.* Not because we believe, surely? No. So why? *Since we shall see him as he is* (1 Jn 3:2).

Hope consoles us on the journey

8. What about hope? Will that be there? There won't go on being hope, when the thing hoped for is there.[11] Certainly hope is very necessary for us in our exile, it's what consoles us on the journey. When the traveler, after all, finds it wearisome walking along, he puts up with the fatigue precisely because he hopes to arrive. Rob him of any hope of arriving, and straightaway his strength is broken for walking.[12] So the hope also which we have here, is part and parcel of the justice of our exile and our journey. Listen to the apostle himself: *Awaiting the adoption*, he says, *we are still groaning within ourselves* (Rom 8:23). Where there is still groaning, we cannot yet say there is the bliss of which scripture says, *Toil and groaning have passed away* (Is 35:10).

So, *we are still*, he says, *groaning within ourselves, as we await the adoption, the redemption of our bodies.* We are still groaning. Why? *For we have been saved by hope. But hope which can be seen is not hope. For if you can see it, why should you hope for it? But if we are hoping for what we cannot see, we wait for it in patience* (Rom 8:25). So it was by this hope that the martyrs won their crowns; they were longing for what they could not see, they were indifferent to what they were enduring. In this hope they said, *Who will separate us from the love of Christ? Tribulation? Or deprivation? Or persecution? Or hunger? Or nakedness? Or the sword? Because for your sake.* And where is he, for whose sake? *Because for your sake,* it says, *we are being put to death all day long* (Rom 8:35-36). For your sake; and where is he? *Blessed are those who have not seen and have believed* (Jn 20:29). There you are, that's where he is, he's in you, because faith is itself also in you. Or is the apostle deceiving us, when he says, *for Christ to live by faith in our hearts* (Eph 3:17)? Now by faith, but then it will be by sight; now by faith as long as we are on the way, as long as we are on the journey in exile. For *as long as we are in the body, we are exiled from the Lord; for we are walking by faith, not by sight* (2 Cor 5:6-7).

God will be all in all

9. If that is faith, what will sight be? Listen to what it will be: *That God may be all in all* (1 Cor 15:28). What's "all"? Whatever you wanted and looked for here, whatever you valued highly here, he will be that for you. What did you want here, what did you love? Eating and drinking? He himself will be your food, he himself will be your drink. What did you want here? Fragile, passing, bodily health? He will be your immortality. What were you looking for here? Wealth? You grasping miser, I mean what can ever satisfy you, if God himself doesn't satisfy you? But what did you love? Glory, honors? God will be your glory; even now we say to him, *My glory, who lift up my head* (Ps 3:3). In fact, he has already lifted up my head. Christ is our head. But why be surprised? Because the head and the other members of the body will be lifted up, that's when God will be all in all.

That's what we now believe, what we now hope. When we get there, we will possess it; and now it will be vision, not faith. When we get there, we will possess it, and now it will be this itself, not hope. What about love? It's surely not the case, is it, that love too has its place now, and won't have it then? If we love while we believe and don't see, how much more will we love when we see and possess! So there will be love there, but it will be perfect. As the apostle says, *Faith, hope, love, these three; but the greatest of these is love* (1 Cor 13:13).

Having this, and fostering it in ourselves, and with his help persevering serenely in him, let us say, *Who will separate us from the love of Christ,* until he himself has mercy, himself brings us to perfection? *Tribulation? Or deprivation? Or hunger? Or nakedness? Or danger? Or the sword? Because for your sake we are being put to death all day long, we have been marked down as sheep for the slaughter.* And who can endure that? Who can put up with all that? *But in all this we overcome.* How? *Through him that has loved us* (Rom 8:35-37). Therefore, *If God is for us, who is against us?* (Rom 8:31).

NOTES

1. So one of the leading Augustinian scholars. Others date the sermon to 418 or 419. There is no indication of where it was preached. As likely as not it was in his home base of Hippo Regius.

2. Grace is precisely what God gives us because he has made a promise. It is the promise which Paul often contrasts with the contract or covenant of the law, just as he contrasts faith with the works of the law. See Galatians 3:15-18 in particular. Here in our text Augustine also brings in a kind of "works of the law"; "because we have done what you told us." But he then hastens to give God the credit even for this, because our doing it has only been made possible by his free gift of grace.

3. Following a reading proposed by previous editors. The reading of the text is rather more cumbersome, but amounts to the same thing: "How were you predestined, if not when you did not exist?" If one leaves out the "if not," *nisi*, which occurs in none of the manuscripts, this could be repunctuated: "How were you predestined? When you did not exist."

4. That is, whether or not you are carried or dragged out feet first. He is alluding to gladiatorial combats, from which both parties did not usually emerge alive.

5. Because they lead the flock; though I believe in English flocks it is usually the bellwether (female) which does this.

6. See 1 Jn 1:1.

7. See Tit 3:5.

8. See 1 Cor 13:13.

9. This extra conceit he throws in, asking the apostle to circumcise his faith, seems a little off-beat, seeing that Paul has just said that being circumcised or not simply does not matter anymore. He has in mind, no doubt, the circumcision of the heart, as in Deuteronomy 10:16; 30:6.

10. See 1 Cor 13:12.

11. His favorite contrast between *spes* and *res*, hope and actuality, or thing hoped for.

12. Most people in those days, we have to remember, when they traveled, even on long journeys like Paul, did so on foot. Not many could afford horses, still fewer carriages or litters.

SERMON 159

ON THE SAME WORDS OF THE APOSTLE, ROMANS 8:30-31, OR ON JUSTIFICATION

Date: 417[1]

When we are finally home, there will only be praising

1. Yesterday, on the subject of our justification, which we receive from the Lord our God, a sermon was delivered by my ministry, thanks to his gracious gift, and your attendance. And while we are burdened in this life with the load of the corruptible flesh, not indeed without sin—because *if we say that we have no sin, we are deceiving ourselves and the truth is not in us* (1 Jn 1:8)—still it was made clear to your graces, I rather think, that even so we have been justified after the measure appropriate to our present journey in exile, while we are living by faith, and until we come to the enjoyment of the final vision.[2] So we start from faith, in order to arrive at vision; we hurry along the road, we are aiming at getting home. On the journey, in our exile, our soul says, *Since all my desire is before you, and my groans are not hidden from you* (Ps 38:9). When we are finally home, though, praying will be out of place, there will only be praising. Why will praying be out of place? Because nothing will be lacking; what here has to be believed is there seen; what is hoped for here is possessed there; what is asked for here is received there.

However, perfection of some kind is to be found in this life, and the martyrs achieved it. That's why, as the faithful know, Church custom has it that at the place where the names of the martyrs are recited at God's altar, we don't pray for them, while we do pray for the other departed brothers and sisters who are remembered there.[3] It is insulting, I mean, to pray for martyrs, to whose prayers we ought rather to commend ourselves. They have tackled sin, after all, to the point of shedding their blood. To people on the other hand, who were still imperfect and yet partly justified, the apostle says in his letter to the Hebrews, *For you have not yet fought to the point of shedding your blood, as you struggle against sin* (Heb 12:4). So if they hadn't yet shed their blood, there can be no doubt that others had. Who had got to the point of shedding their blood? The holy martyrs, of course, about whom we have just heard the reading from the apostle James: *Count it all joy, my brothers and sisters, when you meet with various trials*—he is already speaking to the perfect, who are also in a position

121

to say, *Prove me, Lord, and try me* (Ps 26:2). *Knowing*, he goes on, *that tribulation produces patience, while patience has a perfect work* (Jas 1:2-4).

Delight in justice most

2. We are required, surely, to love justice; and in this justice that we have to love there are stages marking progress. First of all, nothing at all that gives pleasure or delight must be preferred to the love of justice. That's the first stage. What's this that I've just said? That among all the things you delight in, you should delight in justice most; not that you shouldn't take delight in other things, but that you should delight in justice most. There are things, after all, that it is natural for us in our weakness to delight in;[4] like food and drink which delight us when we are hungry and thirsty; like this light which delights us when it pours down on us from the sky after the sun is risen, or shines from the moon and the stars, or is kindled on earth in lamps to relieve our eyes in the dark; we are delighted by a melodious voice and a lovely ditty, delighted by a sweet smell; our sense of touch delighted too by anything to do with the pleasures of the flesh.

And of all these things which delight our bodily senses, some are lawful. Our eyes are delighted, as I said, by these great spectacles of nature; but the eyes are also delighted by the spectacles to be seen in the theaters. The first sort are lawful, the other sort unlawful.[5] A sacred psalm sung sweetly delights our ears, but so too do the songs of the music halls; the first sort lawfully, the second unlawfully. The scent of flowers and spicy smells delight our noses; so too does the incense on the altars of demons; the first sort lawfully, the second unlawfully. Food that is not forbidden delights the taste; so too do the banquets that follow sacrilegious sacrifices; the first sort lawfully, the second unlawfully. The embraces of husbands and wives are delightful; so too are those of harlots; the first sort lawfully, the second unlawfully. So you see, my dearest friends, that our bodily senses provide us with delights both lawful and unlawful. But let our delight in justice be such that it beats even lawful delights; and put justice before the delight that you lawfully enjoy.

One only loves what delights one

3. Because of what I've said, let us set before our eyes the example of a contest or struggle. I ask you whether you love justice; you will answer, "I do." And it wouldn't be a true answer, unless to some extent justice delighted you. One only loves, after all, what delights one. *Take delight in the Lord* (Ps 37:4). Scripture says that. Now the Lord is justice. I mean, you mustn't picture God to yourself as an idol. God is like invisible things; and even in us the things that are invisible are the better ones. Faith is better than flesh, faith is better than gold, and faith is better than silver, than money, than farms, than family, than wealth; and all these things can be seen, faith cannot. So what do we think God is more like, visible things or invisible, precious things or cheap ones?

Let me say something about the cheaper sort.[6] You have two slaves, one misshapen in body, the other very, very beautiful; but the misshapen one is trustworthy, the other one not. Tell me which of them you love the more, and I can see that you love invisible things. What else? When you love the trustworthy slave, even though his body is deformed, more than the beautiful faithless one, have you gone off the rails, and preferred ugly things to beautiful ones? Obviously not; on the contrary, you have preferred the more beautiful to the ugly. You see, you have ignored the eyes in your head, and raised the eyes in your heart. You questioned the eyes in your head, and what information did they give you? This one's beautiful, that one's ugly. You rejected them, turned down their evidence; you raised the eyes in your heart to the faithful slave and the faithless slave; you found the first to have an ugly body, the other a beautiful one; but you gave judgment and said, "What can be more beautiful than fidelity, what more misshapen than faithlessness?"

The interior senses are delighted by the delights of justice

4. So above all pleasures, which include even lawful delights, we must love justice. You see, if you've got interior senses, all those interior senses are delighted by the delights of justice. If you've got interior eyes, observe the light of justice: *For with you is the fountain of life, and in your light shall we see light* (Ps 36:9). It's about that light that the psalm says, *Enlighten my eyes, lest I fall asleep in death* (Ps 13:3).

Again, if you've got interior ears, try to hear justice. Such were the ears he was looking for, the one who said, *Whoever has ears to hear, let him hear* (Lk 8:4). If you have an interior sense of smell, listen to the apostle: *For we are the good odor of Christ for God in every place* (2 Cor 2:15). If you've got an interior sense of taste, listen to this: *Taste and see that the Lord is sweet* (Ps 34:8). If you've got an interior sense of touch, listen to what the bride sings about the bridegroom: *His left hand is under my head, and his right hand embraces me* (Sg 2:6).

The delight of justice should prevail

5. So then, as I started to say, let us provide ourselves with an example.[7] Let us see, my dear brothers and sisters—it can be any of you; I ask the question, and you can answer what I'm going to say—let us see whether you take such delight in justice that you prefer it to those other delights enjoyed by the bodily senses. Here we are then: gold delights you, it delights your eyes; it's a beautiful metal, shining ever so brightly, it's a delight. It's beautiful, I don't deny it, because if I did deny it was beautiful, I would be insulting the Creator. So a tempter comes along, and he says to you "I'll take all your gold, unless you give some false evidence for me; on the other hand, if you do give it, I will get you more."[8]

Two kinds of delight are fighting it out in you; now I ask you the question, which you prefer, which delights you the more, gold or truth; gold, or giving true evidence. Or can it be that the first gleams and glitters, the other doesn't?

What's required of you in giving true evidence is being trustworthy; does gold glitter, and trustworthiness have no gleam to it? You should be ashamed of yourself; bring out those eyes; what you loved in your slave, give back to your Lord and master. Just now, remember, when I was questioning you about your two slaves, one deformed and faithful, the other beautiful and faithless, which of them you loved more; you gave me the right answer, and preferred what ought to be preferred. Go back inside yourself, because now we are dealing with you. Naturally, you loved the trustworthy slave. Does your Lord not deserve to have you as his trustworthy slave?

And what of real value did you promise your faithful slave? The supreme reward of freedom, as you loved him so much. What was the great thing you promised your faithful slave? Freedom in the time of this life. Don't we see, incidentally, many slaves in want of nothing, and free persons begging? And you were demanding fidelity from a man you were promising liberty; and you don't even show fidelity to one who is promising you eternity!

Our actions are motivated by delight

6. It would take too long to run through each of the bodily senses. But what I have said about the eyes, you should apply to the others, putting what delights the mind above what delights the flesh. Your flesh, I mean to say, is delighted even by unlawful pleasures; let your mind take delight in the invisible, beautiful, chaste, holy, melodious, sweet thing that is justice, so that you won't be forced to it out of fear. After all, if you are forced to it out of fear, you don't yet take delight in it. You ought to refrain from sinning, not out of fear of punishment, but out of love of justice.

On this point the apostle says, *I am saying something in human terms, because of the weakness of your flesh. For just as you offered your members to be the slaves of uncleanness and iniquity upon iniquity, so now offer your members to be the slaves of justice for your sanctification* (Rom 6:19).[9] What have I said? I am saying something in human terms; saying something you can bear. When you offered your members to iniquity for the perpetration of disgraceful acts, were you dragged into it by fear, or lured into it by delight? What are you all saying? Answer me, because even those of you who are now living good lives, once upon a time perhaps lived bad lives. When you were sinning, you used to take delight in your sins; was fear dragging you into sinning, or the deliciousness of sin? You will answer, of course, its deliciousness.

So you are led into sin because it's delicious, and prodded toward justice because you're frightened? Test yourselves, take a look at yourselves. Let the man who's threatening you take your gold away. Justice tastes more delicious, justice gleams more brightly. So what, if the man who's promising it doesn't give you the gold? Justice is to be preferred to gold, to be preferred as more delightful. It shines more brilliantly, gleams more brightly, tastes more delicious, is much, much sweeter. So now if any of you are testing yourselves, and find you have been the winner in this contest, you have heard the apostle saying,

I am saying something in human terms, because of the weakness of your flesh.
Undoubtedly he has spared our weakness; and he has tried to say something—
I'm not sure quite how to put it—something even more worthwhile to people
not quite ready for it.

Justice puts up with pain

7. "Look," he says, "I'm saying something you are able to grasp; you have
offered your members to unlawful delights, you have been drawn by the enjoyable element in sins to commit them; let the enjoyable sweetness of justice draw
you on to doing what is right; love justice, as you loved iniquity." Justice
deserves to obtain from you, that you should offer her what you offered iniquity.
That's the meaning of *I am saying something in human terms*; that's all your
weakness can as yet stand.

So what did the apostle keep back? What did he put off saying? Let me tell
you, if I can, what he put off saying. Weigh justice against iniquity; is justice
only worth as much as iniquity was worth? Is it to be loved only in the way
iniquity was loved? Surely, surely not only as much, and in the same way; but
yet again, if only it were at least as much and in the same way. So, more, then?
Certainly, certainly more. In iniquity you followed pleasure; for justice put up
with pain. In the matter of injustice, I repeat, you followed enjoyment, for justice
put up with pain; that's the more that I mean.

Here's some shameless youngster or other, of that dangerously slippery age,
and out to have some fun, he has cast his eyes on another man's wife, he's fallen
in love, he's eager to get to her; and yet he tries to avoid being found out. You
see, he loves pleasure all right, but he's more afraid of pain. Why doesn't he
want to be found out? Because he's afraid of being caught, handcuffed, led
away, shut up, brought before the judge, tortured, put to death.[10] Being afraid
of all that, in his pursuit of pleasure he looks for a secret trysting place, he keeps
an eye open for the husband's absence, he's afraid of finding someone to help
him in his misdeed, because he's terrified of being tied up with anyone who
knows about it. And we see him drawn by the prospect of pleasure; but the
pleasure is not so great that it can also overcome fear and pain and the fear of
punishment.

Now give me the beautiful lady justice, give me the beauty of fidelity; let her
step out in the midst of us, show herself to the eyes of the heart, inspire her lovers
with tremendous ardor. Now she is saying to you, "Do you want to enjoy me?
Despise whatever else you delight in, despise it for my sake." There you are,
you've despised it; that's not enough for her; that's just something human,
because of the weakness of your flesh. "It's not enough that you should despise
whatever you used to take delight in; you must also despise whatever you used
to be terrified of; despise prison, despise chains, despise the rack, despise torture,
despise death. You have overcome these, and you have found me."

Test yourselves as lovers of justice in each grade.

The martyrs are the true and perfect lovers of justice

8. Perhaps we have found some among us who prefer the enjoyment of justice to the pleasures and enjoyment of their bodies; but do you think there is anybody among you who for her sake would despise pains, penalties, and death? Well, at least let us think about what we do not have the audacity to profess. What are our thoughts to be? Where are they to be concentrated? Our eyes gaze on thousands of martyrs all round us,[11] and they are the true and perfect lovers of justice. About them it is said, *Count it all joy, my brothers and sisters, when you meet with various trials; knowing that the testing of your faith produces patience, while patience has a perfect work* (Jas 1:2-4). What more can be added, so that it may have a perfect work? It[12] loves, is full of ardor and fervor; tramples on everything that delights it, and passes on; comes to things that are rough, fearsome, grim, threatening; tramples on them, breaks them, and passes on.

Oh, to love like that, like that to advance, to die to oneself, to come to God! *Whoever loves his life will lose it; and whoever loses his life for my sake will find it unto eternal life* (Mt 10:39). That's the way the lover of justice must arm himself, that's the way to arm himself for the lover of invisible beauty. *What I say to you in the dark, speak out in the light; and what you hear in the ear, proclaim on the rooftops* (Mt 10:27). What's the meaning of *What I say to you in the dark, speak out in the light*? What I say and you hear in the mind, speak out boldly and confidently. *And what you hear in the ear, proclaim on the rooftops*. What's the meaning of *you hear in the ear*? You hear in secret, because you are still afraid of professing it and confessing it openly. So what's *proclaim on the rooftops*? Your houses are your bodies; your houses are your flesh. Go up to the roof, tread on the flesh, and proclaim the word.

Don't imagine that you profit by receiving, and God loses by giving

9. But first, my brothers and sisters, mourn and lament what you used to be, so that you may be able to become what you are not yet. What I'm talking about is a very great thing. And how are we to get hold of a very great thing? It's the last word, it's perfect, it's the best; where are we to get it from? Listen to where we are to get it from: *Every best gift and every perfect gift is from above, coming down from the Father of lights, with whom there is no change, or shadow of movement* (Jas 1:17). That's where the good we have comes from, that's where the good we don't yet have comes from.

Haven't you got it? *Ask, and you will receive* (Mt 7:7). *If you*, says the Savior, *if you, though you are bad, know how to give good gifts to your children, how much more will your heavenly Father give good things to those who ask him?* (Mt 7:11). So let us all, human as we are, examine ourselves, and whatever good we find in ourselves that concerns our justification, let us give thanks for it to the one who gave it us; and in giving thanks to the one who gave it us, let us also ask him for what he has not yet given us. Don't imagine, I mean, that you profit by receiving, and he loses by giving. However capacious the gullet, however capacious the belly you bring, the fountain infinitely surpasses your thirst.

NOTES

1. The text adds to the title, *And also on the words of James 1:2-4, Count it all joy, my brothers, when you meet with various trials, etc.* The sermon appears to follow immediately on the heels of 158, being preached on the following day. However, this is not the view of the leading authority, who dated 158 to the year 417, and this sermon to about 418. So she clearly thinks that the reference in the opening sentence is to another sermon altogether. I do not have access to her arguments.

2. See Sermon 158, 4-6.

3. "The faithful know about this," because the names of the martyrs and the deceased members of the community are recited during the canon, or great eucharistic prayer, from which the unbaptized were excluded.

4. Our weakness here is our natural condition, our dependence for our very existence on material things. To call it weakness betrays indeed decidedly Platonist habits of expression, though not necessarily strict adherence to Platonist philosophy.

5. Such was the severe moral discipline of the Church in those days.

6. This is not yet the example he proposed at the beginning of the section, just a sub-example of something else. In what follows we mustn't take him to mean that slaves as such belong to the cheaper sort of things; what does is their looks, as compared with their characters.

7. An example (in case we had forgotten) of a contest or conflict of delights; though nowadays we talk more readily of a conflict of interests.

8. A favorite illustration of Saint Augustine's. It is nearly always the influential and the powerful that he casts as the villains in his little parables. The sort of false evidence he would usually have in mind would be the kind required in a lawsuit over property rights—cases like that of Naboth's vineyard.

9. It is not the apostle who with this text is making the point about acting from a love of justice instead of from a fear of punishment, but Augustine who is quite ingeniously extracting that point from this text.

10. Was adultery, in Roman law at this time, punishable by death? I think it is unlikely—unless, for example, the licentious youth were a slave, and the woman's husband a senator or other *vir illustris*, person of note.

11. The eyes of our hearts, presumably. But the sermon may well have been preached at the shrine of some martyrs; perhaps, since he says thousands of them, those known as the *massa candida*, the white mass. These were about 300 Christians who in a persecution of about 260 AD were offered the choice of burning incense on an altar dedicated to the emperor, or themselves being burnt in a lime-kiln. With one accord they chose the latter, and leapt into the lime-kiln themselves. Their shrine was at Utica, not far from Carthage.

12. Patience, that is.

SERMON 160

ON THE WORDS OF THE APOSTLE, 1 CORINTHIANS 1:31:
WHOEVER BOASTS SHOULD BOAST IN THE LORD

Date: 397[1]

Glorying in the Lord, you won't be put to shame

1. We have been advised by the apostle that *whoever boasts should boast in the Lord* (1 Cor 1:31); and to the Lord himself we have sung, *In your justice rescue me and free me* (Ps 71:2). So this is what boasting in the Lord means; boasting not in one's own but in his justice. Now this justice has escaped the notice of those who boast in their own justice. And this vice was above all to be found in the Jews who rejected the new covenant, and remained in the old self.[2] It was all in vain and to no good effect that they had read in their service books, and sung, *In your justice rescue me. For being ignorant of the justice of God, and wishing to establish their own, they did not submit themselves to the justice of God* (Rom 10:3).

So none should boast about justice, even if they are just, as though it were their own. To anybody boasting about his own justice, in fact, it says, *For what have you got that you did not receive?* (1 Cor 4:7) So, *whoever boasts should boast in the Lord.* What, after all, could be a safer bet than to boast in one about whom nobody could ever be put to shame? I mean, if you boast in man, something could be found in man, indeed many things could be found in man, about which whoever boasts in him could be put to shame.

Now when you hear that there must be no boasting in man, that means not in yourself either; you are not, after all, a non-man. So if you boast in yourself, you are boasting in man; and this is the most stupid and detestable thing imaginable. Because if you boast in some just man, or in another wise man, the one in whom you are boasting is not boasting in himself. You though, if you boast in yourself, are neither wise nor just; but if you shouldn't boast even in a wise man, much less should you boast in an unwise one. But anyone who boasts in himself is boasting in an unwise person; he is convicted of being unwise by the very fact of boasting in himself.

So, *whoever boasts should boast in the Lord.* Nothing safer, nothing surer. You've got something to hold onto there, if you can; glorying in the Lord, you won't be put to shame. Nothing reprehensible, after all, can be found in the one you are boasting in. And so it is that the psalmist too, who did not say "In my justice rescue me," but *In your justice rescue me*, had first of all said this: *In you have I hoped, Lord; let me not be put to shame for ever* (Ps 71:1-2).

Hold onto the gift, but acknowledge the giver

2. Is there any other point, I mean to say, on which the Jews went wrong, or any other vice for which they were banished from the grace of the gospel, but this single one about which the apostle did not keep quiet, as I reminded you just now? *I bear them witness*, he says, *that they have zeal for God, but not according to knowledge* (Rom 10:2). He praised them here, and he also blamed them. So what put them in the wrong? That while they had zeal for God, of course, it wasn't according to knowledge. And as though we were to consult the apostle, and say, "What's this you said, *not according to knowledge?* What is this knowledge which they don't have, though they do have, all the same, zeal for God?" Do you want to hear what knowledge they don't have? Pay attention to what follows: *For being ignorant of the justice of God, and wishing to establish their own, they did not submit themselves to the justice of God* (Rom 10:3).

So if you have zeal for God, and wish to have it according to knowledge, and to belong to the new covenant, which the Jews were unable to belong to precisely because they did not have zeal for God according to knowledge, acknowledge God's justice, and don't wish to establish this very justice, if you have any, as your own. If you are living a good life, if you are keeping God's commandments, don't think it's all your doing; because that's what wishing to establish one's own justice means. Acknowledge from whom you received and from whom you have what you received. You do not have anything, after all, which you did not receive. *But if you received it, why do you boast as though you did not receive it?* (1 Cor 4:7). When you boast, you see, as though you did not receive it, you are boasting in yourself; and then what's become of *Whoever boasts should boast in the Lord* (1 Cor 1:31)?

Hold onto the gift, but acknowledge the giver. When the Lord promised he was going to give his Spirit, *If anyone is thirsty*, he said, *let him come to me and drink. Whoever believes in me, rivers of living water will flow from his belly* (Jn 7:37-38). Where does this river in you come from? Remember your former dryness. I mean, if you hadn't been dry, you wouldn't have been thirsty; if you hadn't been thirsty, you wouldn't have drunk. What's this, if you hadn't been thirsty, you wouldn't have drunk? Unless you had discovered how empty you were, you wouldn't have believed in Christ. Before saying *rivers of living water will flow from his belly*, he first said, *If anyone is thirsty, let him come and drink.* The reason you will have a river of living water is that you drink; you don't drink if you're not thirsty; but if you were thirsty, why did you want to boast about the river as though it were your own? So then: *Whoever boasts should boast in the Lord.*

3. *And I, brothers*, he says, *on coming to you, did not come in loftiness of word or wisdom to proclaim to you the mystery of God.* He also says, *Did I say that I knew anything among you, except Jesus Christ, and him crucified?* (1 Cor 2:1-2). And if that was the only thing he knew, there was nothing he didn't know. It's a great thing to know Christ crucified; before the eyes of little ones[3] he was placing a treasure, so to say, all wrapped up. Christ, he says, crucified. How many things has this treasure got inside? Then in another place, when he was apprehensive about some people possibly being led astray from Christ through philosophy and empty tricks, he promised them a treasure of God's knowledge and wisdom in Christ. *Beware*, he says, *lest anyone should lead you astray through philosophy and empty propaganda, according to the elements of the world, not according to Christ, in whom are hidden all the treasures of wisdom and knowledge* (Col 2:8.3). Christ crucified, treasures of wisdom and knowledge hidden away. So don't, he says, be taken in by the name of wisdom. Apply yourselves to this packet in its wrapping, pray that it may be unwrapped for you.[4]

You foolish philosopher of this world, what you are looking for is nothing; it's whom you are not looking for that counts.[5] What's the use of being very thirsty, if you trample all over the spring as you pass by?[6] You despise humility, because you don't really understand sovereign majesty. *For if they had known, they would never have crucified the Lord of glory* (1 Cor 2:8; Ps 24:10). Jesus Christ, he says, crucified. *I did not say that I knew anything among you, except Jesus Christ, and him crucified*; that is, his humility, which the proud deride, so that these words may be realized in them: *You have rebuked the proud; for accursed are they who turn aside from your commandments* (Ps 119:21).

And what is his commandment, but that we should believe in him and love one another? In whom are we to believe? In Christ crucified. Let wisdom hear what pride is unwilling to hear. His commandment is that we should believe in him. In whom? In Christ crucified. That's his commandment, that we should believe in Christ crucified.[7] That's it, entirely. But this proud fellow, with his nose in the air, and his gobbling throat, and his big words, and his puffed out cheeks, he sneers at Christ crucified. So, *accursed are they who turn aside from your commandments.* Why do they sneer? It can only be because they see the cheap old shirt wrapped round the outside, and don't see the treasure covered up inside. He sees the flesh, sees a man, sees the cross, sees a death; these are the things he disregards.

Stay, don't go on by, don't scorn him, don't mock. Wait a bit, investigate, perhaps there's something inside which may delight you extremely, if you find *what eye has not seen, nor ear heard, nor has it crossed the mind of man* (1 Cor 2:9). The eye sees flesh; there is something underneath the flesh which the eye does not see. Your ear hears a voice; there's something there which the ear has not heard.[8] What has crossed your mind, like any common or garden thought, is a man crucified and dead; there's something there which has not crossed the mind of man. It is ordinary thoughts, you see, that cross our minds. *It crossed the mind of Moses*, it says, *to visit his brothers* (Ex 2:11). This is just our human situation. And when the disciples were hesitating about the Lord himself, and saying to each other when they could see he had all of a sudden risen again, "It's him, it's not; it's flesh, it's a spirit"; what he says to them is, *Why are such thoughts crossing your minds?* (Lk 24:38).

Many have loved the stately home on high,
but have been ignorant of the humble way there

4. So let's try to discover, if we can, not what may possibly cross our minds, but where our minds may deserve to cross over and up to. You will deserve, you see, to be glorified in the one who reigns, if you have learned to glory in the one who was crucified. That's why the apostle himself, who could see not only where he should cross over to but also how he should cross over—many people, after all, have seen where, and haven't seen how; they have loved the stately home on high, but have been ignorant of the humble way there—so the apostle, who knew about and thought about and reflected in good time on how as well as on where, *Far be it from me*, he said, *to glory in anything but the cross of the Lord Jesus Christ* (Gal 6:14). He could have said "in the wisdom of our Lord Jesus Christ," and he would have said something true; he could have said "in the sovereign majesty," and it would have been the truth; he could have said "in the power," and it would have been the truth. But in fact he said *in the cross*.

Where the philosopher of the world was just embarrassed, there the apostle found a treasure; by not spurning the cheap wrapping, he came to the valuable thing wrapped up in it. *Far be it from me*, he says, *to glory in anything but in the cross of the Lord Jesus Christ*. You have picked up a fine load, everything is there you have been looking for; and you have shown what great thing was concealed in it. How did it help? *Through whom*, he says, *the world was crucified to me and I to the world* (Gal 6:14). When would the world have been crucified to you, if the one through whom the world was made hadn't been crucified for you? So, *whoever boasts should boast in the Lord* (1 Cor 1:31). What Lord? Christ crucified. Where there's humility, there's majesty; where there's weakness, there's might; where there's death, there's life. If you want to get to these things, don't disdain those.

You are aiming at Christ exalted on high;
come back to him crucified on the cross

5. You heard in the gospel about the sons of Zebedee. They were aiming at the heights, suggesting that one of them should sit on the right of such a great proprietor, the other on his left. It was certainly a place of great eminence they were after, very great eminence; but because they were disregarding the how of it, Christ calls them back from the matter of where they wanted to go, to the matter of how they ought to go. There they were, aiming at such dizzy heights, and what answer did he give them? *Can you drink the cup which I am going to drink?* (Mt 20:22). What cup, if not the one of humiliation, the one of suffering?

As he was on the point of drinking it, and transferring to himself our weakness, he said to the Father, *Father, if it can be done, let this cup pass from me* (Mt 26:39). So here, transferring and associating with himself these two in particular, who were not intending to drink such a cup, and were aiming at the heights, while neglecting the way there of humiliation, *Can you drink*, he says, *the cup which I am going to drink?* You are aiming at Christ exalted on high; come back to him crucified on the cross. You want to reign, and take pride in the thrones of Christ;[9] first learn to say, *Far be it from me to take pride in anything but in the cross of our Lord Jesus Christ* (Gal 6:14).

This is Christian teaching, the rule of humility, the recommendation of humility, that we should not take pride in anything except the cross of our Lord Jesus Christ. After all, there's nothing special about taking pride in Christ's wisdom; there is something very special about taking pride in Christ's cross. What the ungodly jeer at you about, that's what the godly take pride in; what the proud jeer about, that's what Christians take pride in. Don't be ashamed or embarrassed about the cross of Christ; that's why you received the sign of it on your forehead, as on the seat of shame.[10] Remember what you have on your forehead, and don't be terrified by someone else's tongue.

Circumcision is the sign of the Old Testament;
the cross is the sign of the New Testament

6. The sign of the old covenant is circumcision in flesh that is covered up; the sign of the new covenant is the cross on the open forehead. There, you see, it's a matter of concealment, here of open revelation; that sign is under the veil of clothing, this one is on the face. *Whenever Moses is read*, you see, *the veil is drawn over their minds*. Why? Because they haven't crossed over to Christ. For when you cross over to Christ, *the veil will be taken away* (2 Cor 3:15-16), so that as you once kept your circumcision hidden, you may now carry the cross on your forehead: *But we with face unveiled gazing at the glory of the Lord, are being transformed*, he says, *into the same image, from glory to glory, as by the Spirit of the Lord* (2 Cor 3:18). Mind you don't put all this down to yourself, don't imagine it's all your doing, and being ignorant of God's justice and wishing to establish your own, fail to submit yourself to the justice of God.[11]

So cross over to Christ, you that are so proud of circumcision. I mean, you want to boast about something you are too bashful to display. It's a sign, it's a true one, it was ordained by God; but it's a sign of concealment. The new covenant, you see, was veiled in the old; the old covenant is being unveiled in the new. For that reason, let the sign change over from being hidden to being manifest, and what was concealed under the clothes start being openly on the forehead.[12]

I mean, that Christ was foretold in that sign, who can doubt? In that connection there was the knife of stone;[13] but the stone was Christ.[14] In that connection there was circumcision on the eighth day, and the Lord's resurrection too.[15] That's why the apostle, crossing over from there, coming from there, crossing over, that is, to Christ, for the veil to be taken away, knew what to boast about, what to glory in: *But far be it from me to glory in anything, but in the cross of the Lord Jesus Christ.* What, after all, had he just been saying before? *For those who have been circumcised do not even keep the law themselves; but they want to have you circumcised, in order to glory in your flesh.* What about you, apostle? "Transfer the sign to the forehead. *But far be it from me to glory in anything except in the cross of our Lord Jesus Christ* (Gal 6:13-14). Here I now have," he says, "what I was ignorant about. The new covenant has come, what was concealed has been revealed. Those who were sitting in the shadow of death, a light has risen for them;[16] what was concealed has been revealed to them, what was hidden is out in the open. The Stone, the Rock itself has come, has circumcised us all in the spirit, and has fastened the sign of his humiliation on the foreheads of the redeemed."

Do not be ungrateful for grace

7. Now let all our pride be in the cross of Christ, let us not be ashamed of the humiliation of the Most High. How long is the distinction of foods to continue, and the circumcision of the flesh? It's only for those whose god is their belly, and their pride in their shameful parts.[17] The things that were to come were foretold to them; now that they have happened, they should be believed. We mustn't be ungrateful to the one who has come, if we have been waiting for him to come.[18]

But how do the Jews come to be banished from this grace, like foreigners, like refugees? *Because they have zeal for God, but not according to knowledge.* What knowledge? *Being ignorant,* he says, *of God's justice, and wishing to establish their own* (Rom 10:2-3); only holding on to God in the commandments, and reckoning that they could carry out the commandments by their own powers, they shunned his help. *For the end of the law is Christ,* the perfection of the law is Christ, *unto justice for everyone who believes* (Rom 10:4). And what does Christ do? He justifies the ungodly. By believing indeed in the one who justifies the ungodly, not the godly but the ungodly; making godly the one he finds ungodly; so *to the one who believes in him who justifies the ungodly, his faith is accounted as justice. For if Abraham was justified by works,* as though he had done it all himself, as though he had bestowed it on himself, *he has something to boast about, but not in God's presence* (Rom 4:5.2).

But *whoever boasts should boast in the Lord,* and should say without a qualm, *In your justice rescue me and free me* (Ps 71:2). Because he does rescue and free those who hope in him, not attributing to their own powers what they have received. *This too,* after all, *belongs to wisdom, to know whose gift it is* (Wis 8:21). Who said that? Someone who asked God to give him self-control. Can justice, can any tiny little bit of justice ever be practiced without some self-control? After all, it's enjoyable to sin, because if it wasn't enjoyable, it wouldn't happen.

Justice, however, is less enjoyable, or not enjoyable at all, or less enjoyable than it deserves to be. What else can be the cause of this, but the disabilities of the soul? Bread is found distasteful, and poison enjoyable. How, I ask you, is this distemper ever to be cured? Is it really to be by ourselves and through ourselves? We were all perfectly capable of wounding ourselves, but which of us is capable of curing what we've done. It's the same with misdeeds; any of you can wound yourselves, can't you, whenever you like. But you can't cure yourself whenever you like. So, have a God-fearing mind, be faithfully a Christian, do not be ungrateful for grace. Acknowledge the doctor; the sick never cure themselves.

NOTES

1. The sermon was preached in Carthage in June, 397, according to the majority of the scholars; but one considers at least a much later date, between 412 and 416. The text adds to the title, "And on the verse of the psalm, 71:2, *In your justice rescue me and free me.*"

2. Literally, "the old man"; see Eph 4:22-24. Augustine enjoys conjugating, so to say, the new man with the new covenant, the new song, the new creation, etc., and the corresponding old entities.

3. See 1 Cor 3:1.

4. The wrapping is Christ crucified; what's wrapped in him are the treasures of wisdom and knowledge. At other times Augustine would explain these as being Christ's divinity, or the Word concealed in the flesh. But in this sermon he doesn't seem to do so. Rather, the treasures seem to be the wisdom of humility, the knowledge that it is the only way by which to reach Christ's glory.

5. There are probably one or two words missing from the text, which runs, *quod quaeris nihil est; quem non quaeris.* I have supposed something like *quem non quaeris interest*—or it could be *totum est* or *magnum est.* On the other hand something could be made of the text as it stands: "It's nothing, *what* you are looking for; you are not looking for *whom.*"

6. See Ez 34:18-19. The philosopher as such is credited with being genuinely thirsty for knowledge and wisdom; but then he foolishly muddies their only source.

7. See Jn 6:29.

8. Respectively, the life under the flesh, and the meaning in the voice; these are simple analogues for the divine mystery hidden under the "cheap wrappings" of Christ crucified.

9. See Mt 19:28, where Christ had already promised the apostles twelve thrones.

10. He is referring in particular to their being the seat of shame (in a good sense); perhaps the blushes of the ancients showed more on their foreheads than in their cheeks.

11. See Rom 10:3.

12. That is to say, it's equivalent; he is being a little careless about how he expresses himself here. It reminds me of a story I heard more than thirty years ago: a lady said to the late Archbishop Downey of Liverpool, "You know, your Grace, I never realized, until Dom N. N. raised his hat to me in the street the other day, that he was circumcised."

13. See Jos 5:2. We are more used to saying in English "the rock was Christ"; but one can scarcely talk about knives of rock. In the Latin it is *petra* and *petrinus*.

14. See 1 Cor 10:4.

15. We usually think of his resurrection being on the third day. But it was on the day after the sabbath, the seventh day, and thus could be reckoned as being on the eighth day. This symbolism of the number eight appears in 1 Peter 3:20. For circumcision on the eighth day, see Lv 12:3; Gn 17:12.

16. See Is 9:2.

17. See Phil 3:19.

18. See Mt 11:3.

SERMON 161

ON THE WORDS OF THE APOSTLE, 1 CORINTHIANS 6:15:
DO YOU NOT KNOW THAT YOUR BODIES ARE MEMBERS OF CHRIST? ETC.

Date: uncertain[1]

Your body is a member of Christ

1. We heard the apostle, when he was read, rebuking and curbing human lusts, and saying, *Do you not know that your bodies are members of Christ? So shall I take the members of Christ, and make them the members of a harlot? Perish the thought!* (1 Cor 6:15). So he said our bodies are the members, or parts, of Christ; since Christ is our head in that he became man for our sakes, the head of which it is said, *He is the savior of our body* (Eph 5:23); his body, though, is the Church.[2] So if our Lord Jesus Christ had only taken on a human soul, only our souls would be his members. But in fact he also took on a body, and thus is a real head for us, who consist of soul and body; and therefore our bodies too are his members.

So if any of you were longing so intensely for a little fornication that you were ready to undervalue yourself, and in yourself to despise yourself, at least don't despise Christ in yourself; don't say, "I'll do it, I'm nothing; *all flesh is grass* (Is 40:6)." But your body is a member of Christ. Where were you off to? Come back. Over what precipice, so to say, were you so keen to throw yourself? Spare a thought for Christ in yourself, recognize Christ in yourself.[3] *So shall I take the members of Christ, and make them the members of a harlot?* The harlot, you see, is the woman who agrees to commit adultery with you; and perhaps she is a Christian, and is also taking the members of Christ and making them the members of an adulterer.

Together you are despising Christ in yourselves, and not recognizing your Lord, or giving a thought to your price, your true value.[4] What sort of Lord is that, do you think, who makes his slaves into his brothers and sisters? Brothers and sisters, though, wasn't enough; he also had to make them into his members. Has such great worth, such tremendous dignity, really grown so cheap? Because it was bestowed so graciously, is it not to be treated with respect? If it hadn't been bestowed, it would be desired; because it has been bestowed, is it to be despised?

Your body is a temple of the Holy Spirit

2. But these bodies of ours, which the apostle says are members of Christ thanks to Christ's body, which he took to himself of the same nature as our bodies; so these bodies of ours the apostle also says are the temple of the Holy Spirit in us, whom we have received from God. Because of Christ's body, our bodies are members of Christ; because of Christ's Spirit dwelling in us, our bodies are the temple of the Holy Spirit. Which of these two within you are you prepared to despise? Christ whose member you are, or the Holy Spirit whose temple you are?

As for that harlot, who agreed to join you in wrongdoing, I don't suppose you will dare to take her into your bedroom, where you have your marriage bed; but you look for some neglected, dirty corner of your house, where you can wallow in your dirty games. So you show respect to your wife's bedroom, and you show no respect to the temple of your God? You don't bring a shameless woman into the place where you sleep with your wife, and you go yourself to a shameless woman, though you are God's temple? I rather think God's temple is something better than your wife's bedroom.

Wherever you go, after all, Jesus can see you; the one who made you, and when you were lost redeemed you, and when you were dead died for you. You don't know who you really are; but he never takes his eyes off you, not to help you this time, but to punish. Yes, *the eyes of the Lord are on the just, and his ears are turned to their prayers*; but he added something immediately, to terrify those who were granting themselves a false security, who were saying to themselves, "I'll do it; after all God doesn't stoop to watching me doing such dirty things." Listen to what comes next, consider who you belong to, since wherever you go Jesus can see you: *But the frown of the Lord is on those who do evil, to destroy their memory from the land* (Ps 34:15-16). From which land? The one of which it says, *My hope are you, my portion in the land of the living* (Ps 142:5).

The immoral person is excluded from the kingdom of God

3. It may well be, after all, that a thoroughly bad man, unjust, an adulterer, quite shameless, a fornicator is glad that he does all this, and he grows old, though lust doesn't grow old in him, and he says to himself, "Is it really true, that *the frown of the Lord is on those who do evil, to destroy their memory from the land*? Here am I, already an old man, who has been doing so many bad things from my first steps right up until today, I've buried many chaste men before myself, have myself led the funeral cortège of many a chaste young man to the grave, and I the old lecher have outlived the chaste and virtuous. What's this that it says here: *The frown of the Lord is on those who do evil, to destroy their memory from the land*?"[5]

There's another land, where there's no lecher, there's another land in the kingdom of God. *Make no mistake; neither fornicators, nor idol-worshippers, nor adulterers, nor the effeminate, nor men who lie with men, nor thieves, nor the grasping, nor the drunken, nor the scurrilous shall possess the kingdom of God* (1 Cor 6:9-10). Which means, he will destroy their memory from the land. Many people, you see, who commit such sins nurse fond hopes for themselves. It's because of people who live abandoned lives, and nurse fond hopes of the kingdom of heaven, where they are not going to get to, that it says, *He will destroy their memory from the earth.* You see, there will be a new heaven and a new earth, where the just shall dwell;[6] there the ungodly, there the evil, there the utterly wicked people are not permitted to dwell. Any of you like that should choose now where you would like to dwell, while there is still time, still the chance for you to change.

Two dwellings: eternal fire and the eternal kingdom

4. There are, in fact, two kinds of dwelling; one in eternal fire, the other in the eternal kingdom. Granted that in the eternal fire this person and that will endure different torments; there they will be, all the same, there they will all be tormented; one less the other more, because it will be more tolerable for Sodom in the day of judgment than for another city;[7] and some people travel round sea and land to make one proselyte, and when they've made one, they make him twice as much a child of gehenna as they are themselves.[8] Granted that some there get double, some single measure; granted that some get more, others less; it's not a district where you would naturally choose yourself a place. Even the milder torments there are worse than any that you dread in this world.

Think how you tremble if someone starts telling tales about you, in case you should be put in prison; and are you yourself going to live a bad life against yourself, to get yourself put in the fire? You quake in your shoes, you're worried to death, you grow pale, you hurry to the church, you beg to see the bishop, you fall at his feet. He asks why.

"Save me," you say.

"What's going on?"

"Look, that man's telling lies about me."

"And what's he going to do to you?"

"My lord, I'm being blackmailed; my lord, I'm about to be put in prison. Take pity on me; save me." That's how much prison is feared by people, how they are afraid of being locked up; and they aren't afraid of being burnt up in gehenna!

Then again, when misfortunes come thick and fast, and affliction strikes more cruelly than ever, and strikes to the point of death, when the one concern is to save the person from dying, from being killed, and everyone starts shouting that first aid must be given, begging for any kind of assistance: "Come and help; quickly, for his life's sake; S.O.S., for his soul's sake."[9] The whole urgency of the disaster lies in the expression "for his life's sake, for his soul's sake." Certainly one must rally round, and not refuse to respond to this fear; what can be done must be done, by whomever it can be done.

5. But all the same, I myself would like to question this person whose life is in danger, and who is tugging at my heart-strings on that account; because he is saying, "Hurry, for my soul's sake." I've an easy answer to make to this: "Certainly I will hurry for the sake of your flesh; if only you would hurry yourself for the sake of your soul. And you know perfectly well that I'm hurrying for the sake of your body, not for the sake of your soul. I prefer to listen to Christ speaking the truth, than to you muttering out of a false fear. I mean, the Lord himself says, *Do not fear those who kill the body, but cannot kill the soul* (Mt 10:28). Sure, you want me to hurry for the sake of your soul. But look, the one you're afraid of, and at whose threats you turn pale,[10] can't kill your soul; he can strike savagely as far as the body is concerned; just stop striking savagely yourself at your soul. It can't be killed by him, it can be by you; not with a spear, but a tongue. The enemy who stabs you puts an end to this life. *But the mouth that lies kills the soul* (Wis 1:11)."

So from the things people are afraid of in this time, they should work out what they really ought to be afraid of. I mean, they're afraid of prison, and not afraid of gehenna? Afraid of the inquisitor's torturers, and not afraid of hell's angels? Afraid of torment in time, and not afraid of the pains of eternal fire? Afraid, finally, of dying for a moment, and not afraid of dying forever?

6. This fellow who's going to kill you, whom you're afraid of, who gives you the shudders, whom you're running away from, dread of whom won't let you sleep, and if you see him in a dream when you are asleep, you're paralyzed with fright—what's he going to do to you? He is going to exclude your soul from your flesh; consider where your soul goes when it's excluded. You see, the only way he can kill your flesh is by excluding from it the soul by which your flesh lives. It is, of course, by the presence of your soul that your flesh lives, and as long as your soul is present in your flesh, your flesh is of necessity alive. But the fellow who's seeking your death wants to eject from your flesh your life, by which your flesh lives.

Do you imagine there isn't some life by which your soul itself lives? The soul, you see, is a kind of life, by which your flesh lives. Do you imagine there's no other kind of life, by which your soul itself lives? Or rather, that just as your flesh has life, namely the soul by which your flesh lives, the same also happens with your soul, that it has some kind of life of its own? And that just as the flesh, when it dies, breathes out the soul which is its life, so too the soul, when it dies, breathes out some life of its own? If we can discover what this life is, not of your body, because that is your soul; but the life of the life of your body, that is, the life of your soul; if we can discover it, then I think that, proceeding from this death in which you are afraid of your soul being ejected from the flesh, you ought to be much more afraid of that other death, afraid of the life of your soul being cast out of your soul.

So let me put it very shortly; and indeed, why am I taking so long about it? The life of the body is the soul, the life of the soul is God. The Spirit of God dwells in the soul, and through the soul in the body, so that even our bodies are the temple of the Holy Spirit, whom we have received from God. You see, the Spirit comes to our souls, because *the love of God has been poured forth in our hearts through the Holy Spirit who has been given to us* (Rom 5:5); and the one who possesses the chief part possesses the whole. In you, of course, the chief part is played by what is the better. God, by holding what is the better, which is your heart, your mind, your soul, automatically through the better part possesses the lower, which is your body.

Therefore, let your enemy rage, let him threaten you with death, let him carry out the threat if he is allowed to, and exclude your soul from flesh; only don't let your soul exclude its life from itself. If you are justified in your lamentations, and imagine yourself saying to that powerful enemy of yours, "Don't strike, spare me the shedding of my blood"; can't God say to you, *Have mercy on your own soul by pleasing God* (Sir 30:24[11])? Perhaps your soul is saying to you, "Ask him not to strike, because otherwise I'm leaving you. I mean, if he does strike, I can't stay with you. Ask him not to strike, if you don't want me to leave you." Now, who is it, saying to you, "if you don't want me to leave you"? It's you yourself; you, I mean, doing the talking, are your soul. So if that man strikes the flesh, it's you that flee away, you that depart, you that emigrate; what's lying in the dust is dust. Where will that thing be that animated the dust? The thing that was given you by the breath of God,[12] where will that be? If it hasn't breathed out its life, that is its God, it will be in him whom it hasn't lost, in him whom it has not excluded from itself. But if you yield to your soul's weakness when it says to you, "He strikes, and I leave you," aren't you afraid of God when he says to you, "You sin, and I leave you"?

If you are afraid of death, love life

7. From a vain, futile sort of fear, let us move on to grasping a useful sort. It's a vain sort of fear which all people have who are afraid of losing temporal things, people who are going to move on some time or other, and are petrified of moving on, always wanting to put off what they cannot finally avoid. This kind of fear people have is futile; and yet it's there, and it's very strong, and it can't be resisted. It's about this that people have to be rebuked and taken to task, about this they should be mourned and wept over, that they are afraid of dying, and the only thing they ever do about it is to die a bit later. Why don't they do something about not dying? Because whatever they do, they can't manage not to die.

"But they can do something, surely, to ensure that they never die?" No way at all. No matter what you do, however vigilant you are, wherever you run away to, whatever defenses you try out, however much money you spend to ransom yourself, however cunningly you trick your enemy, you can't trick that fever. All you are doing to ensure you don't die promptly at the hand of your enemy, only ensures that you will die sometime later on at the hand of a fever.

You do have something, though, you can do in order not to die ever. If you are afraid of death, love life. Your life is God, your life is Christ, your life is the Holy Spirit. You don't please him by behaving badly. He won't live in a tumbledown temple, he won't enter a filthy temple. But plead with him to clean a place out for himself; plead with him to build himself a temple; to construct himself what you have destroyed; to restore himself what you have defaced; to raise up himself what you have thrown down. Cry out to God, cry out inside, cry out where he is listening; because that's also where you sin, and where he sees you;[13] cry out to him there, where he is listening and can hear you.

It's dread of the bad, not yet love of the good

8. And when you've straightened out your fear, and begun to be afraid in a useful sort of way, not of temporal torments but of the pain of eternal fire, and for that reason avoided being an adulterer; because that's what we were talking about, remember, on account of the apostle's saying, *your bodies are members of Christ* (1 Cor 6:15); so when you have refrained from starting on a course of adultery for the very good reason that you are afraid of burning in everlasting fire, you don't yet deserve to be praised. You don't indeed need to be grieved over as before, but still you are not yet deserving of praise.

After all, what's so splendid about being afraid of punishment? There is something splendid, but that's loving justice. I'm going to question you, and find you out. As for you then, observe my interrogating you out loud, and conduct your own interrogation of yourself in silence. So I say to you:

"When lust overpowers you, and the other party is agreeable, why don't you commit adultery?" And you will answer:

"Because I'm afraid of gehenna, afraid of the punishment of eternal fire, afraid of Christ's judgment, afraid of the devil's company, and of being punished by him and burning with him."

What now? Am I going to say, "You are wrong to be afraid," as I did say to you about that rival of yours because he was aiming at killing your body? In that case, yes, I was right to say, "You're wrong to be afraid; God has reassured you, saying *Do not fear those who can kill the body*." But now when you tell me, "I'm afraid of gehenna, I'm afraid of burning, I'm afraid of being punished forever," what am I to say? "You're wrong to be afraid"? "It's futile to be afraid"? I daren't say that, considering that the Lord himself removed fear only to introduce fear; and he went on, after saying *Do not fear those who can kill the body, and afterward have nothing they can do; but fear the one who has the authority to kill both body and soul in the gehenna of fire; yes, I tell you, fear that one* (Lk 12:4-5; Mt 10:28[14]). So when the Lord instills fear, and instills it very forcefully, and by repeating the word gives double emphasis to the threat, am I going to say, "You are wrong to be afraid"? That I will not say. Certainly be afraid, there's nothing better to be afraid of, there's nothing you should fear more.

But I've a further question for you: "If God didn't see you when you do it, and nobody would convict you of it at his judgment, would you do it?" You take a look at yourself. After all, you can't answer all my words openly. Examine yourself. "Would you do it?" If you would, it means you are afraid of punishment, you don't yet love chastity, you don't yet have charity. You are afraid like a slave; it's dread of the bad, not yet love of the good. But go on being afraid, all the same, so that this dread may keep guard over you, may lead you to love. This fear, you see, with which you are afraid of gehenna, and that's why you don't do wrong, is restraining you; and in this way, though your mind inside wants to sin, it won't let it. Fear, you see, is a kind of warder, it's like the pedagogue of the law;[15] it's the letter threatening, not yet grace assisting. All the same, let this fear keep guard over you, while being afraid stops you doing wrong, and in good time charity will come. It enters your heart, and to the extent that it comes in, fear goes out. Fear, you see, was ensuring that you didn't do it; charity is ensuring that you don't want to do it, even if you could entertain the idea with impunity.

The more charity enters, the less fear becomes

9. I have said what you should be afraid of, I have said what you should be desirous of. Set your sights on charity, let charity come in. Open the door to her by being afraid to sin, open the door to love that doesn't sin, open the door to love that lives uprightly. When she comes in, as I had started to say, fear begins to go out. The more she enters, the less fear becomes. When she has come in completely, there will be no more fear left, because *perfect love casts out fear* (1 Jn 4:18).

So charity comes in and drives out fear. She doesn't come in, however, without a companion of her own. She has her own fear with her, and brings him in herself; but he is a chaste fear, *abiding for ever and ever* (Ps 19:9). Slavish fear is the kind which makes you afraid of burning with the devil; chaste fear is the kind which makes you afraid of displeasing God.[16] Consider, my dearest friends, our ordinary human feelings, and question them. A slave is afraid of offending his master, in case he has him flogged, has him put in chains, has him shut up in a dungeon, has him worn out on the treadmill. It's because he's afraid of these things that the slave doesn't sin; but when he judges the eyes of his master are not on him, and there is no witness he can be convicted by, he does it. Why does he do it? Because he was afraid of the punishment, and didn't love justice.

A good man, though, a just man, a free person—because only the just are really free; *everyone*, you see, *who commits sin is the slave of sin* (Jn 8:34)—a free person takes delight in justice in itself; and if he could sin without anybody seeing and being a witness, he dreads God too as a witness. And if he could hear God saying to him, "I can see you when you sin, I won't sentence you to damnation, but you displease me"; he doesn't want to displease the eyes of a father, not of a fearsome judge, and so he's afraid, not of being damned, not of being punished, not of being tortured, but of spoiling his father's joy, of displeasing the eyes of someone who loves him. You see, if he himself loves, and is aware of his Lord loving him, he doesn't do what would displease the one who loves him.

10. Take a look at the smooth, dishonorable sort of lovers; ask yourselves if any wanton and worthless fellow, out of love for a woman, dresses otherwise than in a fashion that pleases her, dresses differently from the way his beloved likes, or wears any jewelry except what she likes. She only has to say, "I don't want you to wear a coat[17] like that"; he doesn't wear it. If she says to him in winter, "I just love you in shirt-sleeves,"[18] he prefers to shiver, rather than displease her. Is she ever going to sentence him to eternal damnation for displeasing her? Is she ever going to send him to prison, ever going to bring along the torturers? The one and only thing he's afraid of is this: "I won't see you"; the one and only thing he trembles at is this: "You shan't see my face." If a shameless hussy can say this and strike terror, does God say it, and not strike terror? Obviously he does, and how! But only if we love him. If we don't love, though, we are not terrified by that. But we are terrified like slaves, are we, of fire, of gehenna, of the horrifically savage threats of hell, of the countless swarms of the devil's angels, and of his punishments? Well, if we don't love that other thing very much, at least let us fear all this.

11. So let's have no more fornications. *You are God's temple, and the Spirit of God dwells in you. If anyone reduces God's temple to ruins, God will ruin him* (1 Cor 3:16-17). Marriage is lawful, you shouldn't go looking for anything more. After all, it isn't a very big burden that has been imposed on you. A greater love has imposed a greater burden on virgins. Virgins have declined to do what was allowed, in order to be more pleasing to the one to whom they vowed themselves. They have aimed at that greater beauty of the heart. "What orders are you giving?" It's as though they said, "What orders are you giving? That we shouldn't live in adultery, is that your command? For love of you, we are doing more than you require."

About virgins, says the apostle, *I have no command of the Lord's*. So why are they doing this? *But I have some advice to give* (1 Cor 7:25). These women, then, are so loving that earthly marriage is not worth much to them anymore, earthly embraces no longer attract them, and they have acknowledged the commandment to the extent of not turning down the advice; in order to be more pleasing to the one they love, they have paid more attention to their make-up and their ornaments. You see, the more attention people pay to the ornaments and finery of this body, that is of the outer self, the greater the neglect of the inner self; while the less attention they pay to finery for the outer self, the more the inner self is decked out with the finery of beautiful behavior.

That's why Peter too says, *Not adorning themselves with braided hair;* as soon as he said "adorning themselves," what else should literal-minded, sensual people think of but these visible ornaments, and visible finery? He immediately turned our thoughts away from what greed would be looking for. *Not*, he said, *with braided hair, and not with gold, or pearls, or expensive dresses; but that hidden self of the heart, who is rich in the sight of God* (1 Pt 3:3-4). God, I mean to say, would not give riches to the outer self, and leave the inner self in want; he has given invisible riches to the invisible self, and invisibly adorned the invisible self.

The love of virgins

12. Eager to please with such adornments, God's young ladies, the holy virgins, have neither desired what was allowed them nor consented to what they were being forced into. Many of them, you see, have had to overcome the contrary efforts of their parents with the fire of heavenly love.[19] Father was furious, mother was in tears; she didn't care, because she had before her eyes *one comely of form above the sons of men* (Ps 45:2). It was for him, and him alone that she longed to adorn herself, in order to care only and wholly for him. Because *the woman who is married thinks about the affairs of the world, how to please her husband; but the one who is unmarried thinks about God's affairs, how to please God* (1 Cor 7:34).

Notice what it means to love. He didn't say, "She thinks about how not to be condemned by God." That, after all, is still that slavish fear, the guardian indeed of bad people, to make them refrain from bad behavior, and by refraining become fit to open their doors to charity. But these women are not thinking how to avoid being punished by God, but how to please God with their inner beauty, with the elegance of the hidden self, the elegance of the heart, where they are naked to his eyes—inwardly naked, not outwardly; both inwardly and outwardly pure and untouched.

At least let the virgins teach married men and women not to go in for adultery. They do more, over and above what is lawful; let these at least not do what is not lawful.

NOTES

1. The heading in the Latin text is rather longer: ". . . 1 Cor 9:9-10. 15, *Make no mistake: neither fornicators, nor idol-worshippers, nor adulterers, nor the effeminate, nor men who lie with men, shall possess the kingdom of God. Do you not know . . .* etc. It is true, he does refer to these verses. But then so he does to many others. The sermon really is on the text of verse 15.

No date has been suggested for it. My inclination would be to date it fairly late, say 415-420, and failing any evidence to the contrary, to assume it was preached in his home territory of Hippo Regius.

2. It is rather strange, and also a little inconvenient for him, that he read in Ephesians 5:23, "He is the savior of *our* body." The Greek simply has "the body," the Latin Vulgate "this body"; and it is this that he immediately goes on to explain.

Calling us, or our bodies, "members of Christ" is really very unsatisfactory as a translation of *membra*, because in current English the word is confined to its secondary sense, signifying belonging to some club, society, or organization. But to find an alternative is difficult; "limbs" is too narrow, since it doesn't include most of our organs, like eyes and ears and so on; in fact we only have four limbs. "Organs" is too medical, "parts" too mechanical. So I think we are stuck with "members," but every now and again need to amplify it with one of these other words.

3. It is refreshing to find Augustine warning us here against having too low an opinion of ourselves, against that self-contempt and self-hatred which can sometimes masquerade as humility. Normally of course, and quite rightly, he has his guns trained on our pride, our excessive self-love and self-esteem.

4. The value of the price paid for you, the blood of Christ.

5. It would no doubt be reading too much into his words to conclude that he was presenting his old rogue as an undertaker or mortician.

6. See 2 Pt 3:13.

7. See Lk 10:12.

8. See Mt 23:15.

9. The Latin just has *propter animam*, which I have to amplify, because he is playing on the word's range of meaning from "soul" to "life." There is no readily equivalent English word. The nearest is the S.O.S., Save Our Souls, distress signal; nowadays, I believe, replaced by "Mayday," whatever that means.

10. The kind of disaster he conjured up in the last paragraph of the previous section, and has been discussing since, seemed to be some kind of act of God or natural calamity like shipwreck, or fire, or a road accident. But now he is returning to the first sort of danger, that coming from a powerful enemy.

11. This verse occurs in the Latin text of Ecclesiasticus, but not in the Greek, or in translations made from it, like the Jerusalem Bible.

12. See Gn 2:19. 7.

13. In the inner chamber of your heart, your thoughts and intentions.

14. The quotation mixes up these two gospels; or indeed it may be from a Latin translation of Tatian's *Diatessaron*, a harmony of the four gospels.

15. See Gal 3:24, and Sermon 156, note 9.

16. This second sort of fear, that accompanies love or charity, is more usually called filial fear, in contrast with servile or slavish fear.

17. *Byrrhus*—a heavy cloak like a Mexican *poncho*, worn against rain and cold; probably the ancestor of the monk's cowl, and even of the Church vestment, the chasuble. It tended to characterize the wearer as belonging to the lower orders.

18. *Lacerna*—apparently a lighter, and more fashionable kind of byrrhus, or just a cloak, and not a poncho-like garment.

19. In the earlier Christian centuries virgins who had vowed themselves to God did not live in convents or communities or sisterhoods; it would hardly have been possible when Christianity was still an unlawful religion. Instead, they lived a secluded life at home with their families. This still continued to be a common practice in Augustine's time; but because many aspiring virgins had to face this kind of parental opposition, religious communities were being established. Augustine himself organized one in Hippo Regius, of which his sister was the superior. Men too were beginning to live the religious, celibate life in communities, as well as in hermitages in remote desert places. It's rather odd that in this context in which he is exhorting primarily the men to shun adultery, he doesn't mention such monks and male celibates—like his own clergy, for example.

SERMON 162

ON THE WORDS OF THE APOSTLE, 1 CORINTHIANS 6:18: *EVERY SIN WHATEVER THAT A MAN COMMITS IS OUTSIDE THE BODY; BUT THE ONE WHO FORNICATES SINS AGAINST HIS OWN BODY*

Date: before 393[1]

The difficult question

1. The question is about the blessed apostle Paul's letter to the Corinthians, where he says, *Every sin whatever that a man commits is outside the body; but the one who fornicates sins against his own body* (1 Cor 6:18); I don't know if it can be definitively cleared up, although with the Lord's help it may be possible to offer a likely solution; it is indeed such a profoundly difficult matter. A little earlier on in the same letter, you see, the apostle was saying, *Make no mistake; neither fornicators, nor idol-worshippers, nor adulterers, nor the effeminate, nor men who lie with men, nor thieves, nor the grasping, nor the drunken, nor the scurrilous, nor the rapacious shall possess the kingdom of God* (1 Cor 6:9-10); and a little later, *Do you not know,* he says, *that your bodies are members of Christ? So shall I take the members of Christ and make them the members of a harlot? Perish the thought! Or do you not know that the one who cleaves to a harlot is one body? For they shall be two, it says, in one flesh. But the one who cleaves to the Lord is one spirit. Flee from fornication;* and that's where he added, *Every sin whatever that a man commits is outside the body; but the one who fornicates sins against his own body. Or do you not know that your bodies are the temple of the Holy Spirit in you, whom you have received from God, and that you are not your own? For you have been bought for a great price; glorify and carry God in your bodies* (1 Cor 6:15-20).

So in this chapter he first lists a whole lot of horrifying sins people commit, which bar their being given the kingdom of God, which people can only perpetrate, however, through their bodies; then he says that these bodies, of the faithful now of course, are the temple of the Holy Spirit which we have from God, having already asserted that the very members of our bodies are members of Christ.[2] It was by way of censuring these sins and to some extent interrogating us about them that he said, *So shall I take the members of Christ and make them the members of a harlot?* And he answered the question himself: *Perish the thought!*

145

He carries on still, and says, *Do you not know that the one who cleaves to a harlot is one body? For they shall be two, it says, in one flesh. But the one who cleaves to the Lord is one spirit.* And he concludes, *Flee from fornication* (1 Cor 6:15-18). But for all that, he goes on to say, *Every sin whatever that a man commits is outside the body; but the one who fornicates sins against his own body*; as though, if you please, all those sins he had listed, saying, *Make no mistake; neither fornicators, nor idol-worshippers, nor adulterers, nor the effeminate, nor men who lie with men, nor thieves, nor the grasping, nor the drunken, nor the scurrilous, nor the rapacious shall possess the kingdom of God*; all these outrageous and shocking deeds, can any of them be done or practiced, except through the body? Could anybody in his right mind deny this? In fact, in this whole passage the apostle was acting on behalf and in defense of the body itself, that has now been bought for a great price, that is, the precious blood of Christ, and been made by the Lord into a temple of the Holy Spirit, to prevent its being polluted by such shocking acts, but rather to preserve it inviolate as a dwelling place for God. So why did he want to add these words, which give rise to such a difficult problem, and say, that is, *Every sin whatever that a man commits is outside the body; but the one who fornicates sins against his own body* (1 Cor 6:18); when not only fornication but other sins of the same sort, sins very like impurity and fornication which only occur through the body, can only be carried out and practiced through the body? I mean, what are we to say? Leaving aside the other things mentioned, could anybody be a thief, or a drunk, or scurrilous, or rapacious without engaging the activity of this body? Although not even idolatry itself and avarice can come to their full use and completion[3] apart from the service of this body.

So what can it mean, *Every sin whatever that a man commits is outside the body; but the one who fornicates sins against his own body?* First of all, because whatever wrongful desires a person living in this body may entertain in the mind alone, such a person cannot be said to do this outside the body, because it is agreed that he is acting like this out of fleshly sensuality and fleshly calculations, being still enclosed all round by this body. I mean, even what it says in the psalm, *The wicked said in his heart, There is no God* (Ps 14:1), the apostle Paul found it impossible to separate from bodily activity, in the place where he says, *We shall all stand before the judicial bench of Christ, to receive, each one, according to what we did in the body, whether good or bad* (2 Cor 5:10); because, of course, it was only as living in the body that the wicked could say, *There is no God.*

To say nothing about what this Teacher of the nations says in another letter: *But the works of the flesh are manifest*; and he proceeds, *which are fornications, impurities, debaucheries, sorceries, enmities, rivalries, jealousies, animosities, dissensions, heresies, envies, drunkenness, and things like them; about which I warn you, as I have warned you before, that those who do such things shall not possess the kingdom of God* (Gal 5:19-21). Are we not inclined to think, after all, that these other things he included there happen without the body, jealousies, animosities, dissensions, envies, heresies? And yet the Teacher of the nations in faith and truth attributed these things too to the works of the flesh. So what does it mean, *Every sin whatsoever that a man commits is outside the body*; and then naming the one sin alone of fornication, he says, *But the one who fornicates sins against his own body?*

The evil of fornication

2. It will thus be apparent to anyone, however dense and slow in the uptake, what a difficult question this is; but if the Lord is kind enough to shed a little light and reveal something to our devout scrutiny of the matter, we may be able to find a reasonable explanation. It seems, you see, that the blessed apostle, in whom Christ was speaking, wished to emphasize the evil of fornication above all other sins, which even though they are committed by means of the body, still do not get the human mind so totally caught up and tied up in fleshly lust as happens in the single activity of bodily fornication. Here the colossal force of the libido[4] makes the mind mingle with the body itself, and somehow or other glue and bond itself into one thing with it; so much so that in the actual moment and experience of this utterly shameful act a person is not permitted to think of or consider anything else at all but this thing that is taking possession of his mind, which is being captured, subdued, drowned, and somehow or other swallowed up by the libido and fleshly lust. So this would seem to be what is being said: *But the one who fornicates sins against his own body*; because that is when the heart of the person fornicating is turned precisely and intimately into the slave of the body, above all at the moment of this utterly vile act. So much so, that the apostle himself, wishing to urge people all the more emphatically to shun this evil, said, *Shall I take the members of Christ and make them the members of a harlot?*; and then answered with vehement detestation, *Perish the thought! Or do you not know*, he went on, *that the one who cleaves to a harlot is one body? For they shall be two, it says, in one flesh* (1 Cor 6:16).

Surely this could not be said, could it, of all or any other human misdeeds whatsoever? The human mind is free, after all, in all other kinds of evil actions, both to commit one of them, and at the same time to let its thoughts wander elsewhere; something that is not permitted to the mind in the act and moment of fornication, to be free to think about something else. Because the whole person is so absorbed, swallowed up by and in the body that now he cannot be said to be his own; but simultaneously the whole man can be said to be what the flesh is, and *a breath that goes and does not return* (Ps 78:39).

So that is how we can understand that *Every sin whatever that a man commits is outside the body; but the one who fornicates sins against his own body*; it seems, as I said, that the apostle wished so to emphasize the evil of fornication, that he considered any other sins at all should be regarded as being outside the body; and that he said by this one evil of fornication alone does one sin against one's own body; because so powerful is the drive of libido here, which no other appetite can match, that bodily pleasure keeps one enslaved and takes one captive.[5]

3. All this may apply to specific fornication with this body. But holy scripture talks about fornication and denounces it in general as well as in specific terms; let us try, with God's help, to say something convincing on this score too.[6] General fornication, then, is plainly indicated in the psalm, where it says, *Since behold, those who set themselves far from you shall perish; you have destroyed everyone who fornicates away from you*; and where he goes on to show in what way this general fornication can be avoided and shunned, by adding, *But for me it is good to cleave to God* (Ps 73:27-28). From this we can easily remark that what general fornication means for the human soul is for anyone not to cleave to God, but to cleave to the world. About this the blessed apostle John says, *If anyone loves the world, the love of the Father is not in him* (Jn 2:15). And the apostle James says, *Adulterers, do you not know that the friendship of the world is at enmity with God* (Jas 4:4). So it is asserted, definitively and shortly, that you cannot have the love of God if you have the love of the world; and that if you want to be a friend of the world, you are an enemy of God's.

Relevant also to this is what the Lord says in the gospel: *No one can serve two masters; for he will either hate the one and love the other; or he will submit[7] to one and ignore the other;* and he concluded, *You cannot serve God and mammon* (Mt 6:24). So this then, as has been said, is the general fornication of the soul, containing absolutely everything in itself,[8] which consists in not cleaving to God while one cleaves to the world. And thus we are in a position to understand as referring also to this general fornication, what the apostle said: *Every sin whatsoever that a person commits is outside the body; but the one who fornicates sins against his own body* (1 Cor 6:18). Because if the human soul avoids fornicating, by cleaving to God and not cleaving to the world, then any other sins whatsoever (provided they are quite unconnected with fleshly lust[9]) that a person can get involved in out of the frailty of our mortal condition, whether by ignorance, or negligence or forgetfulness, all that is what is meant by *Every sin whatsoever that a person commits is outside the body*; because no sin of bodily or temporal lust can be observed in this case, and so it seems that any such sin is quite rightly said to be outside the body. But if a worldly person cleaves to the world and so sets himself far off from God, by fornicating away from God, he sins against his own body; because now the human mind is being dragged around and dragged apart by fleshly lust for every sort of temporal and material reality, by fleshly sensuality and calculation, serving the creature rather than *the Creator, who is blessed for ever* (Rom 1:25).[10]

4. So in this way, it seems to me, saving the faith,[11] the evil of both sorts of fornication, universal as well as specific, can be understood as the subject of this one section of so fine and so great a teacher, where he says, *Every sin whatsoever that a person commits is outside the body; but the one who fornicates sins against his own body.* Thus either a particular emphasis was being placed

by the apostle on the sin of specific fornication, to show that it is rightly understood as a sin against one's own body, because in no other case is the whole person so totally given over to the pleasure of the body itself, and so inexpressibly and inevitably stuck to it; so that in comparison with such a great evil as this, other sins seem to be outside the body, even though they are perpetrated by means of the body. Thus it is only in the case of fornication that some imperious force of libido entirely subjects a person to its own terms, and makes him in the worst degree the possession and plaything of his own body, supremely at the moment of this impurest of acts; so that the human mind is not free to think about or consider anything else besides what it is actually doing in the body.

But if the apostle also wanted to indicate the general kind of fornication, so that it would be with reference to that, it would seem, that he said, *Every sin whatsoever that a person commits is outside the body; but the one who fornicates sins against his own body*, then this is how it must be taken and understood: that anyone who doesn't cleave to God, and cleaves to the world, loving and lusting after all temporal things, is rightly said to sin against his own body; that is, he is given over and subjected to universal fleshly lust, as being wholly the slave of the creature and estranged from the Creator, by reason of that pride which is the beginning of all sin, the pride whose own beginning, as it is written, *is to apostatize from God* (Sir 10:15.14). People who are strangers to this general evil of fornication, whatever other kind of sin they may as corruptible and mortal human beings get involved in, it is to be understood as being outside the body; that is, to be outside the evil of every bodily and temporal lust, alien to it, is, as has been said often enough, to be outside the body.[12]

For it is only by the evil of fleshly and general lust that the soul fornicates away from God in every way. As though bound hand and foot to bodily and temporal desires and enjoyments, it sins against its own body; becoming in every respect the slave of its lust, it bows down to the world and is estranged from God; which is the meaning of *The beginning of the pride of man is to apostatize from God*. In order to beware of this evil of general fornication, the apostle John admonishes us, saying, *Do not love the world, nor the things that are in the world; since the things that are in the world are the lust of the flesh, and the lust of the eyes, and the ambition of the world, which is not from the Father, but from the world. And the world is passing away, and its lust. But whoever does the will of God abides for ever, just as he abides for ever* (1 Jn 2:15-17). So this love of the world, which contains in itself the universal lust of the world, is the general kind of fornication by which one sins against one's own body; in that the human mind is unceasingly enslaved to all bodily and visible desires and pleasures, left marooned and abandoned by the very Creator of all things.

NOTES

1. The title of the Latin text calls this piece a fragment; but it appears on the face of it to constitute a complete whole. What is quite certain is that it is not a sermon. It is indeed characteristic of Augustine; but never of Augustine preaching to a congregation. Rather, it is Augustine thinking aloud in his study to his secretary and stenographer, as he wrestles with a knotty question or problem of scripture, as he says himself right at the beginning. In fact this piece really belongs with works like *A Miscellany of Eighty-three Questions*, or *Eight Questions to Dulcitius*. And it got among the sermons by mistake.

It is certainly not Augustine at his best. In fact I would be prepared to say that, as regards both content and style—or lack of it—it is Augustine at just about his worst. Which leads me to correct what I said about its being Augustine thinking aloud in his study, and to offer a guess about its composition. This is very much, in my judgment, the work of a novice in the interpretation of scripture, and the solution of scriptural "questions." My guess is that here we have Augustine thinking aloud, not in his study, but in the presence of the community of like-minded serious men, which he gathered round him on his family property in Thagaste on his return to Africa from Milan shortly after his conversion. So, I am suggesting, it is Augustine the devout layman, the devout "servant of God" or monk, making his contribution to community reflections on scripture. Even then, there would have been a stenographer in attendance. So this piece would find its way into Augustine's papers, and being what it is, would be forgotten by him and so remain uncorrected (or undestroyed), until it was found after his death by his devoted but uncritical executor Possidius, and placed by him unthinkingly in a collection of sermons. So I would date it before 393, and place its composition at Thagaste.

2. Why he complicates matters by saying that the members of our bodies are members of Christ, where Paul had simply said that our bodies are members of Christ, it is impossible to say. Doubtless there was no reason; it is just an instance of hesitant thinking aloud. But since, in the Latin, we are in the middle of a single sentence, which runs from the second sentence in the first paragraph to the end of this paragraph, he may be excused for getting muddled.

3. He uses the legal expression *usum et fructum*, "usufruct," meaning the use and enjoyment of some property belonging to someone else, rented or on loan.

4. I think it is permissible here to keep Augustine's Latin word, in the sense in which the term is used in modern psychology. His language is in fact suggesting that the libido released in the act of copulation brings about an analogous, quasi-sexual coupling or union between mind and body.

5. There are two weaknesses to Augustine's solution to the problem posed by this text. The first is an incoherence in his argument, taken on his own terms. The text says that by committing fornication (which Augustine together with Paul is treating as a wide term for any sexual sin, including those specified in verse 9), one sins against one's own body; Augustine argues that this is so because in this sin the mind is entirely swallowed up and enslaved by the pleasure of the body; so what he is in fact proving is that it is supremely a sin against one's mind or spirit, against one's human rationality or freedom; and he is doing it without noticing that he is treating "sinning against one's own body" as if it meant "sinning with one's own body." The second weakness is due to his Platonic categories of thought. These lead him automatically to equate body with flesh—and spirit or mind with soul. But this is not being true to Paul. For him, almost all modern commentators agree, "body" means the whole self, the total personality manifested in one's bodily appearance; and this can be either carnal (fleshly) or spiritual, depending on one's relationship to God in Christ and the Holy Spirit. So by fornication in the wide sense, one sins against one's essential self or personality, by taking what is meant to be one spirit with Christ, and making it one flesh with a harlot, or equivalent. This dire effect has little to do with the intensity of libido involved in sexual sin.

6. He is using logical categories very carelessly here. Instead of "specific" and "general" meanings of fornication, he should really say "literal" and "figurative."

7. *Patiens*—a very strange rendering of the Greek.

8. He appears to mean it is a kind of compendium of all sins, which all involve not cleaving to God, and thus cleaving to the world.

9. That is, provided they don't involve what he called specific fornication.

10. His argument about what he so misleadingly calls general, or generic, fornication seems to be even weaker than his first one about specific or literal fornication. Again, what in fact he ends up demonstrating is that "general fornicators" sin against their own human minds, just as the specific fornicators do. Which would be fine, if he had been aware of what Paul really meant by "body."

11. It is hard to see what the faith has got to do with it. But he is simply protecting himself against any possible charges of unorthodoxy, and indicating that his suggested explanation is subject to the correction which it most certainly merits.

12. This shapeless, repetitive sentence is even more shapeless and repetitive in the Latin: Augustine thinking out loud, and very hesitantly and uncertainly at that.

SERMON 162A

ON THE READING OF THE APOSTLE, 1 CORINTHIANS 12:31—13:13, WHERE HE SAYS:
I WILL SHOW YOU A SUPERLATIVE WAY; AGAINST THE DONATISTS

Date: 404[1]

Having prophecy and not having charity, having faith and not having charity

1. It is good to talk about charity to those who love it, since by it you love well and truly whatever you do love. According to the apostle, at any rate, in charity is to be found a really superlative way. It was being read just now, we heard it: *I will show you*, he said, *a superlative way* (1 Cor 12:31). Then he went on to list many gifts, and splendid ones at that, and by no means to be made light of; and yet he said they were no use at all to people who didn't have charity. Among these gifts, he mentioned: speaking with the tongues of men and of angels; having all prophecy, all knowledge, all faith, so as to move mountains; distributing all one's goods to the poor; handing over one's body to burn.[2] These are all great and divine things; but only if they are set up on the foundation of charity, and spring from the root of charity.

Now we would not dare to say that many of these gifts have been found in many people who did not have charity, unless we were so taught, not by examples of any sort of people raked up from any old where, but by the holy scriptures themselves—and if you don't believe them, you cannot have charity. But among the outstanding gifts mentioned here, the really important one seems to be either prophecy or faith. So what about the rest? If having prophecy is no good to anybody who hasn't got charity, and if by having faith you can't reach the kingdom of God unless you have charity, why should we talk about the others? Even speaking with tongues—what is that compared to prophecy and faith? Even distributing all one's goods to the poor—what is that compared with prophecy? And handing over one's body to burn? The rash, headstrong cliff-jumpers often do this.[3] So we have those two important gifts there, about which we may well wonder if anybody could be found having prophecy and not having charity, or having faith and not having charity.

*Saul has become a kind of instrument to be touched by the Spirit,
not one to be cleansed by the Spirit*

2. The book of Kings gives us an example about prophecy.[4] Saul was the persecutor of Saint David. When he was persecuting him he sent guards to drag him away to punishment, and those who were sent to bring David to be slain found him among the prophets; and Saint Samuel was there too, the son of the barren Hannah, whom she had begged the Lord to be able to conceive, whom she had received from the Lord, and whom she had given back to the Lord when he was born. So at that time, when David was around, Samuel was the most outstanding of the prophets; in fact David was anointed by him. And so when he was subjected to persecution by Saul he fled to Samuel, just as nowadays, for example, someone who may be subjected to some persecution flees to the Church.

So he had fled to the place where besides Samuel, the most distinguished of all the prophets, there were also many other prophets. Pushing their way among them, while they were prophesying, came the emissaries of Saul, to drag him off, as I said, to death. The spirit of God leapt upon them and they began to prophesy, having come to lead a holy and just man of God to the execution block, and snatch him away from among the prophets. They were suddenly filled with the spirit of God, and turned into prophets. It's possible this happened because of their innocence; after all, they hadn't come of their own accord to arrest him, but had been sent by their king. And perhaps they had indeed come to the place where David was, but weren't going to do what Saul had told them to; perhaps they too were intending to stay there. Because such things even happen today. Sometimes a bailiff is sent by high authority to drag somebody out of the church; he daren't act against God, and in order not to face execution himself he stays there, in the place he was sent, to haul someone out of it. So you could say, pleasantly surprised and relieved, that these men suddenly became prophets because they were innocent; the very gift of prophecy bore witness to their innocence. They came because they were sent, but they weren't going to do what that bad man had told them to. Let us believe that about them.

Others were sent; the Spirit of God leapt on them too, and they too began to prophesy. Let's count them too with the first lot as being quite innocent. A third lot were sent; the same happened to them too; let them all be innocent. When they delayed, and what Saul had ordered wasn't done, he came himself. Was he too innocent? Was he also sent by some authority, and not ill-intentioned of his own free will? Yet the Spirit of God leapt on him too, and he began to prophesy. There you are, Saul is prophesying, he has the gift of prophecy, but he hasn't got charity. He has become a kind of instrument to be touched by the Spirit, not one to be cleansed by the Spirit.

*God doesn't cleanse everything he touches,
but he touches everything he cleanses*

3. The Spirit of God, you see, touches some hearts to set them prophesying, and yet doesn't cleanse them. And if it touches and doesn't cleanse, is the Spirit

itself, perhaps, soiled? But you see, it belongs to the divine nature to touch everything intimately and in no instance to be soiled. Nor should that surprise you, considering that this light which pours down from the sky, spreads every-where and directly touches every kind of unclean thing, and is in no case smudged by anything unclean. Nor is it just this light from the sky; but even the sort shed by a lamp touches whatever you shine the light on; and suppose someone is going through a sewer, he's defiled himself if he touches anything; but if he takes a lamp, the bright rays of the lamp pass over all the filth without contracting any blotch or stain from it at all.

So if God could endow material lights with such immunity, can he himself, the true and eternal and unchangeable light, ever in any way be defiled? Or can there be anywhere not reached by God's light, of which it is said, *She reaches mightily from end to end, and disposes all things sweetly* (Wis 8:1)?[5] So he touches what he will, and he cleanses what he will; he doesn't cleanse everything he touches, but he touches everything he cleanses.

And so the Spirit of God did not cleanse Saul the persecutor, but all the same it touched him to make him prophesy. Caiaphas, the chief priest, was a perse-cutor of Christ; and yet he uttered a prophecy, when he said, *It is right and proper that one man should die, and not the whole nation perish*. The evangelist went on to explain this as a prophecy, and said, *He did not, however, say this of himself, but being high priest, he prophesied* (Jn 11:50-51). Caiaphas prophe-sied, Saul prophesied, they had the gift of prophecy, but they didn't have charity. Did Caiaphas have charity, considering he persecuted the Son of God, who was brought to us by charity? Did Saul have charity, who persecuted the one by whose hand he had been delivered from his enemies, so that he was guilty not only of envy but also of ingratitude?

So we have proved that it is possible for you to have prophecy, and not to have charity. But prophecy does you no good, according to the apostle: *If I do not have charity*, he says, *I am nothing* (1 Cor 13:2). He doesn't say, "Prophecy is nothing," or "Faith is nothing," but "I myself am nothing, if I don't have charity." So while he has great gifts, he is nothing; although he has great gifts, he is nothing; because these great gifts which he has, he doesn't have to his benefit, but to his condemnation. It isn't a great thing to have great gifts; but it is a great thing to use great gifts well; but you don't use them well if you haven't got charity. The fact is, it is only a good will that uses anything well; but there cannot be a good will where charity is not to be found.

The demons have believed what we believe,
and don't love what we love

4. What about faith? Can we find anybody who also has faith, and hasn't got charity? There are many people who believe and don't love. There's no point in counting all the human beings; we find that the demons have believed what we believe, and don't love what we love. When the apostle James, you see, was reproving those people who thought it was enough for them to believe, and

didn't want to live good lives, which can only be done out of charity—the good life, after all, goes with charity, and a person who has charity cannot live a bad life, because living a good life is exactly the same as being filled with charity; so when some people were patting themselves on the back for having come to believe in God, and were unwilling to live good lives, in a way that suited the wonderful faith they had received, he compared them with the demons and said, *You*, he said, *say that there is one God. You believe well and truly; but the demons too believe, and tremble* (Jas 2:19). So if you only believe and don't love, it's so far only something you have in common with the demons.

Peter said, *You are the Son of God*, and was told, *Blessed are you, Simon Bar Jona, because flesh and blood did not reveal it to you, but my Father who is in heaven* (Mt 16:16-17). We find that demons too said, *What is there between us and you, Son of God?* (Mt 8:29). The apostles confess the Son of God, the demons too confess the Son of God; the confessions are alike, the love quite unlike. Those ones believe and love; these believe and fear. Love looks forward to a reward, fear to punishment.

So we find it is possible for someone also to have faith, and not have charity. So nobody should boast about any kind of gift of the Church, if you happen to stand out in the Church for some gift allotted to you, but you should rather see whether you have charity. Because the same apostle Paul spoke to list the many gifts of God to be found among the members of Christ, which is what the Church is; and he said that appropriate gifts have been distributed to each of the members, and that it cannot happen that all should have one and the same gift. Nor on the other hand will anyone be left without any gift: *Apostles*, he said, *prophets, teachers, interpreters, speakers in tongues, those who have powers of healing, those who have abilities to help, to govern, to speak languages* (1 Cor 12:28). That's what he said; and in fact we see different gifts in different people. So don't any of you feel hurt because you haven't been granted what you see has been granted to someone else; have charity, don't envy what others have, and you have it with them. You see, whatever my brother or sister has, if I'm not jealous, and I love, then it's also mine. I don't have it in myself, but I have it in them; it wouldn't be mine, if we weren't in one body and under one head.

Love one another in the same way as the members of the body
love each other in the body

5. In your body your left hand, for example, has a ring on it, and your right hand doesn't; does that mean that it is left without an ornament? Look only at each hand in turn, and you will see that one has something, and the other doesn't; look at the whole body complex, into which both hands are integrated, and observe that the one which doesn't have a ring, does in fact have it in the one which does. Your eyes can see where you are going, your feet go where your eyes are looking ahead; the feet can't see, and the eyes can't walk. But your foot answers you, "I too have the light; not in myself, though, but in the eye; the eye, after all, doesn't see only for itself, and not for me." Your eyes too say, "We too

can walk, not in ourselves but in the feet; the feet, after all, don't only carry themselves, and not carry us."

So every single member is allotted each to its own proper duty, and they all carry out what the mind commands them to; yet they are all set up together in one body, maintaining their unity; and they don't claim for themselves what other members have, if they don't happen to have it themselves; nor do they think it's no concern at all of theirs, because in fact they all have it together in the one body.

Finally, brothers and sisters, if something nasty happens to one member of the body, do any of the other members at all refuse to help it? What is there in a person so apparently remote from the center of things as the foot? And in the foot, what is so remote as the sole? And in the sole of the foot, what is so remote as the skin, with which you tread on the earth? And yet this remotest extremity is held so closely in the complex of the whole body, that if a thorn is trodden on in that place, all the members of the body come crowding round to help pull out the thorn; straightaway the knees are bent, the spine is twisted,[6] you sit down to extract the thorn; already, sitting down to do this is a matter for the whole body. How tiny the place where the trouble is! The place is as minute as the thorn could puncture; and yet the discomfort felt in that remote and tiny spot is not left alone by all the rest of the body; the other members are not hurt at all, and in that one spot they are all hurt.

On this point the apostle himself gave the example of charity, when he was urging us to love one another in the same way as the members of the body love each other in the body. *If one member suffers*, he said, *the other members also suffer with it; and if one member is honored, all the members rejoice with it. You are the body of Christ and his members* (1 Cor 12:26-27). If the members of a body which have their head on earth love each other, how should members love each other whose head is in heaven? It's true, the first sort don't love each other if they are severed from their head. But since this head is head in such a way, and raised up and seated at the right hand of the Father in heaven in such a way, that nonetheless he is afflicted on earth, not in himself but in his members, so that he can say at the end,[7] *I was hungry, I was thirsty, I was a stranger*, when he will be asked, *When did we see you hungry and thirsty?*, and he can in effect reply, "I the head was in heaven, but my members were thirsty on earth," and in fact he said, *When you did it for one of these least of mine, you did it for me*, and again to those who didn't do it, *When you failed to do it for one of the least of mine, you failed to do it for me* (Mt 25:35-45)—well, our only connection with this head is charity.[8]

What health is in the members of the body,
that charity is among the members

6. That, after all, brothers and sisters, is how we see each of our members doing its own proper work, all according to their several functions; so that the eye sees, but doesn't work; while the hand works, though it doesn't see; the ear

hears, and neither sees nor works; the tongue talks, and neither hears nor sees; and while each and every one of them has its own separate and distinct function, nonetheless being bound together in the one body complex, they have something common to and in all of them. Their functions are different, their health is one and the same. So what health is in the members of the body, that charity is among the members of Christ.

The eye is situated in the best place, a very eminent one, and established, as though for giving directions, in the watchtower, from where it can look out, can see, can point things out. The eyes are esteemed very highly, both for their position, and their keener sensitivity, and nimbleness, and a certain energy which other members don't have.[9] So it is that people frequently swear by their eyes,[10] rather than by any other member. Nobody has ever said to someone else, "I love you like my own ears"; and the sense of the ears is almost equal and very close to the eyes. What can I say about other parts? Every day people say, "I love you like my own eyes." And the apostle indicated that the eyes are more highly valued than other members, when he said, to state how much he was loved by the Church, *For I bear you witness that, if it could be done, you would have plucked out your eyes and given them to me* (Gal 4:15).

So there's nothing in the body more sublime and valued than the eyes; and probably nothing in the body more way out than the little toe of the foot. While that is so, it's still more use to be a toe in the body, and to be healthy, than to be an eye, and be inflamed with conjunctivitis. Health, after all, which is common to all parts of the body, is more precious than the functions of any of them.

And so it is that you can see in the Church a person who only has some little gift, and yet has charity; another person very eminent in the Church with some greater gift, who however doesn't have charity. Let the first be the little toe, the second one be the eye; the former belongs more effectively to the whole body complex, seeing that it has been able to share in its health. Finally, anything that gets ill in the body is a nuisance to the rest of the body; and all the members cooperate to get what is unwell cured, and very often it is cured. but if it isn't cured, and turns septic and festers so badly that it can't be cured, in that case it is in the interest of all the other members that it should be amputated from the body's organic unity.[11]

God is not yet presiding in judgment;
he's already presiding in the gospel

7. So let's grant that somebody or other called Donatus was a kind of eye in the body, let that be so. We don't actually know what sort of man he was, but certainly let's allow him to have been such as he is said to be;[12] what good did it do him to excel like that in honor and glory? He couldn't keep hold of his health, because he didn't have charity. Finally, those people became so septic with gangrene, that they simply had to be cut off; and as for their saying that they have some people of their own, well they are the maggots in the gangrene; the maggots have been cut off, and are incapable of letting health into them-

selves. You see, a member can let health into itself just as long as it is not cut off from the body, because health flows from the rest of the body to the place of the wound. But when the member where the wound is has been cut off, there is no means by which or source from which health can come to it.

That's why they are also compared to branches that have been cut off, and the gospel reading goes along with the reading from the apostle. There too, you see, the Lord, to make sure we remain in him, recommended to us above all nothing but charity. *I am the vine,* he said, *you are the branches. My Father is the cultivator. Every branch that bears fruit in me, he prunes, that it may bear more fruit; but what does not bear fruit in me, he cuts off* (Jn 15:1-2). What the fruit comes from is charity, because fruit only proceeds from the root, and the apostle says, *As rooted and founded in charity* (Eph 3:17). So that's where the root is, from which all the fruit springs. Any who start to part company with the root, although they may seem to remain for a time, are either secretly cut off, or else to be openly cut off; in any case they cannot by any stretch of the imagination bear any fruit.

Those people[13] were once upon a time in the unity. They were cut off. What were they cut off from? From the unity. "But it's you," they say, "who were cut off." What are we to do?

I say, "You were cut off."

You say, "No, you were cut off." Let God be the judge. And so we have put the question off, have we, and sent it up on appeal to God's judgment? Not at all. In many cases we do do this, where God's judgment is not yet apparent. But where it is apparent we apply it, we don't put the matter off till later. I cite scripture, and there I can see who was cut off from what. Because if scripture has borne witness to the party of Donatus, to some Church set up in some part of the world, as the party of Donatus is set up in part of Africa, then let them say that we have been cut off and let them say that they have remained rooted. But if scripture only bears witness to a Church spread throughout the whole world, why are we looking for a man to judge our quarrel? We've got God; he is not yet presiding in judgment; he's already presiding in the gospel.[14]

Crispinus the Donatist appeals to the emperor

8. Recently judgment was given against Crispinus as a heretic.[15] But what did he say? "I wasn't convicted by an evangelical judgment, was I?" His reason for asserting that he wasn't really defeated, is that it was the proconsul who gave judgment against him, not Christ. So if he values a human judgment so lightly, why did he appeal from the proconsul to the emperor? He himself had demanded to be judged by the proconsul; he said himself, "Hear my case, I'm not a heretic." You requested his judgment, and does his judgment displease you? Why? Because it went against you. If he had given judgment for you, it would have been a good judgment; because he gave it against you, it was a bad judgment. Before he gave judgment, he was a good judge, and you said to him, "I'm not a heretic; hear my case."

"But the proconsul," he says, "gave judgment according to the laws of the emperors, not according to the laws of the gospel."[16] Suppose he did do that, suppose the proconsul did give judgment according to the laws of the emperors; so if the emperors make bad laws against you, why did you appeal from the proconsul to their tribunal? Were there already imperial laws in force against you, or weren't there any as yet? If there weren't any yet, the proconsul did not give judgment according to them; if they were already in force, do you imagine the emperors are going to give judgment for you against their own laws?[17]

Then I have another question for you: about these imperial laws against you; what happened? Instruct me, please. It's well known, you see, and nobody denies it, that there are many imperial laws against them. How did this come about? How did this happen? We persecuted you, perhaps, and said many bad things about you people to the emperors? That indeed is what they say to these wretched, uneducated people they mislead. The actual case, you see, as it unfolded at that time,[18] they totally conceal from those they wish to mislead. But however much they conceal it, out it comes, out into the open, published far and wide, brought to the knowledge even of people who don't want to know and refuse to know. They mustn't be allowed to pretend ignorance of what is common knowledge; mustn't be allowed to turn their eyes away from what's plain as a pikestaff; mustn't be allowed to cover up what has been opened up. We must press upon them with the plain truth.[19]

It was you people who demanded a judgment from the emperor. "You lie," he says. There are public documents extant to prove it; it was the Donatists themselves, of the party of Majorinus, who was the first one to be ordained in opposition to Caecilian, that approached the proconsul of that time, Anulinus, and brought written accusations against the name of Caecilian, which were sealed in a pouch. They said they had written the charges against Caecilian in that document, and asked him to send their accusation to the imperial court. The report of Anulinus the proconsul is extant, which he wrote to the emperor Constantine, saying that persons from the party of Majorinus had come to him with written accusations against Caecilian, and asked him to send them to the emperor. And he says he did what they asked. The emperor wrote to Miltiades the bishop and Marcus, transferring the ecclesiastical case to them and withdrawing it from himself. In the same letter the emperor writes that he has sent on the documents sent by Anulinus; and in the letter he says he does not know what the documents contain, but that it is stated in Anulinus' report, which is available today in the public records.[20]

Then Constantine wrote to Anulinus to dispatch the parties to Rome to the episcopal tribunal. Finally, Anulinus replies that he has sent the parties. So it was you people who went to the emperor; you that referred a cause of the Church to human authority. He was better than you, because you referred it to the emperor, while he referred it to the bishops. The case was put in the bishop's court, where they made their accusation. Judgment was given for Caecilian. They were not satisfied with the ecclesiastical judgment and started grumbling; they again approached the emperor, seeking an imperial judgment after the episcopal judgment.

He gave them another ecclesiastical trial at Arles;[21] from that verdict too they appealed to the emperor again. Overcome by their persistence, he was willing to take cognizance of the case himself. He did so; he found Caecilian completely innocent; and so now we have all those imperial edicts against them.

Hardly surprising, is it? You insisted on his judging the case, and you have the nerve to reject his judgment? Why did you want to take the case to his court in the first place? You had the Church in Africa; didn't you have it in the whole world? But of course, where could they go to? To what they had already cut themselves off from?[22] They were no longer attached to the Church; but the emperor to whom they referred their case, was attached to it.[23] Even then with admirable modesty he wanted the bishops to try the case; and then later on, he gave in to these people and also tried it himself. That's how there come to be laws against you; just see if they don't tell against you. You yourselves started it all; you began by accusing, you ended up by appealing, and now last of all you are complaining. "For all that," he says, "was I overcome from the gospel?" You were overcome from the judgment which you yourself had chosen.

Have the courage to be grafted again

9. But we for our part are not fighting shy of the verdict of the gospel; even if he[24] hadn't referred to it, we would read it ourselves, extract it ourselves, demonstrate it ourselves. Let the gospel be recited; let us see where the Lord Jesus Christ says the Church is. To him, surely, both our ears and hearts should be open; let us listen to him, let him tell us where the Church is. If he says his Church is in Africa, let's all go streaming together into the party of Donatus. If he says his Church is in the whole world, let the members that have been cut off return to the body, because the branches weren't broken off in such a way that they cannot be grafted in afresh. You have the words of the apostle Paul: *But you say, the branches were broken off so that I might be grafted in. True. They were broken off because of their unbelief; while you stand by faith. Do not be high-minded, but fear. For if God did not spare the natural branches, neither will he spare you* (Rom 11:19-21).

The Jews, you see, were broken off, like the natural branches, and the nations were grafted in, like a wild olive into the olive tree. We all, from these engrafted branches and from this engrafted wild olive, have a share in the olive tree. But, as the apostle threatened the wild olive branches when they were getting proud, precisely by getting proud they became such as to deserve to be cut off themselves for pride, together with those natural branches that had already been lopped. But what did the apostle say? *They too,* he says, *if they do not remain in unbelief, will be grafted in* (Rom 11:23); and you, if you don't remain in faith, will be cut out. So nobody in the vine should start getting proud, and nobody outside the vine should despair. If you start getting proud in the vine, take care you aren't cut off; if they find themselves outside the vine, they mustn't despair; let them have the courage to be grafted in again.[25] Because it isn't by their own hands that they have to be grafted in; he says, you see, *God has the power to graft them in again* (Rom 11:23).

They mustn't say, "And how can it happen that a thing cut off, a branch broken off, should be grafted in afresh?" You're right to say it can't happen if you are questioning human capacity, but not if you are questioning divine greatness. I mean, I ask you, can any cultivator you care to think of do what has already been done by the Lord? He took a wild olive and grafted it onto an olive tree; and the wild olive grafted onto the olive tree produced, not bitter berries, but olives. Somebody does the same thing now; let him graft a wild olive onto an olive tree, and he will see that it produces nothing but wild olive berries.[26] So God had the power, not to graft the olive onto the wild olive, but the wild olive onto the olive tree, and make the wild olive share in the olive tree's fatness, thus shedding its own bitterness and putting on fatness; and won't he have the power to graft you in again by way of humility, after you had been cut off through pride?

"Fine," he says, "you're pressing and inviting me so nicely; but first show me that I have been cut off; in case perhaps you should be pressing yourself to come to me, not me to be grafted onto you." I'm bold enough to say, Listen to me; and yet I'm afraid to say, Listen to me. I'm afraid, you see, that he may ignore a mere man. Or rather, I exhort him to ignore a mere man; if he ignored mere men, you see, he wouldn't belong to the party of Donatus; Donatus, after all, was a mere man. So then, if I utter my own words, let me be ignored; if I utter Christ's words, let him be listened to, because he isn't listened to for nothing, and he isn't ignored for nothing. Listening to him means a reward, not listening to him means punishment. Let us listen to him; let the Lord himself tell us.

As a Catholic keep a firm grip on the whole

10. He points to the Church in innumerable places; but all the same, let me remind you of just one. After his resurrection, as you know, brothers and sisters, he showed himself to his disciples, he indicated his scars, presenting them to be handled and felt, as well as to be seen. They however, while holding him, and touching and recognizing him, still for all that hesitated for sheer joy, as the gospel tells us, and not to believe that is impious. But while they were still hesitating and doubting for joy, the Lord brought some definite certainty into the situation from the scriptures, and said: *I told you this while I was still with you, that it is necessary for everything to be fulfilled that is written about me in the law and the prophets and the psalms. Then he opened their minds to understand the scriptures, and he said to them: That thus it was necessary for the Christ to suffer, and rise again on the third day, and for repentance and forgiveness of sins to be preached in his name throughout all nations, beginning from Jerusalem* (Lk 24:44-47).

For you, there's no place there; for me, there is a place there. Why wait for a mere man to give judgment about you from the bench? Listen to Christ giving it from the gospel. *Throughout all nations,* he says, *beginning from Jerusalem.* Any sign of you, there? Do you communicate with all nations? Are you in communion with that Church which is spread throughout all nations, beginning from Jerusalem? If you are in communion with it, then you are there, you're in the vine, you haven't been cut off; it, you see, is the vine, which has grown and filled the whole wide world,[27] the body of Christ, the Church of Christ, whose head is in heaven. But if you are only in communion with Africans, and from Africa send people where you can to provide comfort for your emigrants,[28] then don't you find that you have remained in a part only, and been cut off from the whole?

What did you say in the proconsul's court?[29] "I am a Catholic." Those are his words, quoted from the record. As a Catholic keep a firm grip on the whole; *holon*, you see, means whole, and that's why the Church is called Catholic, because it is throughout the whole. Was it ever called *Katamerike*,[30] and not Catholic? *Meros*, you see, means part, *holon* means whole; the Church is called Catholic from a Greek word, meaning "according to the whole." So, are you in communion with the entire world? "No," he says. So you are just in a part, a party; how can you be a Catholic? There's a great difference between the whole and a part, from where it gets the name Catholic. You, after all, have taken your name from the party of Donatus; the Catholic Church has taken its name from the entire world.

But are we saying it's in the entire world, and God perhaps is not saying it? I reminded you of the gospel, I quoted from the gospel: *Throughout all nations*, he said, *beginning from Jerusalem*. Didn't it come to Africa from there? You see, if it began from Jerusalem, it came to you by filling everything on the way, not by drying up. Who could ever say, "A channel was led off from the spring to come to me; it dried up on the way and reached me?" If it dries up along the way, how did it reach you? Of course it reached you by filling everything on the way.[31] Ungrateful stream, why do you speak ill of the spring? Unless it flowed, you wouldn't fill up. But what I'm afraid of is that you may dry up; obviously every stream cut off from the spring is bound to dry up. It's from the experience of drought that they speak harshly against the Church; they would speak mildly, if they were well watered.

"I'm a Catholic." What does Catholic mean? Someone from Numidia?[32] At least I shall ask the Greeks. Clearly, "catholic" isn't a Punic word, but a Greek one. Look for a translation. You are bound to be mistaken in language, when you don't agree with any other language.

The meaning of speaking in all languages

11. When the Spirit came down from heaven, and filled those who had believed in Christ, they spoke in all languages; and this was a sign, for that time, that you had received the Holy Spirit, if you talked the languages of all people.[33] Is the Holy Spirit not given to the faithful nowadays? Heaven forbid we should think so, otherwise we won't have any hope. They too, of course, confess that the Holy Spirit is given to the faithful; and we also say this, we believe this, we agree that this happens chiefly and only in the Catholic Church.[34]

But all right, suppose they are Catholics, the Holy Spirit is given there; suppose we are Catholics, the Holy Spirit is given here; for the moment let's not ask what the difference is between us, ask who are the real Catholics. Either way, it's clear that the Holy Spirit is still being given. So why do those who receive the Holy Spirit not speak nowadays in the languages of all peoples? It can only be, can't it, because at that time something was being prefigured in a few people which would afterward be manifest in all peoples?

What, after all, did the Holy Spirit foretell, when he moved the hearts of the people he filled at that time, and taught them all languages? It's hard enough to learn two or three, either from teachers or by a kind of familiarity with them by living in different places; at most three or four languages.[35] They spoke *all* languages, those who were filled with the Holy Spirit; what's more they spoke them immediately, not by learning them gradually. So what was the Spirit indicating at that time? Tell me why he doesn't do this now, if not because he only did it then to signify something. And what was he signifying, but that the gospel would be proclaimed in all languages? I make so bold as to say that even now the Church speaks in all languages, because the gospel cries out in all languages; and what I was saying just now about members, I also say about languages. And just as the eye says "The foot walks for me," so too the foot says, "The eye sees for me," so too I say, "My language is Greek, my language is Hebrew, my language is Syriac," because one faith holds them all together, one network of charity enfolds them all. What was demonstrated by the Lord had been foretold earlier on by the prophets: *Their sound went out into all the earth, and their words to the ends of the world.* There you have the extent to which the Church has grown, the Church which is called, from the whole, Catholic. And notice that all languages went through all lands: *There are no dialects or forms of speech whose voices are not heard* (Ps 19:4.3).

Return and be grafted in

12. So I hold onto this Church, you don't; so if you have been cut off, recognize what you have been cut off from. Come back, and be grafted in, or else you will wither and be thrown on the fire.[36] The prophets speak, the apostles speak, the Lord speaks about the Church spread throughout the world; these all give judgment against you. From the proconsul to the imperial tribunal; from the gospel, where to? Well, what about to Donatus? Will Donatus give judgment against Christ, or does Christ judge Donatus? What's Donatus going to say to you? "I have preached my Christ from Africa"? What's he going to say? What about, "I have set myself up instead of Christ, and I have succeeded Christ"? That's about all that's left to him to say, that he has dared to cut people off from the body because he has succeeded Christ.[37]

Look, there's Christ's verdict, look, there are the gospels. *Throughout all nations,* he said, *beginning from Jerusalem* (Lk 24:47). He began from Jerusalem; that's where the Holy Spirit came; that's where the gospel began to be preached from, to spread from there throughout all the nations; that's where it eventually came to Africa from. Has it deserted the people, where it came eventually? Indeed it has not, if they don't want it to. After all, we too are Africans. Of course the gospel, which came to Africa, stays here among Catholic Africans, just as it stays among all nations. Because throughout all nations there are also heretics, some there, others here; and the ones in those nations were not born Africans.[38] They have been cut off from the vine. The Catholic Church, you see, knows them all; they don't know each other. The vine, of course, from which the branches have been cut off, knows all its branches, both those that stay in it and those that have been cut off from it. The Catholic Church, after all, has spread everywhere. Those branches have remained where they were cut off; they haven't been able to reach other parts.[39]

She, however, spread everywhere, everywhere keeps her own people, everywhere mourns those who have been cut off. She cries out to all of them to return and be grafted in. Her cry is not heard, and yet her loving maternal breasts never cease to pour forth her exhortations. She is anxiously concerned for those who have been cut off. She cries out in Africa to the Donatists, cries out in the East against the Arians and Photinians, against this group and that. Because, you see, she is spread everywhere, she finds everywhere ones against whom to cry out; because they were in her and have been cut off from her. The branches began to be unfruitful and were cut off; if they don't persist in their infidelity, they will be grafted in again.

Hear this, brothers and sisters, with fear, and don't start getting proud; also with love, and don't forget to pray for them too.

Turning to the Lord, etc.

NOTES

1. Preached in Carthage in June, 404.

2. See 1 Cor 13:1-3.

3. That is, do its equivalent. He is clearly referring to the fanatical and violent Donatists known as Circumcellions, who as well as roaming the countryside beating up and killing Catholics, would also when on the run from the security forces often lay a claim to martyrdom (which of course Augustine treated as spurious) by throwing themselves over cliffs. The technical means for the modern method of protest-suicide by dousing oneself in petrol or gas and setting oneself afire were not available in those days.

4. See 1 Sm 19:18-24. The Greek and Latin bibles call the books of Samuel, 1 and 2 Kings, and the books of Kings, 3 and 4 Kings.

5. Actually said of the divine wisdom, who has however in the preceding verses been called the brilliance of eternal light. Christ, who is identified with the wisdom of God, 1 Cor 1:24, is also the light of the world, Jn 8:12.

6. In Latin the word for spine, *spina*, is the same as the word for thorn. So he adds an explanatory phrase which would be pointless in English: ". . . the spine is twisted—not the one stuck in the sole of the foot, but the one which holds the whole back together."

7. At the end of the world, that is.

8. It is impossible to make a proper sentence, or even a series of sentences, out of this very concentrated stream of homiletic consciousness.

9. Augustine assumed that the sense of sight is active, as well as simply receptive of light stimuli; the eyes, he thought, literally flash; they emit rays, which so to say feel the objects they touch. This, I think, must be the energy, the *vis*, a kind of electrical charge, which they have and other organs don't.

10. Or, as he tells us in another sermon, "by their lights," meaning their eyes.

11. On the face of it, the ecclesiastical equivalent of such amputation is excommunication. But in fact excommunication was usually imposed and accepted as itself a remedial act, to be terminated when its purpose of bringing the affected member to repentance had been achieved. Evidently he has something much graver in mind here. In fact, as the next part of the sermon immediately goes on to suggest, he is thinking of the exclusion from the Church of leading heretics or schismatics like Donatus.

12. By the Donatists. He is in fact known to the historians as Donatus the Great.

13. The Donatists. As for the phrase "the unity," unity for Augustine is more than an abstract name signifying oneness. It is a name for the Catholic Church.

14. Augustine's central and constant argument against the Donatists is that they in fact rejected the universality or catholicity of Christ's Church, which he promised it in a great many biblical texts, one or two of which Augustine goes on to quote; and that in effect they assumed that Christ's Church only continued to exist in one corner of the world, in North Africa. He accuses them of putting the part—he constantly calls them the party, *pars*, part of Donatus—before the whole.

In the actual circumstances of the time it was a good argument against the Donatists, because they did, both in fact and in principle, unchurch all the other local churches that were in communion with their enemies, the Catholic Church in Africa. But it cannot be generalized into an argument against all or any schismatical bodies at any time or place, though Augustine occasionally suggests that it can, by assuming that all heresies are, like Donatism, local phenomena. His argument from worldwide universality could scarcely be used today, for example, in support of the Catholic Church's claims against the Protestant churches, because they too now have worldwide membership and outreach.

15. The Donatist bishop of Calama, a town about 40 miles southwest of Hippo Regius, whose Catholic bishop was Augustine's friend and later biographer and executor, Possidius. Augustine does not here give the background to the case, which was fairly complex (see *The Donatist Church* by W.H.C. Frend, Oxford, 1952, reprint, 1971). Not long before this, Possidius had been attacked by Circumcellions led by a Donatist presbyter, one of Crispinus' clergy it was presumed, and had been lucky to escape alive. So he and Augustine had brought a case against Crispinus in the local magistrate's court. It was from there that Crispinus appealed to the proconsul, who—at least according to Frend's interpretation of Possidius' account of the affair in his *Life of Augustine*, and Augustine's own account in his *Answer to Cresconius*—did not find against Crispinus quite so straightforwardly as Augustine here suggests (Frend, pages 260-261).

16. There had been imperial laws against heretics since the reign of Theodosius, the father of the emperors reigning at this time: Honorius in the West at Ravenna, Arcadius in the East at Constantinople. But it was only from 401 that imperial rescripts had applied these laws to the Donatists, who could indeed say with some justification that they were not heretics, since their faith on central points of doctrine then much in dispute, such as the Trinity and the incarnation, was quite orthodox.

17. In fact they—that is he, Honorius, the emperor of the West—did no such thing, but imposed a fine of 10 pounds of gold (lbs., not £; a huge sum) on Crispinus, which the emissaries of the African Catholic bishops at court intervened to get waived, in order to avoid making Donatist martyrs (Frend, *op. cit.*)

18. The time of the beginning of the Donatist schism, at the end of the great persecution, in 313. The line that the Catholics were the persecutors was put out very effectively by one of the leading Donatist controversialists, Petilian, to whom Augustine replied in his *Answer to Petilian*.

19. *The Plain Truth* is, unfortunately, the name of a rather poisonous little publication put out by the sect of a certain Dr. Armstrong, which finds its way into all corners of the third world.

20. Here Augustine is harking back to events at the beginning of the schism. The appeal to Constantine was made in 313. Caecilian was the man ordained bishop of Carthage in 311, to whom

the Donatists objected. Majorinus was the first rival bishop they installed against him, but he died in 313, and was succeeded by Donatus the Great, who gave his name to the schism. Anulinus the proconsul seems also to have been in charge of the persecution ten years earlier! Miltiades was the bishop of Rome, and Marcus possibly one of his suffragan bishops, who is otherwise unknown. See Frend, pages 147-151.

21. In the south of France. The Donatists themselves had indicated that they would rather the case was tried by bishops of Gaul, instead of the Italian bishops whom Miltiades had called in to assist him at the first trial. Bishops from Gaul, Spain, Britain, and Italy attended the Council of Arles in 314. It not only decided against the Donatists, but also gave a definitive judgment on the doctrinal point of the validity of heretical or apostate baptism, condemning the Donatist practice of rebaptizing.

Meeting over ten years before the Council of Nicaea, it can be seen as kind of trial run for that council. While it has never been officially listed as an ecumenical council, it is clear from various texts that Augustine in effect regarded it as such. It only represented, it is true, the Western or Latin Churches; but then Nicaea in fact if not in principle only represented the Eastern or Greek Churches.

22. He is ironically explaining why they had to have recourse to the emperor.

23. In spirit, no doubt. But Constantine was not baptized until he lay dying in 336. Like Herod the Great, he had too many rival members of his family to dispose of first.

24. Crispinus.

25. This is a direct appeal to the Donatists, following his warning to the Catholics against pride. It needed courage, a definite moral effort, for ordinary Donatists to switch over to the Catholic Church.

26. I think most commentators just assume that Paul, being a city man and a tentmaker, made an agricultural gaffe with his parable. Augustine rather ingeniously saves the apostle's face. Grafting, of course, is always of the more highly bred, and thus more delicate variety, onto the tough wild stock.

27. See Ps 80:8-11.

28. There was quite a large emigrant African community in Rome, for example, and in Ostia its port, too, one imagines. The Donatists appear to have had a church there.

29. He is addressing Crispinus. See the beginning of section 8 above.

30. He makes up a Greek word, on the lines of "catholic," meaning "according to the part." The Latin text gives it in Greek characters—very inaccurately.

31. His point is that the gospel could not have reached Africa directly from Jerusalem without passing through other countries on the way. How in fact it reached Africa is unknown. The most likely route would have been via Rome; but possibly also through Egypt, Cyrene, and Libya.

32. Crispinus' and Augustine's home province, and the seedbed and hotbed of the most fanatical brand of Donatism.

33. See not only Acts 2:1-4, but also 10:44-46 and 19:6.

34. This last point is something we don't actually agree to nowadays.

35. Augustine himself never felt very good at languages.

36. See Jn 15:6.

37. This does seem to be what some African Independent Churches (in black Africa) say about their founders, even if their founders didn't quite say it about themselves.

38. Reading *nati Afri* with the manuscript (or earliest edition) instead of *noti Afri* with the later editor; this would mean, "they were not known as Africans."

39. He would discover he was mistaken on this point when toward the end of his life the Arians turned up in Africa in force.

SERMON 162B

DISCOURSE OF SAINT AUGUSTINE ON THE WOMAN BENT DOUBLE, LUKE 13:11-17
(FRAGMENT)

Date: unknown[1]

We heard the apostle telling us, *We are undertaking an embassy for Christ, exhorting you to be reconciled with God* (2 Cor 5:20). He wouldn't be exhorting us to be reconciled, unless we had been enemies. So the whole world was the Savior's enemy, the captor's friend; that is, God's enemy, the devil's friend. And the whole human race, like this woman, was bent over and bowed down to the ground.[2] There is someone who already understands these enemies, and he cries out against them, and says to God, *They have bowed my soul down* (Ps 57:6). The devil and his angels have bowed the souls of men and women down to the ground; that is, have bent them forward to be intent on temporal and earthly things, and stop them from seeking the things that are above.[3]

Because of course that is what the Lord says about this woman, whom Satan had bound, look, *for eighteen years* (Lk 13:16);[4] and now it was high time for her to be released from her bondage on the sabbath day. But they criticized him for straightening her up, quite unjustly. Who but people who were bent double themselves? Since they quite failed to understand the very things God had commanded,[5] they regarded them with earthbound hearts. Thus they used to celebrate the sacrament of the sabbath[6] in a literal, material manner, and not notice its spiritual meaning.

NOTES

1. This fragment is printed in PL 39, 1709-1710, as the first chapter of a long sermon, 392, entitled "To married couples," which is now generally supposed, however, to be a stitching together of several fragments. Only this one, apparently, is definitely authentic.

2. See Lk 13:11.

3. See Col 3:1.

4. What he said about her was that it was Satan who had bound her, just as he had bound, or bowed down, the whole human race.

5. Meaning here, above all, the commandment about the sabbath, Ex 20:8-11.

6. The text actually says *baptism*, and the editors reasonably suggest that that is a mistake for *sabbath*. But this very mistake may also suggest that this fragment was part of a sermon mainly concerned with baptism; and hence mainly directed at the Donatists (the rebaptizers), whom Augustine would be urging, in Paul's words, to be reconciled with God. And this in turn would suggest that the most likely date for the fragment would be about 405.

SERMON 163

ON THE WORDS OF THE APOSTLE, GALATIANS 5:16-21: *WALK BY THE SPIRIT, AND DO NOT CARRY THROUGH THE LUSTS OF THE FLESH*; PREACHED IN THE HONORIAN BASILICA ON 24 SEPTEMBER

Date: 417[1]

God can walk in us

1. If we consider, brothers and sisters, what we were before receiving the grace of the Lord, and what we have begun to be through the grace of the Lord, then we actually discover that just as we human beings have been changed for the better, so too the places on the ground which were previously against the grace of God are now being dedicated to the grace of God.[2] *For we*, as the apostle says, *are the temple of the living God; wherefore God says, I will dwell and walk about among you* (2 Cor 6:16[3]). The idols that were here knew how to be fixed in place; but they didn't know how to walk. The presence of divine greatness, on the other hand, does walk among us, if it finds among us the space of charity.

It was to encourage us in this respect that the apostle said, *Open yourselves wide, in order not to bear the yoke with unbelievers* (2 Cor 6:13). If we open ourselves wide, God can walk in us; but for us to make space in ourselves, God himself must set to work in us. If charity, you see, which is innocent of narrowness, creates space, notice how God makes a space for himself in us, with the apostle saying, *The love of God has been poured out in our hearts, through the Holy Spirit who has been given to us* (Rom 5:5). It is because of this space, I'm saying, that God can walk in us.

What used to serve the impurity of greed may henceforth serve the grace of love

2. Just now, when the apostle's letter was chanted, we heard, *Walk by the Spirit, and do not carry through the lusts of the flesh. For the flesh lusts against the spirit, and the spirit against the flesh. For these are opposed to each other, so that you may not do what you would* (Gal 5:16-17). He was talking to people who had been baptized; but he was still building the temple of God, not yet dedicating it. Notice, my dear brothers and sisters, how when these material

169

buildings are being converted to better use,[4] some things are destroyed and broken up, others are just changed and put to better use; it's the same with us. The works of the flesh used to be in us. You heard the list of them: *But the works of the flesh*, he said, *are manifest; such as fornications, impurities, worship of idols, sorceries,[5] quarrels, enmities, heresies, jealousies, drunkenness, and things like them; they are to be hurled down, not changed; about which*, he says, *I am warning you, as I warned you before, that those who do such things will not possess the kingdom of God* (Gal 5:19-21). These things in us, like idols, are to be smashed. But the actual members of our bodies are to be turned to better use, so that what used to serve the impurity of greed may henceforth serve the grace of love.[6]

Our building work is now going on by faith,
so that our dedication too may take place at the final resurrection

3. But observe what he has been saying, and take careful note of it.[7] We are God's work force, God's temple is still being built. In its head it has already been dedicated, since the Lord has risen from the dead, conquering death, and swallowing mortality has ascended into heaven; because the psalm for the dedication of the house was written about him.[8] Thus he says after his passion, *You have turned my grief into joy for me, you have cut away my sackcloth, and girded me with cheerfulness; so that my glory may play psalms to you, and I may not be deflated* (Ps 30:11-12). So that dedication was celebrated after the passion in the resurrection. So too our building work is now going on by faith, so that our dedication too may take place at the final resurrection.

Again, after this psalm for the dedication of the house, in which we are shown the restoration of our head to life, there is another psalm—after this one, not before it—which has this title: *When the house was being built after the captivity* (Ps 95, LXX). Recall the captivity in which we have previously been, when the devil had the whole world in his possession, like a vast lump of unbelievers. It was because of this captivity that the redeemer came on the scene; he shed his blood as our ransom; having shed his blood, he canceled the documentary proofs of our captivity.[9] *The law*, says the apostle, *is spiritual; but I am of the flesh, sold under sin* (Rom 7:14). Previously sold under sin, but afterward set free by grace. It is after that captivity that the house is now being built; and for it to be built, the gospel is preached. That, you see, is how this psalm begins: *Sing to the Lord a new song*. And in case you should imagine that this house is being built in a corner, the way schismatics or heretics build, notice how it goes on: *Sing to the Lord, all the earth* (Ps 96:1).

Let what is old be pulled down, what is new rise up

4. *Sing to the Lord a new song*, against the old song; a new covenant, because there was first an old covenant; the new self, so that the old self may be laid aside. *Strip yourselves*, he says, *of the old self with its deeds; and put on the*

new, who has been created according to God in justice and the holiness of truth.[10] Therefore, *Sing to the Lord a new song; sing to the Lord, all the earth.* Sing, and build; sing, and sing well. *Proclaim day from day his salvation* (Ps 96:1-2). Proclaim day from day his Christ; what, after all, is his salvation but his Christ? It was for this salvation that we were praying in the psalm, *Show us, Lord, your mercy, and grant us your salvation* (Ps 85:7). The just people of old were longing for this salvation, about whom the Lord said to his disciples, *Many have wished to see what you people see, and have not been able to* (Lk 10:24).

And grant us your salvation. That's what the just ones of old said: "*Grant us your salvation.* Let us see your Christ while we are still in this flesh. Let us see in the flesh the one who is to set us free from the flesh. Let flesh come, purifying flesh. Let flesh suffer, and redeem both soul and flesh. *And grant us your salvation, Lord.*" Such was the desire of that holy old man Simeon; such, I say, was the desire of that holy old man who deserved so well of God, Simeon. Without a shadow of doubt he also used to say, *Show us, Lord, your mercy, and grant us your salvation.* Expressing this desire with prayers such as that, he received the reply that he would not taste death unless he had seen the Christ of the Lord. Christ was born, once he had come the other departed; but until he came, the other was unwilling to depart. Ripe old age was already ushering him out, but genuine piety was holding him back. But when he came, but when he was born, but when he saw him carried in his mother's arms, and devout old age recognized divine infancy, he took him in his arms and said, *Now, Lord, you are letting your servant go in peace; since my eyes have seen your salvation* (Lk 2:29-30). That's what proves that he used to say, *Show us, Lord, your mercy, and grant us your salvation.* The old man's desire was satisfied, when the world itself was verging on old age.[11] He came to an old man, because he found the world grown old.[12] So if he found the world grown old, let the world listen to the words, *Sing to the Lord a new song; sing to the Lord, all the earth.* Let what is old be pulled down, what is new rise up.

Evangelize

5. *Sing to the Lord a new song, sing to the Lord.* Observe the struggle the builders are engaged in. *Sing to the Lord, bless his name. Proclaim well*—which in Greek is "evangelize." What? *Day from day.* Which day from day? *His salvation.* Which day from day? Light from light, the Son from the Father, *his salvation. Proclaim among the nations his glory, among all peoples his wonders.* There you have how the house is being built after the captivity. *He is terrible above all gods.* Above which gods? *Since all the gods of the nations are demons; but the Lord made the heavens* (Ps 96:1-5). He made the saints, he made the apostles, since *the heavens declare the glory of God. There are no languages nor dialects, of which the voices are not heard. Into all the earth has their sound gone forth* (Ps 19:1.3-4), because all the earth is singing the new song.

6. So let us listen too to the apostle, the architect of the master: *Like a wise architect*, he says, *I laid the foundation* (1 Cor 3:10). So let us listen to this architect, constructing some new buildings, pulling down some old ones. *Walk by the Spirit*, he says; that's the new construction; *and do not carry through the lusts of the flesh*; that's the destruction of the old. *For the flesh*, he says, *lusts against the spirit, and the spirit against the flesh. For these are opposed to each other, so that you may not do what you would* (Gal 5:16-17). You are still being built, you see, not yet being dedicated. *So that you may not do what you would.*

What would you like, I mean? That there should be absolutely no lusts at all for evil and unlawful delights. Which of the saints wouldn't like that? But none achieve it; as long as you are living here, this is not fulfilled. *For the flesh lusts against the spirit, and the spirit against the flesh. For these are opposed to each other, so that what you would like to do*, that there should be absolutely no lusts whatever in you for unlawful things, *you cannot*. So what's left for you to do? *Walk by the Spirit*, and, because you cannot manage to annihilate the lusts of the flesh, *do not carry through the lusts of the flesh*. You ought indeed to want to annihilate them and finish them off and totally eradicate them in every possible way; but as long as they are in you, and there is another law in your members fighting back *against the law of your mind* (Rom 7:23), *do not carry through the lusts of the flesh.*

What is it, after all, that you want? That there should simply not be any lusts of the flesh. They don't allow you to achieve what you want; don't allow them to achieve what they want. What do you want? That they should simply not be there. But they are there. *The flesh lusts against the spirit*; let the spirit lust against the flesh. *So that you may not do what you would*, that is, that there should not be any lusts of the flesh in you; don't let them do what they would, that you should carry through their work. If they don't give way totally to you, don't you give way either. First you must square up to the battle, in order eventually to gain the victory.

7. Because it will be gained, my dear brothers and sisters; of that there is no doubt at all. Let us believe, let us hope, let us love; some time or other victory will be gained, at the dedication of the house which is now being built after the captivity. *For death, the last enemy, shall be destroyed* (1 Cor 15:26), *when this corruptible thing puts on incorruption, and this mortal thing puts on immortality*. Savor in advance the words of the triumph: *Where, death, is your striving?* (1 Cor 15:54-55).

But the voice of battle is, *Have mercy on me, Lord, since I am weak; heal me, Lord, since my bones are vexed, and my soul is sorely troubled; and you, O Lord, how long?* (Ps 6:2-3). Notice how hard he finds the struggle. What's the answer to *How long?* "Until you experience the truth that I do bring help. You see, if I brought help straightaway, you wouldn't feel the brunt of the struggle; if you didn't feel its brunt, it's likely you would get proud of your own powers; and as a result of that pride, you would never gain the victory." It says indeed, *While you are still speaking I will say: Look, here I am* (Is 58:9); but God is here even when he puts off helping, and he is here because he puts off helping, and he is here by putting off helping. He doesn't want to carry out your hasty and impatient wishes, and thereby fail to bring about your complete restoration to health.

The medical treatment of Paul

8. After all, my dear brothers and sisters, we can't say that God wasn't there with the apostle Paul, who was afraid, while he was engaged in combat, he might get swollen-headed. *In case*, he says, *I should get swollen-headed over the greatness of my revelations.* Notice him engaged in combat and conflict, not yet securely triumphant. *In case I should get swollen-headed over the greatness of my revelations.* Who is saying *In case I should get swollen-headed*? How terrifying, how really frightening! Who is it, saying *In case I should get swollen-headed*? So many of his words directed at cutting pride down to size, restraining any swollen self-esteem, and he says *In case I should get swollen-headed*!

That's nothing, that he says *In case I should get swollen-headed.* Notice the medical treatment he says was applied to him: *In case I should get swollen-headed*, he says, *there was given me a goad in my flesh, an angel of Satan.* What a poison, that can only be cured by poison! *There was given me a goad in my flesh, an angel of Satan to knock me about* (2 Cor 12:7). His head was beaten, to stop his head swelling. What an antidote, put together it seems from the serpent itself![13] It was that serpent, after all, who induced the sin of pride: *Taste, and you will be like gods* (Gn 3:5); that's an inducement to pride. That's what caused him to fall, and he used it to bring down others.

So it's fitting that the serpent's poison should be cured by means of the serpent. How did the apostle go on? *For that reason I begged the Lord three times to take it from me.* Where is that saying now, *While you are still speaking, I will say: Look, here I am*? *For that reason*, not just once, but again and yet a third time, *I begged the Lord.* At that, didn't even he say, *And you, O Lord, how long*? But surely it doesn't mean that because God was putting off helping, he wasn't there with Paul, and so the words were false, *While you are still speaking, I will say: Look, here I am*?

Well, what's the answer? When the doctor gives you what you desire, he is there present; when he cuts you, isn't he still there, present? Under the doctor's scalpel don't you cry out to him to spare you? And because he is indeed there present, he goes on cutting more than ever. Anyway, to show you that God was there present, notice what answer he gave to Paul's thrice repeated plea: *He said to me*, says Paul, *My grace is sufficient for you; for strength is perfected in weakness* (2 Cor 12:8-9). "I know"; God is saying, "I am the best doctor there is. I know," he says, "what a swelling the malady can produce which I wish to cure. Keep still; let me apply my knowledge. *My grace is sufficient for you*; your will is not sufficient for you." Those were the words, of course, of one engaged in the struggle, and in danger in the struggle, and requesting divine aid.

Let there be truth in the battle, to win security in the victory

9. But what will his words be when he triumphs? The words of a struggler, while the house is being built; words of a triumphant conqueror when the house at the last is dedicated. *Where, death, is your striving? Where, death, is your sting? Now the sting of death is sin* (1 Cor 15:55-56). The apostle said that, as though he were already there himself. In any case, after these words,[14] which clearly refer to the future reward, not the present conflict, seeing that he says, *Then will come about*; not "Now is coming about," but *then will come about*. What will come about then? *The word that is written: Death has been swallowed up in victory. Where, death, is your striving? Where, death, is your sting?* Then it will come about that the sting of death is nowhere to be found, that sin cannot be found anywhere.

Why the hurry? *Then will come about, then will come about*. Let humility in you deserve that it should then come about in you, or pride may not permit that even then it should come about in you. *Then will come about*. Meanwhile now, while you are fighting, while you're in difficulties, while you're in danger, say, yes say, *Forgive us our debts* (Mt 6:12). Say particularly while you're fighting, say it, say it as the truth, say it from the heart, *If we say that we have no sin, we are deceiving ourselves*. You, in that case, will be acting the devil's part to yourself.[15] *We are deceiving ourselves, and the truth is not in us* (1 Jn 1:8). After all, we are not telling the truth by saying we have no sin, since here we cannot be without sin. So let us tell the truth, in order one day to discover true security. Let there be truth in the battle, to win security in the victory. *Then will come about: Where, death, is your sting? For the sting of death is sin* (1 Cor 15:55-56).

The law without grace

10. But you are presumptuously relying on the law, because the law has been given you, and the commandment has been given you. What you need is for the Spirit to give you life, not for the letter to kill you.[16] I want you to want this; but it is not sufficient for you to want it. You need to be helped to want it fully, and to achieve what you want.[17] Do you want to see, I mean, what the letter commanding is worth without the Spirit assisting? He has told you here. After saying, *Where, death, is your sting? Now the sting of death is sin*, he added straightaway, *but the power of sin is the law* (1 Cor 15:55-56). What does that mean, *the power of sin is the law*? It isn't by commanding bad things, or forbidding good things; on the contrary, it's by forbidding bad things, and commanding good things. *The power of sin is the law*, because, he says, *law was introduced so that delinquency might abound*. What's the meaning of *so that delinquency might abound*? That where there was no grace, prohibition

increased desire; and when one apparently relies entirely on one's own virtue, the result is a great vice.[18]

But what has grace done? *Where sin abounded, grace abounded all the more* (Rom 5:20). The Lord came; everything you contracted and caught from Adam, everything you have added by your own crooked behavior, he forgave it all, erased it all; he taught you prayer,[19] he promised you grace; he organized the contest, he assisted you when you were losing, he has given you the prize when you won. *And so,* says the apostle, *the law indeed is holy, and the commandment holy, and just, and good. So has what is good become death for me? Perish the thought! But sin, that it might be seen to be sin* (Rom 7:12-13). It was there, you see, even when you were not being forbidden; but it wasn't clearly seen as such. *For I would not know lust,* he says, *unless the law said, You shall not lust. Therefore, seizing its opportunity, sin through the commandment deceived me, and through it slew me* (Rom 7:7-8). There you have the meaning of *The letter kills* (2 Cor 3:6).

Necessity of divine help

11. So if you wish to escape the threats of the law, take refuge in the assistance of the Spirit. What the law gives orders for, you see, faith hopes for. Cry out to God, let him help you. You shouldn't remain guilty under the letter, but let God help you with his Spirit; don't let the proud Jew be your model.[20] I mean, since the sting of the law was sin, and the power of sin the law, what was human weakness to do, with its weariness of will? *To will,* he said, *is available to me; but the power to carry through with the good I cannot find* (Rom 7:18). So what was he to do? Look, *the sting of death is sin,* look, *the power of sin is the law* (1 Cor 15:56). *But the law was introduced, in order that delinquency might abound* (Rom 5:20). *For if the law could give life, then justice would come entirely from the law. But scripture locked all things up under sin* (Gal 3:21-22). How did it lock them up? To prevent you wandering off, tumbling over a cliff, getting drowned, the law made you a kind of cage or pound, so that finding no way out, you would take wing, and fly away to grace.

But scripture locked all things up under sin, so that the promise. Anybody who promises, makes the promise about what he does, not about what you do. But if it were you that were going to do it, God would be foretelling it, not promising it. *But scripture,* he says, *locked all things up under sin, so that Jesus Christ's promise out of faith might be given to those who believe* (Gal 3:22).[21] Listen: *might be given.* What have you got to grow proud about? Listen: *might be given. For what have you got that you have not received?* (1 Cor 4:7).

So then, because the sting of death is sin, while the power of sin is the law; and this by God's good providence, so that all people should be locked up under sin, and look for someone to help them, look for grace, look for God, not rely presumptuously on their own powers and virtue; that's why here too, after saying *But the sting of death is sin, while the power of sin is the law*—what are you afraid of, why are you making such heavy weather of it, why are you in such a sweat? Listen to what comes next: *But thanks be to God, who has given us the victory through our Lord Jesus Christ* (1 Cor 15:56-57). Is it really you, that give yourself the victory? *Thanks be to God, who has given us the victory through our Lord Jesus Christ.*

Call on the Lord for help

12. So when you begin to find the going hard in your fight against the lusts of the flesh, walk by the Spirit, call upon the Spirit, start seeking the gift of God.[22] And if the law for your members is fighting back against the law of your mind from the lower part, that is from the flesh, is holding you captive under the law of sin, even that will be corrected, even that will be changed into the rights of victory. All you have to do is cry out, all you have to do is call upon him. *It is necessary to pray always and not grow slack* (Lk 18:1). Just go on calling on him constantly, calling on him for help. *While you are still talking, he will say, Look, here I am* (Is 58:9). Next, try to understand,[23] and you hear him saying to your soul, *I am your salvation.*

So since the law of the flesh has begun to fight back against the law of the mind, and to take you prisoner under the law of sin which is in your members, say in prayer, say in confession, *Wretched man that I am.* What else, after all, is man? *What is man, except that you remember him?* (Ps 8:5; 144:3).[24] Say, *Wretched man that I am*, because unless the Son of man had come, man would have perished.[25] Cry out from the fix you are caught in, *Who will deliver me from the body of this death* (Rom 7:24), where the law in my members is fighting back against the law of my mind? *For I take delight in the law of God according to the inner self* (Rom 7:22). *Who will deliver me from the body of this death?* If you say this faithfully, say this humbly, you will receive the truest answer there can be: *The grace of God through Jesus Christ our Lord* (Rom 7:25).

Turning to the Lord, etc.

NOTES

1. There is unanimity among the scholars about this date. The Honorian basilica was presumably so called because it had been built, in Carthage, at the expense of the emperor Honorius, on the site of a pagan temple. See note 4 below.

2. The reference is to the adaptation of pagan temples to Christian worship.

3. Quoting Lv 26:11-12.

4. See Ps 115:7, for example. This sentence indicates that this basilica had been a pagan temple, or was built on the site of one.

5. *Veneficia* in the Latin, translating the Greek *pharmakeia*, both of which literally mean "poison making." But as this was always associated with the casting of magic spells, it came to mean sorcery.

And here Augustine adds a short aside, which would be meaningless in English, but which is clear proof that in African Latin then, as in Spanish today, the sounds of v and b were indistinguishable. After *veneficia* he adds: *non beneficia, id est non a bonis dicta, sed a venenis:* ". . . not benefits, so called, that is, from good things, but what gets its name from poisons."

6. See Rom 6:19.

7. His next actual reference to the Galatians text will be at the beginning of section 6. Right now he prepares the ground for it by a long reflection on the titles and text of Psalms 30 and 96.

8. He means Psalm 30, alluding to its title. It was actually composed, one presumes, for the dedication of the house, namely the second temple; or just possibly for the dedication of David's house. That at least would be the idea of whoever affixed the title to the psalm. Augustine is within his rights as a Christian interpreter of the Old Testament in saying it was written about Christ; only he leaves out a step, and if one does not realize this, one is tempted to dismiss his interpretation as fanciful and illegitimate.

He took it for granted that the psalm titles were part of the inspired text; modern scholars and textbooks take it for granted that they are not. For my part, I cannot see why not. The conclusion does not in fact follow from the certainty that they were not composed by the actual psalmists; though that is the only grounds for it that I have ever seen stated.

9. See Eph 2:15; Col 2:14.

10. He is freely conflating Eph 4:22-24 with Col 3:9-10.

11. In Augustine's reckoning the birth of Christ ushered in the sixth and final age of this world. The seventh will be the eternal sabbath of the new heaven and the new earth.

12. There is a play on words here; on *venit*, he came, and *invenit*, he found.

13. Here he adds a clause, *et propterea theriacum nuncupatur*; "and that's why it's called theriacum." This is the Greek word for antidote, commonly used, evidently, by Latin speakers. The point is, this word is derived from another Greek word meaning wild animal. None of this would mean anything to English ears, so I left it out of the text.

14. He doesn't get on to what the apostle says after these words until well on in the next section.

15. Because the devil is the supreme deceiver or seducer. The Latin word here translated by deceiving is *seducere*.

16. See 2 Cor 3:6.

17. In the immediate context it looks as if what you want and what I want you to want, is for the Spirit to give you life. But that would reduce his argument to a pointless tautology. Obviously, that is what you should want. The trouble is, you are likely to be wanting something good without also wanting this: namely to keep the law. That, after all, is how he began this section, saying that you are relying on the law.

18. Greater, presumably, than it would have been before the law, because the illicit desire has increased, and one's own virtue cannot restrain it. Elsewhere when discussing this point, he says that what law adds to sin committed when there was no law, is the specific note of transgression.

Some manuscripts here give what one could call a distinctly Lutheran reading: "when one relies entirely on one's own virtue, virtue has become a great vice." Augustine could indeed have said this; but it does not seem quite to fit this context.

19. Specifically what we call the Lord's Prayer. This is the *oratio* without qualification.

20. This is the only way I can make sense of the text, which appears to say, "Don't let the proud Jew be like you," or "lest the proud Jew should be like you": *ne tibi similis sit superbus Judaeus*. The Jew is proud, because he relies on his own powers to keep the law.

21. For this translation of the verse, see Sermon 156, 2, note 7.

22. In Augustine's trinitarian theology the gift of God is the most proper name, almost, for the Holy Spirit.

23. Understand what? That that *here I am*, I take it, is by no means usually experienced in an obviously comforting way; that it is to be interpreted in the light of the next divine utterance quoted, *I am your salvation* or health; for we have already seen that recovery of health usually requires painful medicine.

24. *Nisi quod memor es ejus*. The addition of *nisi*, unless or except, makes the question even more radical.

25. The language cannot here, I regret, be "desexisticated" without rendering either the quotations unrecognizable or the argument void. We must just take it that "man" is being employed in its inclusive sense.

SERMON 163A

ON THE WORDS OF THE APOSTLE, GALATIANS 5:16: *WALK BY THE SPIRIT, AND DO NOT CARRY THROUGH THE LUSTS OF THE FLESH*, ETC. A SERMON PREACHED ON A SUNDAY

Date: 416[1]

Faith gives us courage

1. I would hardly dare speak to you, unless I had the faith to believe that you were praying for me. I know, you see, that I am in your hearts for dying together and living together;[2] the warmth of your charity encourages this hope in me.

Flesh and spirit are locked in combat

2. We heard the apostle Paul, when his letter was read, admonishing us with apostolic authority, and saying, *Walk by the Spirit*, he says, *and do not carry through the lusts of the flesh; for the flesh lusts against the spirit, while the spirit lusts against the flesh; for these are opposed to each other, so that you may not do what you would* (Gal 5:16-17). He has set before our eyes a kind of war, in which flesh and spirit are so locked in combat, that we may not do what we would; and since the lust of the flesh has to be subjected to God's imperial rule, he has harangued us where we are engaged in the contest, and said, *Walk by the Spirit, and do not carry through the lusts of the flesh*. "Fight bravely," he is saying, "and defeat, not some foreign nature rebelling against you,[3] but the lust which is reigning in your own members."

I see, says the apostle, *another law in my members* (Rom 7:23). It's fighting hard, outfight it; it's rebelling, put it down; don't yield your members to it, and it cannot kill your soul. *Do not let sin*, he says, *reign in your mortal bodies, and do not present your members to sin as weapons of iniquity* (Rom 6:12-13). Deny lust its weapons, and your victory is assured. Fight, strive; no athlete gets the prize without sweat. You are out there in the stadium, in the match, in the thick of the contest; the lust of the flesh is putting up a struggle against your spirit. *The flesh lusts against the spirit, and the spirit lusts against the flesh*. The flesh suggests lechery, let the spirit order chastity; the flesh is sparking off anger, let the spirit order mercy. Engaged as you are in this contest, when you don't give

178

rebellious lust those members of yours which were weapons of iniquity for sin, they become weapons of justice for God.

3. So, dearly belovèd, *walk by the Spirit, and do not carry through the lusts of the flesh.* While engaged in this battle, do not presume to rely on the powers of your freedom of choice, because your opponent can defeat you. Implore the aid of God's grace, and then you can defeat the lust of the flesh rebelling against you. But perhaps you have already been defeated, and you will say, perhaps, "I've already been defeated, lust is already up in arms against me, sin is already reigning in my mortal body to make me obey its desires."

Cry out, and say with Paul, *Wretched man that I am, who will deliver me from the body of this death?* (Rom 7:24) *I take delight in the law of God according to the inner self; but I see another law in my members, fighting back against the law of my mind, and taking me prisoner to the law of sin, which is in my members* (Rom 7:22-23). "Such a great master of the field of war was taken prisoner; what am I to do as a prisoner, and weak into the bargain?" So implore the assistance of grace; you will be told in reply, *The grace of God, through Jesus Christ our Lord. Who will deliver me,* he says, *from the body of this death?* You Manichee there, *from the body of this death* is what he said, not "from the captivity of that race." [4] *The grace, he says, of God through Jesus Christ our Lord* (Rom 7:24-25). You Pelagian there, *through Jesus Christ our Lord* is what he said, not through our free choice and free will.[5]

4. And so, dearly beloved, *if we live by the Spirit, let us also follow the way with the Spirit. Let us not become greedy for empty glory* (Gal 5:25-26). You heard the reading from the apostle: *Walk by the Spirit, and do not carry through the lusts of the flesh. For the flesh lusts against the spirit and the spirit against the flesh; but these are opposed to each other, so that you may not do what you would. And so, if you are being led by the Spirit, you are not still under the law. The works of the flesh,* he goes on, *are manifest; they are fornications, impurities, lechery, the worship of idols, sorceries, enmities, quarrels, jealousies, animosities, dissensions, envies, drunkenness, conspicuous consumption, and things,* he says, *like them; about which I warn you, as I have warned you before, that those who do such things shall not gain possession of the kingdom of God* (Gal 5:16.18-21).

With the help of God's grace slay in yourselves the lust of the flesh; turn your backs on the works of the flesh, love the fruit of the Spirit. *For the fruit of the Spirit is joy, peace, patience, kindness, goodness, faithfulness, gentleness, self-control* (Gal 5:22-23). *Do all this,* and continue in it,[6] *and the God of peace shall be with you* (Phil 4:9).

NOTES

1. Or a year or two later. The opening words of the sermon indicate pretty clearly that Augustine was not preaching in his own church of Hippo Regius, or anywhere in his own diocese. But the next ones indicate a very special relationship with the congregation; more than just the familiarity of a frequent visitor, as he was in Carthage. My guess would be that he may have been addressing a community of monks, "servants of God," and possibly in his home town of Thagaste, where the great friend of his youth, Alypius, was the bishop.

2. See 2 Cor 7:3.

3. That is how a Manichee would describe this warfare.

4. Our souls, or at least the particles of light in us, according to the Manichee myth, are held captive by the race of darkness, servants of the "dark lord," the author of evil, identified with matter. As Augustine interprets them, they thereby deny any personal responsibility for sin.

5. Pelagius on the other hand so stressed personal responsibility, that he said we can and should deliver ourselves from the dominion of sin by our own free will and force of character.

6. See 1 Tm 4:15.

SERMON 163B

ON WHAT THE APOSTLE SAYS TO THE GALATIANS (6:1): *BROTHERS, IF A MAN HAS BEEN CAUGHT OUT IN SOME WRONGDOING, YOU WHO ARE SPIRITUAL INSTRUCT SUCH A ONE,* ETC. A SERMON PREACHED IN CARTHAGE AT THE SHRINE OF THE MARTYR CYPRIAN ON THE EIGHTH DAY OF SEPTEMBER

Date: 410[1]

The reading of Paul

1. Please call to mind what the reading from the apostle's letter was reminding us of: *Brothers,* he says, *if a man has been caught out in any wrongdoing, you who are spiritual instruct such a one in a spirit of mildness, watching yourself lest you too should be tempted. Bear one another's burdens, and in this way you will fulfill the law of Christ. For whoever thinks he is anything, while he is nothing, is deceiving himself. But let each one prove his own work, and then he will have glory in himself alone, and not in someone else. For each one will carry his own burden.*

But let the one who is being instructed in the word share in all goods with the one who is instructing him. Make no mistake, God is not to be made fun of; for what a man has sown, that he shall also reap; because whoever has sown in the flesh, from the flesh will reap corruption; while whoever has sown in the Spirit, from the Spirit will also reap eternal life. But doing good, let us not grow feeble; for we shall reap in good time, if we don't tire. And so, while we have time, let us do good to all, but specially to those at home in the faith (Gal 6:1-10).

We bear one another's burdens

2. That's as far as the apostle's letter was chanted; thus far I have, it seems, been just playing the part of the reader for you. But, my dear brothers and sisters, if the reader has been understood, what is the commentator needed for? Look, we've heard, we've understood; let's do it, and live. And what need is there for me to burden your memories? Hold on to these things, and think about them.

Or perhaps some of you are puzzled about how we should understand what he said: *Bear one another's burdens*; and a little later he says, *Each one will carry his own burden* (Gal 6:2.5). I imagine you are saying to yourselves, those

181

of you at least who noticed this, "How can we carry each other's burdens, if everybody is carrying his own burden? How will each one carry his own burden, if we are carrying each other's burdens?" I admit, it's a problem. *Knock, and it will be opened to you* (Mt 7:7; Lk 11:9). Knock by concentrating, knock by being interested, knock also for me, that I may be able to say something worthwhile to you, by praying. By knocking like that, you are helping me, and the problem will soon be solved. If only the speed by which it will be solved could be matched by the thoroughness with which we each put into practice what we have understood!

As regards the weight of our weakness, we carry one another's burdens; as regards the account to be rendered of duty, every one of us will carry our own burden. What's this I've just said? All of us human beings, what are we but human, and thereby weak, and people who are certainly not without sin? It's in this regard, I mean, that we bear one another's burdens. After all, if you feel disgust at your brother's sin, and he at yours, you are neglecting each other, and really committing a serious sin. If you, though, tolerate what he cannot cope with, and he in turn tolerates what you cannot cope with, then you are carrying each other's burdens; and because you are carrying each other's burdens, you are fulfilling the most sacred law of charity. That, you see, is the law of Christ; the law of charity is the law of Christ. That's why he came, because he loved us; and there was nothing there for him to love, but by loving us, he made us lovable.

You have heard what it means, *Bear one another's burdens, and in this way you will fulfill the law of Christ*. So what about, *Each one will bear his own burden*? Each one will render account for his own sin; nobody is going to render an account for anybody else's sin. We each of us have our own case; each of us is going to render our own account to God. Yes even prelates themselves, who must give an account of Christ's flocks, render an account for their own sin, if they have neglected Christ's flocks.

Love and do whatever you wish

3. So, brothers and sisters, *if a man has been caught out in some wrongdoing, you who are spiritual*, whoever you are that are spiritual, *instruct such a one in a spirit of mildness* (Gal 6:1). And if you shout at him, love him inwardly; you may urge, wheedle, rebuke, rage; love, and do whatever you wish.[2] A father, after all, doesn't hate his son; and yet if necessary a father gives his son a whipping; he inflicts pain, to ensure well-being. So that's the meaning of *in a spirit of mildness*. You see, if a man has been caught out in some wrongdoing, and you say, "It's no business of mine," and I say to you, "Why isn't it your business?" and you answer me, "Because *each one will bear his own burden*"; then I will answer you, "Why, you certainly have been willing to hear and understand *Bear one another's burdens!*"[3]

So then, *if a man has been caught out in some wrongdoing, you who are spiritual instruct such a one in a spirit of mildness*. He, certainly, is going to give an account of his own sin, because *each one will carry his own burden*; but you, if you neglect his wound, are going to have a bad account to give of your sin of negligence. And thus, if you don't bear one another's burdens, you will all have a bad account to render, inasmuch as each one will bear his own burden. Do that, so that you carry one another's burdens, and God will spare you when you are each carrying your own burden. Because if you carry someone else's burden, when he is caught out in some wrongdoing, by instructing him in a spirit of mildness, you will come to the place where, as you heard, *Each one will carry his own burden*, and then you can say to God with a good conscience, *Forgive us our debts* (Mt 6:12).

So remember, brothers and sisters, *If a man has been caught out in some wrongdoing*—don't just skip lightly over that word, *a man*. He could, after all, have said, "If someone has been caught out, if anybody has been caught out." He didn't say that, but he did say, *a man*. Now it is extremely difficult that a man should not be caught out in some wrongdoing; because what is man?

Pray, beg, someone not to sin

4. But now these spiritual people, whom he admonished to instruct in mildness that man who had been caught out in wrongdoing: perhaps they were saying to themselves, "Let us bear the burdens of those who are caught out in various misdeeds, because we haven't got anything that they could help us carry." Listen, because you shouldn't be too sure of yourself, to the words that come next; notice: *Watching yourself, lest you too should be tempted* (Gal 6:1). The spiritual people mustn't get proud, mustn't think highly of themselves; although if they are really spiritual, they won't think highly of themselves. I'm afraid the reason they may think highly of themselves is that they are indeed unspiritual; all the same the spiritual people too must watch themselves, in case they too are tempted.

After all, just because they are spiritual, does it mean they are not human, belonging to the species man? Because they are spiritual, does it mean they do not carry around *a perishable body which weighs down the soul* (Wis 9:15)? Just because they are spiritual, have they done with this life, the whole of which *is a temptation on earth* (Jb 7:1)?[4]

So they were properly told, very properly indeed, *Watching yourself, lest you too should be tempted*. And when he had admonished them, that is the spiritual people, he immediately delivered that general judgment, *Bear one another's burdens, and in this way you will fulfill the law of Christ* (Gal 6:2). What's meant by *one another's*? Let the unspiritual person carry the burden of another unspiritual person, the spiritual person carry another spiritual person's? *Carry your burdens for each other*; do not ignore and neglect each other's sins. Reprimand those who have confidence enough in you to take it;[5] give a friendly warning to those who don't trust you enough to take a reprimand; and should it come to that, pray, beg someone not to sin.

Or do you perhaps find it humiliating that I have told you to beg, sometimes, on your knees? Listen to the apostle: *But while commanding you*, he says, *we also beg you not to receive the grace of God in vain* (2 Cor 6:1).[6] If a doctor finds his sick patient strong enough, he rebukes him sharply; but if he finds he hasn't got the strength, and is afraid he may possibly just fade away under the bitterness of a rebuke, he implores, begs him to listen, to do what he prescribes, to live.

So it's agreed that the reason the apostle said, *Bear your burdens for one another*, is that he had been admonishing spiritual people, and had said *Watching yourself, lest you too should be tempted*; and was afraid that these spiritual people might claim so much for themselves, that they imagined they didn't have any burdens which needed another person to take some of the weight.

Flatterers and deceivers

5. Listen to him again, going on about pomposity, about swollen heads, about hot air; listen to him again: *for anyone who thinks he is anything, while he is nothing, is deceiving himself* (Gal 6:3). It couldn't be better said: he is deceiving himself. The devil mustn't be blamed for everything; sometimes human beings can act the devil to themselves. After all, why do we have to beware of the devil? Clearly for this reason, in case he deceives you. So aren't you being your very own devil, when you deceive yourself?

What comes next? *But let each one prove his own work, and then he will have glory in himself alone, and not in someone else* (Gal 6:4). You do some good deed; if the reason you like doing it is because someone else praises you for it; while if nobody else praised you for it, you would give up doing good, being deprived of a praise-singer's words; then you have praise in someone else and not in yourself. If he praises you, you do it; if your good deed happens to have displeased a silly man, you stop doing it. Don't you see people pouring out their money on actors, and offering nothing to the poor, and how they are praised to the skies on the lips of many? Is what they are doing good, just because they get praised for it? Come on, wake up at last: *The sinner is praised in the desires of his soul*. You all shouted out, because you know the holy scripture whose testimony I have reminded you of; let those who don't know it hear it too.

Holy scripture has said, holy scripture has said in advance, *Since the sinner is praised in the desires of his soul, and the one who behaves unjustly is blessed* (Ps 10:3). Now then, if the sinner is praised in the desires of his soul, and the one who perpetrates iniquitous deeds is blessed, now go looking for praise-singers. Let evil desires tear you to shreds; perpetrate iniquities every day to satisfy your desires, and go looking for people to praise you. Believe me, all you will find will be flatterers or deceivers.

Why flatterers, why deceivers? I'm bound to give you an account of the words I chose. Flatterers are those who know what you are doing is bad, and yet praise you all the same. Those however who praise you when you do something bad, because they think what you are doing is good, are not flatterers, because they are praising you sincerely; but they are deceivers, because by their repeated praises they are deceiving you, seducing you into evil behavior, and not letting you even breathe. You see, you are running before the vain wind of popularity,[7] you think what you are doing is good; all the time you are jettisoning your possessions, emptying out your house, leaving your children stripped of everything. All that praise has sent you round the bend; you run around, wave your arms, accept favors, blow kisses;[8] you drain your house dry, you collect wind.

"How," you ask, "can these people be my deceivers, who are praising me sincerely?" They are deceiving you precisely because they first went wrong and deceived themselves. Do you really suppose that someone who is deceiving himself will go to all that trouble to scale your walls, and not try to deceive you too? So, *the sinner is praised in the desires of his soul, and the one who perpetrates iniquitous deeds is blessed.* As for you, watch out for people praising you like that, avoid the givers of that sort of blessing. As for you, do good instead.

"But," you will say, "I will displease So-and-so if I do that." Go ahead, and both displease him, and please God; because if you displease him and please God, you will have glory in yourself and not in somebody else. But bad people pull the good to pieces, and the lovers of this world speak ill of those who despise the world, they spread scandal, they look for things to find fault with; as soon as anything bad is said, they believe it straightaway. If anything good is said, they refuse to believe it. And your heart is troubled, so that you falter in doing good, because you haven't found anyone to praise you as either a flatterer or a deceiver, and you are not satisfied with the testimony of your own conscience, in the theater of your bosom, where God is your audience. Why are you troubled, please tell me; why are you upset? "Because they are saying so many nasty things about me." You really say that? You wouldn't be troubled in the boat of your heart, unless Christ was asleep there.

Let Christ wake up and talk to you

6. You heard the story when the gospel was read; a great storm burst, the boat was being tossed about and the waves breaking over it. Why? Because Christ was asleep.[9] When does Christ go to sleep in your heart, if not when you forget your faith? Faith in Christ in your heart is like Christ in the boat. You hear nasty stories about yourself, you lose heart, you get upset; Christ is asleep. Wake Christ up, wake up your faith. You've something you can do, even when you are upset; stir up your faith. Let Christ wake up and talk to you: "Does abuse and nasty talk upset you? What didn't I myself hear first for your sake!" That's what Christ says to you, that's how your faith talks to you. Listen to it, and just see that it does talk to you like that—unless of course you've forgotten that Christ suffered for us,[10] and that before he suffered such dreadful things for us, he heard a lot of abuse and nasty talk. He used to cast out demons, and he was told, *You have demons.*[11]

Of him it was said through the prophet, *The abuse of those who abuse you has fallen on me* (Ps 69:9). So rouse up Christ, and he will say to you in your heart, *When people disparage you, and speak all kinds of evil against you for my sake, rejoice and exult, because your reward is lavish in heaven* (Mt 5:11-12). Believe what is said, and a great calm will settle in your heart.

So if a person *thinks he is something when he is nothing, he is deceiving himself; but let each one prove his own work, and then he will have glory in himself, and not in someone else* (Gal 6:3-4). You, whether they praise or blame you, have glory in yourself, because your glory is your God in your conscience; and you will be like the wise virgins, who took oil with them in their flasks, so that they wouldn't have glory in someone else, but in themselves. Because those others, who didn't take oil with them, begged it from these, and their lamps went out and they said, *Give us some of your oil* (Mt 25:1-8). What does *Give us some of your oil* mean? What else but, "Praise our works, because our own consciences don't satisfy us?"

What seemed to be obscure in the reading from the apostle, I have explained as the Lord has enabled me to. The rest is plain enough; it doesn't look for someone to explain it, but for people to do it. But that we may do what we have heard, let us beg him without whose help we won't be able to do anything good, since he said himself to his disciples, *Without me you can do nothing* (Jn 15:5).

Turning to the Lord, etc.

And after the sermon because the people requested us not to depart before the birthday[12] of the blessed Cyprian he added:

I am telling your graces the truth, that we cannot bear to ignore any longer the desire and the complaints of our own people which reach us by letters. But because what you are asking is also the command of the holy Primate,[13] let me conclude the sermon like this: The blessed Cyprian's birthday is certainly already very close;[14] because of that great feast day you are prepared to be violent in keeping me back. Therefore, as we are so eager for the word, it would be a good thing for us also to fast in the body.

NOTES

1. For once there is unanimity among the scholars about the date of this sermon. Augustine seems to have been in Carthage some time, and was eager to return to Hippo Regius, as we gather from the tailpiece at the end. It was the year before the great conference with the Donatists, which would be held in June, 411; and no doubt there were a lot of preparations to be made. It was also the year in which Rome was sacked by the Goths under Alaric. But perhaps news of that event had not yet reached Carthage.

2. One of the more famous Augustinian paradoxes. He also uses it in his commentary on 1 John, where he is talking, as he goes on to do here, about parents beating their children. "Whatever you wish," of course, has to be interpreted as meaning "whatever you think best."

3. Heavy irony, of course.

4. One would normally translate "a trial on earth"; but in the context of his commenting on Gal 6:1, we have to keep "temptation" here.

5. *Apud quos fiducia est vobis.* This could probably also mean, "those in whom you have con-

fidence." For giving and receiving a severe reprimand, where, to make it effective, does the confidence have to be above all? I would say, primarily in the recipient, in the subordinate, who can say, "I can take that from you, but I wouldn't take it from anybody else."

6. Augustine's version is a rather idiosyncratic translation of the Greek.

7. *Is in auras inanes*; literally, "you are going after empty breezes"; he is thinking of the man who pours out his money on actors, who puts up the money, in fact, to stage popular shows.

8. This is a guess at the meaning of an idiomatic expression: *ad os ponis*; literally, "you put to mouth." I am assuming what you put is your fingers.

9. See Mk 4:36-41.

10. See 1 Pt 2:21.

11. Jn 7:20, which here, as he does elsewhere, he is conflating with a text like Lk 11:14-16, in which they say that he casts out demons by Beelzebub, the prince of demons.

12. Meaning his birthday into glory, that is, the day of his martyrdom. This interesting little tailpiece tells us that Augustine traveled with at least a skeleton office staff of secretaries and stenographers.

13. Literally, "the holy old man," *sanctus senex*; this was the title given to African provincial primates; in this case it referred to Aurelius, bishop of Carthage and primate of all Africa.

14. Just under a week away, on 14 September.

SERMON 164

ON THE WORDS OF THE APOSTLE, GALATIANS 6:2. 5: *BEAR YOUR BURDENS FOR EACH OTHER*, AND ON THOSE OTHERS: *EACH ONE WILL BEAR HIS OWN BURDEN*; AGAINST THE DONATISTS, PREACHED SHORTLY AFTER THE CONFERENCE HELD AT CARTHAGE

Date: 411[1]

The law of Christ won't be fulfilled, unless we carry our burdens for each other

1. Truth[2] is urging us through the apostle to bear our burdens for each other;[3] and in so urging us to bear our burdens for each other, he shows how profitable it is for us to do that, by going on to say: *And in this way you will fulfill the law of Christ* (Gal 6:2); which won't be fulfilled, unless we carry our burdens for each other. What these burdens are, and how they are to be carried—since of course we must all try as best we can to fulfill the law of Christ—I will try with the Lord's help to show you. Remember to exact to the last farthing what I have proposed to demonstrate; and when I have paid the debt, don't go on claiming it.[4] This is what I have proposed to demonstrate, with the Lord assisting both my intention and your prayers on my behalf: what the burdens are which the apostle tells us to carry for each other, and how they are to be carried. If we do this, the value he placed on it, that we would be fulfilling the law of Christ, will accrue automatically.

We must distinguish between burdens

2. Somebody says, "Well, did the apostle speak all that obscurely, that you should try to explain what these burdens are, or how they are to be borne for one another?" There is a problem there, which forces us to distinguish between burdens. Right in this very same section of the reading you have this statement: *But each one will bear his own burden* (Gal 6:5). So it's already crossed your minds: if *each one will carry his own burden*, how can he say, *Carry your burdens for each other*? The only answer is that we must distinguish between burdens, or the apostle will be thought to be contradicting himself. I mean, it isn't in some quite different place, not in another letter, after all, not after all much earlier or later in this letter, but in this very same place, so that these same

188

words come next to each other, that he stated both things; both that each one will carry his own burden, and that he urged and exhorted us to carry our burdens for each other.

Two kinds of burdens

3. So there are some burdens of a sort that each carries his own, and one doesn't carry it with another, nor throw it onto another. And there are other burdens of a sort that you quite rightly say to your brother, "I'll carry it with you," or "I'll carry it for you." So if such a distinction has to be made, understanding is not all that easy.

So against those who thought that a person can be contaminated by somebody else's sins, the apostle answered, *Each one will bear his own burden.* Again, against those in whom this could make room for indifference, so that being assured they wouldn't be contaminated by other people's sins, they wouldn't bother to correct anyone: *Carry your burdens for each other.* It's briefly stated, the distinction briefly made; and this, I rather think, hasn't prevented the truth being made plain. I mean, you both heard it briefly, and understood it quickly. I haven't seen into your minds; but I heard your voices bearing witness to your minds. So now, as being sure of what we have understood, let us discuss the matter a little more widely, not to gain understanding, but to appreciate better what has been understood.

The burdens are sins

4. The burdens, of which we all have to carry our own, are sins. To human beings carrying the loads of these detestable burdens, and sweating under them all to no purpose, the Lord says, *Come to me, all you who labor and are overburdened, and I will refresh you* (Mt 11:28). How does he refresh them, burdened with sins, except by pardoning sins? Delivering an address to the whole world from the platform, so to say, of his sublime authority, he cries out, "Listen, human race; listen, children of Adam; listen, race of unproductive toilers! I can see your toil; you just see what I have to give. I know, you are laboring and overburdened; and what is even more pitiable, you are strapping loads of calamity onto your own shoulders; worse still, you are asking for burdens to be added to these, not asking for them to be laid aside."

Avarice and laziness

5. Could any of us in a short time run through the vast number and variety of these loads? However, let us mention a few of them, and from these make an informed guess about the rest. Consider a man burdened with the load of avarice; look at him sweating, gasping, thirsty under this load—and with all his efforts adding to the load. What are your expectations, money-grubber, as you hug your burden, and harness the evil load to your shoulders with the straps of greed?

What are your expectations? Why all the toil? What are you panting for, what are you lusting after? "To satisfy Avarice, of course."

Oh vain hopes, and good-for-nothing business! So you are really expecting to satisfy Avarice? She can weigh you down, you can't satisfy her. Or perhaps she doesn't weigh very much? Under this load have you lost your wits as completely as that? Avarice doesn't weigh very much? So why does she wake you up from sleep, why does she sometimes not even allow you to sleep? And perhaps together with her you have another burden of laziness, and these two absolutely worthless loads, which fight each other into the bargain, weigh you down and tear you apart. After all, they aren't giving you the same orders, they aren't issuing similar commands. Laziness says, "Sleep"; Avarice says, "Get up." Laziness says, "You don't need to endure cold weather." Avarice says, "You must even put up with storms at sea." The first says, "Have a nice long holiday." The other won't let you take a holiday.

Her command is not only, "Carry on," but also, "Sail across the sea, seek out countries you do not know. There is merchandise to be exported to India." You don't know the language of the Indians, but the lingo of Avarice seems universally intelligible. You will come, unknown, to someone unknown to you; you give, you receive, you buy, you bring. You have braved dangers to arrive, you experience more dangers on your return. Tossed about in a storm at sea, you cry out, "God, deliver me!"

Can't you hear him answering, "Why should I? Did I send you? It was Avarice who told you to go and acquire what you didn't have. What I told you to do, was to give what you did have to the poor at your door, without any bother. She sent you to the Indies to bring back gold. I set Christ at your door,[5] from whom you could buy the kingdom of heaven. You work so hard at the bidding of Avarice; at my bidding you don't work at all. We have both issued instructions; you haven't listened to me; you've obeyed her, let her deliver you."

Let charity lay upon you a yoke that will do you good

6. How many people are carrying these loads! How many of you, shouldering such loads, applaud me now as I speak against them! They have come in with their loads, they go out with their loads. They have entered in love with money, they depart in love with money. I, in speaking against these loads, have been working very hard. If you applaud, drop what you are carrying.

Finally, don't listen to me; listen to your emperor as he cries out, "*Come to me, all you who labor and are overburdened.*" You don't really come, you see, unless you stop laboring. You want to run to me, but you can't do it with those heavy loads. "*Come to me*," he says, "*all you who labor and are overburdened, and I will refresh you* (Mt 11:28). I am pardoning your past sins, I will take away what was blinkering your eyes,[6] I will heal the sores on your shoulders. I will certainly relieve you of your loads, but I won't let you go entirely free of loads. I will relieve you of bad loads and place good ones upon you." After saying, you see, *and I will refresh you*, he added, *Take my yoke upon yourselves* (Mt

11:29). Greed had laid an evil yoke upon your neck, let charity lay upon you a yoke that will do you good.

Carry the feathers of peace, accept the wings of charity

7. *Take my yoke upon you, and learn from me.* If any and every kind of human teaching[7] has lost all value for you, *learn from me.* Christ the teacher, the master, is calling out, the only Son of God who alone is truthful, true, the truth, is calling out, *Learn from me.*

Learn what? That *in the beginning was the Word, and the Word was with God, and the Word was God, and all things were made through him* (Jn 1:1-3)? Shall we ever be able to learn that from him, to manufacture a world, to fill a sky with lights, to arrange the changes of day and night, to instruct the seasons and ages how to run their course, to endow seeds with their energy, to fill the earth with animals? The heavenly master is not telling us to learn any of that. He does all that as God.

But because this God was also willing to be man, insofar as he is God, listen to him for your renewal; insofar as he is man, listen to him so that you can imitate him. *Learn*, he says, *from me*; not how to manufacture the world and create various natures; nor even those other things which he achieved here, hiddenly as God, manifestly as man. He doesn't mean them either: "Learn from me how to drive out fevers, put demons to flight, raise the dead, command the winds and the waves, walk on the waters"; he doesn't mean that either by *Learn from me.* Yes, he did give these powers to some of his disciples, to others he didn't give them. But what he says here, *Learn from me*, he says to everyone; nobody is to be excused from this commandment: *Learn from me, since I am meek and humble of heart* (Mt 11:29).

Why hesitate to pick up this load? This load's heavy, is it, humility and a sense of duty? This load's heavy, is it, faith, hope, charity? These, you see, are the things that make you humble, make you meek. And notice that you won't be overburdened if you listen to him: *for my yoke is easy, and my load is light* (Mt 11:30). What does he mean by light? That if it weighs anything, it's still less? That avarice weighs more, justice less? I don't want you to understand it like that. This load is not a weight to burden you with, it's wings to help you fly. Birds too, after all, have the load of their feathers. And what are we to say? They carry them, and are carried by them. They carry them on the ground, they are carried by them in the sky. If you want to show kindness to a bird, especially in summer, and say, "This poor little bird is burdened with feathers," and start pulling off this burden, the poor little bird you wanted to help will remain grounded. So carry the feathers of peace, accept the wings of charity. That's the load for you, that's how the law of Christ will be fulfilled.

Each one carries a burden

8. There are other kinds of burden. Look now, some money-grubber or other comes in. You know he's a money-grubber, he stands beside you, and you are

not a money-grubber. You are even kind-hearted, you give what you have to the poor, you don't pant after what you haven't got; you listen to the apostle saying, *Command the rich of this world not to be haughty, nor to hope in the uncertainty of riches, but in the living God, who provides us abundantly with everything to enjoy; let them be rich in good works, to give readily, to share, to treasure up for themselves a good foundation for the future, that they may lay hold of true life* (1 Tm 6:17-19). You've heard this, acknowledged it, learnt it, held onto it, done it. Go on doing what you are doing, don't slack off, don't stop. *It is the one who perseveres to the end that shall be saved* (Mt 10:22).

You have done a person a good turn, the person's ungrateful; don't be sorry for having done a good turn, don't pour away by being sorry what you have filled up by being kind. Say to yourself, "This one I've done it for doesn't notice; that other one for whose sake I've done it does notice. If this one did notice, if he wasn't ungrateful, it would do him more good than me. Let me hold fast to God, since what I do doesn't escape his notice; not only what I do, but even what I do in my heart. Let me place my hopes in his rewarding me, since he doesn't require a witness for my good deed."

That's the sort of person you are, and perhaps here among the people of God a money-grubbing grabber of other people's property, who always has his eyes on other people's goods, comes and stands next to you. You know what he is, and he's a believer, or rather he's called a believer. You can't drive him out of the church, there's no way you can correct him by punishing or rebuking him; he's going to approach the altar with you. Don't worry. *Each one will bear his own burden* (Gal 6:5). Remember the apostle, and approach the altar yourself without anxiety; *each one will bear his own burden.*

Only don't let him say to you "Carry it with me"; because if you agree to share avarice with him, it won't lessen the burden, but instead the two of you will be weighed down by it. So let him carry his load, and you yours, seeing that when your Lord tossed that sort of load off your shoulders, he placed another one on them; he tossed aside the load of greed, replaced it with the load of love. So each person, according to the nature of his desires, carries his own load, a bad person a bad one, a good person a good one.

The burdens of poverty and riches

9. Now turn again to that other precept: *Carry your burdens for each other* (Gal 6:2). What you have, you see, is Christ's burden, which enables you to carry with someone else his own burden. He's poor, you're rich; his burden is poverty; you haven't got a burden like that. Take care you don't say, when the poor man pleads with you, *Each one will carry his own burden.* Pay heed in this case to the other precept: *Carry your burdens for each other.*

"Poverty is not my burden, it's my brother's burden." Consider whether riches aren't a greater burden for you. You haven't got poverty as a burden, but you have got riches as a burden. If you look at it in the right way, this is a burden. He's got one burden, you another. Carry his with him, and let him carry yours with you, so that you end up by carrying your burdens for each other. What's the burden of poverty? Not having anything. What's the burden of riches? Having more than is needed. He's overburdened, and you're overburdened too. Carry his having nothing with him, let him carry your having more than enough with you, so that your loads may be spread equally.

You see, if you give to a needy person, who's got nothing, you reduce his load for him, which consisted of having nothing; if you give him something, he starts having something; his burden, that's called not having anything, is reduced. And he in turn is reducing your burden, which is called having more than enough. The two of you are walking along God's road in the journey through this world. You were carrying vast superfluous provisions, while he didn't have any provisions at all. He has attached himself to you, desiring to be your companion; don't ignore him, don't turn him away, don't leave him behind. Can't you see how much you are carrying? Give some of it to him, since having nothing he's carrying nothing, and you will be helping your companion, and he will be relieving you. I rather think that is a sufficient explanation of the apostle's considered judgment.

The Donatists

10. Don't let them sell you smoke, those who say, "We are holy, we don't carry your loads, that's why we don't communicate with you."[8] Those big men[9] carry loads of division, the big men are carrying loads of exclusion, loads of schism, loads of heresy, loads of dissension, loads of animosity, loads of false testimony, loads of trumped up accusations. We have tried and we are continuing our efforts to lift these loads from the shoulders of our brothers. They, I'm afraid, love them and hug them to themselves, they refuse to become a little smaller,[10] because their heads have been swollen by their very loads. It's true, I suppose, a person who puts down a load which he was hoisting on his neck seems to grow smaller; but it's a weight he has put down, not his own stature.

Don't break the Lord's nets

11. "But I," you say, "am not communicating with other people's sins"—as though what I'm saying to you were "Come and communicate with other people's sins!" That's not what I'm saying. I know what the apostle would say, and I say the same. Just because of other people's sins, if they really were such and not rather your own, you shouldn't desert God's flock which is a mixture of sheep and goats; you shouldn't leave the Lord's threshing floor, as long as the straw is being threshed; you shouldn't break the Lord's nets, as long as they are hauling both good and bad fish to the shore.

"And how," you say, "am I to put up with someone whom I know to be bad?" Isn't it better you should put up with him than that you should put yourself down outside? Here's how you are to put up with him: you only have to pay attention to the apostle saying *Each one will carry his own burden* (Gal 6:5); that judgment should set you free. It means you wouldn't be communicating with him in avarice, but you would be communicating with him at the table of Christ. And what harm would it do you, if you communicated with him at the table of Christ? The apostle says, *For whoever eats and drinks unworthily is eating and drinking condemnation to himself* (1 Cor 11:29). To himself, not to you. Certainly if you are a judge, if you have received authority to judge according to Church rules, if he is accused before you, and convicted by true documents and witnesses, place restrictions on him, rebuke, excommunicate, degrade him. Tolerance must keep awake in such a way that discipline doesn't go to sleep.

The case of Caecilian

12. "But," they say, "Caecilian was condemned." Condemned? By whom? First in his absence, then though innocent by betrayers.[11] These things have been formally alleged, inserted in the records, proved. They did indeed try to weaken the force of truth, and attempted as best they could to cloud its clear skies over with the clouds of unsubstantial considerations.[12] The Lord stood by us, his clear sky overcame their clouds. And notice how, without meaning to, they absolved the Church of the whole world,[13] in whose communion we rejoice, whatever sort of people we may be in her. It's not ourselves but she that we are protecting, defending, preserving, as we defend the Lord's threshing-floor.

Yes, it's on behalf of the Lord's threshing-floor that I am loudly claiming a hearing.[14] As for who I may be on the floor, you don't have to care about that; I'm waiting for the winnowing. I don't want you, I say, to care about that; or if you insist on caring, don't do it by wrangling, but in a way that will enable you to heal your brothers. Take care of the straw, if you can; but don't abandon the grain if you can't take care of the straw. Sometimes the straw too is pushed off the threshing-floor; occasionally even some grains, but not far off.[15] But there are good workmen who go round the threshing-floor, and with rakes and brooms clean up what has been pushed off the edge, and pull it and summon it back onto the floor, even if it means pulling and compelling.[16]

The rakes and brooms for cleaning up are these secular laws.[17] Call them back, drag back the wheat even with some earth mixed up with it, or the wheat may be lost because of the earth. Caecilian was condemned, they say. He was condemned once in his absence, cleared three times when present. We answered them; and though they are the sort of men you can't teach anything, we reminded them briefly about their own doings, and said, "Why do you bring up against Caecilian the council of seventy bishops which passed judgment on him in his absence? Several judgments were passed by a council of Maximianists against Primian in his absence."[18] We said, "Caecilian was condemned by those people in his absence, Primian was condemned by these in his absence. Just as these aren't prejudicial to the absent Primian, so in the same way those couldn't have been prejudicial to the absent Caecilian."

The Donatists condemned by their own opinions

13. What do you suppose they answered, when caught in this cleft stick? What could they say, after all? How could they avoid being trapped in the nets of truth? In order to break these nets by violence, what do you think they said, very briefly, and absolutely in *our* favor? As a matter of fact much, practically everything they said, worked in our favor, as the Acts will indicate, which your graces are of course going to read as soon as ever they are published. But as regards this particular point,[19] I beg and beseech you by Christ to hold onto it, to repeat it, to have it always on your lips. You see, a briefer, surer, clearer judgment in our favor could not have been given.

So what did he say, when we made this objection: "These cannot be prejudicial to Caecilian, any more than those are to Primian"? Their spokesman replied, "You cannot prejudge one case by another, nor one person by another."[20] What a perfectly short, clear, true reply! You see, he didn't know what he was saying, but like Caiaphas when he was high priest, he prophesied.[21] "You cannot prejudge one case by another, nor one person by another." If you can prejudge neither one case by another, nor one person by another, it follows that each one must bear his own burden.

Now let him go and make his objection about Caecilian to you; not to you, any individual, but to the whole world; let him cast Caecilian in its teeth. When he does that, in fact, he is casting an innocent man in the teeth of innocent people; the records will show this in the clearest possible way. Caecilian was cleared. But suppose he wasn't cleared, suppose he was found guilty; listen to the echo of your own voice coming from the whole world: "You can neither prejudge one case by another nor one person by another." You incurably spiteful, heretical soul, since you are giving judgment against yourself, why do you accuse the judge? If I bribed him to give judgment for me, who bribed you to condemn yourself?[22]

The error of the Donatists

14. If only some time or other they would just think about this, think about it even late in the day, think about it at least when their spite and arrogance is on the wane; if only they would come to their senses, question themselves, examine themselves, answer themselves, for the sake of the truth not be afraid of the people whom they have so long palmed off with falsehood. They are afraid of shocking them, you see; they blush for shame before human weakness, and they don't blush for shame before the unconquerable truth.

What they are afraid of, of course, is people saying to them, "So why did you deceive us? Why did you lead us astray? Why did you say so many bad and untrue things?"

Their answer should be, if they feared God, "It was human to be mistaken, it's diabolical to remain in the mistake out of spiteful animosity. It would indeed have been better if we had never gone wrong; but at least let us do the next best thing and finally correct our error. We deceived you, because we were deceived ourselves. We preached untruths, because we believed others who preached untruths."

They should say to their people, "We have gone wrong together, let us together withdraw from our error. We were your leaders into the ditch, and you followed us when we led you into the ditch;[23] and now follow us when we lead you back to the Church." They could say that; they would be saying it to indignant people, saying it to angry people; but they too would sooner or later lay aside their indignation, and come, even though late in the day, to love unity.

We must be patient with the Donatists

15. We, however, brothers and sisters, must be patient with them. The eyes we are trying to care for are inflamed and swollen. I am not saying we should stop caring for them, but that we should avoid provoking them to greater bitterness by crowing over them. Let us mildly give a reasonable account of the affair, not proudly brag about victory. *The servant of the Lord*, says the apostle, *should not wrangle, but be gentle with everyone, willing to learn,*[24] patient, correcting those who think differently with modesty, in the hope that God would grant them repentance, and they would recover their wits from the devil's snares, by whom they are being held captive according to his will.[25]

So put up with them patiently if you are sound of mind and body yourselves; put up with them patiently insofar as you are of sound health yourselves. Which of us, after all, is perfectly sound of mind and body? When the just king sits upon his throne, which of us will be able to boast that he has a pure heart, or which of us will be able to boast that he is clean of all sin?[26] So as long as we are such, this is what we owe ourselves, that we should carry our burdens for one another.

Turning to the Lord, etc.

NOTES

1. Preached at Hippo Regius shortly after Augustine's return from the conference, say in September or October. It is only in the last part that he turns his attention to the Donatists, having provided a convenient general framework by his commentary on the two texts from Galatians.

2. That is, Christ.

3. In the previous sermon, 163B, preached about a year before at Carthage, he reads the text of this verse as "Bear one another's burdens," *Alter alterius onera portate*, but frequently slips into the equivalent "Bear your burdens for each other," *Invicem onera vestra portate*. That is the text consistently used in this sermon. From this we may conclude that the received Carthaginian text differed in this respect from the one he was more familiar with in Hippo Regius.

4. He himself is here positively exacting full audience participation—but within limits!

5. The poor man.

6. *Quod premebat oculos vestros*. His image, I take it, is of porters, or stevedores, or coolies, whose heavy loads on their shoulders were partly supported by straps round their foreheads, which either partly covered their eyes, or made them keep their heads down.

7. The word he uses is *magisterium*.

8. The Donatists.

9. The Donatist bishops recently assembled in Carthage for the conference with the Catholics. Most of them not surprisingly refused to accept the judgment of the imperial tribune Marcellinus in favor of the Catholic case.

10. By adhering to the Catholic Church the Donatist bishops would lose their flocks, and in many cases at least would cease to exercise their office, though they would not lose their episcopal rank and dignity.

11. For a brief outline of the events at the beginning of the Donatist schism, involving Caecilian, elected bishop of Carthage in 311, see Sermon 162A, notes 20 and 21.

The Donatists justified their schism by accusing the Catholics of condoning the sin of *traditio*, the betrayal of the sacred books to the persecutors; they maintained both that Caecilian had been guilty of this and that he had been ordained by a bishop guilty of it, which in their view rendered his ordination invalid.

Here Augustine, with some justification from the historical evidence, is saying that the bishops who condemned Caecilian were themselves, or at least several of them, *traditores*, and that Caecilian was innocent and, as he will go on to say, cleared three times by three tribunals.

12. He is referring to the tactics of the Donatist bishops at the conference.

13. He only comes back to this point in section 13.

14. *Clamo.* I think that in late Latin it was coming to mean more than just shouting; to mean a kind of legal procedure, precisely making a *claim*—by shouting, presumably—in court. It has this meaning in the Norman French law of the Channel Islands: the procedure of the *clameur*, according to which anybody feeling wronged by someone else kneels down in the presence of two witnesses, recites the Our Father in Norman French, and cries "*Haro! Haro! Haro! A l'aide, mon Prince, on me fait tort!*"

15. He is not here referring to the final winnowing of the last judgment, but to the rough and ready kind that is going on all the time in the course of the historical process.

16. A reference to Lk 14:23, "compel them to come in"; a text which by the date of this sermon Augustine had come to regard as justifying the imperial laws against heretics.

17. *Leges mundanae.* He is punning on the things for cleaning up, *mundatoria instrumenta.*

18. Primian was the Donatist bishop of Carthage at this time. About 12 to 15 years previously a faction among the Donatists had so disapproved of him that they installed Maximian in his place, so that now there was a schism within the Donatist ranks. Augustine taunts the Donatists with this awkward fact *ad nauseam*, pointing out that their predecessors had treated Caecilian in exactly the same way as the Maximianists treated Primian.

19. Reading either *hoc locum*, treating *locum* as a neuter, which is unusual but possible; or if it is too unusual to be likely, *hunc locum*, instead of *hoc loco*. The verbs demand an object. This could be just the pronoun *hoc*, treated as unconnected with *loco*, which could then be translated as "instead," that is, instead of the many other clumsy things the Donatists said. But this would to my mind be even more unusual than my first suggestion. We must bear in mind that *hoc locum* would have sounded almost exactly the same as *hoc loco*.

20. *Summary of the Conference with the Donatists* 3, 28.

21. See Jn 11:51.

22. The Donatists were presumably saying that the Catholics had bribed or otherwise corrupted Marcellinus to pronounce in their favor.

Augustine's point here against them, if he hasn't made it clear enough himself, is that since each one must carry his own burden, that is be responsible for his own sins alone, a principle their spokesman endorses with his saying about not prejudging one person by another, then even if Caecilian had been guilty of the sins they accuse him of, that was his responsibility, not that of other bishops and local Churches.

23. See Lk 6:39.

24. *Docibilem*, which properly means teachable, and that is how I translate it; but here it renders the Greek *didaktikon*, which has the active sense of being good at teaching, and *docibilis* may have acquired this sense in Church Latin.

25. See 2 Tm 2:24-26.

26. See Prv 20:8-9.

SERMON 164A

ON THE UNIVERSALITY OF ALMSGIVING

Date: before 396[1]

To whom should we give alms?

1. There are some people who think that alms should only be given to the just, while we ought to give nothing of the kind to sinners. The ones who take the lead in this error are the sacrilegious Manichees, who believe that pieces of God are mixed up and bundled together, and thus imprisoned, in every kind of food; and so they reckon we must spare these from being polluted by sinners and tied up in even more unpleasant knots. Better, perhaps, than bothering to rebut this insanity, is simply to state it and leave it to offend the good sense of all sane people.

There are others, however, with no such opinions, who think that the reason why sinners ought not to be fed, is that we would be striving against God, whose displeasure at them is being manifested;[2] as though he could also get angry with us too as a result, because we want to help those whom he wants to punish. They also produce proof texts from the holy scriptures, where we read: *Give alms, and do not support the sinner, and to the ungodly and sinners pay back vengeance. Do good to the humble person, and give nothing to the ungodly. Since the Most High also hates sinners, and will pay back vengeance to the ungodly* (Sir 12:4.6.7). They don't understand how these words should be taken, and so they clothe themselves in dreadful cruelty. That's why, brothers and sisters, I have to address your graces on this matter, or else a crooked way of thinking may bring you into disagreement with the divine will.

Alms should be given to everyone

2. The apostle Paul teaches us in the clearest possible way that alms are to be distributed to everybody, when he says, *Let us be tireless, while we have the time, in doing good to all, though supremely to those at home in the faith* (Gal 6:10). This indeed makes it plain enough that in works of this kind the just are to be given preference. Who else, after all, are we to understand by *those at home in the faith*, since elsewhere it is stated plainly, *The just person lives by*

faith?[3] That doesn't mean, though, that we must close our hearts to other people, even sinners, not even if they adopt a hostile attitude toward us. The Savior himself says, after all, *Love your enemies, do good to those who hate you* (Lk 6:27). Nor is the point passed over in silence in the books of the Old Testament; one reads there, you see, *If your enemy is hungry, feed him; if he is thirsty, give him a drink* (Prv 25:21); a text the apostle also makes use of in the New (Rom 12:20).

No human being is to be excluded from kindness and compassion

3. This does not mean, however, that what we quoted above is false, because these too are divine precepts: *Give alms, and do not support the sinner* (Sir 12:4). The reason this was said was to make sure you don't do good to any sinner because he is a sinner, but that you do good to the person who hates you, not because he's a sinner, but because he's a human being. In this way you will keep each commandment, and be neither slack about punishing, nor callously inhuman about giving relief. Everyone, after all, who rightly takes a sinner to task, what else does this show but that he doesn't want him to be a sinner? So he is hating in him what God also hates, in order to get what man has made eliminated, and what God has made set free. What man has made is sin, what God has made is the man himself. And when we speak these two words together, man and sinner, they are certainly not spoken needlessly. Because he's a sinner, rebuke him, and because he's a man, be sorry for him. And you certainly won't set him free as a man, unless you chase him up as a sinner.

All discipline is alert to the performance of this duty, in whatever way is the appropriate responsibility of anyone put in charge of others; not only of the bishop in charge of his people, but also of the poor man in charge of his own house,[4] the rich man in charge of his family and servants, the husband in charge of his wife, the father in charge of his children, the judge in charge of his province, the king in charge of his nation. All these, when they are good men, naturally wish them well, those they govern, and according to the authority allotted to them by the Lord of all, who also governs governors, they take pains to ensure that those they govern should be preserved as human beings and perish as sinners. In this way they fulfill the text, *Show mercy, and do not support the sinner,* by not wanting the fact of his being a sinner to flourish in him; *and to the ungodly and sinners pay back vengeance*—here too, let the fact of their being ungodly and sinners be eliminated in them; *do good to the humble person,* precisely because he's humble, *and give nothing to the ungodly,* precisely as being ungodly, *since the Most High also hates sinners, and will pay back vengeance to the ungodly* (Sir 12:4.6.7). He though, because they aren't only sinners and ungodly, but are also human beings, *makes his sun rise upon the good and the bad, and sends rain upon the just and the unjust* (Mt 5:45). In this way no human being is to be excluded from kindness and compassion, no sinner to be allowed to go unpunished.

4. And so what we have above all to conclude from all this, is how very much almsgiving is not to be made light of, which is bestowed on any poor people by right of humanity, seeing that the Lord himself relieved the wants of the poor even from those funds which were supplied from other people's contributions.[5] If anyone, though, should happen to say that neither those cripples and beggars whom the Lord advised us to invite for preference,[6] nor those to whom he was in the habit of contributing from his funds, were sinners; and that therefore it doesn't follow from these gospel quotations that he is giving instructions that even sinners should be supported and fed by the kindhearted; this objector should pay attention to what I have already mentioned earlier on, that the most dastardly of sinners are of course those who hate and persecute the Church,[7] and yet about them we are told, *Do good to those who hate you* (Lk 6:27). And this is supported by the example of God the Father, *who makes his sun rise on the good and the bad, and sends his rain upon the just and the unjust* (Mt 5:45).

So then, we are not to support sinners, precisely insofar as they are sinners; and yet because they are also human beings, we must treat them too with humane consideration. Let us relentlessly pursue their own wickedness in them, while showing mercy to their and our common condition. And in this way, *let us be tireless, while we have the time, in doing good to all, though supremely to those at home in the faith* (Gal 6:10).

NOTES

1. This is the suggestion of Dom Lambot, who edited this sermon. The sermon was known earlier to the Maurists, but they questioned its authenticity, though it has a genuine Augustinian ring to it. If it was preached while Augustine was still only in priest's orders, as Lambot suggests, then the strong presumption would be that it was preached in Hippo Regius.

2. By their penury or other misfortunes.

3. Hab 2:4, a favorite Pauline quotation; Rom 1:17; Gal 3:11; Heb 10:38.

4. *Domum suam.* One manuscript has the intriguing alternative reading *dominum suum*, the poor man in charge of his master. I would like to think Augustine said this. As a bishop he might well have done, but as a priest it is less likely, and if he had done so he would probably have made the paradox more stark by saying "the slave servant in charge of his master"—the old retainer responsible for correcting the peccadilloes of his employer, an Augustinian Jeeves. It is harder, all the same, to explain how a copyist could have changed *domum suam* into *dominum suum*, than to see how the reverse alteration could have occurred.

5. See Jn 13:29, where the disciples thought Jesus was telling Judas to give something to the poor; and also Lk 8:3, which tells us of the women who supported Jesus and his disciples out of their own means.

6. See Lk 14:13.

7. He hadn't mentioned this earlier on; but he had quoted the text he goes on to quote now.

SERMON 165

ON THE WORDS OF THE APOSTLE, EPHESIANS 3:13-18: *I ASK YOU NOT TO BE WEAKENED BY MY TRIBULATIONS ON YOUR BEHALF, WHICH IS YOUR GLORY*, ETC. AND ON GRACE AND FREE WILL AGAINST THE PELAGIANS, DELIVERED IN THE BASILICA OF THE ANCESTORS

Date: 417[1]

We should place our hopes not in ourselves, but in God

1. We have heard the apostle, we have heard the psalm, we have heard the gospel;[2] all the divinely inspired readings agree that we should place our hopes not in ourselves, but in God. *I ask you*, says the apostle, *not to be weakened by my tribulations on your behalf, which is your glory* (Eph 3:13). *I ask you*, he says, *not to be weakened*,[3] when you hear that I suffer tribulations on your behalf; because that is your glory. So he's asking them not to weaken; which he wouldn't do, unless he wanted to rouse their wills. I mean, suppose they answered, "Why do you ask us for what we don't have in our power?" Wouldn't it seem they had given him a fair answer? And yet unless the apostle knew that there was in them such a thing as the consent of their own will, when they too were to do something themselves, he wouldn't have said *I ask you*. And if he said "I order you," the word would come from his mouth quite pointlessly, unless he knew they could apply their wills to his order.

But again, he knew that without God's help man's will is weak. So he didn't only say *I ask you*, to stop them saying "We haven't got free will"; but in addition, to stop them saying, "Free will is all we need," notice how he continued: *For this reason.*[4] For what reason, if not because he had just said, *I ask you not to be weakened by my tribulations on your behalf, which is your glory*? So because you have free will, *I ask you*; but because free will is not all you need to carry out what I ask, *For this reason I bend my knees to the Father of our Lord Jesus Christ, from whom all fatherhood in heaven and on earth is named, that he would give you* (Eph 3:14-16). That he would give you what? What I ask from you, I beg him to give you. I ask it of you, because of free will; I beg him to give it you, for the sake of help from on high.

201

Paul's asking from God what he's demanding from human beings

2. But we have anticipated the apostle's words. You are still waiting, perhaps, to hear, those of you who don't remember the actual text of this reading here, whether in fact the reason the apostle bent his knees to the Father was that he should give them what he himself had said to them: *I ask you*. So remember what he had asked of them: *I ask you not to be weakened by my tribulations on your behalf* (Eph 3:13); that's what he had asked of them. Now notice what he asks for them: *I bend my knees to the Father of our Lord Jesus Christ, that he would give you according to the riches of his glory, to be strengthened with power*. What else is that but not to be weakened? *To be strengthened with power*, he says, *through his Spirit* (Eph 3:14-16). This is the Spirit of grace. Notice what he's asking for. He's asking from God what he's demanding from men; because for God to be willing to give, you for your part have to accommodate your will to receive. How can you really wish to receive the grace of divine goodness, if you don't open the lap of your will to receive?

That he would give you, he says. After all, you don't have anything, unless he gives it you. *That he would give you to be strengthened with power through his Spirit*. If he gives you to be strengthened with power, I mean, he will thereby give you not to be weakened. *In the inner self, for Christ to dwell through faith in your hearts*. That he would give you all this. *Rooted and founded in charity, that you may win through to comprehend with all the saints*. Comprehend what? May he give you through his spirit to be strengthened with power, and to have Christ dwelling in your inner selves through faith, and that thus being rooted and founded in charity, you may be able to comprehend with all the saints: what? *What is the width, the length, the height and the depth* (Eph 3:16-18).[5]

In the four dimensions is the cross

3. So what now, my brothers and sisters? Shall I, here, explain this to you? If anybody else should possibly find it easier, what then? Because I am less suited to understanding and stating the width, length, height, and depth, these four dimensions the apostle mentions, shall I pass on from this point? Or shall I rather knock, and also be assisted by your prayers, that I may offer you something sound and wholesome? Why travel in thought, Christian man or woman, through the width of the earth, the length of the ages, the height of the sky, or the depth of the abyss? When can you comprehend these either by mind or body? That is, whether by thinking or by looking with your eyes of flesh, when can you comprehend these? Listen to the apostle saying to you, *But far be it from me to boast, except in the cross of our Lord Jesus Christ* (Gal 6:14).

Let us too make it our boast, if only because we lean totally upon it. Let us all boast of it, good brothers and sisters, let us make it our boast. Perhaps it is there that we shall find both width, and length, and height, and depth. These words of the apostle, you see, somehow set up the cross before our very eyes. I mean, it has width, where the hands are fixed; it has length, where the post goes down from there to the ground; it also has height, which goes up a little from the crossbar on which the hands are fixed, where the head of the crucified is laid; and it also has depth, that is, the part fixed in the ground which cannot be seen. Notice what a great, significant mystery[6] it is; from that depth which you cannot see rises everything that you can see.

Let the one you love be himself the reward

4. So where is the width? Turn your mind to the life and behavior of the saints, who say, *Far be it from me to boast, except in the cross of our Lord Jesus Christ* (Gal 6:14). We find in their way of life and behavior the width of charity; which is why the apostle himself gives them this advice: *Open yourselves wide, lest you should be bearing the yoke with unbelievers* (2 Cor 6:13-14). And to show that he was wide open himself, as he urged upon them width and breadth of mind, listen to what he says: *Our mouth is open to you, O Corinthians, our heart is open wide* (2 Cor 6:11). So width means charity, which alone does good works. It is this width that ensures that God can *love a cheerful giver* (2 Cor 9:7). I mean, if you're being squeezed tight, you will give sadly; if you give sadly, your giving will lose all value. So you need the width of charity, to save whatever good you do from losing its value.

But because the Lord said, *When iniquity abounds, the charity of many will grow cold* (Mt 24:12), give me also length. What is meant by length? *Whoever perseveres to the end shall be saved* (Mt 24:13). This is the length of the cross, where the whole body is stretched; where after a fashion it is standing, the kind of standing by which one perseveres. So if you are seeking, you that make the cross your boast, to have the width of the cross, make sure you have the virtue to do good. If you want to have the length of the cross, make sure you have the long suffering capacity to persevere.

But if you want to have the height of the cross, make sure you know the meaning of the words you hear, "Lift up your hearts," and of where you hear them.[7] Well, what does it mean, "Lift up your hearts"? Place your hope up there, place your love up there, ask for strength from up there, look for your reward from up there. Because if you do good, and give cheerfully, you seem to have the width; if in these same good works you persevere to the end, you seem to have the length. But if you don't do any of this for the sake of the reward up above, you won't have the height; which means you won't have the real width and real length either. What, after all, does having the height mean, but thinking about God, loving God, and freely loving God as being himself the helper, himself the spectator, himself the prize-giver, himself the bestower of the reward; finally indeed, reckoning him to be the reward himself, and looking for nothing else from him but himself? If you love him, love him freely; if you love him truly, let the one you love be himself the reward. Or can it be that all things are precious to you, and the one who established them all is worthless?

The depth of the cross

5. That we might be able to do all this, the apostle bent his knees on our behalf, precisely, of course, that it might be given to us. Then there is also the frightening passage of the gospel: *To you it has been given to know the mystery of the kingdom, but to them it has not been given. For whoever has, will be given.* But who does have, so as to be given, except the one to whom it has been given? *But whoever does not have, even what he has will be taken away from him* (Mt 13:11-12). But who doesn't have, except the one to whom it has not been given? So why was it given to this one, and not given to that one?

It doesn't embarrass me to say, this is the depth of the cross. From heaven knows what deeps of God's judgments, which we are quite unable to scrutinize or contemplate, proceeds everything that we can. From heaven knows what depths, I repeat, of the judgments of God, which being inscrutable we cannot contemplate, which we are quite incapable of scrutinizing, proceeds everything that we can. What I can, I see; how I can, I don't see—except that I can see this far, that I know this comes from God. But why this person and not that—it is too much for me, it is an abyss, the depth of the cross; I can cry out in wonder, I cannot explain by reasoned argument.

What can I cry out about this unfathomable depth? *How magnificent are your works, O Lord!* (Ps 92:5). The nations are enlightened, the Jews are reduced to blindness. Some babies are washed clean in the sacrament of baptism, but some babies are left in the death of the first man. *How magnificent are your works, O Lord! How deep have become your thoughts!* And it continues, *The thoughtless man does not know this, and the fool does not understand* (Ps 92:5-6). What doesn't the foolish and thoughtless person understand? That there is even anything deep there. Because if the fool doesn't understand, and the sage does, the matter can't be too deep. But if the sage does understand that it is deep, the fool doesn't understand even that it is deep.

Souls carrying on in heaven before the body

6. So it is that many people, in trying to give an account of this deep matter, have strayed away into futile fables. Some have said that souls sin above in heaven, and according to their sins are dispatched to bodies and locked up in them as in appropriate prisons.[8] They have followed in the tracks of their own thoughts; wishing to theorize about the depths of God, they have been drowned in the deeps themselves. The apostle, you see, counters them when he is wishing to put the case for grace; and he chose those twins in Rebecca's womb, and says, *For when they were not yet born, or such as had done anything good or bad* (Rom 9:11). Notice how he deprives these triflers of their fantasies about souls carrying on in heaven before the body. I mean, if they have already carried on a life there, they have already done something good or bad, and been thrust down into earthly bodies for their deserts. By all means, if you like, let us contradict the apostle, who said, *When they were not yet born, or such as had done anything good or bad.*

But because Catholic faith, thanks to the apostle's clear statement, rejects the opinion that souls first live and carry on in heaven, and there qualify for the bodies they are to receive as they deserve; these people with newfangled ideas don't dare to say that anymore.[9]

Infants and sin

7. What do they say, though? Some of them, so we have heard, argue as follows: "Beyond question," they say, "all people die as they deserve, because they have sinned. For there wouldn't be any such thing as death, except as coming from sin." Very well and truly said, indeed; there wouldn't be any death, except as coming from sin. But the reason I applaud when I hear this, is that I am fixing my gaze on that first death and the sin of that first man. You see, I'm listening to the apostle: *Just as in Adam all die, so also in Christ shall all be made alive* (1 Cor 15:22). *Through one man sin entered into the world, and through sin death; and thus it passed into all men, in that all have sinned* (Rom 5:12). All, you see, were that one man.

"Is that how I hear you saying that death comes from the sin of man?"

"No," he says.

"And what are you saying?"

"God creates every human being immortal now."

"What a wonderful new idea! What do you say, again?"

"Beyond question," he says, "God creates every human being immortal."

So why do infant children die? I mean, if I said, "Why do adults die?" he would say to me, "They have sinned." So I won't argue about people who have come of age; I will summon to testify against you the infancy of babies. They can't talk, and they convict you; they are silent, and they prove what I am saying. Here we have infants, obviously innocent in their actions, having nothing sinful about them apart from what they have contracted from the first man. The reason they need the grace of Christ is to be made alive in Christ, after having died in Adam; after being defiled by being born, to be purified by being reborn.

So these are the witnesses I will call. Answer me: why do they die, if all human beings are born immortal, and the only reason they die is that they sin? What, do you think, the answer could have been? Whose ears could tolerate it? "They too have sinned." Where have they sinned? I'm asking you, when have they sinned? How have they sinned? They don't know what good and evil are. Do they get saddled with sin, though they can't even understand a command-ment? Prove to me that infants are sinners. That's what you said, in truth because you have forgotten what you were; prove to my satisfaction the sins of infants. Or is it because they cry, that they sin? Because with movements like those of dumb animals they push away what annoys them, accept what gives them pleasure, is that why they sin? If such motions are sins, they become much more thorough sinners in baptism, because when they are baptized, they struggle against it most vigorously. Why is such resistance not imputed to them as sin, if not because there is still no deliberate choice of will?

Did infants sin in the womb?

8. But I have something else to say. These sinned, so you consider, because they were born; because if they didn't sin, you say, they wouldn't die. What do you say about those who die in the womb? That's got you! "They too," he says, "have sinned, that's why they die." Are you lying, or just kidding yourself? The apostle contradicts you: *Not yet born, nor doing anything good or bad* (Rom 9:11). I prefer to listen to the apostle rather than you; I prefer to believe the apostle rather than you: *Not yet born, nor doing anything good or bad.*

But if you reject that evidence, take yourself off, rather, on those other ramblings, and say that they sinned in heaven, and from there were flung down into bodies.

"I don't say that," he says.

"Why don't you say it?"

"Because the apostle says, *Not yet born, nor doing anything good or bad.*"

"So if you don't accuse them of sin in heaven, why do you accuse them of sin in the womb? The apostle's answer meets both points; it meets those who say they sinned in heaven, and it meets those who say they sinned in the womb, because the words which say that before they were born they did nothing either good or bad, are good against either point. So why do they die? Am I going to listen to you here too, and not rather to the teacher of the nations?

In the end, grace

9. You tell me, Paul the apostle, why they die. *Through one man sin entered into the world, and through sin death; and thus it passed into all men, in that all have sinned* (Rom 5:12). There you are, the first man has made the whole lump fit only for condemnation. Let him come, let our Lord come, the second man; let him come, let him come from another line, let him come by the virgin.[10] Let him come alive, let him find the dead; let him die, to relieve the dying,[11] to transfer the dead to life, to redeem the dead from death, to preserve life in death, to slay death with death. This is the only grace there is for children, the only grace for adults; the only grace to set free the little ones together with the great.[12]

Why this one and this one; why not that one and that one; don't ask me. I'm just a man; I notice the depth of the cross, I can't penetrate it; I shudder with dread, I don't poke and pry. *Inscrutable are his judgments, unsearchable are his ways* (Rom 11:33). I'm just a man, you're just a man, he was just a man, the one who said, *O man, who are you to answer back to God?* (Rom 9:20). It was a man saying it, saying it to a man. Let the man listen, or else the man may perish, for whose sake God became man.

So in this great depth of the cross, in this profound darkness of things, let us hold onto what we have been singing. Let us not presume to rely on our own virtue, let us not lay claim in this problem to any capacity for our own little intellects. Let us say the psalm, let us say with the psalm, *Have mercy on me, God, have mercy on me.* Why? Because I have some virtue by which I deserve well of you? No. Why? Because I can make deliberate choices of will, whereby my merit can precede your grace? No. But why, then? *Because in you my soul trusts* (Ps 57:1).

Turning to the Lord, etc.

NOTES

1. "Basilica of the ancestors" translates *basilica majorum*. Sermon 16A is also noted as having been preached there. It was one of the principal churches of Carthage. Who the *majores* were, I do not know; I only guess they were ancestors, but then which ancestors and whose? It may possibly have been the name of a pagan temple, or shrine, which was converted into a church.

2. What we would call the epistle, the responsorial psalm, and the gospel at Mass. It is to be noted that the usual Sunday Masses in Christian Africa did not include an Old Testament reading, as our reformed liturgy now makes them do. This is not to criticize the liturgical reforms put into effect as a result of the Second Vatican Council. Perhaps it just indicates that these reforms were not antiquarian in spirit.

3. Here he adds an explanatory phrase which would be purely tautological in English. His Latin text is not quite as precise as its English translation; it runs simply *Peto non infirmari*, without actually saying *vos*, you. So it is heard as "I ask not to be weakened," and Augustine adds, *id est, ut non infirmemini*, "that is, that you should not be weakened."

4. *Hujus rei gratia*. While *gratia* here is no more than a preposition meaning "because of," it is still also the word for grace, and he is well aware of that as he quotes the phrase. That is why he pauses here, though he will not in fact base his argument on this use of the word here.

5. Here we have another explanation of a peculiarity of Latin, which in a translation properly belongs to a footnote. He adds, "Height *(altitudo)* indeed in the Latin language signifies each thing; both what points upward has the name of *altitudo*, and what is vast *(altum)* in depth has the name of *altitudo*. That is why the Latin translator answers well to what is above by calling it height *(altitudo)*; and to what is deep *(altum)* below by calling it depth."

6. *Sacramentum*. Augustine gives a similar explanation of the dimensions of the cross in several other places: Sermon 53, 15, 16; *Homilies on the Gospel of John* 118, 5; *Expositions on the Psalms* 104, 14; Letters 55, 14, 25; 140, 26, 64; 147, 14, 34; *Teaching Christianity* II, 41, 62.

7. In the preface at Mass.

8. This appears to be an application of a theory of Origen's (died 253) on the matter.

9. The Pelagians.

10. In saying "let him come from another line, *ex alio tramite*," he is not suggesting that Jesus was not descended from Adam; he is only putting in other words what he goes on to say next: "let him come by the virgin." His virginal conception is the other line, since in Augustine's view it cut, so to say, the connection through which the flaw of original sin is transmitted. This, for him, was specifically the sexual act, and even more specifically the sexual act of the male partner.

Modern theologies of original sin are never so specific. They will see it simply as the consequence of being born into the same flawed nature as we derive from Adam, flawed by his sin. And the immunity of both Mary and Jesus from that flawed inheritance is seen purely and simply as a prime effect of divine grace.

11. A triple play on words here: *vivus veniat, mortuos inveniat; moriatur ut morienti subveniat*.

12. See Ps 115:13.

SERMON 166

ON WHAT THE APOSTLE PAUL SAID, EPHESIANS 4:25: *PUTTING ASIDE LYING, SPEAK THE TRUTH*, AND ON WHAT IS SAID IN PSALM 116:11: *EVERY MAN IS A LIAR*

Date: after 409[1]

Lying

1. Let me explain briefly, if the Lord helps us to understand, how these words spoken by the apostle, *Putting aside lying, speak the truth* (Eph 4:25), do not contradict the ones spoken in the psalm, *Every man is a liar* (Ps 116:11).[2] So what is meant by *Putting aside lying, speak the truth*, and by *Every man is a liar*? Could God, through the apostle, be commanding the impossible? No. So what is he commanding? I make so bold as to say—but you mustn't take offense at what I say, because I'm saying it against myself too—what God is commanding is that we should not be men. I mean, if I said, "God is commanding you not to be men," you would possibly take it hard; and so I have included myself as well, so that nobody need get angry.

If you put aside lying, take off Adam;
if you speak the truth, put on Christ

2. You see, I've something more to tell your holinesses: that the apostle has objected to people as a kind of crime precisely that they are men; he said it, I mean, by way of scolding them. Just as when we are angry, and say to someone, "You're a beast"; so he, to rebuke them with the stick of the Lord's discipline, objected to people that they were men. What did he want them to become, if it was a crime for them to be men? *For since there is among you*, he says, *jealousy and quarreling, are you not of the flesh, and walking by merely human standards? For when someone says, I, for sure, am Paul's man, while another says, I am Apollo's, are you not men?* (1 Cor 3:3-4). He is taking them to task and scolding them when he says *Are you not men?*

So what did he want them to become, if not what it says in the psalm, *I said, You are gods, and sons of the Most High* (Ps 82:6)? It's God, certainly, who said that; that's what he is calling us to, after all. But what did he add? *You, however, shall die like men, and fall like one of the princes* (Ps 82:7). Here too they are

208

being reproached and objected to, when it says, *You, however, shall die like men*. Adam, you see, was man, and not son of man;[3] Christ, however, is Son of man, and God.

It is to lying that the old man belongs, that is, Adam; to the truth that the new man belongs, the Son of man, that is, Christ who is God. If you put aside lying, take off Adam; if you speak the truth, put on Christ;[4] and you won't find the texts quoted just now from the scriptures to be contradictory. Because the apostle for his part is advising us to take off the old man and put on the new, when he says *Putting aside lying, speak the truth*; and the psalm, in turn, was warning them and lamenting them, because they didn't want to take off Adam and put on Christ, and were eager to be, not new men, but just mere men, of the sort to whom it is said, *Are you not men?* and on whom the statement falls, *Every man is a liar*.

Put on Christ, and you will be truthful

3. If you desire to be man, you will be a liar; don't desire to be man, and you won't be a liar. Put on Christ, and you will be truthful; so that whatever you speak won't be like your very own, and established by you, but will belong to the truth which shines on you and enlightens you.[5] I mean, if you are stripped of light, you will remain in your own darkness, and all you will be able to speak is lies. The Lord said himself, after all, *The one who speaks a lie, speaks from what is his own*,[6] because *Every man is a liar* (Ps 116:11).

So the one who speaks the truth, does not speak from what is his own, but from what is God's. Not indeed in the sense that we say he speaks what belongs to someone else; you see, it becomes his own when he loves what he receives, and gives thanks to the one who gave it. Because if a man is deprived of illumination by the truth, he will remain as though stripped naked of the garment of light, and will be able to speak nothing but lies. The judgment, you see, will remain on him that is written in the psalm: *Every man is a liar*.

God wants to make you a god, by his gift and by adoption

4. So there are no grounds for anybody to misrepresent the case and say to me, "I'm going to tell lies, because I am a man." Because I will say to him in my turn, and with the utmost confidence, "Don't be a man, so that you won't have to tell lies." "So," he says, "I won't be a man?" "No, of course not. You see, it is in order not to be a man that you have been called by the one who became man for your sake. Don't take umbrage. I mean, you are not being told not to be a man, in the sense that you are to be a beast, but rather that you are to be among those to whom *he gave the right to become children of God* (Jn 1:12). God, you see, wants to make you a god; not by nature, of course, like the one whom he begot; but by his gift and by adoption.[7] For just as he through being humbled[8] came to share your mortality; so through lifting you up he brings you to share his immortality. Give him thanks, therefore, and cling onto what

you have been granted, so as to deserve to enjoy what you have been called to. Don't be Adam, and you won't be man. If not man, then of course not a liar, because *every man is a liar*. And when you begin not to tell lies anymore don't take the credit yourself and get a swollen head, as though it's all your own doing; otherwise you are liable to be snuffed out by the wind of pride, like any lamp that is lit from another, and to remain once more in your own falsehood."

So don't tell lies, brothers and sisters. Just a short while ago, you see, you were the old sort of man; you have approached the grace of God,[9] you have become the new sort of man. Lying belongs to Adam, truth to Christ. So, *putting aside lying, speak the truth* (Eph 4:25), in order that this mortal flesh too, which you still have from Adam, may itself earn renewal and transformation at the time of its resurrection, having been preceded by newness of spirit;[10] and thus the whole man being deified and made divine may cleave forever to the everlasting and unchangeable truth.

NOTES

1. The sermon was preached at the shrine of the Twenty Martyrs at Hippo Regius on the Sunday after Easter. The Twenty Martyrs were Christians of Hippo martyred during the persecution of Diocletian, 303 to 313, and included the bishop of the city, Fidentius. Augustine mentions them in Sermons 148, 257, and 325; and also in *The City of God* XXII, 8.

2. This short sermon makes great play with the word *homo*, which occurs first in this quotation from the psalm. Now there are many times when one can avoid translating *homo* by "man," and instead use "person," "human," "human being," "the new self," "the old self" and so on, in order to avoid sounding sexist. But to resort to these alternatives in this sermon—and it would be impossible to use the same one consistently all through—would completely obscure the preacher's point. So readers must please just accept that here "man" is employed in its inclusive, not its exclusive, sense.

3. Because he wasn't born of human parents, but fashioned from the slime of the earth.

4. See Eph 4:22-24; Col 3:9-10; Rom 13:14.

5. This truth, of course, he understands as Christ, as the light which enlightens every man coming into the world (Jn 1:9).

6. Jn 8:44. But in fact Jesus is talking here about the devil, not making a general remark about men.

7. See Gal 4:5-6.

8. Reading *per humilitatem*, in an allusion to Phil 2:8, instead of the *per humanitatem* of the text. There is no manuscript support for this emendation of mine. I just think it is more likely to be what Augustine said, and that his stenographer misheard him.

9. A term for baptism. It is this passage, presumably, that leads Lambot, reasonably enough, to the conclusion that the sermon was preached on the Sunday after Easter to the newly baptized.

10. See Eph 4:23.

SERMON 167

ON THE WORDS OF THE APOSTLE, EPHESIANS 5:15-16:
WATCH HOW YOU WALK CAREFULLY; NOT AS UNWISE, BUT AS WISE PEOPLE; REDEEMING THE TIME, SINCE THE DAYS ARE EVIL

Date: 410-412[1]

Two things make days evil: malice and misery

1. You heard the apostle, when he was read; or rather we all heard him telling us, *Watch how you walk carefully; not as unwise but as wise people; redeeming the time, since the days are evil* (Eph 5:15-16). Two things, brothers and sisters, make days evil: malice and misery. It is through human malice and human misery that days are called[2] evil. Otherwise these days, as far as their hourly divisions are concerned, are very regular; they follow each other in turn, they lead along the seasons. The sun rises, the sun sets, the seasons pass. Who would be vexed by times and seasons, if people weren't vexatious to each other? So evil days, as I said, are made by two things: human misery and human malice.

But human misery is common to us all; malice ought not to be common. From the very moment Adam fell, and was driven out of paradise, there have never been any days that weren't evil. Let's question the very babies as they are born, why they begin by crying, though they are also capable of laughing. It's born, and straightaway it cries; after I don't know how many days it laughs. When it started crying at birth, it was a prophet of its own future misfortunes; tears, after all, bear witness to misery. It can't yet speak, and it is already prophesying. What is it prophesying? That it is going to live in toil or in fear. Even if it lives a good life and is just, finding itself in the midst of trials and temptations, it will certainly always be afraid.

Start living loyally in Christ

2. What does the apostle say? *All who wish to live loyally in Christ will suffer persecution* (2 Tm 3:12). There you are, it's because the days are evil that the just cannot live here without persecution. Those who live among evil people suffer persecution; all the bad people persecute the good, not with steel and stones, but by their life and behavior. Was anyone persecuting the holy man Lot

211

in Sodom? Nobody was bothering him; and yet he was living among the ungodly, and amid the impure, the proud, the blasphemers he was suffering persecution, not by being beaten, but just by seeing the wicked.[3]

Any of you listening to me and not yet living loyally in Christ, start living loyally in Christ, and you will discover the truth of what I am saying. Finally, when the apostle was reminding us of the dangers he ran, *From dangers*, he said, *in the sea, dangers in rivers, dangers in the desert, dangers among robbers, dangers among false brethren* (2 Cor 11:26); the rest of the dangers can cease; dangers from false brethren cannot possibly cease until the end of the world.

Redeeming the time

3. Let us redeem the time, since the days are evil. You are waiting to hear from me, perhaps, what is meant by redeeming the time. I am going to say something that few can listen to, few put up with, few attempt, few can do. I will say it, all the same, since those few who are going to listen to me are living among the bad. Redeeming the time is this: when someone brings a lawsuit against you, lose something, so that you have time to spend on God, not on lawsuits. So lose it; what you lose is the price you pay for time.

Certainly when you go off downtown to supply your needs, you give cash and you buy yourself bread, or wine, or oil, or wood, or some household goods; you give and you receive, you lose something, gain something; that's what buying is. I mean, if you lose nothing, and start having what you didn't have, you have either found it, or received it as a gift, or inherited it. But when you lose something in order to get something, then you are buying; what you get is bought, what you lose is the price. So just as you lose cash in order to buy yourself something, in the same way lose cash in order to buy yourself peace and quiet. There you have what redeeming the time is.

A Punic proverb

4. There is a well-known Punic proverb, which I will of course quote to you in Latin, because you don't all know Punic. It's an old Punic proverb: "Pestilence is begging for a penny; give it two, and let it take itself off." Doesn't this proverb appear to have been born of the gospel? After all, what else did the Lord say but *Redeeming the time*, when he said, *If anyone wants to go to law with you and take away your shirt, let him have your coat as well* (Mt 5:40). He wants to go to law with you and take your shirt, he wants to distract you with lawsuits from your God; you won't have tranquillity in your heart, you won't have a quiet mind, your thoughts will be all upside down, you're exasperated against this opponent of yours. Just look, you see, you've lost, you've wasted, time. So how much better it is to lose cash, and redeem, buy back time!

My brothers and sisters, in your disputes and business cases which you bring to me for judgment,[4] if I tell a Christian person he should be ready to lose something of his in exchange for redeeming the time, how much more strictly am I bound in trust to tell him to restore what belongs to another? You see, both parties that I hear are Christians. Now that swindler, who wants to bring a case against another person and get something from him, at least by way of settlement, is delighted at these words: "The apostle said, *Redeeming the time, since the days are evil* (Eph 5:16). So now I can swindle that Christian; willy-nilly, he'll give me something to redeem the time, because he's heard what the bishop said."

Tell me though: if I am going to say to him, "Be prepared to lose something, in order to have leisure," am I not going to say to you, "Swindler, incorrigible spawn of the devil, why do you put so much effort into grabbing other people's property? You've no case at all, and you're full of trickery." So if I say to him, "Give him something, to get him to drop his false claims," where will you be, seeing that you will be getting money out of making false claims? He, having redeemed the time from you in order to avoid all that chicanery, puts up with evil days here; but you, because chicanery is your bread and butter, will have evil days here, and after these days you are going to get much worse ones on the day of judgment.

But you're probably laughing at this, because you've got away with the money. Laugh away, laugh, and turn away with a shrug. I for my part can only lay out an investment in you; the one who will demand the interest is yet to come.

NOTES

1. From what he says in section 4 below about a Punic proverb, and not all his congregation knowing that language, though the implication is that some did; and about their bringing him their disputes for arbitration, it seems clear to me that the sermon was preached in his own diocese, though not necessarily in the city of Hippo Regius itself.

2. Reading *dicuntur* with many manuscripts instead of the *ducuntur* of the text: that days are spent as evil, or that evil days are spent.

3. *Sed malos videndo.* The text actually reads *sed malos vivendo*, but I take this to be a misprint, as it makes no sense. Or, perhaps more likely, the word *inter*, among, has dropped out, and we should have, "but just by living among the wicked."

4. The arbitration of bishops in civil lawsuits was widely sought, and their decisions were upheld by imperial law. As his remarks show, they would commonly be inspired by evangelical and moral principles, rather than by legal rules and precedents. It was the one part of his duties as bishop that Augustine cordially detested, and indeed resented.

SERMON 167A

SERMON OF SAINT AUGUSTINE ON EPHESIANS 6:12

Date: unknown[1]

Our struggle

1. *Our struggle is not against flesh and blood,* because it is not only man that persecutes you, but also the devil acting through him; and before he hurts you in your body, he kills you in your mind.[2] *Our struggle is not against flesh and blood,* not one of human beings against human beings, who are flesh and blood, *but against princes and powers, the rulers of this darkness* (Eph 6:12). Because just as Christ governs and guides those who are light, so the devil pushes and prods those who are darkness into every kind of evil. So what the apostle is urging upon us, is that we should direct our prayers, not against the bad man, but against the devil who is operating with him, and that we should do whatever we can to get the devil driven out and the man set free.

Suppose, for example, you are stationed in the line of battle, and from the opposite side an armed man comes at you seated on a horse, you don't get angry with the horse but with the horseman, and you are eager to do what you can to hit the horseman and get possession of the horse. We should act in the same way with bad men, and work hard with everything we've got, not against them, but against the one who is prodding them from behind, so that while the devil is defeated, that unfortunate whom he had begun to possess may be set free.

If we wish to imitate Christ, we ought to run along the same road as Christ

2. *Whoever says he abides in Christ, ought himself to walk too, just as he walked* (1 Jn 2:6). What is the way along which Christ walked? What else can it be but charity, about which the apostle says, *I can show you a still more superlative way* (1 Cor 12:31)? So if we wish to imitate Christ, we ought to run along the same road as Christ was prepared to walk along, even while hanging on the cross. You see, he was fixed immovable to the cross, and yet running along the road of charity, by making supplication for his persecutors. In a word, this is what he said: *Father, forgive them, because they do not know what they are doing* (Lk 23:34). So let us also make continuous supplication for all our

214

enemies, that the Lord may grant them reform of their behavior and pardon for their sins.[3]

NOTES

1. A somewhat lost fragment of a sermon. The heading, taken I presume from the principal, or perhaps the only manuscript, actually runs, "Sermon of Saint Augustine on the same words of the apostle." They are not, however, on the same words as Sermon 167 is, so it would be absurd to put that heading here. What it suggests to me is that the manuscript is an anthology of short patristic comments on Eph 6:12; and the collector gives this as Augustine's contribution. The truth of the matter, as far as it is available, may be learned from the *Revue Bénédictine*, 84 (1974), to which I myself have not had access.

2. Another reading has "he kills himself in his heart." This clearly took the persecuting man as the subject, while our text assumes the devil to be the subject.

3. The second section is related in theme to the first, but starts from quite a different text. So it is more than likely that the sermon of which this is a fragment was not specifically on the Ephesians text at all.

SERMON 168

ON THE WORDS OF THE APOSTLE, EPHESIANS 6:23:
PEACE TO THE BRETHREN, AND CHARITY WITH FAITH, OR ON THE GRACE OF GOD,
ACCORDING TO THE CONFESSION AND TEACHING OF THE CHOSEN VESSEL,
THAT FAITH IS A GIFT OF GOD'S MERCY

Date: 416[1]

What you promise God carries out

1. May the Lord build up your minds through the readings, psalms and hymns, and divine utterances, and first and foremost by his grace, so that the truth you hear may be heard by you not to your condemnation but to your being rewarded. He will do this for you, because having made his promise, he has the power also to carry it out. Thus Abraham believed, giving God the glory, and thereby in fact most fully believing that he also has the power to carry out what he has promised. A great joy for us; he promised us to Abraham; we are *the children of the promise* (Gal 4:28). You see, when Abraham was told, *In your seed shall all the nations be blessed* (Gn 22:18), it is we that were promised.

So it was he that made us into children of the faith of Abraham, the one who has the power to do what he has promised. Nobody should say, "I did it." It's hardly the case, after all, that God makes the promise, and you keep it. It can, however, correctly be said that what you promise, God carries out. You, I mean, are weak, you are not almighty. So when you make a promise, unless God carries it out, your promise is an empty one. God's promise, on the other hand, doesn't depend on you, but on him.

"But I," you say, "have believed."

"I grant you. What you say is true; it is you that have believed; but it wasn't you that gave you faith. Now what did you believe by, if not by faith? Faith is in you the gift of God."

The faith of the demons is to be distinguished from the faith of the saints

2. Listen to the apostle, the very promoter of faith, the great champion of grace; listen to him saying, *Peace to the brethren, and charity with faith* (Eph 6:23). Three great things he mentioned: peace, charity, faith. He began at the

216

end, ended at the beginning. The beginning, you see, lies in faith, the end in peace. What we believe by, after all, is faith. But it should be the faith of Christians, not of demons; because, as the apostle James says, *The demons too believe, and tremble* (Jas 2:19). The demons too said to Christ, *You are the Son of God* (Mk 3:11). Demons confessed what men would not believe; they trembled at him, while these killed him. I mean, so what, just because the demons said, *You are the Son of God, we know who you are* (Mk 1:24)? Does that mean they are going to reign with the Son of God? Perish the thought!

So the faith of demons is to be distinguished from the faith of the saints. Certainly to be distinguished with all care and alertness. You see, Peter too said the same thing to the Lord when he asked, *Who do you say that I am? You are the Christ, the Son of the living God.* And the Lord answered, *Blessed are you, Simon Bar Jona* (Mt 16:15-17). "O Lord, the demons said the same thing to you; why aren't they blessed?"

"Why not? Because the demons said this out of fear, Peter out of love."

So one begins from faith. But what sort of faith? The sort defined by the apostle: *Neither circumcision is worth anything, nor uncircumcision, but faith.* Tell us what faith. *Which works through love* (Gal 5:6). This faith the demons don't have, the sort that works through love; but only the servants of God have it, only the saints of God, only the children of promise; that's why it also said, *and charity.*

Those are the three things mentioned by the apostle: *Peace to the brethren, and charity with faith* (Eph 6:23). *Peace to the brethren.* Where does peace come from? *And charity.* Where does charity come from? *With faith.* If you don't believe, you see, you don't love. So the apostle said, beginning like that from the end, and coming back to the beginning, *Peace, charity, with faith.* Let us, though, say, "Faith, charity, peace." Believe, love, reign. If you believe, you see, and don't love, you still haven't distinguished your faith from those who trembled and said, *We know who you are, the Son of God.* You, then, love; because charity with faith will itself escort you right through to peace. What peace? True peace, complete peace, solid peace, carefree peace; where there's no disease, no enemy. That peace is the final goal of all good desires. *Charity with faith*; even if you say it the other way round, you are saying it well: faith with charity.

Peace, charity with faith, only comes to you from God

3. So they are splendid goods, which the apostle has mentioned: *Peace to the brethren, and charity with faith*; splendid goods. But let him tell us where these good things come from; where are they from, ourselves, or from God? If you say, "From ourselves," you are boasting in yourself, not in God. But if you have learned the truth of what the apostle also says himself, *That whoever boasts, should boast in the Lord* (1 Cor 1:31); then confess that peace, charity with faith, only comes to you from God.

But you answer me, "That's what you say; prove what you are saying."

"I'll prove it; I'll call the apostle himself as a witness. Here you have it: the apostle said, *Peace to the brethren, and charity with faith.* He said it himself."

"What did he say?"

"Look; he continues, *Peace to the brethren, and charity with faith, from God our Father and the Lord Jesus Christ* (Eph 6:23). So *what have you got that you did not receive? But if you received it, why do you boast as though you did not receive it?* (1 Cor 4:7)."

Because if Abraham boasted, he boasted out of faith. What is complete and perfect faith? The faith that believes that all our good things come from God, even faith itself. Again the apostle says, *I obtained mercy*. What a marvelous confession! He didn't say, "I obtained mercy because I was faithful," but *in order that I may be faithful, I obtained mercy* (1 Cor 7:25).[2]

Saul was an unbeliever, but he obtained mercy

4. Let us come now to his origins, let us look at Saul raging, observe him raving, observe him breathing out hatred and thirsting for blood. Let us take a good look at him, brothers and sisters, a stupendous sight. Here we are, after the slaughter of Stephen, after the shedding of the blood of God's witness[3] with stones, when he kept the coats of those who were doing the stoning, so that he too was doing the stoning with their hands; that's when the brethren who had been gathered in Jerusalem were scattered abroad. And he, not satisfied in his rage with having seen and shed the blood of Stephen, received a commission from the chief priests to go to Damascus, and bring back in chains any Christians he found there.

And off he went. This was the road of Paul, whose road or way was not yet Christ, who was himself still Saul, not yet Paul. Off he went. What did he have in his heart? What else but evil? Give me any merits he had. If you're looking for merits in him, they are deserving of condemnation, not of liberation. So off he went to rage against the members of Christ, off he went to shed blood, off went the wolf who was going to be the shepherd. That's how he went on his way. There was no other way he could go about his business, given the reasons he had for going about it. And while he's walking along like that, thinking, breathing out slaughter; while wrath is guiding his feet, hatred moving his limbs, while he goes walking steadily on, the compliant slave and instrument of cruelty; and lo and behold, a voice from heaven, *Saul, Saul, why are you persecuting me?* (Acts 9:1-4).

There you are, that's why he said, *I obtained mercy, that I should be faithful* (1 Cor 7:25). He was an unbeliever: that's nothing; he was cruel in his unbelief. But he obtained mercy, that he should be faithful. What are you going to say to God, as he says, "That's my wish"?

"So, Lord, that man who did such dreadful things, who was only too eager to do such dreadful evils against your saints, you think he is worthy of such mercy as that?"

"That's my wish. *Or is your eye evil, because I am good?* (Mt 20:15)."

5. Have faith; but in order to have faith, pray in faith. But you wouldn't be able to pray in faith, unless you had faith. It is only faith, after all, that prays. *How,* you see, *will they call upon one in whom they have not believed? Or how will they believe one whom they have not heard? But how will they hear without a preacher? Or how will they preach, if they are not sent?* (Rom 10:14-15). That's why I'm talking, because I have been sent. Listen to me, listen to him through me.[4]

"So," somebody says, "we call upon God to grant us the ability to persevere in these good things that we have, and to add good things which we don't have. So the faith which makes the request has come first. Certainly God gives everything; after all it was in order that he should give to me that I made my request; to make my request, I first believed. So he gave me what I believed, and God gave me what as one believing I asked for."

The problem remains, and it's no small one. What I see you saying, is that you first gave something to God, so that he might give all the rest to you. You gave him, that is to say, your faith and your prayer. And where do you fit in what the apostle says: *For who has known the mind of the Lord, or who has been his counselor? Or who first gave to him, and will be repaid?* (Rom 11:34-35). There's the sort of person you want to be. So you first gave to God, and you gave him what God hasn't given to you? Did you find a supply to give it from? Beggar man, where did you get it from? So from what supply could you give it? Did you have anything? What, after all, have you got that you have not received?[5] So you give to God from what belongs to God; he receives from you some of what he has given you. Because your indigence and beggary, unless he had first given you something, would have remained a total void.

6. Listen to how you may satisfy yourselves on this point more clearly still. Yes, granted that you, because you have believed, have received; what can we say about those who haven't yet believed, such as Saul was, who hadn't yet believed? But he did receive that he should believe; after he believed in Christ, then he began to call upon Christ. It was from him that he received that he should believe, and by believing should call upon him, and by calling upon him should receive other things. What do we think, brothers and sisters? Before Saul believed, were those who did believe praying for him, or were they not? I would like to be told, if they weren't praying for him, why Stephen said, *Lord, do not hold this sin against them* (Acts 7:59). Prayer was being made both for him and for other unbelievers, that they might come to believe. There you are, they didn't yet have faith, and they received faith by the prayers of the faithful. They didn't yet have anything to offer to God, because they had not yet obtained mercy, *in order to be faithful* (1 Cor 7:25).

Finally, after this Saul had been converted, by a single voice hurled down, and lifted up, hurled down a persecutor, lifted up a preacher; after he had begun to proclaim the good news of the faith which he previously tried to devastate, what did he say about himself? *But I was unknown in person to the Churches of Judaea which are in Christ; they had only heard, though, that the one who used once upon a time to persecute us is now preaching the good news of the faith which he once tried to devastate; and in me they glorified God* (Gal 1:22-24). Did he say "And in me they glorified me"? And in me, who was proclaiming the good news of the faith I once tried to devastate, they didn't glorify me, but God. So he brought it about that Saul should lay aside the old garment, ragged with sins, bloody with slaughter, that he should lay aside that garment, and receive the garment of humility, and from Saul be turned into Paul.

What you were, you were by your own iniquity;
what you are, you are by God's grace

7. What does Paul mean? The least.[6] *For I am the least of the apostles.* There you have what Paul means; the Latin *paulum* means "a little." That's how we speak when we say "After a little I will see you; a little later I will do that." What's "*paulo* later"? A little later; "after *paulum*, after a little." So why the name Paul? Because little. Little because last. *For I am*, he said, *the last of the apostles, who am not worthy to be called an apostle, because I persecuted the Church of God* (1 Cor 15:9). You put it very well; from the one by whom you deserved to be condemned, you received what you would deserve to be given the prize for. From whom did you receive what you would deserve to be given the prize for?

Do you want to hear who he received it from? Don't listen to me, listen to him. *I am not worthy*, he said, *to be called an apostle, because I persecuted the Church of God; but by the grace of God I am what I am.* So what you were, you were by your own iniquity; what you are, you are by God's grace. *And his grace*, he goes on, *in me has not been idle.* There he is, preaching the good news of the faith he once tried to devastate; nor is grace idle in him, seeing he can say, *In me it has not been idle, but I have worked harder than all of them.*

"Watch it! You've started to boost yourself. Where are you, Paul, Tiny? Certainly you used to be little. *I have worked harder than all of them.* Tell us how you managed it. I mean, what have you got that you didn't receive?"

Immediately he had second thoughts; and after saying *I have worked harder than all of them*, it's as though his own words really scared him, and he straightaway submitted himself as the humble Paul: *Not I, however, but the grace of God with me* (1 Cor 15:9-10).

Pray for those who have not yet come to believe

8. So, my brothers and sisters, to help you realize that faith comes to us from the Lord God, pray for those who have not yet come to believe. If any of you has a friend who is not a believer, I urge you to pray for him. But is there really any need for me to urge you? The husband is a Christian, the wife an unbeliever;

doesn't he pray for his wife, that she may come to believe? The wife is a Christian, the husband an unbeliever; doesn't the religious woman pray for her husband, that he may come to believe? Whenever those who pray, pray for this, what are they praying for, but that God would give that person faith? So faith is a gift of God. Nobody should get a swollen head, nobody claim the credit for himself, as though he had given himself anything. *Whoever boasts, should boast in the Lord* (1 Cor 1:31).

NOTES

1. Paul is referred to in the title as "the chosen vessel," one presumes, because Augustine does allude in the sermon to his conversion, though without using this phrase himself. See Acts 9:15.

2. "Faithful" here, not in the elementary sense of being a believer, but in the sense, as is clear from the context, of being a faithful steward, trustworthy, true to his commitments and responsibilities. We have indeed constantly to remind ourselves that all these aspects are included in what Augustine means by faith. First and foremost it means *trusting* God absolutely. "Trust" would often be a better English word for it than "faith."

3. He uses the Latin word *testis*, where one might expect the Greek word, taken over into Latin as into English, "martyr."

4. One could take these last two sentences as words which Augustine is putting into Paul's mouth. But I think he is also asserting his own commission to preach the gospel.

5. 1 Cor 4:7.

6. That, or rather "small," or "tiny," is the meaning of the Latin word *paulus*. See Sermon 77, 3, note 7.

SERMON 169

ON THE WORDS OF THE APOSTLE PAUL, PHILIPPIANS 3:3-16: *FOR WE ARE THE CIRCUMCISION, WHO SERVE THE SPIRIT OF GOD*, ETC. AGAINST THE PELAGIANS

Date: 416[1]

The spirit governs; the flesh is governed

1. Would your holinesses please turn your ears and minds to the reading from the apostle, assisting me with your eagerness in the presence of the Lord our God, so that whatever he is pleased to reveal to me there, I may be able suitably and profitably to pass on to you. So, when it was read, you heard the apostle Paul saying, *For we are the circumcision, who serve the Spirit of God* (Phil 3:3). I know that several codices read *who serve God in spirit*. But as far as I have been able to examine them, most Greek texts have this reading: *who serve the Spirit of God.*[2]

But there is no particular problem there. Each, after all, is clear, and in harmony with the rule of truth; both that we serve the Spirit of God, and that we serve God not in the flesh but in spirit. You serve God in the flesh, you see, or in the manner of flesh, when you hope to please God with things of the flesh.[3] But when the flesh is itself subjected to the spirit for the performance of good works, then we serve God in the spirit, because we tame the flesh, so that the spirit may submit to God. The spirit, surely, governs, the flesh is governed; nor does the spirit govern well, if it is not governed itself.

We are justice

2. So when he says, *We are the circumcision*, consider what he wanted us to understand by that circumcision which was given as a shadow signifying things to come,[4] and set aside at the coming of the light. Why, though, he didn't say, "We have the circumcision," but *We are the circumcision*, take it as the apostle wanting to say, "We are justice." Circumcision, you see, stands for justice.[5]

Now by saying we are justice, he makes his point more effectively than he would if he said we are just; in such a way, however, that when he says "justice" we should understand "just." We are not, after all, that unchangeable justice of which we have been made partakers;[6] but just as one says "There's a lot of youth there," meaning many young people; so one can say justice, and understand by it just people. Listen to the same apostle saying the same thing more plainly: *That we*, he says, *may be the justice of God in him* (2 Cor 5:21). That we may be, not our justice, but God's; received from him, not taken over by us; imparted, not usurped; granted, not grabbed. Someone, in fact, did think equality with God was something to be grabbed;[7] and since he tried grabbing, he discovered missing his grip and falling.[8]

Our Lord Jesus Christ, however, *since he was in the form of God, did not think equality with God was something to be grabbed*; equality with God, after all, was natural to him, and so not something to be grabbed. *But*, all the same, *he emptied himself, taking the form of a servant* (Phil 2:6-7), *that we might be the justice of God in him* (2 Cor 5:21). You see, if he had shunned poverty, we would never be rid of poverty. In fact, *he became poor, though he was rich, in order that by his poverty*, as it is written *we might be enriched* (2 Cor 8:9). What are his riches going to make us, if his poverty made us rich?

So the apostle, then, hasn't denied you circumcision, but explained it; he has held up the light, displaced the shadow.[9]

The Lord's day

3. *We*, he says, *are the circumcision, who serve the spirit of God, and boast in Christ Jesus, and do not put our trust in the flesh* (Phil 3:3). He had certain people in mind who did put their trust in the flesh; they were the ones who boasted about circumcision in the flesh. In another place he says about them, *Whose God is their belly, and their boast in their shameful parts.*[10] As for you, understand circumcision, and be circumcision; understand and be; *understanding*, you see, *is good*; but *for all who carry it out* (Ps 111:10).

It was certainly not for nothing that the commandment was given for the child *to be circumcised on the eighth day* (Gn 17:12; Lv 12:3); it can only have been because the rock, the stone with which we are circumcised, was Christ. It was *with knives of rock*, or stone,[11] that the people was circumcised (Jos 5:2); *now the rock was Christ* (1 Cor 10:4). So why on the eighth day? Because in seven day weeks the first is the same as the eighth; once you've completed the seven days, you are back at the first. The seventh is finished, the Lord is buried; we are back at the first, the Lord is raised up. The Lord's resurrection, you see, promised us an eternal day,[12] and consecrated for us the Lord's day. It's called the Lord's, because it properly belongs to the Lord, because on it the Lord rose again. The rock has been restored to us, let those be circumcised who wish to say, *For we are the circumcision* (Phil 3:3).

You see, *He was handed over on account of our sins, and rose again on account of our justification* (Rom 4:25). Your justification, your circumcision, doesn't come from you. *It is by grace that you have been saved through faith; and this not from yourselves, but it is God's gift; not from works* (Eph 2:8-9). In case by any chance you should say, "I deserved it, that's why I received it." Don't think you received it by deserving it, because you wouldn't deserve it unless you had received it. Grace came before your deserving, or merit; it isn't grace coming from merit, but merit from grace. Because if grace comes from merit, it means you have bought it, not received it free, gratis, for nothing. *For nothing*, it says, *you will save them* (Ps 56:7).[13] What's the meaning of *For nothing you will save them*? You can find no reason in them to save them, and yet you save them. You give for nothing, you save for nothing. You precede all merits, so that my merits follow your gifts. Of course, of course you give for nothing, save for nothing, since you can find no reason for saving, and many reasons for condemning.

What is putting one's trust in the flesh?

4. So *we*, he says, *are the circumcision, who serve the Spirit of God, and boast in Christ Jesus* (Phil 3:3). *Whoever boasts should boast in the Lord* (1 Cor 1:31). *And do not put our trust in the flesh*. And what is putting one's trust in the flesh?

"Listen," he says. "*Although I*," he says, "*might have confidence even in the flesh. If anybody else thinks he has confidence in the flesh, I more so* (Phil 3:4). Don't imagine," he says, "that I am making light of something I haven't got. What's so wonderful if some marginal person, working class, common, makes light of nobility, and then shows true humility? *Although I*," he says, "*might have confidence even in the flesh*. That's how," he says, "I'm teaching you to make light of it, because you can see that I have got what I am making light of. *If anybody else thinks he has confidence in the flesh, I more so*."

Understand the sort of person Paul was

5. And just listen to his confidence in the flesh: *with circumcision of the eighth day*; that means, "I am not a proselyte, not a newcomer to the people of God, not circumcised as an adult, but born a Jew of my parents, I have the circumcision of the eighth day. *Of the race of Israel, of the tribe of Benjamin, a Hebrew of the Hebrews, according to the law a Pharisee* (Phil 3:5).

There were some people of the first rank, set apart, so to say, as a Jewish aristocracy, not mixed up with the common people of no account, who were called Pharisees. This word, you see, is said to signify a sort of segregation, like a word we have from the Latin, "egregious," as it were separated from the *grex* or flock.[14] Even those groups who had separated themselves, however, from the temple, were Israelites, that is, of the race of Israel. But there remained attached to the temple the tribe of Judah and the tribe of Benjamin. The tribe of Levi in the priests, the royal tribe of Judah, and the tribe of Benjamin; that was all that remained attached to Jerusalem and the temple of God, when that separation took place under the servant of Solomon. So you mustn't take lightly what he says, *of the tribe of Benjamin*; sticking to Judah, not withdrawing from the temple.

A Hebrew of the Hebrews, according to the law a Pharisee, as regards zeal, persecuting the Church (Phil 3:5-6). Among his merits he mentions the fact that he was a persecutor; *as regards zeal,* he says. What zeal? "I wasn't," he is saying, "a slack Jew. Anything that seemed to be hostile to my law, I took it badly, I had no patience with it, I would hunt it down mercilessly." That, with the Jews, is nobility; but with Christ what is looked for is humility. That's why he is Saul there, Paul here. He was called after Saul; you know who Saul was; he was chosen for his tall stature. That's how scripture describes him, that he was head and shoulders above them all, when he was chosen to be anointed as king.[15] It wasn't like that with Paul, but he became Paul.[16] *Paulus,* you see, means small; therefore Paul means little.

And so, *"As regards zeal,"* he says, *"persecuting the Church.* From this let people understand the sort of person I was among the Jews, persecuting the Church of Christ out of zeal for the ancestral traditions."

Saul was walking in the law without reproach

6. He adds: *As regards the justice which is in the law, in which I was without reproach* (Phil 3:6). Your graces know that Zachary and Elizabeth were said to have walked in all the justifications of the Lord without reproach. *In all the justifications of the Lord,* says scripture, *walking without reproach* (Lk 1:6). And here's our Paul exactly the same, when he was Saul. He was walking in the law without reproach; and it was precisely what was without reproach in him, that made of him a great reproach.[17]

So what are we to think, brothers and sisters? That being without reproach as regards the justice which is in the law, is something bad? If it's bad to be without reproach as regards the justice which is in the law, then is the law something bad? But we have the same apostle saying, *And so the law indeed is holy, and the commandment is holy, and just, and good* (Rom 7:12). If the law is holy, and the commandment holy and just and good, how can it not be good to conduct oneself without reproach as regards the justice which is from the holy law? How can it not be holy?

Or is it in fact holy? Let's listen to the apostle himself; see what he says: *The things that were for my profit, I have considered to be losses because of Christ.* He calls them his losses, and among his losses he reckons the fact that he was without reproach in the justice which is in the law. *All the same,* he says, *I also count everything as loss because of the surpassing knowledge of Christ Jesus our Lord.* I take a look, he says, at my several distinctions; I compare them with the surpassing eminence of our Lord Jesus Christ. As that's what I thirst for, I think nothing of this. That's saying nothing: *On whose account,* he says, *I not only judge all things to be a waste, but I have even reckoned them to be dung, that I may gain Christ* (Phil 3:7-8).

The law was a hindrance to Paul's coming to Christ

7. This has raised a major problem, Paul. If you were conducting yourself without reproach as regards the justice which is in the law, and if you count this as part of your waste material, your losses, as dung, in order to gain Christ, then

that justice was keeping you away from Christ, was it? I beg you, please explain this a little. Or rather let us ask God to enlighten us as well, just as he enlightened the man who wrote this letter to us, not in ink, but in the Spirit of the living God.[18]

You can see, dearly beloved, how hard, how difficult it is to understand this; when it's agreed that *the law is holy, and the commandment holy, and just and good* (Rom 7:12); and it's certainly agreed among faithful Catholics, so that nobody would disagree unless he doesn't want to be a Catholic, that this law was given by none other than the Lord our God;[19] how are we to understand that conducting himself without reproach as regards that justice which is in the law, was for the apostle a hindrance to his coming to Christ; and that he wouldn't have come to Christ, unless he had reckoned the fact of his having been without reproach according to the justice which is in the law, as so much loss, and wastage, and dung? So let us continue, and read a little further, and perhaps some light may dawn on us from the apostle's own words, by which this obscurity can be removed and dispelled.

I have come to believe, he says, *that all these things are waste, and I have reckoned them to be dung, that I might gain Christ.* Pay close attention, please. As losses, wastage, dung have I reckoned these things, among which I also mention the fact that I was without reproach as regards the justice which is in the law. So, *I reckoned all these things as wastage and dung, that I might gain Christ, and be found in him, not having my justice, which is from the law.*

(Those of you who have anticipated the solution in your minds, please think of yourselves as fast walkers traveling the road with slower people. Let your speed be held in check a little, in order not to leave your slower companion behind.)[20]

That I might gain Christ, he says, *and be found in him, not having my justice, which is from the law.* If he said *mine*, why did he add *from the law*? I mean, if it's from the law, how is it yours? Did you impose the law on yourself? God gave the law, God imposed the law, God commanded you to comply with the law. If the law didn't teach you how you ought to live, how could you have justice according to the law without reproach? If you have this according to the law, how can you say, *not having my justice, which is from the law, but that which comes through the faith of Christ, which is from God* (Phil 3:8-9)?

The apostle remembered God and was delighted

8. So now I will explain as best I can; may the one who holds you in his keeping give you a better insight, and grant you both understanding and appreciation. You see, if he grants you appreciation, he will also grant you application.[21] This, you see, is what I want to say: once the law of God has been stated—it has said itself, after all, *You shall not lust* (Ex 20:17; Rom 7:7)—so once the law of God has been stated, apart from those fleshly sacraments which were shadows of things to come;[22] anyone who felt afraid when the law of God had been stated, and thought he could fulfill its requirements by his own powers,

and did what the law commands, not for love of justice but for fear of punishment; such a person was indeed, as regards the justice which is from the law, a person without reproach; he doesn't steal, doesn't commit adultery, doesn't bear false witness, doesn't commit murder, doesn't covet his neighbor's property; he can do this, yes perhaps he can. How? Out of fear of punishment.

Although anyone who doesn't covet or lust for fear of punishment, well I think he does covet. Even a lion can be shooed off its prey by the terrifying threat of arms and weapons and the crowd of people perhaps surrounding it or coming to attack it; and yet the lion comes, the lion returns. It hasn't seized its prey, it hasn't either laid aside its evil intention. If that's what you're like, your justice is still the sort by which you take care not to get tortured. What's so great about being afraid of punishment? Who isn't afraid of it? What robber, what rascal, what villain? But this is the difference between your fear and the robber's; that the robber is afraid of the laws of men, and that's why he commits his robberies, because he hopes to get round the laws of men.[23] But you are afraid of the laws, afraid of the punishment, of one whom you cannot get round. I mean, if you could get round him, what wouldn't you have done? So with your lust too; it isn't love that eliminates it, but fear that represses it. The wolf at the sheepfold; when the dogs bark, it isn't love that removes him, but fear that drives him off. The wolf comes to the sheepfold; at the barking of the dogs and the shouting of the shepherds, the wolf slinks away from the sheepfold; still he always remains a wolf. Let him turn into a sheep; the Lord, you see, can even do that. But then it's his justice, not yours. Because as long as you have yours, you can fear punishment, not love justice.

So, my dear brothers and sisters, does iniquity have its delights, and justice not have any? Does what is evil delight us, and not what is good? It certainly does have its delights; but *The Lord will give delightfulness, and our land will yield its fruit* (Ps 85:12). Unless he first gives delightfulness, our land will have nothing but barrenness. So this is the justice that the apostle longed for, delighted in; he remembered God, and was delighted; his soul lusted and was on fire for the courts of the Lord;[24] and all the things that he used to value highly grew worthless, became losses, wastage, dung.

Paul was stumbling over the stone of stumbling

9. Hence also, you see, the fact that he persecuted the Church according to his zeal for his ancestral traditions;[25] it came about because he was establishing his own justice, not seeking God's justice.[26] Just notice, I mean, that was precisely why he was persecuting the Church. *So what shall we say?* says the same apostle in another place. *That the nations which were not pursuing justice, seized hold of justice.* But what sort? *The justice, though, which comes from faith* (Rom 9:30). *But the nations which were not pursuing justice,* the sort that is from the law, as though it were their very own, the sort that arises from the fear of punishment, not from the love of justice; because they *were not pursuing justice, they seized hold of justice; the justice, though, which comes from faith.*

But Israel, he says, *chasing after the law of justice, did not attain to the law.*[27] Why? Because not from faith. What does it mean, *Because not from faith*? He didn't hope in God, didn't ask for it from God, didn't believe in the one *who justifies the ungodly* (Rom 4:5) wasn't like the tax-collector casting his eyes to the ground, beating his breast and saying, *God, be gracious to me a sinner* (Lk 18:13).[28] Therefore, *chasing after the law of justice, he did not attain to the law. Why? Because not from faith, but as it were from works. For they stumbled over the stone of stumbling* (Rom 9:30-32).

There you have why Saul was persecuting the Church; when he was persecuting the Church, you see, he was stumbling over the stone of stumbling. Christ was lying, humble and lowly, on the ground; he was also, to be sure, in heaven, his flesh that had been raised from the dead having been lifted up there. But unless Christ were also lying on the ground, he wouldn't cry out to Saul, *Why are you persecuting me?* (Acts 9:4). So he was lying there, because he was displaying and had a preference for humility;[29] the other stumbled, because he couldn't see. And where did all this not seeing come from? From the tumor of pride. What's the tumor of pride? As though from his own justice; from the law indeed, but his own. What's "from the law"? Because in the commandments of the law. What's "from his own"? As though from his own powers. Love was lacking, the love of justice, the love of Christ's charity.

And where would he get love from? Fear alone possessed him, but it was keeping a place in his heart for the charity that was to come. While he was raging, head held high, boastful, priding himself among the Jews for persecuting the Church in the measure of his zeal for the ancestral traditions; while he seemed to himself to be right on top and high up, he heard from still higher up above the voice of our Lord Jesus Christ, already seated in heaven, and still recommending humility: "*Saul*," he said, "*Saul, why are you persecuting me? It is hard for you to lift your heels against the goad* (Acts 26:14).[30] I could leave you to it; I mean, it's you that would be hurt by my jabs, not me that would be broken by your heels. But I'm not leaving you to it. You are raging with fury, I am moved with pity. *Why are you persecuting me?* You see, I'm not afraid of you, that you may crucify me over again; but I want you to acknowledge me, in case you should kill, not me, but yourself."

Paul was horrified at his own justice

10. So the apostle was petrified, knocked down and laid low, raised up and patched up. The words, you see, were realized in him: *It is I that will strike, and I that will heal* (Dt 32:39). You see, it doesn't say, "I will heal and I will strike," but *I will strike, and I will heal.* I will strike you, and give myself to you. Thus being laid low, he was horrified at his own justice, in which he was certainly without reproach, praiseworthy, great, even glorious among the Jews; he reckoned it was waste, he thought it was loss, he counted it dung, *that he might be found in him, not having his own justice, which is from the law; but that which is through the faith of Christ, which is*, he says, *from God* (Phil 3:9).

But those now who stumbled over the stone of stumbling; what does the same apostle say about them? *Because not from faith*, he says, *but as though from works*. Because they, as though through their own justice, *stumbled at the stone of stumbling; as it is written: Behold, I am placing in Zion a stone of stumbling, and a rock of scandal; and whoever believes in him shall not be confounded* (Rom 9:32-33). Whoever believes in him, you see, will not have his own justice, which is from the law, though the law is good; but he will fulfill that very law not with his own justice but with that given by God. And in that way he will not be confounded. *Charity*, after all, *is the fullness of the law* (Rom 13:10). And where is this charity poured out from in our hearts? Certainly not from ourselves, but *through the Holy Spirit which has been given to us* (Rom 5:5).

So those people stumbled over the stone of stumbling and the rock of scandal. And he says about them, *Brothers, the good will of my heart and my prayer to God is for them unto salvation*. The apostle is praying for those who don't believe, that they may believe; for those who have turned away, that they may turn back to God. You can see how not even this turning back or conversion happens without God's help. *My prayer*, he says, *to God is for them unto salvation. For I bear them witness that they have the zeal of God*. Just as he too used to have it himself; he used to have the zeal of God. *But not according to knowledge*. What's this, *not according to knowledge*? *For being ignorant of God's justice, and wishing to establish their own* (Rom 10:1-3). That's why, when this man was put right, he said, "*Not having my own justice* (Phil 3:9). While they wish to establish their own, still enjoy lying in the muck, I on the other hand do not have my own justice, but that which is through the faith of Christ, justice from God; justice, I repeat, from God, *who justifies the ungodly* (Rom 4:5)."

Let there be justice in you, but let it be from grace

11. Remove yourself, remove, I repeat, yourself from yourself; you just get in your own way. If it's you that are building yourself, it's a ruin you're building. *Unless the Lord has built the house, they have labored in vain, who build it* (Ps 127:1). So stop wishing to have your own justice. Certainly it's from the law, yes obviously it's from the law; certainly God has given the law—and because justice is from the law, don't let it be yours. It's the apostle Paul speaking; those who love their own justice mustn't put the blame on me. Here's where you can find him.[31] Open it, read, listen, see. Don't have your own justice; the apostle counts it as dung, even though it's from the law, but still because it's his own. *For being ignorant of God's justice, and wishing to establish their own, they did not subject themselves to the justice of God* (Rom 10:3).

Don't think that just because you call yourself a Christian, you cannot for that reason stumble over the stone of stumbling. When you disparage his grace, you stumble over him. It's less serious to stumble at Christ hanging on the cross than at Christ seated in heaven. Let there be justice in you, but let it be from grace, let it come to you from God; don't let it be your own. *Let your priests*, it says, *vest themselves with justice* (Ps 132:16). A vestment is received, it doesn't grow with your hair; sheep are clothed with what is their own. This is what the apostle Paul preached: "Let it come to you from God." Sigh to obtain it, weep to obtain it, believe in order to obtain it. *Whoever calls upon the name of the Lord*, he says, *shall be saved* (Rom 10:13; Jl 2:32). Or do you suppose that when it says, *Whoever calls upon the name of the Lord shall be saved*, it means from malaria, or the pox, or the gout, or any other pain of the body?[32] Not so, but *will be saved* means "will be just." Because, *The doctor is not needed by the healthy, but by the sick*; he explained that when he said, *I have not come to call the just, but sinners* (Mk 2:17).[33]

Recognize the power of Christ's resurrection

12. So notice what comes next: *And may be found*, he says, *in him, not having my own justice which is from the law*; still mine, though, even if from the law; *but that which is through the faith of Christ*, which is obtained from God; *which is from God, justice in faith, in order to know him and the power of his resurrection* (Phil 3:9-10). It's something great, to recognize the power of Christ's resurrection. Are you thinking that this is what's great, that he raised up his own flesh? Is that what he meant by the power of his resurrection? Won't it also be our resurrection at the end of time? Won't this perishable thing of ours also put on imperishability, and this mortal thing put on immortality?[34] Just as he has risen from the dead, and now dies no more, and *death will have no more dominion over him* (Rom 6:9), won't the same happen to us too, and if I may say so, more wonderfully still? His flesh, after all, did not see corruption,[35] but ours is to be restored from ashes.

It is indeed something great that he went first as an example, and gave us something to hope for; but that's not all there is to it for this man, who was talking about a justice not his own, but the sort which is from God, and in that connection mentioned the power of Christ's resurrection; recognize here your own justification. You see, it's as a result of his resurrection that we are justified, as though we were being circumcised by a flint knife, by rock. That's why he began from there: *We are the circumcision* (Phil 3:3). Circumcision by what? By rock. By what rock? By Christ. How? On the eighth day—just as the Lord rose again on the Lord's day.

Without your will, there will be no justice of God in you

13. So, my brothers and sisters, let us hold onto this justification insofar as we have it, and let us grow in it insofar as we are still small and immature, and let us bring it to perfection when we arrive at the place where we shall say, *Where, death, is your victory? Where, death, is your sting?* (1 Cor 15:55). But the whole thing is from God; not however as though we were asleep, as though we didn't have to make an effort, as though we didn't have to be willing. Without your will, there will be no justice of God in you. The will, indeed, is only yours,

the justice is only God's. There can be such a thing as God's justice without your will, but it cannot be in you apart from your will. You have been shown what you have to do. The law has laid down, "Don't do that, nor that; do this and that." It's been shown to you, laid down for you, your mind has been opened for you,[36] you have understood what you should do. Beg for the power to do it, if you know the power of Christ's resurrection.

He was handed over, you see, *because of our wrongdoing, and he rose again because of our justification* (Rom 4:25). What does *because of our justification* mean? In order to justify us, to make us just. You will be God's work, not only because you are human, but also because you are just. It is better, after all, to be just, than for you just to be human. If it was God that made you human and if it's you that make you just, it means you are making something better than God made.

But God made you without you. You didn't, after all, give any consent to God making you. How were you to consent, if you didn't yet exist? So while he made you without you, he doesn't justify you without you. So he made you without your knowing it, he justifies you with your willing consent to it. Yet it's he that does the justifying (in case you should think it's your justice, and go back to the dead losses, the wastage and the muck), for you to be found[37] in him not having your own justice, *which is from the law, but the justice through the faith of Christ, which is from God; justice from faith, to know him and the power of his resurrection, and a share in his sufferings* (Phil 3:9-10). And that will be your power, your strength; a share in Christ's sufferings will be your strength.

God can only be loved by virtue of God's gift

14. What, though, will be sharing in the sufferings of Christ, if charity isn't? Can't brigands be found, of such physical courage under torture, that some of them have not only refused to betray their accomplices, but haven't even deigned to confess their own names? In agony, in torment, their flanks torn to ribbons, their bodily organs practically destroyed, the spirit has remained worthlessly obstinate to the bitter end. So consider what it was they loved. At least they couldn't have done all that without some great love.

But that's not what the lover of God is like. God can only be loved by virtue of God's gift. That man loved goodness knows what else by virtue of the flesh, as a man. Whatever he loved, whether he loved his comrades, loved the consciousness of his crimes, loved the renown gained by his misdeeds; whatever he loved, he loved it very much, if he could be tortured, and could not be broken down. So if he couldn't—the man who could be tortured and couldn't be broken down—so if he couldn't endure such terrible things without love; then neither can you share in Christ's sufferings without love.

Receive this rich guest. Your space will be widened,
not narrowed down

15. But what I'm asking you, is what sort of love? Don't let it be cupidity, but let it be charity. *If,* he says, you see, *I hand over my body to burn, and do not have charity, it does me no good* (1 Cor 13:3). For a share in Christ's sufferings to do you good, charity must be present. Where can you get charity from? O most needy and indigent infirmity, where can you get God's charity from? Do you want me to show you where you can get it from? Ask the Lord's own storekeeper here.[38] You see, if God's charity is found in you, you will really share in Christ's sufferings and will be a true martyr; the person in whom charity is given the prize, that's who will be the true martyr. So where can you get it from? *We have this treasure in earthen vessels,* says this same apostle, *so that the prominence of the power may be God's and not from us* (2 Cor 4:7). So where do you get charity from, if not because *it has been poured out in our hearts through the Holy Spirit who has been given to us* (Rom 5:5)?

There you have what you should be sighing for. Ignore your own spirit, receive the Spirit of God. Don't let your spirit be afraid that when the Spirit of God takes up residence in you, your spirit will be squeezed into a corner of your body. When the Spirit of God takes up residence in your body, it won't shut your spirit out; don't worry. If you receive some rich man as a guest, you suffer from lack of space; you can't find anywhere to stay yourself, where to get a bed ready for him, where to put his wife, his children, his retinue. "What am I to do?" you say. "Where am I to go, where am I to move to?"

Receive this rich guest, the Spirit of God. Your space will be widened, not narrowed down. "You have widened your steps under me," you say.[39] To this guest of yours you are going to say, *"You have widened my steps under me"* (Ps 18:36). When you weren't here, I was enduring straightened circumstances. "You have filled my apartment, and not shut me out, but my straightened circumstances." You see, when it says, *The charity of God has been poured out,* that very pouring out signifies spaciousness and width. So don't be afraid of being squeezed out; receive this guest, and don't let him be one of those passing guests. You see, he has nothing to give you on departure.[40] Let him come and take up residence in you, and he has given it you. Be his, don't let him leave you, don't let him move on from there; hold on to him altogether, and say to him, *Lord our God, take possession of us* (Is 26:13 LXX).

The apostle recognizes that he is not perfect

16. So to this end, he says, let us have the justice which is from God, in order to know him, and the power of his resurrection, and a share in his sufferings, being conformed to his death. *For we have been buried,* he says, *together with Christ through baptism into death; in order that, just as Christ rose from the dead, so we too may walk in newness of life* (Rom 6:4). Die, in order to live; be buried, in order to rise again. When you've been buried, you see, and risen again, then will really come true, "Lift up your hearts."[41] You like what I said; would

this sermon be to your taste, if there wasn't already within you some internal sweetness?

Being conformed, he says, *to his death, if somehow I might attain to the resurrection of the dead* (Phil 3:10-11). He was talking about justice, the justice which is from the faith of Christ, the justice which is from God, and in this way he has followed everything up. And while he was looking for justice when he said, *That I may be found in him not having my own justice which is from the law, but the justice which is from the faith of Christ, which is from God* (Phil 3:9); he now says, *If somehow I might attain to the resurrection of the dead.* Why did you say "If somehow I might attain"? *Not that I have already obtained it, or am already perfect; but I follow after, if somehow I might grasp it, insofar as I have also been grasped by Christ Jesus* (Phil 3:11-12). His justice has gone ahead of me, let mine follow him. Mine, though, will only follow him when and if it is not mine.

If somehow I might attain. Not that I have already obtained, or am already perfect. When people heard the apostle saying, *If somehow I might attain; not that I have already obtained, or am already perfect*, it started them wondering. What is there that he hadn't yet obtained? He had faith, he had virtue, he had hope, he was aflame with charity, he worked miracles, he was an unsurpassable preacher, he bore with all kinds of persecution, patient in all circumstances, loving the Church, carrying in his heart his concern for all the Churches.[42] What hadn't he yet obtained? *Not that I have already obtained, or am already perfect.* What's this you're saying? You say it, and we wonder; you say it, and we are amazed. I mean we know what we are hearing; what are you saying?[43] *Brothers*, he says. What is it you're saying? What are you saying? *I do not consider myself to have grasped.* "Don't," he says, "have false ideas about me; I know myself better than you do. If I don't know what I'm lacking, I don't know what I've got. *I do not consider myself to have grasped. One thing, though* (Phil 3:13); this is what I do not consider I have grasped. I have many things, and one thing I have not yet grasped. *One thing I have asked of the Lord, this will I seek.* What have you asked, and what are you seeking? *That I may dwell in the house of the Lord for all the days of my life.* What for? *To contemplate the delight of the Lord* (Ps 27:4). That's the one thing which the apostle was saying he had not yet grasped; and to the extent he still lacked it, to that extent he was not yet perfect.

Martha and Mary

17. You remember, my brothers and sisters, that gospel reading where the two sisters received the Lord, Martha and Mary. Of course you do. Martha was going about all the business of serving, and was taken up with the care of the house; she had, of course, received the Lord and his disciples as guests. She had her hands full, taking care most religiously to see that these holy people came to no harm in her house. So while she was taken up with all the service, Mary her sister was sitting at the Lord's feet, and listening to his talk. Martha, working hard, got very cross when she saw her sitting there and not caring about her

work, and she appealed to the Lord: *Do you think it right, Lord*, she said, *that my sister has deserted me, and here I am, working so hard at the serving? And the Lord said, Martha, Martha, you are busy with so much. On the other hand, one thing is necessary. Mary has chosen the better part, which will not be taken away from her* (Lk 10:38-42).

You have chosen a good part, but she a better one. You a good one—it is good, after all, to spend one's time in attending to the saints—but she a better one. And then, what you have chosen comes to an end. You are serving the hungry, serving the thirsty, making beds for people to sleep on, offering your house to those who wish to stay there. All these things come to an end. The time will come when nobody's hungry, nobody's thirsty, nobody sleeps. So your concern will be taken away from you. *Mary has chosen the better part, which will not be taken away from her.* She has chosen to contemplate, chosen to live on the Word.[44] What will life on the Word be like without any word? Right now she was living on the Word, but on the word that makes a sound. There is going to be life on the Word, with no word making a sound. The Word itself is life. *We shall be like him, since we shall see him as he is* (1 Jn 3:2). That was the one and only life, to contemplate the delight of the Lord (Ps 27:4). This we cannot do, though, in the dark night of this world. *In the morning I will stand before you and contemplate* (Ps 5:3). Therefore, *I*, he says, *do not consider myself to have grasped. One thing, though* (Phil 3:13).[45]

Keep on walking

18. So what am I to do? *Forgetting what lies behind, stretched out to what lies ahead, I follow the direction*—I'm still following—*toward the palm of God's summons up above in Christ Jesus* (Phil 3:13-14).[46] I am still following, still forging ahead, still walking, still on the road, still extending myself; I haven't yet arrived. So if you too are walking, if you are extending yourself, if you are thinking about the things that are to come, forget what's past, don't look back at it, or you may stick there where you turn to look back. *Remember Lot's wife* (Lk 17:32).

As many then as are perfect, let us have this mind. He had just said, "I am not perfect," and now he says, *As many as are perfect, let us have this mind! I do not consider myself to have grasped. Not that I have already obtained, or am already perfect*; and he says *As many as are perfect, let us have this mind!* Perfect, and not perfect; perfect travelers, not yet perfect possessors.

And to show you that he means perfect travelers—those who are now walking along the road are perfect travelers—to show you he meant travelers, not residents, not possessors, listen to what follows. *As many then as are perfect, let us have this mind. And if you have other ideas*, in case perhaps the idea creeps into your mind that you are something; but *whoever thinks he is something when he is nothing, is deceiving himself* (Gal 6:3). And *whoever thinks he knows something, does not yet know as he ought to know* (1 Cor 8:2). Therefore: *And if you have other ideas*, like little children, *that too God will reveal to you.*

Nevertheless, to the extent that we have arrived, let us go on walking in it (Phil 3:15-16). That God may reveal to us even what we have other ideas about to the extent that we have arrived,[47] that we should not stay in it, but go on walking in it. You can see that we are travelers.

You ask, "What does walking mean?" I'll tell you very briefly; it means forging ahead, in case you should possibly not understand, and start walking sluggishly. Forge ahead, my brothers and sisters; always examine yourselves without self-deception, without flattery, without buttering yourselves up. After all, there's nobody inside you before whom you need feel ashamed, or whom you need to impress. There is someone there, but one who is pleased with humility; let him test you. And you, too, test yourself. Always be dissatisfied with what you are, if you want to arrive at what you are not yet. Because wherever you are satisfied with yourself, there you have stuck. If, though, you say, "That's enough, that's the lot," then you've even perished. Always add some more, always keep on walking, always forge ahead. Don't stop on the road, don't turn round and go back, don't wander off the road. You stop, if you don't forge ahead; you go back, if you turn back to what you have already left behind; you wander off the road, if you apostatize. The lame man on the road goes better than the sprinter off the road.

Turning to the Lord, etc.

NOTES

1. Preached at the shrine of Saint Cyprian in Carthage.

2. Not exactly Augustine the textual critic, which he was not, in any sense at all; but Augustine the serious student of scripture, aware of scriptural problems. However, he was a little hasty in assuming that his Greek texts supported his first Latin text unequivocally. He should have remembered that Greek has no ablative case in addition to the dative, like Latin. So while the Greek does indeed support the genitive "of God," it could mean, in fact probably does mean, "we serve (worship) in the Spirit of God." The alternative Latin texts are: *qui Spiritui Dei servimus*, and *qui spiritu Deo servimus*; a more likely rendering of the Greek he mentions would be *qui Spiritu Dei servimus/colimus*.

3. He has in mind, presumably, naively superstitious modes of worship—or the kind of absolute reliance on rituals and sacrifices satirized in Ps 50.

4. See Heb 10:1.

5. He nowhere spells out his justification for this somewhat arbitrary identification of circumcision with justice, though it could be teased out of the complexities of his sermon. The steps would be something like this: circumcision, eighth day, resurrection, justification, justice. Readers may decide for themselves whether I have got it right.

6. He means the Platonic idea of justice: Justice-in-itself.

7. See Phil 2:6. He is referring to Adam, in stark contrast to Christ.

8. Neater in the Latin: *et quoniam quaesivit rapinam invenit ruinam*.

9. An extremely confused section, which must have left his congregation's heads reeling.

10. Phil 3:19. Augustine (or possibly his text) makes Paul's words "in their shame" more coarsely explicit: *in pudendis eorum*.

11. The connection between Christ and the flint knives with which Joshua circumcised the people is easier to make in Augustine's Latin, where the knives are *cultelli petrini*, the adjective from *petra*, rock.

12. Which is precisely the first day, considered as the eighth after the sabbath of the seventh.

13. Even in the Latin text, this verse means in its context something quite different from what Augustine understands: "In no way at all will you save them"; or else it is an indignant question: "Will you let them off scot-free?"

14. He is correct in his explanation of the name Pharisee. It was a genuine *apartheid* concept. He goes on immediately to mention another, apparently less worthy, kind of separation, that of the tribes of the northern kingdom breaking away from the son of Solomon; see 1 Kgs 12.

15. See 1 Sm 10:23; also 9:2, and indeed the whole two chapters 9-10.

16. What he seems to mean is that Paul did not get his name from any intrinsic quality of greatness comparable to Saul's stature, but that he *became* Paul, changed his name, or had it changed for him, to signify littleness: the opposite of Saul's stature.

The text here is possibly dubious. The manuscripts have what I have translated: *Non fuit sic Paulus, sed factus paulus*. But some printed editions read *Non fuit sic Saulus, sed* . . . : "It wasn't like that with Saul," meaning *this* Saul of the New Testament. For the Latin distinguishes between *Saul* for the Old Testament character and *Saulus* for the pre-conversion apostle.

17. That is, I take it, it was his irreproachable observance of the law that made him a persecutor.

18. See 2 Cor 3:3.

19. This is an allusion to the Manichees' denial that the old law was given by the God and Father of our Lord Jesus Christ.

20. Some rather noisy demonstration of having got the point must have prompted this mild rebuke to the quicker wits of the class.

21. Better in Latin: *Donabit enim effectum, si donabit affectum.*

22. See Heb 10:1. He means what the scholastics will classify as the ceremonial precepts of the law, as distinct from the moral ones.

23. I don't think he has in mind the robber's hope of not being caught. He talks of deceiving, *fallere*, the laws of men. So what he has in mind appears to be the robber's hope, the big criminal's, of "perverting the course of justice."

24. He is echoing a mixture of Ps 77:3 and 84:2.

25. See Gal 1:14.

26. See Rom 10:3.

27. Omitting "of justice" with most of the manuscripts. It reflects the Latin Vulgate reading, but not the most authentic Greek text.

28. The "he" of this passage is both Israel and Paul while still Saul the persecutor.

29. I translate *humilitatem praeferebat* twice, giving both possible senses of *praeferebat*.

30. This is the only place in the most authentic Greek texts where the second sentence occurs. Naturally enough, however, it found its way also into the first account of Paul's conversion, Acts 9:4-5, though not always quite in the same place. Had you asked Augustine which passage he was quoting from, he would no doubt have found it impossible to tell you.

31. At this point, one imagines, he thumped the book of Paul's letters on the pulpit in front of him, or waved it at the people.

32. The Latin *salvus* primarily means "safe and sound," in good health. Augustine is at pains to stress that it more profoundly means what being saved ordinarily means in English.

33. And so "being saved," *salvus*, means being changed by the doctor from sick to healthy, by Christ from being a sinner to being just.

34. See 1 Cor 15:53.

35. See Ps 16:10; Acts 2:27.

36. See Lk 24:45. Reading with several manuscripts, *apertum est tibi cor*, instead of the text, *apertum est tibi, si tibi est cor*: it has been opened to you, if you have a mind.

37. Reading *inveniri* instead of the text's *invenire*, which is probably just a misprint.

38. He means Saint Paul.

39. You say this, presumably, to the rich cuckoo you have taken into your nest, parodying the psalm which you will quote in its proper form to the Holy Spirit.

40. Such as payment for board and lodging given by passing guests on their departure.

41. Appreciative applause at this point.

42. See, chiefly, 2 Cor 11:22-29.

43. "We" in this passage are dramatically the Philippians, interrupting Paul after verse 12, and being answered from verse 13 on.

44. He will be playing on the word "word" for all he is worth, so that it becomes difficult to decide sometimes whether to spell it with a capital W or not. When in doubt, capitalize!

45. I am sure Augustine knew he was being very willful in punctuating Paul's text like this. He had few scruples about doing this sort of thing, if it yielded good sermon or meditation material. He couldn't resist the word "One."

46. I am following my usual practice of keeping the translation of scriptural quotations as literal as possible; which makes this particular text rather hard to decipher. "Direction" renders *secundum intentionem*, which is more obscure than the Greek, which has "toward the mark." Paul himself was probably getting his images a little mixed—not unusual for him. He is both answering a summons from on high, and running in a marathon toward a distant mark, to win a prize.

47. He takes the other ideas that people may have (which are by implication wrong ideas) as being the notion that we have already arrived. Well, maybe, he says, we have arrived somewhere. May God reveal to us that we shouldn't stay there, but keep on walking.

SERMON 170

ON THE SAME WORDS OF THE APOSTLE, PHILIPPIANS 3:6-16: *ACCORDING TO THE JUSTICE WHICH IS FROM THE LAW, I WAS WITHOUT REPROACH,* ETC.

Date: 417[1]

Justice from the law

1. The divinely inspired readings are all so connected with each other, that they almost make one reading; because they all proceed from one mouth. Many are the mouths of those who exercise the ministry of the word; but he that fills the ministers has only one mouth.

We heard the reading from the apostle, and perhaps some of you may be worried by what is written there: *According to the justice which is from the law, I was without reproach. Whatever was a gain for me, that I have regarded as a dead loss on account of Christ.* Then he went on to say, *I have reckoned it to be not only a dead loss, but even muck, that I may gain Christ, and may be found in him, not having my own justice which is from the law, but the justice which is from the faith of Jesus Christ* (Phil 3:6-9). The question is, how could he consider conducting himself without reproach according to the justice which is from the law, to be so much muck and loss? After all, who gave the law? Wasn't the one who first put the law in place, the same as the one who later came with relief for those whom the law held to be guilty? Did the law, though, hold guilty those who behaved without reproach according to the justice which is from the law? So if the Lord brought relief and pardon of sins for those guilty under the law, didn't he bring any for the apostle Paul, who says he conducted himself without reproach under the law?

But let us listen to what he says in another place: *It was not as a result of works,* he says, *which we have done ourselves, but according to his own mercy that he saved us, by means of the bath of rebirth* (Tit 3:5). And again: *I, who was previously a blasphemer and persecutor, and an overbearing man; but I obtained mercy,* and so on (1 Tm 1:13). On the one hand he affirmed that he conducted himself without reproach; on the other he confessed he had been a sinner of such proportions, that no sinners need despair of themselves, precisely because even Paul had qualified for remission.[2]

238

They were given a law, not to cure them
but to prove to them that they were sick

2. Consider, brothers and sisters, and take a good, hard look at this expression, how the apostle Paul reckons as a dead loss and as muck the time when he says he conducted himself without reproach. On the one hand fulfilling the law, on the other hand guilty under the law, all at one and the same time, before baptism, before grace. But it is not without reason that he says it is all a dead loss:[3]—and don't let poisonous thoughts creep in, such as that the reason the apostle Paul said this is that there was one giver of the law and another giver of the gospel. That's what the Manichees suppose, with their twisted minds, and the other heretics[4] who said that there was one giver of the law which was given through Moses, and another bestower of the grace of the gospel; the first a bad God, the second a good God.

Why should we be surprised, brothers and sisters? In the obscurity of the law, as though behind locked doors, they endured thick darkness because they didn't knock with humble devotion.[5] We find the same Paul saying as plainly as could be *that the law is good* (Rom 7:12); yet the reason it was given, he says, was that sin might abound; and the reason sin abounded was that *grace might abound all the more* (Rom 5:20). You see, people were presumptuously relying on their own powers, and while doing whatever they judged was allowed them, they were sinning against a hidden law of God.[6] That's why this law was brought out into the open, and promulgated to people who considered themselves to be entirely guiltless. They were given a law, not to cure them but to prove to them that they were sick. The law ran ahead of the doctor, so that the sick person who thought he was in good health might discover how sick he really was; and it said, *You shall not covet* (Rom 7:7; Ex 20:17).

And because there was no transgression before the law was given—*for where there is no law*, he says, *neither is there any transgression* (Rom 4:15)—sins were indeed committed previously without the law; but once the law was given, committing sin was a graver matter, because it involved transgression. When, what's more sin involved transgression,[7] man discovered that he was being overcome by his greedy appetites, which he had been fostering against himself by his bad habits, seeing that from Adam on the race had been propagated together with the drag and liability of sin. That's why the apostle says, *We too were once by nature children of wrath* (Eph 2:3). So it is that not even a baby one day old is said to be clean of sin[8]—not the sin it has committed, but the sin it has contracted.

Absence of sin in Christ

3. Listen to the psalm speaking of our inner life, and singing about the more hidden aspects of our sins. Christ is being addressed by the psalmist, speaking for the human race as a whole: *Against you alone have I sinned, and done what is evil in your presence.* David is not saying this as an individual, but in the person of Adam, from whom comes the human race.[9] I mean, listen to what

follows: *Against you alone have I sinned, and done what is evil in your presence; that you may be justified in your words.* Christ is being spoken to; how can we tell this? Listen to what follows: *and may overcome when you are judged* (Ps 51:4). God the Father wasn't judged; God the Holy Spirit wasn't judged; we find that the Son alone was judged, in this flesh, which he was prepared to accept from our human lump—not by way of the lust of a man and a woman; his mother believed as a virgin, conceived as a virgin, bore him as a virgin, remained a virgin.

And that's why it says, *and may overcome when you are judged.* He was judged, you see, and he overcame because he was without sin when he was judged. For him, to be put on trial was a matter of patience, not of guilt. Many innocent people, sure, are put on trial; but they are innocent of whatever they are accused of; because for the rest they are not lacking in sin; because just as for a human court sin is a matter of a deed done, so for God's judgment sin is also a matter of thoughts thought. In God's eyes your thoughts are also your deeds. The witness to this deed is the judge himself; the prosecutor is your own conscience.

So he really was innocent when he was judged, and that is why he overcame. He alone won the case, not from the judge Pontius Pilate, nor from the Jews raging against him, but from the very devil himself, who pries into all our sins with the busy industry of envy.

Original sin

4. And what had the Lord Jesus got to say about this very devil? *Behold, the prince of this world is coming* (Jn 14:30). Now your graces have often been told that by "this world" sinners are being referred to. And why are sinners referred to under the name of the world? Because they live in the world by loving the world. Those, you see, who don't love the world, don't live in what they don't love. *The company we keep,* he says, *is in heaven* (Phil 3:20). So if those who love God live in heaven with God, those who love the world live in the world with the prince of the world.

And so it's all the lovers of the world who are themselves the world. They live in the world, not only in the flesh which all the just do too; but also in the spirit, which only sinners do, whose prince is the devil. It's the same as the way "house" can mean the inhabitants of the house; in this way of speaking we can say a mansion of marble is a bad house, and a shack full of smoke is a good house. You find a shack full of smoke where good people live, and you say, "It's a good house." You find a mansion, all marble and fine panelling, owned by wicked people, and you say, "It's a bad house," meaning by "house" not the walls and the rooms for bodies to be put in, but its actual occupants. In the same way scripture meant by "world" those who live in the world by their greedy love of it, not just by their bodily presence in it.

So, *Behold,* he says, *the prince of the world is coming, and in me he can find nothing.* He was the only one in whom the devil could find nothing. And as though he were asked, "So why must you die then?" he continues there: *But that all may know that I do my Father's will, arise, let us go hence* (Jn 14:30-31). He rises, and goes to his passion. Why? *Because I do my Father's will.*

So it is because of this quite unique innocence that the psalm says, *Against you alone have I sinned, and done what is evil in your presence, that you may be justified in your words, and may overcome when you are judged,* because he could find not a hint of evil in you. Why could he find it in you, though, O human race? Because it goes on to say, *For I myself was conceived in iniquity, and in sins did my mother conceive me* (Ps 51:4-5). It's David saying this; inquire how David was born; you will discover that it was of a lawful wife, not of adultery. So in terms of what sort of propagation does he say *I was conceived in iniquity*? It can only be that there is here a kind of propagation or transmission of death, which every person contracts who is born of the union of man and woman.

We know we are sick, let us cry for the doctor

5. So since we all have lustful or covetous appetites, let us pay attention to the law which says, *You shall not covet* (Rom 7:7; Ex 20:16). We find in ourselves something the law forbids, we become guilty under the law. Since, though, we also find within ourselves the one to whom we are subject,[10] let us now start saying, *I take delight in the law of God according to the inner self; but I see another law in my members, fighting back against the law of my mind, and taking me prisoner to the law of sin, which is in my members* (Rom 7:22-23). We know we are sick, let us cry for the doctor: *Unhappy man that I am; who will deliver me from the body of this death?* Let the doctor reply: *The grace of God, through Jesus Christ our Lord* (Rom 7:24-25).

The grace of God, not your own merits. So why then did you say that you conducted yourself in the law with justice without reproach? Pay attention, please: he meant without the reproach of men. There is, you see, a kind of justice which a person can fulfill, so that no other human person can complain about that person. It says, after all, *Do not covet what belongs to another* (Ex 20:16). If you, though, don't grab what belongs to another, there will be no reproach or complaint against you from men. So sometimes you covet, and don't grab. But God's judgment hangs over you, because you covet; you are guilty under the law—but only in the eyes of the lawgiver.

You are living without reproach; so why is this all a dead loss, why is it so much muck? This knot is being pulled somewhat tighter; but it will be undone by the one who has the knack of doing that.[11] But we all have to earn this by our dutiful attention; you can't leave it to me alone, all by myself, to earn it by my dutiful submission. Whatever the Jews used to do that people could not complain about, so that their conduct in the law was without reproach, they used to take the credit themselves, and attribute this justice in terms of the law to their own powers. They weren't able to fulfill it completely, but they did so as far as they could; by taking the credit for this themselves, they didn't even fulfill this much in a truly devout and dutiful way.

Let me draw upon the Lord's mercy

6. So this is what he says fulfilling the law is: that is, not coveting, or lusting. Who among the living can do that? Let the psalm which has just been sung come to our aid: *Hear me out in your justice* (Ps 143:1), that means, not in mine. If he said, "Hear me out in my justice," it would be as if he were calling it merit. In some places he does indeed call it his own justice also; but here he distinguishes the matter better, because even when he says it's his own, he says he has been given it;[12] as we say, *Give us today our daily bread* (Mt 6:9). In what way "our," in what way "give"? So here, speaking more precisely, he says, *Hear me out in your justice*; and he continues, *and do not enter into judgment with your servant*. What's *Do not enter into judgment with your servant*? "Do not stand with me in judgment, demanding from me an account of everything you have commanded, an account of everything you have ordered. Because you will find me guilty if you enter into judgment with me. So what I need," he is saying, "is your mercy, rather than your clearest judgment."

So why *do not enter into judgment with your servant*? He goes on and tells us: *since nobody living will be justified in your sight* (Ps 143:2). "I am a slave, after all; why stand with me in judgment? Let me draw upon the Lord's mercy." Why? *Since nobody living will be justified in your sight.* What has he said? As long as we live in this life, none of us is justified—in the sight of God, though. It was not for nothing that he added *in your sight*. It was because a person can be justified in the sight of men, to verify the words, *According to the justice which is from the law, I was without reproach* (Phil 3:6) in the sight of men. Turn back to the sight of God: *Nobody living will be justified in your sight.*

A sinner who is humble is better than a just person who is proud

7. So what are we going to do? Let us cry out, *Do not enter into judgment with your servant* (Ps 143:2). Let us cry out, *Unhappy man that I am; who will deliver me from the body of this death? The grace of God through Jesus Christ our Lord* (Rom 7:24-25). So this is what we heard the psalm saying, what we heard the apostle saying; because when that justice comes by which the angels live, when that justice comes with which there will be no lust or covetousness— that's what we should, each one of us, measure ourselves by; what we are now, and what we will be then. And we will find that in comparison with that justice, this sort is just a dead loss and so much muck.

Any people, though, who think they live good and harmless lives, as human reckoning approves it, well, they have got stuck on the road. They don't desire anything better, because they think they have completely fulfilled it all; and especially if they take the credit to themselves, they will be proud. And a sinner who is humble is better than a just person who is proud.

That's why he says, *and that I may be found in him, not having my own justice which is from the law*, as the Jews supposed; *but the justice which is from the faith of Christ Jesus*. Then he went on and said, *if somehow I may attain to the resurrection of the dead* (Phil 3:9.11). That's where he believed he would completely satisfy justice, that is, would have complete justice. In comparison with that resurrection, the whole of this life we are living now is just muck. Listen further to the apostle saying it even more plainly: *If somehow I may attain to the resurrection of the just. Not that I have already received it, or am already perfect.* And then he added, *Brothers, I do not reckon that I have grasped it* (Phil 3:12.13). How he compares justice with justice, well-being with well-being, faith with sight, wandering exile with the heavenly city!

Live by faith in the hope of eternal salvation

8. Observe how thoroughly he does this: *Brothers, I do not reckon that I have grasped it. One thing, though.* What one thing, but to live by faith in the hope of eternal salvation, where there will be full and perfect justice, compared with which everything that is going to pass away is a dead loss and so much muck to be thrown out? So what, then? *One thing, though; forgetting what lies behind, stretched out to what lies ahead, I follow the direction toward the palm of God's summons up above in Christ Jesus.*[13] And to those who might rely presumptuously on their own perfection: *But as many of us as are perfect, let us have this mind. And if perhaps you have other ideas, that too God will reveal to you* (Phil 3:13-15); that is, that if you judge yourselves to be justified by some spiritual progress you have made, you may discover by reading the scriptures and finding out what true and perfect justice is, that you are guilty, and in your desire for things to come may spurn things present, may live by faith and hope and charity; and may understand that what you still believe you cannot yet see; what you still hope for you cannot yet grasp; what you still desire you cannot yet fulfill.

And if that is what the charity of wandering exiles is like, what must be the love of those who can see? So this man who was teaching the justice of God, and not establishing his own, cried out in the words of the psalm, *Hear me out in your justice, and do not enter into judgment with your servant; since nobody living will be justified in your sight* (Ps 143:2).

At the end what has been promised will be given us

9. As regards this life, Moses is told, *Nobody has seen the face of God and lived* (Ex 33:20). You see, we are not meant to live in this life in order to see that face; we are meant to die to the world, in order to live forever to God. Then we won't sin, not only by deed, but not even by desire, when we see that face which beats and surpasses all desires. Because it is so lovely, my brothers and sisters, so beautiful, that once you have seen it, nothing else can give you pleasure. It will give insatiable satisfaction of which we will never tire; we shall always be hungry, always have our fill. Listen to two sentences from scripture: *Those who drink me,* says Wisdom, *will be thirsty still, and those who eat me will be hungry still* (Sir 24:21). But in case you should suppose that that means there will be want and famine there, listen to the Lord: *Whoever drinks of this water will never thirst* (Jn 4:14).

But you are saying, "When will this be?" Whenever it will be, still watch for the Lord, *wait for the Lord, do manfully and let your heart take courage* (Ps 27:14). Are there as many ages left as have already passed? Think of the time from Adam up to the present day; how many ages have rolled by, and hey presto, they are now no more. In a manner of speaking, only a few days remain. That, at least, has to be said in comparison with the ages that have passed. Let us encourage each other; may we be encouraged by the one who has come to us, who has run the course, and said, "Follow me"; who has ascended first into heaven, in order that as head he may help from a higher point of vantage his other members who are toiling away on earth; who said from heaven, *Saul, Saul, why are you persecuting me?* (Acts 9:4). So nobody must despair; at the end, what has been promised will be given us; there that justice will be completely realized.

Let our desire be directed toward nothing but heaven

10. You also heard how the gospel agrees with these words. *The Father's will,* he said, *is that all that he has given me should not perish, but should have eternal life; and I will raise them up on the last day* (Jn 6:39). Himself on the first day, us on the last day. The first day belongs to the head of the Church. Our day, the Lord Christ, you see, does not end in a sunset.[14] The last day will be the end of the world and its age.

Don't say, "When will it come?" For the human race it will be a long time yet; for each individual human being it will be soon enough, because each person's last day is the day of his death. And indeed, when you depart from here you will receive according to what you deserve, and you will rise again to receive what you have achieved.[15] Then God will set the crown, not so much on your merits as on his gifts. Whatever he has given you, if you have kept and preserved it, he will recognize.

So now, brothers and sisters, let our desire be directed toward nothing but heaven, to nothing but eternal life. We must none of us be pleased with ourselves, as people who have lived uprightly here, nor compare ourselves with those who live bad lives, like that Pharisee who justified himself,[16] who evidently hadn't heard the apostle saying, *Not that I have already received, or am already perfect* (Phil 3:12). So he hadn't yet received what he still desired. He had received a pledge; he said so himself: *Who has given us the pledge of the Spirit* (2 Cor 1:22; 5:5). The thing which this was a pledge of, that's what he longed to reach. A measure of participation—but at a distance. We participate one way now, we will participate then in quite another. Now by faith, by hope in the same Spirit; then, though, it will be by sight, it will be the thing itself;[17] but the same Spirit, the same God, the same fullness. He is crying out to us while we are absent, he will show himself to us when we are present; he is calling us as we wander in exile, he will foster and feed us in the home country.

Walk securely in Christ without anxiety

11. Christ became the way for us, and do we despair of arriving? This way cannot be closed down, cannot be cut, cannot be broken up by rain or floods, nor blocked by bandits. Walk securely in Christ without anxiety; walk. Don't stumble, don't fall, don't look back, don't stick on the road, don't wander away from the road. Only beware of all these things, and you have arrived.

When you arrive, then start boasting about it—but not in yourself. I mean, those who praise themselves aren't praising God, but turning away from God. Just as when you decide to move away from the fire, the fire remains hot but you grow cold; just as when you decide to move away from the light, as soon as you've done so the light remains bright in itself, but you find yourself in the dark. Let us not move away from the warmth of the Spirit, from the light of the Truth.[18] Just now we heard his voice, but then *we shall see him face to face* (1 Cor 13:12). We must none of us be pleased with ourselves, none of us pour scorn on others. We should all so wish to make progress that we neither envy those who do, nor pour scorn on those who fail. And then there will be accomplished in us with joy what has been promised in the gospel: *And I will raise them up on the last day* (Jn 6:40).

NOTES

1. The title given in the text continues: "And on the words of the psalm, 143:1-2, *Hear me out in your justice*, etc.: and finally on the reading of John's gospel, 6:39, *The will of the Father is that all that he has given me should not perish*, etc."

2. The Latin actually says, *meruit indulgentiam*; but clearly Augustine cannot be using *meruit* in the formal sense of meriting or deserving.

3. He does not, however, for the time being say at all clearly what the reason is; he merely goes on to warn against assuming a wrong reason for Paul's words. Not until section 5 will he return to this Philippians text, with some kind of explanation.

4. Like Marcion in the second century.

5. One normally thinks of the gospel image of knocking at the door as a begging to be let in. Here he reverses it; we should knock to be let out. There is also an allusion to the ninth plague of Egypt, the darkness so thick you could touch it (Ex 10:21-23).

6. There is more than one idea, I think, struggling for expression here. It was, of course, in Augustine's estimation, a sin to rely presumptuously on one's own strength of character. But that is not precisely what he primarily has in mind by God's hidden law here; that, it is clear from what follows, is the law forbidding covetousness or lust. Augustine is presuming they sinned against this law (they must have done, he would say, because they were riddled with original sin, just like us), even though they may have confined their external activities to what was permitted them. In fact, of course, the biblical record of Gn 3—11, and from then onward to the giving of the law in Ex 20, makes it quite clear that they did nothing of the sort.

7. There is some textual overloading and uncertainty here. The phrase just before this note, "When, what's more . . . ," is found in several manuscripts, but omitted from the printed text. In my view it is required in order to give coherence to the train of thought, which is indeed both complex

and elusive. Earlier, in the previous sentence, after "once the law was given," and before "committing sin was a graver matter," the text includes the phrase "after sin was committed." It seems to me to be not only redundant, but meaningless. Some reader, I suggest, stuck it in the margin to balance the preceding little sentence, and then it crept into the text, and was adjusted to make some sort of grammatical sense.

I reconstruct the text's history as follows: i) Originally it read, *antea sine lege peccabatur; data vero lege, amplius peccatum est, quia cum praevaricatione peccatum est. Ubi vero cum praevaricatione peccatum est, invenit se homo vinci a cupiditatibus suis* . . . ii) A marginal scribble (roman type) gets incorporated into the text: *antea sine lege peccabatur; data vero lege* postea peccatum est, *amplius peccatum est* . . . iii) A copyist tidies up the grammar: *antea sine lege peccabatur; data vero lege,* posteaquam peccatum est, *amplius peccatum est* . . . iv) Editors, rightly feeling the text to be overloaded, wrongly delete *Ubi vero cum praevaricatione peccatum est* . . .

8. See Jb 14:4, LXX.

9. The Hebrew editors of the psalms, who gave them their titles, ascribed this one to David as speaking in his own person, by assigning it to the occasion of his sin with Bathsheba against Uriah the Hittite. Of course, he is then seen in the liturgical tradition as representative of every sinner, so that this psalm soon becomes the pre-eminently penitential psalm. Augustine is carrying this process a step further here, to its ultimate conclusion.

10. Augustine's fundamental axiom that God is to be found within ourselves at the deepest level.

11. Presumably the Holy Spirit, whose inspiration he is hoping for, as he goes on immediately to suggest.

12. But Augustine gives no instances with justice as the subject, though he illustrates with bread.

13. See Sermon 169, note 44.

14. A phrase that echoes, or is echoed by, the *Exultet* in praise of the paschal candle at the Easter vigil.

15. See 1 Cor 8:15. It is not clear whether Augustine is here distinguishing between what we will receive at the moment of death, and what at the resurrection of the dead; between what later came to be known as the particular and the general or universal judgment. I think myself it is unlikely, and that he regards them as somehow coinciding, outside time.

16. See Lk 18:11.

17. *Res* in the future contrasted with present *spes*.

18. Christ.

SERMON 171

ON THE WORDS OF THE APOSTLE, PHILIPPIANS 4:4-6: *REJOICE IN THE LORD*, ETC.

Date: uncertain

Even while we do find ouselves in this world, we should be rejoicing in the Lord

1. The apostle commands us to rejoice, but in the Lord, not in the world. *Whoever wishes*, you see, *to be a friend of this world*, as scripture says, *will be counted God's enemy* (Jas 4:4). Just as a person *cannot serve two masters* (Mt 6:24), so too nobody can rejoice both in the world and in the Lord. These two joys differ enormously from each other, and are entirely opposed to one another; when there's rejoicing in the world, there's no rejoicing in the Lord; when there's rejoicing in the Lord, there's no rejoicing in the world. Let joy in the Lord go on winning, until joy in the world is reduced to nothing. Let joy in the Lord always go on growing, joy in the world always go on shrinking, until it is reduced to nothing.

By saying this, I don't mean that as long as we are in this world we ought not to rejoice; but that even while we do find ourselves in this world, we should already be rejoicing in the Lord. But someone may argue, "I'm in the world; obviously, if I rejoice, I rejoice where I am." Well, what then? Because you are in the world, does it mean you are not in the Lord? Listen to the same apostle talking to the Athenians, and saying about God, and about the Lord our Creator, in the Acts of the Apostles, *In him we live, and move, and are* (Acts 17:28). Seeing that he is everywhere, after all, is there anywhere he isn't? Wasn't he urging precisely this point upon us, for our encouragement? *The Lord is very near; don't be anxious about anything* (Phil 4:5-6). This is something tremendous, that he ascended above all the heavens, and is very near to those who dwell anywhere on earth. Who can this be that is both far away and near at hand, but the one who became our near neighbor out of mercy?

Christ the Samaritan, the guardian of the weak

2. The whole human race, you see, is that man who was lying in the road, left there by bandits half dead, who was ignored by the passing priest and Levite, while the passing Samaritan stopped by him to take care of him and help him.[1]

247

Now what was the reason for telling that story? Somebody was asking which were the best and most important commandments in the law, and he pointed out to him that there were two: *You shall love the Lord your God with all your heart, and with all your soul, and with all your mind; and you shall love your neighbor as yourself.* He said, *And who is my neighbor?* (Lk 10:27. 29) and the Lord told the story, *A certain man was going down from Jerusalem to Jericho.* He indicated somehow that the man was an Israelite. And he fell into the hands of bandits. When they had robbed him, and inflicted serious wounds on him, they left him in the road half dead. A priest came along, related to him in nationality of course, and walked past him lying there. A Levite came along, also related by nationality, and he too ignored the man lying there. A Samaritan came along, far removed from him in nationality, a near neighbor in mercy, and did for him what you know.

In this Samaritan the Lord Jesus Christ wanted us to understand himself. "Samaritan," you see, means "Guardian."[2] That's why, *rising from the dead, he dies no more, and death has no further dominion over him* (Rom 6:9); because, *he neither sleeps nor slumbers, the one who guards Israel* (Ps 121:4). Finally, when the Jews were speaking ill of him with so many insults, they said to him, *Are we not right in saying that you are a Samaritan, and have a devil?* (Jn 8:48). So since there were two derogatory words cast in the Lord's teeth, and he was told, *Are we not right in saying that you are a Samaritan, and have a devil,* he could have answered, "I am not a Samaritan, and I don't have a devil." What he did answer, though, was, *It is not I who have a devil* (Jn 8:49). What he answered, he refuted; what he kept quiet about, he confirmed. He denied he had a devil, knowing himself to be the expeller of devils; he did not deny that he was the guardian of the weak. So then, *The Lord is very near* (Phil 4:5), because the Lord has become very near to us.

Christ, in order to be our near neighbor,
took on our punishment, did not take on our fault

3. What is so far away, so remote, as God from men, the immortal from mortals, the just one from sinners? Not far away by space, but by unlikeness. We are used to talking like that, you see, when we say about two people of very different morals, "This one is far away from that one." Even if they are standing next to each other, even if they are next-door neighbors, even if they are tied together with one pair of handcuffs, the godly person is a long way away from the ungodly, the innocent a long way away from the guilty, the just a long way away from the unjust. If you can say this about two men, how much more about God and men?

So when the immortal and just one was far away from us, as from mortals and sinners, he came down to us, to become, that far distant being, our near neighbor. And what did he do? Since he himself had two good things, and we two bad things; he the two good things of justice and immortality; we the two bad things of iniquity and mortality—if he had taken on each of our bad things, he would have become our exact equal, and would have been in need of a deliverer along with us. So what did he do, in order to be our near neighbor? Our neighbor, not by being what we are, but by being near us. Keep your eye on two things: he is just, he is immortal. As for your two bad things, one is fault, the other is punishment; the fault is that you are unjust, the punishment that you are mortal. He, in order to be your near neighbor, took on your punishment, did not take on your fault; and if he did take it on,[3] he took it on in order to cancel it, not to commit it.

Just and immortal, a long way away from the unjust and the mortal. A sinner, and mortal, you were a long way away from the just immortal one. He didn't become a sinner, which you are; but he did become mortal, which you are. While remaining just, he became mortal. By taking on your punishment, while not taking on your fault, he canceled both fault and punishment. So, *the Lord is very near, do not be anxious about anything* (Phil 4:5-6). Even if he has ascended above all the heavens in his body, he has not withdrawn in his greatness. He is present everywhere, seeing that he made everything.

Joy in the world

4. What is joy in the world? Rejoicing in iniquity, rejoicing in infamy, rejoicing in what is dishonorable, rejoicing in what is vile. These are all the things the world rejoices in. And none of them would exist, if people didn't want them to. There are some things people do; others that are done to them, they endure even if they don't like it. So what is this world, and what is the joy of this world? I will tell you, brothers and sisters, as briefly as I can, as far as God helps me. Briefly, quickly, I'll tell you. What the world relishes is villainy that no one punishes.[4] Let people indulge in dissolute living, in fornication, in the frivolities of the games; let them drown themselves in drink, befoul themselves with infamy—and suffer no harm: and there you have the joy of the world. Let these evil things I've listed not be chastised by famine, or by fear of war, or any other fear; not by any disease or any misfortunes at all; but let them all pass in material plenty, in bodily ease, in peace of mind—an evil mind: and again, there you have the joy of the world.

But God doesn't think like man; God's way of thinking is one thing, man's another. It is an aspect of his great kindness not to leave villainy unpunished; and he is ready to chastise now with whips, in order not to be forced to consign to gehenna at the end.

Rejoice in truth, not iniqiuty

5. Well, do you want to know what a very heavy punishment going unpunished is—not of course for the just person, but for the sinner, on whom temporal punishment is inflicted in order to prevent the eternal variety following? So do you want to know how heavy a punishment going unpunished is? Ask the psalm: *The sinner has provoked the Lord.* It's a vehement exclamation; he observed,

he reflected, he exclaimed, *The sinner has provoked the Lord*. Why, I ask you? What have you seen? Well, the person who uttered this exclamation saw the sinner playing the rake with impunity, doing wrong, loaded with good things, and he exclaimed, *The sinner has provoked the Lord*. Why did you say this? I mean, what have you seen? *So great is his wrath, he does not inquire* (Ps 19:3-4).

Brothers and sisters, Christians, try to understand God's mercy and kindness. When he chastises the world, it's because he does not want to condemn the world. *So great is his wrath, he does not investigate*. The reason he doesn't investigate is that he is so angry. Great is his wrath. It is by way of sparing us that he is savage, but he is savage with justice, all the same. Severity, you see, is, you might say, "savage verity" or truth.[5] So if he is sometimes savage by way of sparing us, it's good for us that he should come to our help by way of chastising us.

And yet, if we consider all that the human race has done, what do we really suffer? *He has not treated us according to our sins* (Ps 103:10). You see, we are sons and daughters. How do we prove this? The only Son died for us, in order not to remain the only one. He didn't want to be the only one, though he died as the only one. The only Son of God made many sons and daughters of God. He bought himself brothers and sisters with his blood, he accepted us though rejected himself, he redeemed us though sold himself, he did us honor though dishonored himself, he gave us life though slain himself. Can you doubt that he will give you good things, seeing that he did not decline to take upon himself your bad things?

So then, brothers and sisters, *rejoice in the Lord*, not in the world; that is, rejoice in the truth, not in iniquity; rejoice in the hope of eternity, not in the brief flower of vanity. Rejoice like that, and wherever and as long as ever you are here; *The Lord is very near; do not be anxious about anything* (Phil 4:5-6).

NOTES

1. See Lk 10:30-37.

2. At least the Hebrew form of the name Samaria is connected with the verb *shamar*, meaning to guard or keep.

3. He has to qualify his first clear-cut statement, because of such texts as 1 Pt 2:24, echoing, for example, a passage like Is 53.

4. *Saeculi laetitia est impunita nequitia.*

5. *Severitas* is *saeva veritas*; but the *quasi* with which he introduces this conceit suggests indeed that that is all it is, a conceit, not a seriously suggested derivation of *severitas*.

SERMON 172

ON THE WORDS OF THE APOSTLE, 1 THESSALONIANS 4;13:
*BUT WE DO NOT WISH YOU TO BE IGNORANT, BROTHERS, ABOUT THOSE WHO ARE
ASLEEP, SO THAT YOU SHOULD NOT BE SADDENED, LIKE THE REST WHO HAVE NO
HOPE* AND ABOUT THE WORKS OF MERCY, BY WHICH THE DEAD ARE HELPED

Date: unknown[1]

It's nature, not belief, that has a horror of death

1. The blessed apostle warns us not to be saddened about those who are asleep, that is about our dearest dead, like the rest who have no hope, hope namely in the resurrection and eternal imperishability. The reason why scripture usually and most appropriately says that they are asleep, is that when we hear that word "asleep," we need not despair in the least about their one day waking up. That's why we sing in the psalm, *Will the one who is asleep not be sure to rise again* (Ps 41:8)?[2] So about the dead, those who love them naturally feel a certain sadness. It's nature, not belief, that has a horror of death. And death would not have happened to man but for the punishment that had been preceded by a grave fault.

And so if animals, which were so created that they would all die, each kind in due course, run away from death, cling to life, how much more should human beings do so, who would have lived without end if they had been willing to live without sin? And so it is that we cannot help being sad when those we love abandon us by dying. Because even if we know that it is not forever that they are leaving us while we have to stay behind, but that it is only for a short time that they are going ahead of us, and that we are going to follow; still, when death, so abhorrent to nature, overtakes someone we love, our very feeling of love for that person is bound to grieve. That's why the apostle did not advise us not to feel sad, but *not like the rest who have no hope.* So when our dear ones die, we are saddened by the necessity of losing them, but still cherish the hope of receiving them back again. Grief on the one hand, consolation on the other; there we are affected by human weakness, here restored by faith; there we feel pain according to our human condition, here we are healed by the divine promise.

251

We will only be able to enjoy after this life
what we have earned in the course of it

2. So it is that funeral processions, crowds of mourners, expensive arrange-ments for burial, the construction of splendid monuments, can be some sort of consolation for the living, but not any assistance for the dead. It is not to be doubted, though, that the dead can be helped by the prayers of holy Church, and the eucharistic sacrifice, and alms distributed for the repose of their spirits; so that God may deal with them more mercifully than their sins have deserved. The whole Church, I mean, observes this tradition received from the Fathers, that prayers should be offered for those who have died in the communion of the body and blood of Christ, whenever their names are mentioned at the sacrifice in the usual place, and that it should be announced that the sacrifice is offered for them. When, however, works of mercy are performed for their sakes, who can doubt that this benefits those for whom prayers are not sent up to God in vain?

There can be no doubt at all that these things are of value to the departed; but to such of them as lived in such a way before they died, as would enable them to profit from these things after death. For those, you see, who have departed from their bodies without *the faith that works through love* (Gal 5:6) and its sacraments, acts of piety of this sort are performed in vain.[3] While they were still here they lacked the guarantee of this faith, either because they did not receive God's grace at all, or received it in vain, and so stored up for themselves not mercy but wrath.[4] So no new merits are won for the dead when their good Christian friends do any work on their behalf, but these things are credited to them as a consequence of their preceding merits. It was only while they lived here that they could ensure that such things would be of help to them after they ceased to live here. And so it is that when any of us finish this life, we will only be able to enjoy after it what we have earned in the course of it.[5]

Tears should be quickly dried by the joy of faith

3. And so it is perfectly in order for loving hearts to grieve at the death of their dear ones, but with a sorrow that will let itself be assuaged; and to shed the tears that suit our mortal condition, but that are also prepared to be consoled. These should be quickly dried by the joy of the faith with which we believe that when the faithful die, they depart from us for only a little while, and pass on to better things. Let mourners also be comforted by the good offices of their fellow Chris-tians, whether these consist of helping with the funeral arrangements or comforting the bereaved; or else there would be just cause for people to complain, *I waited for someone to share my grief, and there was none; for people to console me, and I could not find any* (Ps 69:20). Let proper care be taken, according to one's means, over burying the dead and constructing their tombs, because the holy scriptures count these things too among good works. People were praised in them, and held up as an example to us, not only as regards the respect shown to the remains of the patriarchs and other holy men and women, and to the corpses of any human beings left lying unburied,[6] but also as regards the body of the Lord himself.

By all means let us perform these last offices for our dead, and thereby soothe our natural human grief. But we should be much more punctilious, more pressing and more generous in seeing to those things which can help the spirits of the dead, such as offerings, prayers, and expenditure on good works and almsgiving; that is, if we love those who have died in the flesh, not the spirit, with an affection that is not merely of the flesh, but also spiritual.

NOTES

1. The sermon was evidently preached at a commemoration of the dead, an occasion like All Souls day in our present calendar.

2. The psalm verse actually means almost the exact opposite!

3. The sacraments of the faith are what we now call the sacraments of initiation: baptism, confirmation, and eucharist. So he means principally people who have shown no interest in becoming Christians; but of course he goes on to include bad Christians.

4. See 2 Cor 6:2, Jas 5:3 (Latin). Both the guarantee of faith and the grace of God here refer to baptism.

5. We should notice how Augustine's strong doctrine of grace does not oblige him to repudiate any notion of merit, or of somehow earning our heavenly reward, and the right, so to say, of profiting from prayers and works of mercy offered for us after our death. But such merit and earning power, so to put it, always presupposes a kind of foundation of entirely gratuitous divine grace.

6. See, for example, Gn 23; 25:9-11. 50; and in particular Tb 1:17-19; 2:1-9.

SERMON 173

ON THE SAME WORDS OF THE APOSTLE, 1 THESSALONIANS 4:13-17

Date: 418[1]

We are alive if we believe

1. When we celebrate days in remembrance of our dead brothers and sisters, we ought to bear in mind both what we should be hoping for and what we should be afraid of. We have reason to hope, you see, because *Precious in the sight of the Lord is the death of his holy ones* (Ps 116:15); but reason to be afraid, because *The death of sinners is very evil* (Ps 34:21). That's why, as regards hope, *The just will be kept in mind for ever*; while as regards fear, *he will not fear an evil hearing* (Ps 112:6-7). There will be something heard, you see, than which nothing could be worse, when those on the left hand are told, *Go into everlasting fire* (Mt 22:41). That is the evil hearing which the just will not fear, because he will be among those on the right hand who will be told, *Come, blessed of my Father, receive the kingdom* (Mt 22:34).

In this life, though, which is spent halfway between and before ultimate good and ultimate evil things, in the midst of middling goods and evils, in neither case the ultimate—because whatever good things come one's way here are just nothing in comparison with the good things of eternity; and whatever evils one may experience in this life are not to be counted at all in comparison with eternal fire—so in this halfway kind of life we must hold onto what we heard just now in the gospel: *Whoever believes in me,* he said, *even though he dies, is alive.* He both proclaims life and does not deny death. What does it mean, *even though he dies, is alive*? Even though he dies in the body, he is alive in the spirit. Then he adds, *and whoever is alive and believes in me, will not die for ever* (Jn 11:25-26).Well now, *even though he dies*; but how, if *he will not die*? Yes, but even though he dies for a time, *he will not die for ever*. That's how we solve that problem, and see how the words of Truth[2] do not contradict each other, and how they can support our loving devotion. So then, although we are going to die in the body, we are alive if we believe.

2. Our faith, however, is totally different from any beliefs of the heathen in the resurrection of the dead.[3] I mean, they absolutely refuse to accept this faith of ours; because they haven't any space, so to say, to accept it in. It is by the Lord, you see, that a person's will is prepared[4] to be a receptacle of faith. The Lord says to the Jews, *My word does not take in you* (Jn 8:37). So it does take in those people in whom it finds something to take. The word which takes, you see, finds something to take hold of in those whom God does not disappoint by his promises.[5] It is he, after all, who goes looking for the sheep that was lost,[6] and he knows both which one to look for, and where to look, and how to gather together its[7] scattered limbs and bring it back into the one place of salvation, and in this way so restore it that he doesn't lose it again.

So let us comfort one another, even with these words of ours.[8] It is possible for the human heart not to grieve for a dear one who has died; it's better, though, that the human heart should feel grief and be cured of it, than by not feeling any grief to become inhuman. Mary was clinging to the Lord, and grieving for her dead brother. But why be surprised that Mary was grieving, when the Lord himself was weeping?[9] You may well be wondering how he could weep for a dead man, when he was going to order him the next minute to come back to life. Well, he wasn't weeping for the dead man whom he brought back to life, but for death, which man brought on himself by sinning. After all, if sin had not come first, death would most certainly not have followed. So the death of the body as well followed on the death of the soul. The soul died first by deserting God, and the death of the body followed when the soul deserted it. In the first case the act of desertion was voluntary and deliberate; the second was performed under compulsion and involuntarily. It's as though the soul were told, "You withdrew from the one you ought to love; now withdraw from the thing you have loved." Who, I mean to say, wants to die? Nobody whatsoever; nobody indeed—so much so that the blessed Peter was told, *Another will gird you and carry you where you do not wish to go* (Jn 21:18). So if there were nothing bitter about death, there would be nothing heroic about martyrdom.

3. That's why the apostle too says, *About those who are asleep I would not have you ignorant, brothers, so that you may not be saddened like the heathen, who do not have any hope* (1 Thes 4:13). He didn't just say *that you may not be saddened*, but *that you may not be saddened as the heathen are, who do not have any hope*. It's unavoidable, after all, that you should be saddened; but when you feel sad, let hope console you. I mean, how can you not feel sad, when the body which lives by the soul[10] becomes inanimate, as the animating soul departs from it? The person who used to walk lies still, who used to talk is silent; the eyes are closed and take in no light, the ears are not open to any voices; all the functions of the body's limbs and organs have been stilled; there is no one there to move the feet to walk, the hands to work, the senses to be aware. Isn't this a house

which I don't know what sort of invisible inhabitant used to distinguish? The one who was not to be seen has departed, there is only left what can only be seen with pain.

That's what causes sadness. If that's what causes sadness, let there be some consolation for this sadness. What consolation? *Because the Lord himself with a shout of command and the voice of an archangel and the last trumpet call will come down from heaven, and the dead in Christ will rise first; then we who are alive, who have been left, will be snatched up with them in the clouds to meet Christ in the air.* Will all this too just be for a time? No; but what's really the case? *And thus we shall always be with the Lord* (1 Thes 4:16-17). Let sadness vanish where such consolation as that is to be had; let grief be wiped from the soul, let faith drive out sorrow.

With hope like that it's not right for God's temple to be sad. A good Comforter is dwelling there, a Promiser there who cannot disappoint. Why should we go on mourning the dead for a long time? Because death is bitter? The Lord too passed through it. Let these few words be enough for your graces. May the one who does not abandon your hearts give you more abundant consolation. But may he be pleased so to dwell there, that he is also pleased to transform us at the end.

Turning to the Lord, etc.

NOTES

1. Another sermon on the same theme as the preceding one. The date is suggested by La Bonnardière. There is no indication of where it was preached.

2. He almost certainly means Christ here.

3. It is not obvious what pagan beliefs he may have had in mind. He is probably speaking rather loosely, and referring to pagan beliefs about the afterlife in Hades (Hebrew, Sheol), or for select heroes in the isles of the blest. None of these really included the idea of bodily resurrection.

4. See Prv 8:35, LXX.

5. *Quos Deus pollicendo non decipit.* Literally, whom God does not deceive by his promises, implying that there are some people whom he does deceive by his promises, which is hardly acceptable. So I am assuming that *decipere* could already mean in the Latin of that time what the French *décevoir* can mean, to disappoint. This places the onus of disappointment on those who are disappointed, not on God.

6. See Lk 15:4.

7. He seems to be picturing the sheep as not only lost but as torn to pieces. Just possibly, he also had Am 3:12 in mind.

8. Contrasted, I think, with the Lord's word which "takes" in those in whom it finds something to take hold of. He can hardly be referring simply to the words of his own sermon.

9. See Jn 11:32-35.

10. The soul, *anima*, which *animates* the body to make it alive. This immediate reference of *anima* to life is unfortunately rather lacking with the English word "soul."

SERMON 174

ON THE WORDS OF THE APOSTLE, 1 TIMOTHY 1:15:
*IT IS A HUMAN WORD, AND WORTHY OF TOTAL ACCEPTANCE, THAT CHRIST JESUS
CAME INTO THE WORLD TO SAVE SINNERS,* ETC.; AGAINST THE PELAGIANS
PREACHED IN THE BASILICA OF CELER, ON A SUNDAY

Date: 412[1]

The human race would not have been set free,
unless the word of God had agreed to be human

1. We heard the blessed apostle Paul saying, *The word is human*[2] and *worthy of total acceptance, that Christ Jesus came into the world to save sinners, of whom I am the foremost* (1 Tm 1:15). So it's a human word, and worthy of total acceptance. Why human, and not divine? Without the slightest doubt, unless this word were also divine, it would not be worthy of total acceptance. But this word is both human and divine in the same sort of way as Christ himself is both man and God. So if we are right in understanding this word to be not only human but also divine, why did the apostle prefer to call it human rather than divine? I mean, it's obvious that since he wouldn't be lying if he called it divine, he must have had a reason for preferring to call it human.

So the aspect he chose was the one by which Christ came into the world. He came, after all, insofar as he was man. Because insofar as he was God, he was always here. Is there anywhere God isn't, I mean, seeing that he said, *Heaven and earth do I fill* (Jer 23:24)? Christ is certainly the power of God and the wisdom of God;[3] and of this wisdom it says, *She reaches from end to end mightily, and disposes all things sweetly* (Wis 8:1). So then, *he was in this world, and the world was made through him, and the world did not know him* (Jn 1:10). He was here, and yet he also came; he was here by divine greatness, he came by human weakness. So because he came by human weakness, that's why Paul declared his coming by saying *The word is human.* The human race would not have been set free, unless the word of God had agreed to be human. After all, people are said in particular to be human who show some humanity, above all by giving hospitality to human persons. So if human beings are called human because they receive human beings into their homes, how human must that one be who received humanity into himself by becoming human?

257

2. So then: *The word is human, and worthy of total acceptance, that Christ Jesus came into the world to save sinners* (1 Tm 1:15). Remember the gospel: *For the Son of man came to seek and to save what had got lost* (Lk 19:10). If man had not got lost, the Son of man would not have come. So man had got lost, God did come as man, and man was found. Man had got lost through free will; God came as man through the grace that sets free. Do you want to know what freedom of decision is capable of for the worse? Call to mind man sinning. Do you want to know what the one who is God and man is capable of for the better? Observe in him the grace that sets free.

Nowhere could it be demonstrated to better effect just what use the will of man is, when taken over by pride, for avoiding evil without God's help; nowhere could it be set out more effectively and plainly than in the first man. And lo and behold, the first man got lost, and where would he be now if the second man had not come? It's just because that one is a man that this one too is a man, and that's also why *the word is human.* Again, absolutely nowhere could the kindness of God's grace and the generosity of his omnipotence appear to better effect than in the man, the mediator between God and men, the man Christ Jesus.[4]

What, after all, are we saying, my brothers and sisters? It's to people brought up in the Catholic faith that I'm speaking, or to those won over to the Catholic peace.[5] We know, and we hold firmly to the truth, that the mediator between God and men, the man Christ Jesus, insofar as he was man, was of exactly the same nature as we ourselves are. I mean our flesh and his flesh are not of different natures, nor our soul and his soul of different natures. He took on precisely that nature which he judged to be in need of saving. He had nothing less than we do as regards nature, but he also had nothing by way of fault. Nature in its purity, but not only human nature. God was there too, the Word of God was there. And just as you, one human being, are soul and flesh, so too he, one Christ, is God and man.[6]

So will anybody have the face to say that our nature in that mediator first deserved well of God by an act of free decision, and in this way earned the right to be taken on in order to be man and God, one Christ Jesus? Yes, we to be sure can say that it is by our virtues, by our good habits, by our style of life that we have earned the right to be made into children of God; we can say, "We have received the commandment; if we keep it and live good lives, we will be received among the number of the children of God."[7] But did he too first live as a son of man, and by living a good life become the Son of God? That's where he got it from,[8] that's where he began from, and became man by being taken on. *The Word,* you see, *became flesh, in order to dwell among us* (Jn 1:14). The Word of God, the only Son of God, assumed the soul and flesh of a man, not of one who previously deserved well of him and worked hard to attain that sublime height by his own virtue; it was an act of pure, gratuitous grace. There was nothing, you see, that preceded that act of taking on; it was by being taken on that that man came to be. The virgin conceived; did the man mediator exist before that conception of the virgin's? Obviously, he wasn't previously a just man. I mean, how could he be just when he didn't yet exist? The virgin conceived, and from that taking on of a human being, he began to be.

Most appropriately does it say, *We saw his glory, the glory as of the only begotten from the Father, full of grace and truth* (Jn 1:14). You, though, are very fond of your free will; you're going to say to your father, *Give me the property which belongs to me* (Lk 15:12). Why entrust yourself to yourself? The one who was able to create you before you existed can look after you much better. So acknowledge Christ, he is full of grace. He wants to pour out into you what he's full of himself; this is what he's saying to you: "Look for my gifts, forget your own merits; because if I went looking for your merits, you wouldn't come to my gifts. Don't exalt yourself; be little, be Zacchaeus."

Climb the tree on which Jesus hung for you, and you will see Jesus

3. But you're going to say, "If I become Zacchaeus, I won't be able to see Jesus." Don't let that get you down; climb the tree on which Jesus hung for you, and you will see Jesus. And what kind of tree did Zacchaeus climb? A sycamore. It doesn't grow at all, or very rarely perhaps, in our part of the world. But in those parts this kind of tree and fruit is very common. Sycamores are what a fruit is called that is like figs; and yet there's a definite difference, which those who've seen or tasted them can tell. However, as far as the meaning of the name goes, sycamores translate into English as "silly figs."[9] Now look at my friend Zacchaeus, look at him please, wanting to see Jesus in the crowd and not being able to. He was lowly, you see, the crowd was proud; and the crowd, as is the way with a crowd, was hindering itself from seeing the Lord well. He climbed away from the crowd and saw Jesus, without the crowd getting in his way.

The crowd, you see, says to the lowly, to people walking the way of humility, who leave the wrongs they suffer in God's hands, and don't insist on getting their own back on their enemies; the crowd jeers at them and says, "You helpless, miserable clod, you can't even stick up for yourself and get your own back." The crowd gets in the way and prevents Jesus from being seen; the crowd which boasts and crows, when it is able to get its own back, blocks the sight of the one who said, as he hung on the cross, *Father, forgive them, because they do not know what they are doing* (Lk 23:24). So this was the one then, the one in whom all the humble are represented, that Zacchaeus wanted to see; and so he ignored the crowd that was getting in his way, but instead he climbed a sycamore tree, a tree so to say of silly fruit. *We*, you see, as the apostle says, *preach Christ crucified, a stumbling block indeed to the Jews*; now notice the sycamore; *but to the Gentiles folly* (1 Cor 1:23). Finally, the wise of this world jeer at us about the cross of Christ, and say, "What sort of minds have you people got, who worship a crucified God?" What sort of minds have we got? Certainly not your sort. *The wisdom of this world is folly with God* (1 Cor 3:19). No, we haven't got your sort of mind. But you call our minds foolish. Say what you like; for our part, let us climb the sycamore tree and see Jesus. The reason, after all, you can't see Jesus, is that you are ashamed to climb the sycamore tree.

Let Zacchaeus grasp the sycamore tree, the humble person climb the cross. That's little enough, merely to climb it; we mustn't be ashamed of the cross of Christ, we must fix it on our foreheads, where the seat of shame is;[10] yes, there, there above all where our blushes show, that's where we must firmly fix what we should never blush for. As for you, I rather think you make fun of the sycamore; and yet that's what has enabled me to see Jesus. You, though, make fun of the sycamore, because you are just a man; but *the foolishness of God is wiser than men* (1 Cor 1:25).

> *You wouldn't have come to the cleanser of sin,*
> *unless he had first seen you in the shadow of sin*

4. And the Lord saw Zacchaeus too. He was seen, and he saw; but unless he had been seen, he wouldn't have been able to see. *Those whom he predestined he also called* (Rom 8:30). He's the one who said to Nathanael—who was in a way helping the proclamation of the gospel by asking, *Can anything good come out of Nazareth?*; so the Lord said to him, *Before Philip called you, while you were under the fig tree, I saw you* (Jn 1:46.48).

You know what the first sinners, Adam and Eve, made themselves aprons from. When they had sinned, they made themselves aprons from fig leaves, and covered their shameful parts; because it was by sinning that they caused themselves to feel shame about them. So if the first sinners made themselves aprons, the couple from whom we derive our origins, in whom we had got lost, so that he would come to seek and to save what had got lost;[11] if they made them out of fig leaves to cover their shameful parts; what else could it mean, *When you were under the fig tree I saw you*, but "You wouldn't have come to the cleanser of sin, unless he had first seen you in the shadow of sin"? In order for us to see, we have been seen; in order for us to love, we have been loved. *My God, his mercy will go before me* (Ps 59:10).

> *Welcoming Jesus means welcoming him into your heart*

5. So now then the Lord, who had already welcomed Zacchaeus in his heart, was ready to be welcomed by him in his house; and he said, *Zacchaeus, hurry up and come down; since I have to stay in your house* (Lk 19:5). He thought it was a marvelous piece of good luck to see Christ. While imagining it was a marvelous piece of luck, quite beyond words, to see him passing by, he was suddenly found worthy to have him in his house. Grace is poured forth, faith starts working through love,[12] Christ who was already dwelling in his heart is welcomed into his house. Zacchaeus says to Christ, *Lord, half my goods I give to the poor; and if I have cheated anyone of anything, I am paying back four times over* (Lk 19:8). It's as if he were saying, "The reason I'm keeping back half for myself, is not in order to have it, but to have something to pay people back from."

So there you are, that's really what welcoming Jesus means, welcoming him into your heart. Christ, I mean, was already there, he was in Zacchaeus, and through him was saying for himself what he was hearing from his mouth.[13] That, you see, is what the apostle says: *For Christ to dwell by faith in your hearts* (Eph 3:17).

Jesus came to save sinners

6. So now, because it was Zacchaeus, because he was a head tax collector, because he was very much of a sinner; that crowd being, so it would seem, of sound mind and good health, though it was preventing people from seeing Jesus, that crowd was astonished and expressed disapproval of Jesus entering the house of a sinner. This amounted to disapproving of the doctor entering the house of a sick person. So because Zacchaeus was scoffed at as a sinner, scoffed at though by those of unsound mind after being restored to sound health himself, the Lord answered the scoffers, *Today salvation came to this house* (Lk 19:9). There you are, that's why I entered; *salvation came to this house*. Clearly, if the Savior hadn't entered, salvation wouldn't have happened in that house.

So why are you astonished, sick man? Call in Jesus yourself as well, don't regard yourself as being in good health. It's with hope that a person is sick who welcomes the doctor; but desperately sick indeed is the one who in a frenzy beats the doctor. So what sort of frenzy must possess the person who kills the doctor? And on the other hand, what must the goodness and power of the doctor be, who from his own blood made a medicine for his crazy killer? After all, the one who had come to seek and to save what had got lost didn't say in vain as he hung there, *Father, forgive them, because they do not know what they are doing* (Lk 23:24). "They are in a frenzy, I'm the doctor; let them rave and rage, I bear it patiently; it's when they've killed me that I will heal them."

So let us be among those whom he heals. *The word is human and worthy of total acceptance, that Christ Jesus came into the world to save sinners* (1 Tm 1:15); whether great or small, to save sinners. *The Son of man has come to seek and to save what had got lost* (Lk 19:10).

Christ is Jesus for all believing infants

7. Those who say that infancy has nothing in it for Jesus to save, are denying that Christ is Jesus for all believing infants. Those, I repeat, who say that infancy has nothing in it for Jesus to save, are saying nothing else than that for believing infants, infants that is who have been baptized in Christ, Christ the Lord is not Jesus. After all, what is Jesus? Jesus means Savior.[14] Jesus is the Savior. Those whom he doesn't save, having nothing to save in them, well for them he isn't Jesus. Well now, if you can tolerate the idea that Christ is not Jesus for some persons who have been baptized, then I'm not sure your faith can be recognized as according with the sound rule.[15] Yes, they're infants, but they are his members. They're infants, but they receive his sacraments. They are infants, but they share in his table, in order to have life in themselves.[16]

What are you telling me? That the child is perfectly all right, nothing wrong with it? Then why are you running with it to the doctor, if it's perfectly all right?

Aren't you afraid he may say to you, "Take this child away, since you consider it to be perfectly all right; the Son of man only came to seek and to save what had got lost; why bring the child to me, if it hadn't got lost?"

You shall call his name Jesus

8. *The word is human, and worthy of total acceptance, that Christ Jesus came into the world.* Why did he come into the world? *To save sinners.* There was no other reason at all why he should come into the world. It wasn't our good merits that brought him down from heaven to earth, but our sins. That's the reason he came, *to save sinners* (1 Tm 1:15). *And you shall call his name*, it says, *Jesus.* Why shall you call his name Jesus? *For he it is who will save his people from their sins* (Mt 1:21). You shall call his name Jesus. Why *Jesus*? Listen why: *For he it is who will save his people.* What from? *From their sins.* His people from their sins. Don't little children belong to this people, whom Jesus will save from their sins? They belong, they certainly do, my brothers and sisters. Keep that firmly in your minds, believe that, with that faith carry your little ones to the grace of Christ; or else if you don't have this faith in your hearts, you may be killing with your tongues those for whom you are giving the answers.[17]

There's not the slightest doubt, brothers and sisters, that those who run with their babies to the church without this faith are just pretending. "It's healthy, has nothing wrong with it, has no faults; but I'll take it to the doctor just the same." Why? "Because that's what's always done." Aren't you afraid the doctor may say to you, "Be off with you; *it's not the healthy who need the doctor, but the sick*" (Mt 9:12)?

Nobody can pass to the second man from the first
except by the sacrament of baptism

9. Let me put the case to your graces for those who cannot speak for themselves. All babies should be considered as orphans, even those who haven't yet buried their own parents.[18] The whole multitude of predestined infants is seeking a guardian in the people of God, just as they are waiting for a Savior in the Lord. That poisonous serpent struck the total mass of the human race in the first man; nobody can pass to the second man from the first except by the sacrament of baptism. In babies who have been born and not yet baptized one should recognize Adam; in babies who have been born and baptized and thereby born again, one should recognize Christ. If you don't recognize Adam in babies as they are born, you won't be able to recognize Christ in those who have been reborn.

"But why," they ask, "does a baptized believer, whose sin has already been forgiven, beget a child who is still burdened with the first man's sin?" Because he begets him from the flesh, not from the spirit. *What is born of the flesh is flesh* (Jn 3:6). *And if the outer self*, says the apostle, *is decaying, yet the inner self is being renewed from day to day* (2 Cor 4:16). It's not from what is being renewed in you that you beget a child; you beget a child from what is decaying in you. You, in order not to die forever, were born and reborn. This child is already born, not yet reborn. If you're alive as a result of being reborn, allow it too to be reborn and live. Allow it, I repeat, to be reborn, allow it to be reborn. Why oppose this? Why try to smash the ancient rule of faith with new objections? After all, what is this that you are saying: "Little children don't have even original sin in the least degree"? What does this that you say amount to, but that they shouldn't come to Jesus? But Jesus cries out to you, *Let the little children come to me* (Mk 10:14).

Turning to the Lord, etc.

NOTES

1. The Latin text adds to the title, "And on the reading from Luke's gospel about Zacchaeus: 19:1-10." The date is not quite as definite as 412; the scholars suggest between 411 and 413.

2. The usual reading is "faithful." But Augustine's Latin text had this odd reading "human."

3. See 1 Cor 1:24.

4. See 1 Tm 1:15.

5. That is, converts above all from the Donatist schism. Those brought up in the Catholic faith would, I imagine, include adult converts from Judaism and paganism who had been baptized in the Catholic Church; by being baptized they had become "newborn infants" again (1 Pt 2:2), and so were reared in the Catholic faith from scratch, so to say. But ex-Donatists had been baptized outside the Catholic Church, in a sect "at war" with Catholic peace. So when they were reconciled, they were not baptized again, did not again become newborn infants, but were accepted as fellow Christians into "the Catholic peace"—one of his favorite names for the Catholic Church.

6. An analogy (not one to be pushed too far) echoed in that very Augustinian document, the Athanasian creed.

7. We can say it, it makes sense, apparently, to say it—and the Pelagians did say it. But Augustine certainly did not. He is going to reduce the idea to absurdity in the particular case of the man Jesus himself.

8. Reading *cepit* instead of *coepit*, which is synonymous with the next verb, *incepit*.

9. He said "Latin," of course. An ingenious but mistaken etymology. The Greek *suko-moron* is a combination of fig and mulberry, *moron*, with the first o short. The Greek for silly or foolish is *moros* with the first o long. The sycamore, at least as known in those parts, seems to have been a kind of mulberry, not the sycamore one meets in northern Europe.

10. For us the "seat of shame" is the face as a whole or the cheeks; for the ancients, the forehead. The cross is fixed on our foreheads, first in the sacrament of confirmation, and secondly every time we make the sign of the cross, which presumably in Augustine's time was only made on the forehead, where we now sign ourselves at the beginning of the gospel.

11. See Lk 19:10.

12. See Gal 5:6.

13. A very condensed clause: *et de illo sibi dicebat quod ex ore ejus audiebat.* From the structure of the sentence Christ, and not Zacchaeus, must be the subject. *De illo* in a sentence governed by *dicebat* would normally mean "about him." But Christ wasn't saying anything so far about Zacchaeus. So one has to take it as meaning "from him," that is, through his words. It was Christ in Zacchaeus making that magnificent declaration. I rather doubt if Augustine's congregation was able immediately to catch his meaning. I am not at all sure I have managed to catch it myself.

14. In its Hebrew form, Joshua, it strictly means "Yahweh saves." In this passage he is directly attacking the Pelagians, who said that infant baptism was unnecessary and meaningless; or when they didn't go as far as that, because they recognized the weight of tradition behind the practice, they said that by baptism infants were made members of Christ's body but not forgiven any sins, not saved from any sins, because they didn't have any sins to be saved from.

15. The Latin has literally "in the sound rule." This recalls a dream of Augustine's mother Monica, which he records in the *Confessions* III, 11. He was still, to her continued distress, a Manichee. And then she had this dream in which she was standing on a rule, and saw him standing on the other end of it. This reassured her that he would one day become a Catholic Christian.

16. This indicates that when infants were baptized, they received all the sacraments of initiation, confirmation and eucharist also, immediately after baptism, as is still the custom today in the Oriental Churches.

17. Quite how he thought this might happen it is hard to see. He certainly didn't suppose the baptism would be invalid. And one can scarcely believe that he thought the babies would be saddled with the sin of falsehood, which he goes on to say their parents or sponsors would be committing. Perhaps he was expressing his doubts about the kind of faith they would be brought up in.

18. A very odd expression to use about babies! In his Latin, *qui nondum parentes proprios extulerunt*, literally "who haven't yet carried out their parents."

SERMON 175

ON THE SAME WORDS OF THE APOSTLE, 1 TIMOTHY 1:15-16: *THE WORD IS FAITHFUL AND WORTHY OF TOTAL ACCEPTANCE*, ETC.

Date: 412[1]

One man without sin came, who would save them from sin

1. The apostle Paul also says much the same as was read just now from the holy gospel.[2] These are his words: *The word is faithful and worthy of total acceptance, that Christ Jesus came into the world to save sinners, of whom I am the first* (1 Tm 1:15). There was no reason for Christ the Lord to come, except to save sinners. Eliminate diseases, eliminate wounds, and there's no call for medicine. If a great doctor has come down from heaven, a great invalid must have been lying very sick throughout the whole wide world. This invalid is the whole human race. But *not all have faith* (2 Thes 3:2). *The Lord knows who are his own* (2 Tm 2:19).

The Jews were behaving proudly, thinking highly of themselves, having big ideas, considering themselves to be just, and on top of all that they found fault with the Lord for picking up sinners. So those who were behaving proudly and were full of big ideas were left on the mountains, they belong to the ninety-nine.[3] What does it mean, left on the mountains? Left in a state of earthly fear. What does it mean, belonging to the ninety-nine? Being on the left hand, not on the right.[4] The ninety-nine, you see, are counted on the left hand; add one and you switch to the right.[5] So he came, as he says himself in another place, *The Son of man came to seek and to save what had got lost* (Lk 19:10). The whole lot, after all, had got lost. From the moment the one man sinned, in whom the whole race was contained, the whole race was lost. But one man without sin came, who would save them from sin. These people, though, by behaving proudly, were worse off than ever; as well as being sick, they thought they were in perfectly good health.

Jesus was always the doctor

2. People who have lost their minds through fever are much more danger-ously ill. They laugh, and sane people cry. What's more, those of sound mind

cry for the crazy ones who are laughing. If, to begin with, you propose a choice between these two things: which is better, to laugh or to cry; is there anybody who wouldn't prefer to laugh? And then, because repentance involves a salutary sorrow, the Lord presented tears as a requirement, laughter as the resulting benefit. How? When he says in the gospel, *Blessed are those who cry, because they shall laugh* (Lk 6:21). So crying is a requirement, laughter the reward, of wisdom. He put laughter for joy; not guffawing but jumping for joy.

So if you put the choice between these two things, if you ask which of these is the better, to laugh or to cry, everybody wants to laugh and would rather not cry. But now if you add particular persons to these expressions of feeling, and put the choice with persons included: which is better, for a crazy person to laugh or a sane person to cry; everyone prefers tears with sanity to laughter with madness. Such is the value of mental health that it is preferred even with lamentation.

Those people who thought they were sane were much more dangerously and desperately ill; and as a result of the very illness which lost them their minds, they even set about beating the doctor. That's not the half of it, that they set about beating him; let me state the whole of it; they set about not only beating him, but also killing him. He, though, even when he was being killed, remained the doctor; he was being flogged, and he was effecting a cure; he was suffering at the hands of a raving lunatic, and never despaired of the patient. He was caught, bound, slapped about, struck over and over with a cane, jeered at, taunted. Finally he was brought to trial, condemned, hung up on the wood, howled at from all sides; and he was still the doctor.

Christ applied his death to the preparation of the cure

3. You recognize the raving lunatics, now recognize the doctor too. *Father, forgive them, because they do not know what they are doing* (Lk 23:34). They were raving and raging, out of their minds, and in their savagery shedding the doctor's blood; he, on the other hand, was making medicines out of this very blood of his for their sickness. It wasn't in vain, you see, that he said, *Father, forgive them, because they do not know what they are doing.* The Christian prays, and is heard; Christ prays, and isn't he heard too? I mean, he hears with the Father, because he's God; so how can he not be heard as the man which he became for us? Of course he was heard. There they were, raving and raging; they were among the ones who had found fault with him and said, *Look, he eats with tax-collectors and sinners* (Mk 2:16; Lk 15:2). They were in that crowd of people by whom the doctor was being killed, and from his blood a cure was being prepared even for them.

The Lord, you see, didn't only shed his blood, but he also applied his death to the preparation of the cure; and so he rose again to present us with a sample of resurrection.[6] He suffered with a patience all his own, to teach us the patience we should have; and in his resurrection he showed us the reward of patience. Again, as you know and we all confess,[7] he ascended into heaven, and then the

Holy Spirit was sent by him as he had previously promised. He had said to his disciples, you remember, *Stay in the city until you are clothed with power from on high* (Lk 24:49). So his promise came true, the Holy Spirit came, he filled the disciples, they started speaking with the tongues of all nations; a sign of unity was being enacted in them. I mean, one person spoke then in all languages, because the unity of the Church was going to speak in all languages.

Those who heard them were filled with dread. After all, they knew they were uneducated men, speaking only one language; and they were astonished and dumbfounded that men of one language, or at most two, should be speaking in the languages of all nations. They were struck dumb with amazement, they lost their high opinion of themselves, from being a mountain they became valleys. If they are now humble, they are valleys; they retain what you pour into them, they don't let it run off. If water comes down on a height, it runs down and flows away; if water comes into a hollow and lowly place, it is retained and stays there. These people were now like that; they were dumbfounded, they were astonished, they lost their savage rage.

The conversion of those who killed Christ

4. In short, while Peter was speaking to them they were pricked to the heart, and there came about in them what the psalm had foretold: *I was converted to distress, when the thorn was stuck in* (Ps 32:4).[8] What's the thorn? Repentance pricking the conscience. You have the very words of scripture saying that in the Acts of the Apostles: *They were pricked to the heart, and said to the apostles, What shall we do?* (Acts 2:37). Why did they say *What shall we do?* "We know what we've done; what shall we do? As far as what we've done goes, we can only despair of salvation; so if it's at all possible, let us find in your advice some hope of health and sanity.[9] We know what we did; tell us what we should do. What is it we did? Well, it wasn't just any sort of man we killed; and we would have been doing something very evil if we had killed just anybody who was innocent. We chose a robber, we killed an innocent man; we chose one who was dead, we killed the doctor. Tell us, *What shall we do?*"

And Peter answered, "*Repent, and be baptized, each one of you, in the name of our Lord Jesus Christ* (Acts 2:38), in order to switch from the ninety-nine to the hundred. Because when you were the ninety-nine, you didn't think you had any need to repent, and what's more you used to taunt the Lord with picking up sinners and wanting to make penitents of them. So now that you have been pricked to the heart, because you acknowledge your sin, *repent and be baptized, each one of you, in the name of our Lord Jesus Christ*; be baptized in the name of the one you slew for no crime; and your sins are at once forgiven you." They were restored to hope. They grieved, they sighed and groaned, they were converted, they were cured. They were the "them": *Father, forgive them, because they do not know what they are doing.*

The doctor comes to the sick so that they won't always be sick

5. So, dearly beloved, when you hear that the Lord Jesus Christ did not come because of the just but because of sinners, you must none of you be attached to being sinners, and perhaps start saying to yourselves, "If I'm just, Christ doesn't love me; he loves me if I'm a sinner, because he came down for sinners, not for the just." You see, he can well answer you, "If you admit I'm the doctor, why weren't you afraid of the fever?" Of course the doctor comes to the sick, we all agree on that; but the reason the doctor comes to the sick is so that they won't always be sick.

So what are we saying? What statement are we making? What's our final conclusion? Does the doctor love the sick or the healthy? He loves what he wants to make, not what he finds. Sure, he comes to the sick, he doesn't come to the healthy. Don't be mesmerized by his coming to those and not coming to these; the fact is, he loves the healthy more than the sick. I mean, to prove to you that he loves the healthy more than the sick, would he bring about something he hated?[10]

How is Paul the first of sinners?

6. So pay attention to the apostle Paul: *The word is faithful and worthy of total acceptance, that Christ Jesus came into the world to save sinners, of whom I am the first* (1 Tm 1:15). He said, *of whom I am the first*. How was he the first? Weren't there so many Jews who were sinners before him? Weren't there any sinners before him in the whole human race? Was there no one, in the whole of humanity, held in the grip of sin before him? Didn't Adam come before him, who was the first to sin, and to plunge us all into death?

What do you mean, *of whom I am the first*? I'm the first of what he came for? But this isn't true either. Peter was chosen before you, Andrew before you, the other apostles before you. As for you, you're the last of the apostles;[11] how can you say, *of whom I am the first*? So the last apostle, the first sinner. Here too, how can you be the first sinner? Peter sinned before you did, when he denied the Lord himself three times. I don't like to say it, but unless he too had been found to be a sinner, he wouldn't have switched from the left hand to the right.[12]

He meant us to understand worst

7. So what's the meaning of *of whom I am the first*? That I am worse than all of them. By first he meant us to understand worst. As in trades and crafts; what does anybody say who wants to build? "Who's the first builder round here, who's the first carpenter?" Or if he wants to be cured of something, "Who's the first doctor round here?" He isn't of course inquiring who's the oldest, or who's the senior in the profession, but who's number one in competence and skill. Just as they come first in competence, so this one came first in iniquity.

Why did Paul come first in iniquity? Remember Saul, and you'll discover why. You are paying attention to Paul, you've forgotten Saul; you're paying attention to the shepherd, you've forgotten the wolf. Isn't he the one who wasn't satisfied with only one hand to stone Stephen, and who took care of the coats of the others?[13] Isn't he the one who persecuted the Church everywhere? Isn't he the one who accepted letters from the chief priests? Because it wasn't enough for him to persecute the Christians who were in Jerusalem; he also wanted to go to other places, to find them out, and bind them, and bring them back for punishment. Wasn't he breathing out slaughter on his journey, when he was struck from heaven, and heard the Lord's voice like a thunderbolt for his salvation? While he's walking along, he's laid low; in order to see, he's blinded. So he it is who was the number one persecutor; there was none worse than he.

Paul's conversion

8. Listen to something which will help you understand the point even better. The same Lord Christ was talking to Ananias, after Saul had already been laid low, already set on his feet again; and he said to him, *Go to that street; there you will find Saul from Tarsus; talk to him, because he has seen a man called Ananias coming in to him* (Acts 9:11-12). When he heard the name Saul, he trembled in the hands of the doctor himself.

There's an even nicer touch; I think you remember, and for those who don't, let me remind you, after whom he was called Saul. Saul was that persecutor of David.[14] In David there was Christ, in David Christ was prefigured, while Saul was prefigured in Saul; it was as though David were speaking to his Saul from heaven, *Saul, Saul, why are you persecuting me?* (Acts 9:4). Now the name Ananias means sheep;[15] the shepherd was talking to the sheep, and the sheep was afraid of the wolf. The wolf's notoriety had gone ahead of him so effectively, that the sheep didn't think it was safe, even while it was in the hands of the shepherd. And the Lord spoke to him as if he were a frightened sheep.

Ananias, you see, said when he heard this news, *"Lord, I have heard of this man, how much evil he has done to your saints in Jerusalem; and now it is said he has received letters from the chief priests to bring any he can seize back to them in chains* (Acts 9:13). Where are you sending me? A sheep to a wolf?" But the Lord wouldn't listen to this excuse. After all, he had already told some of his little sheep, *Behold, I am sending you like sheep in the midst of wolves* (Mt 10:16). If sheep have been sent into the midst of wolves, why are you dreading to go, Ananias, to one who is no longer a wolf? You were afraid of the wolf; but the Lord your God can answer you, "I have made the wolf into a sheep; I am making the sheep into a shepherd."

Saul was made into an apostle out of a persecutor

9. So how this Saul, later Paul, congratulates himself on having attained to the mercy of God, because he was found to be the first, that is the most outstanding, in sins! *And yet I obtained mercy, so that Christ Jesus might demonstrate in me all his forbearance, for the sake of those who are going to*

trust him for eternal life (1 Tm 1:16); so that they could all say to themselves, "If Paul was cured, why should I despair? If such a desperately sick man was cured by such a great doctor, who am I, not to fit those hands to my wounds,[16] not to hasten to the care of those hands?" That people might be able to say that sort of thing, that's why Saul was made into an apostle out of a persecutor. Because when a doctor comes to a new place, he looks for someone there who's been despaired of, and cures him; even if he finds he's very poor, provided he finds him a desperate case; because he is not looking for a fee, but advertising his skill.[17]

So let me say what I started out to: so notice how Saul congratulates himself on having been taken up and cured by Christ, because he was a sinner, and how he didn't say, "Let me remain in sin, because Christ came on my account, not on the just man's." In the same way you too, having heard that Christ came on account of sinners, don't let yourself go on sleeping on that nice comfortable bed; rather, listen to Paul himself saying, *Rise, you that are sleeping, and arise from the dead, and Christ will shed his light on you* (Eph 5:14). Don't grow fond of the bed of sin. *You have turned his whole bed in his infirmity* (Ps 41:3) is what was said earlier. Get up, get well, be keen on good health, and don't once more through pride move from the right hand to the left, from the valley to the mountain, from humility to a swollen head. When you've been made well, that is, when you've begun to live a just life, give God the credit, not yourself. After all, you weren't saved by singing your own praises, but by pronouncing judgment on yourself. Because if you flatter yourself through pride, you will be more seriously ill than ever. *For everyone who exalts himself shall be humbled, and who humbles himself shall be exalted* (Lk 18:14).

Turning to the Lord, etc.

NOTES

1. Here his reading of this passage is the one we are familiar with, "The word is faithful," not the more eccentric one of the last sermon, "The word is human." And yet the two sermons seem to have been preached at much the same time, so it's hardly a case of his having learned of a better version later on. We may infer that the two sermons were preached in different Churches, which had different versions of this epistle. Sermon 174 was preached in Carthage, so this one may have been preached in Hippo Regius—unless there is evidence from any other sermon definitely preached there that there too the reading was found, "The word is human."

2. Probably Lk 15:7.

3. See Lk 15:4. But this talks of leaving the ninety-nine in the desert. It's the parallel text in Mt 18:12 that talks about leaving them in the mountains. Yet that text is not connected with the accusations of the Pharisees, as is the text in Lk 15. Again, it's possibly an indication that the Church he was preaching in was using a Latin version of Tatian's harmony of the gospels, the *Diatessaron*.

4. See Mt 25:33. It is a very idiosyncratic interpretation of the parable of the lost sheep, and not quite, we may feel, what Jesus intended by it.

5. An extremely arbitrary symbolism, by no means self-evident. It illustrates his fascination with the mystique of the number one.

6. A sample, I think, which demonstrates the effectiveness of the cure, of the medicine he has just been talking about.

7. In the creed.

8. As in the Greek and Latin. Modern versions, while confessing that the Hebrew is obscure, render quite differently.

9. Salvation, *salus* is in Latin almost synonymous with health and sanity, *sanitas*.

10. His way of putting the issue is a trifle disconcerting. But perhaps it makes his point more effectively than if he had said, what our own idiom would certainly prefer, that the doctor loves people to be healthy rather than sick.

11. See 1 Cor 15:8.

12. A strange statement, which begins, *Nolo dicere quia*, "I don't want to say that . . ." But it is clearly Augustine's intention precisely to say that Peter, like everyone else, could only switch from the left hand to the right by being shown up to be a sinner, and contritely acknowledging it. Hence my admittedly very free translation—Augustine being reluctant to talk about the sins of the great apostles. I would be happy to hear of a better explanation.

13. See Acts 7:58. Augustine is giving Saul a greater direct responsibility for the stoning of Stephen than the passage really warrants.

14. See 1 Sam 18 onward.

15. Of course it means nothing of the kind; it means "Yahweh, be gracious to me." Where Augustine got this notion from I cannot imagine.

16. A curious inversion of Jesus' words to doubting Thomas, Jn 20:27.

17. I take it that Augustine is here presenting a general case, as an analogy to what Christ did in the case of Saul, even though it seems a rather sweeping generalization. But he could just be talking about "the" doctor, that is Christ, in these general terms.

SERMON 176

ON THREE READINGS: FROM THE APOSTLE, 1 TIMOTHY 1:15-16: *THE WORD IS FAITHFUL AND WORTHY OF TOTAL ACCEPTANCE*; FROM PSALM 95:6: *COME, LET US WORSHIP, AND PROSTRATE OURSELVES BEFORE HIM*; AND FROM THE GOSPEL, LUKE 17:12-19, ABOUT THE TEN LEPERS CLEANSED BY THE LORD; AGAINST THE PELAGIANS

Date: 414[1]

The readings and the psalm

1. Listen carefully, brothers and sisters, to what the Lord is pleased to remind us of from the readings of God's word; he of course provides the fare, I just serve it up. We heard the first reading from the apostle: *The word is faithful and worthy of total acceptance, that Christ Jesus came into the world to save sinners, of whom I am the first. But the reason I obtained mercy was that Christ might show in me complete forbearance, for the instruction of those who are going to trust him for eternal life* (1 Tm 1:15-16). That's what we got from the reading of the apostle.

Then we sang the psalm, in which we were inviting one another, saying with one heart and voice, *Come, let us worship, and prostrate ourselves before him, and weep before the Lord who made us*; and in another verse, *let us come before his face with confession, and with psalms let us acclaim him* (Ps 95:6.2).

After that the reading from the gospel showed us the ten lepers cleansed, and one of them giving thanks to the one who cleansed him.[2] Let us examine these three readings as much as time allows, saying a little about each of them; and I'll try, with the Lord's help, not to linger so long on any one of them, that we are blocked off from the other two.

Infant baptism

2. The apostle sets out for us the science of saying thank you. Remember what the last reading from the gospel left ringing in our ears, how the Lord Jesus praises the one who says thank you, blames the others who were ungrateful; their skins had been cleansed, their hearts remained leprous. So what does the apostle say? *The word is faithful and worthy of total acceptance.* What is this

word? *That Christ came into the world.* Why? *To save sinners.* What about you? *Of whom I am the first* (1 Tm 1:15). Whoever says either "I am not a sinner," or "I haven't been one," is ungrateful to the Savior.

There is no human being in this whole mass of mortals that comes down from Adam, not a single human being who hasn't been sick, not a single one who has been cured without the grace of Christ. What about the little ones, you ask;[3] are they infected with sickness from Adam? Well, they too are carried along to the Church; even if they can't trot along on their own feet, they do so on other people's, in order to be cured. Mother Church lends them other people's feet to come by, other people's hearts to believe with, other people's tongues to confess with;[4] thus since they are burdened with their sickness through another person sinning, it is right that when they recover health here[5] they should be saved by another person confessing on their behalf.

So don't let any of you go about whispering strange doctrines. This is what the Church has always done, always held; this is what it has received from the faith of our ancestors; this is what it will persevere in maintaining to the end. Because *It is not the healthy who need the doctor, but the sick* (Mk 2:17). What need did the infant have of Christ if it wasn't sick? If it's healthy, why through those who love it does it seek out the doctor? If infants are said to be entirely without any inherited sin, when they are brought along and come to Christ, why aren't those who bring them along told in the Church, "Take away these innocents; *it is not the healthy who need the doctor, but the sick*; Christ *did not come to call the just, but sinners*" (Mk 2:17). This has never been said; and never will be, what's more.

So, brothers and sisters, let each of you be ready, if you can, to speak for those who cannot speak for themselves. It's considered a matter of great importance to entrust bishops with the legacies of orphans; how much more important is the grace of infants! The bishop acts as the orphans' guardian, to protect them from exploitation by strangers when their parents are dead. Let him plead more loudly still for the babies, for whom he's afraid of their being killed by their parents.[6] Let him plead, together with the apostle, *The word is faithful and worthy of total acceptance, that Christ Jesus came into the world,* for no other reason but *to save sinners* (1 Tm 1:15). Those who come to Christ have something about them to be cured; if they haven't, there's no point in presenting them to the doctor.

Parents can choose one of two things: either admit that sin is being cured in their babies, or stop presenting them to the doctor. This simply amounts to wanting to present the doctor with a perfectly healthy patient.

"What are you bringing me?"

"Someone to be baptized."

"Who?"

"A baby."

"Who are you presenting it to?"

"To Christ."

"Really, to the one who *came into the world*?"

"Yes," he says.

"Why did he come into the world?"

"To save sinners."

"So the baby you're presenting him with has something in it to be saved from?"

If you say, "It has," by confessing it you are blotting it out; if you say, "It hasn't," by denying it you are keeping it in place.

Paul called himself the first of sinners in the magnitude of the sin

3. *To save sinners,* he said, *of whom I am the first.* Weren't there any sinners before Paul? Certainly Adam at least was before all of them, and the earth that was wiped out by the flood was full of sinners, and how many there have been from then on! So how can it be true, *I am the first*? He called himself the first, not in the whole series of sinners, but in the magnitude of the sin. He considered the magnitude of his sin, for which he called himself the first of sinners; just as among lawyers, for example, some are called first; this one's first, not because he has been handling cases for more years than others, but because from the time he began he has surpassed them. So let the apostle tell us in another place why he is the first of sinners: *I,* he says, *am the last of the apostles, not worthy to be called an apostle, because I persecuted the Church of God* (1 Cor 15:9). Nobody fiercer among persecutors; so nobody ahead among sinners.

No need to despair

4. *But I obtained mercy,* he said. And he explains the reason why he obtained mercy: *so that in me,* he goes on, *Christ might show complete forbearance, for the instruction of those who were going to trust him for eternal life* (1 Tm 1:16). Christ, he is saying, was going to grant pardon to sinners who turned back to him, including his enemies; so in me, the first, he chose his fiercest enemy; when he cured this one, none of the others would need to despair. Doctors do this sort of thing; when they arrive in places they are not known in, they choose the desperate cases to cure first, in order to put into practice on them their benevolence, and to advertise their learning, so that everyone in that place will start saying to the neighbors, "Go to that doctor, don't worry, he can cure you." "Cure me?" he says. "Can't you see what I'm suffering from?" "I know the sort of thing; I too suffered myself from what you've got." [7]

In the same way Paul is saying to any sick people, who are ready to despair of themselves, "The one who cured me has sent me to you, and told me: Go to those despairing people and tell them what you had wrong with you, what I cured in your case, how quickly I cured you. I called from heaven; with one word I struck you and threw you down; with another I raised you up and chose you; with a third I filled you and sent you; with a fourth I set you free and crowned your efforts. [8] Go, tell the sick, cry out to the despairing, *The word is faithful and worthy of total acceptance, that Christ Jesus came into the world*

to save sinners. What are you afraid of? What are you dreading? I," he says,
"am speaking to you, a healthy man to the sick, one standing on his two feet to
you lying there abjectly, one with no worries to you who are in despair. You
see, *the reason I obtained mercy was so that in me Christ Jesus might show
complete forbearance.* He put up with my disease for a long time, and in that
way put an end to it. Like the good doctor he is, he patiently tolerated the
madman, he endured my beating him, he granted me the privilege of being
beaten for his sake.[9] *He showed complete forbearance,"* he says, *"in me, for the
instruction of those who were going to trust him for eternal life."*

The one who died for you will come and give you life

5. So don't despair. You're sick, approach him and be healed; you're blind;
approach him and be enlightened (Ps 34:5). Those of you who are healthy, thank
him for it; those of you who are sick, run to him to be healed;[10] and all of you,
say, *Come, let us worship, and prostrate ourselves before him, and let us weep
before the Lord who made us* (Ps 95:6); made us human beings, and made us
saved. You see, if it was he that made us human beings, while we ourselves
made us saved, it means we have done something better than he has. I mean, a
saved human being is better than just a mere human being. So if God made you
a human being, and you made yourself a good human being, what you made is
better. Don't lift yourself up above God; submit yourself to God, worship,
prostrate yourself, confess to the one who made you; because nobody can
recreate except the one who creates; nobody can make you new, but the one
who made you in the first place.

You get this too in another psalm: *It is he who made us, and not we ourselves*
(Ps 100:3). Clearly, when he made you, you didn't have anything you could do
yourself; but when you already exist, you yourself also have something you can
do; you can run to the doctor, implore the help of the doctor, who can be found
anywhere and everywhere. And he it is that stirred your heart to implore his
help, and that gave you the ability to implore it. *For it is God*, it says, *who works
in you both to will and to work with good will* (Phil 2:13). Because for you even
to have a good will, his calling of you had to come first. Cry out, *My God, his
mercy will anticipate me* (Ps 59:10). For you to exist, for you to perceive, for
you to hear, for you to consent, his mercy anticipated you.

He has anticipated you all round; you in your turn, anticipate in some way
his anger. "In what way," you ask, "in what way?" Confess that you have all
these things from God, anything good you have, and that anything bad you have
from yourself. Don't pride yourself on your good things, and ignore him; don't
blame him for your bad things, and excuse yourself; then you are making a true
confession. He has anticipated you, gone before you, in so many good things;
he is going to come to you and inspect in you his good things, your bad things;
he's inspecting you to see how you've used his goodness. So because he has
gone before you with all these gifts, see how you can go before the face of the
one who is to come. Listen to the psalm: *Let us go before his face in confession*

(Ps 95:2). Let us go before his face, anticipate his coming; before he comes, appease him; before he's here, placate him.

You do have a priest, after all, through whom you can placate your God; and he with the Father is God to you, the same one who is man for you. In this way you will acclaim him with psalms, going before his face in confession. Acclaim him with a psalm; going before his face in confession, accuse yourself; acclaiming him in a psalm, praise him. If you accuse yourself and praise the one who made you, the one who died for you will come and give you life.

Lift up your hearts

6. Hold on to this truth, persevere in it. Let none of you vary it with spots, none of you be leprous. A changeable teaching, which doesn't have a uniform color, indicates a mental leprosy; and this is what Christ cleanses. It's possible that you varied it somehow, and examined it, and changed your opinion for the better; and that what was varied and spotty has been made uniform in color. Don't give yourself the credit for it, in case you find yourself among the nine who did not say thank you. Only one said thank you. The others were Jews, he was a foreigner, representing the foreign nations; the number which has given tithes to Christ.[11]

So it is to Christ that we owe the fact that we are, that we live, that we have understanding; that we are human, that we have lived good lives, that we have understood things rightly,[12] we owe it all to him. Of our own, there's nothing, except sin, that we have. *For what do you have that you have not received?* (1 Cor 4:7). You therefore, especially those of you who understand what you have heard, lift up your hearts to be cured of sickness, already purged of leprous variety, and give thanks to God.

NOTES

1. It is unusual for Augustine to preach quite so formally on all three readings of the Mass. Notice, incidentally, how he counts the responsorial psalm as a reading. Since here his version of 1 Timothy has the familiar "The word is faithful" and not the eccentric text of Sermon 174, "The word is human," we may infer that this sermon 176 was at least not preached in Carthage. The tone of the sermon suggests to me that it was preached to his own people in Hippo Regius.

2. See Lk 17:12-19.

3. Reading *Quid de parvulis, quaeris,* following a neat suggestion of the editors, instead of the text's *Quid de parvulis pueris,* "What about the baby boys?"

4. Though he is talking about the sinful condition of infants, he probably means the confession of faith here, not the confession of sins, because the rite of baptism does not include a confession of sins. This notion, that infants being baptized believe with the faith of their parents or godparents (or with the faith of the Church), is a key point in the Catholic apologetic for the practice of infant baptism. It means that in Catholic teaching the necessity of faith in the recipient for effectively

receiving the sacrament is definitely acknowledged. The concept of vicarious faith, like that of vicarious sin or vicarious suffering for that matter, is not readily acceptable or comprehensible in an individualistic society like ours; but it makes good sense to people for whom social solidarity is a primary value.

5. In the Church.

6. By not bringing them to be baptized; though infanticide, usually by exposing newborn infants, was still, I believe, a common practice; one which Christians naturally abominated. As a kind of background fact of life, this would have given Augustine's plea added significance, added poignancy.

7. See Sermon 175, note 17. What we have here removes any cause for the hesitation expressed there.

8. Augustine is envisaging Paul speaking from his glorious apostolic throne in heaven. Christ saying "I have crowned your efforts" (literally, just "I have crowned you") echoes 2 Tm 4:8.

9. See 2 Cor 11:23-30; also Col 1:24.

10. Perhaps we need to remind ourselves that he is talking all the time in a metaphor about spiritual and moral sickness and health.

11. An obscure remark—only made, presumably, because there were ten lepers, and it was one out of ten, a tithe or tenth part, who gave thanks.

12. According to orthodox teaching, that is to say.

SERMON 176A

FRAGMENT FROM A SERMON ON WHAT A BISHOP SHOULD BE LIKE

Date: unknown[1]

So a bishop ought to be without reproach (1 Tm 3:2). Can anyone deny this? But while a bishop ought to be without reproach, is it right for a Christian not to be irreproachable? "Bishop" is really a Greek word, which in English can be rendered as supervisor or visitor. We are bishops, but with you we are Christians.[2] We get our name from visitation, but the common name of all of us comes from anointing.[3] If the anointing is common to us all, so is the wrestling match. But why should we visit or oversee, if there's nothing good for us to see in you?

NOTES

1. The title adds "and on the passage where Paul blames Peter" (Gal 2:11-12). But the fragment does not touch on that topic, so I leave the phrase out. It is presumably given in the source from which the fragment comes. The fragment occurs here in the volume of sermons, because it starts with the text of 1 Timothy.

2. See Sermon 340, 1, from which a similar but more strongly worded statement is quoted in Vatican II's Constitution on the Church, *Lumen Gentium*, 32: "When I am frightened by what I am for you, I am consoled by what I am with you. For you I am a bishop, with you I am a Christian. The first is a duty, the second a grace; the first a danger, the second salvation."

Here, since he talks of bishops in the plural, he was probably preaching during an episcopal synod. The word "visitor" here is used in its ecclesiastical sense, of one making a formal visitation, or tour of inspection.

3. Christian from Christ, from the Greek *chrio*, I anoint. Hence also "chrism." Augustine here does not dwell on the anointing of kings, but of athletes, particularly wrestlers, before a match. It is to this that in Christian ritual the anointing with the "oil of catechumens" is compared.

SERMON 177

ON THE WORDS OF THE APOSTLE, 1 TIMOTHY 6:7-19: *WE BROUGHT NOTHING INTO THIS WORLD, AND WHAT IS MORE WE CANNOT TAKE ANYTHING OUT OF IT,* ETC.; A DISCOURSE ON AVARICE

Date: 397[1]

Avarice

1. I propose to preach on the reading from the apostle. *We brought nothing, he says, into this world, and what is more we cannot take anything out of it; but having board and lodging, with these let us be content. For those who wish to become rich fall into temptation and a snare, and into many foolish and harmful desires, which plunge people into ruin and perdition. For the root of all evil is avarice, and some people, setting their hearts on it, have strayed from the faith, and involved themselves in many pains* (1 Tm 6:7-10). A serious matter, which calls for close attention from you, and careful exposition from me.

In these words avarice is set before our very eyes; it is being prosecuted; don't let it be defended by anyone. Indeed, as it's being prosecuted it must be convicted; take care you aren't convicted with it by coming to its defense. I don't know how it is, but avarice manages to act on people's hearts in such a way that everybody—or to speak more accurately and carefully, nearly everybody—pronounces it guilty in talk, and in behavior wants to have it protected. Many things, many fine and weighty and true things have been said against it by both poets and historians and orators and philosophers; and every kind of literature and public pronouncement has had much to say against avarice. It's a great thing to be without the lady, and it's much more important to be without her than not to keep silent about what's wrong with her.

Avarice should not hold us in her grip

2. But what's the difference between philosophers, for example, finding fault with avarice, and the apostles finding fault with her too? What's the difference? If we pay attention, we can learn about something which is peculiar to the school of Christ.[2] Here's what I have just reminded you of: *We brought nothing into this world, and what is more we cannot take anything out of it; having board*

279

and lodging, with these let us be content. Many people have said that. Also this: *The root of all evil is avarice*; there have been people who would say that. What follows, none of them has said: *You though, man of God, flee from these things; rather, pursue justice, faith, charity, with those who call upon the Lord from a pure heart* (1 Tm 6:11).[3] Things like that none of them has ever said. Far from their pompously pontificating cheeks is such solid piety.[4]

So, dearly beloved, since there are people outside our company who have both found fault with and despised avarice,[5] it was in order to save us, or men of God, from thinking too highly of them, that he began, *You though, man of God.* To forestall any real comparison, what we must first and foremost discern and hold onto is, that it is for God's sake that we do whatever we do. I mean, if you leave aside the worship of the true God, the lovers of avarice are still disapproved of. Nonetheless, our truer rule of religion ought to instill in us a greater watchfulness in the matter. It's disgraceful, after all, and altogether too shameful and lamentable, if the worshippers of idols are found to be tamers of avarice, and the worshipper of the one God is put in harness by avarice, and becomes avarice's slave, when the blood of Christ was the price of his freedom.

The apostle went on to say to Timothy, *I call you to witness, in the presence of God who gives life to all things, and of Christ Jesus, who bore witness with a good confession under Pontius Pilate* (you can see how far this is from their kind of language), *that you should keep the commandment without reproach until the coming of our Lord Jesus Christ, who at the proper time will be revealed by the blessed and only mighty one, the King of kings and Lord of lords, who alone has immortality and dwells in light inaccessible, whom no human being has seen or can see, to whom honor and glory are due for ever and ever* (1 Tm 6:13-16). It is of this God that we have become the family, into his family that we have been adopted; we are his children, not by our own merits but by his grace. It's simply too unbearable, too horrible, that avarice should hold us in her grip on earth, when we are saying to him, *Our Father, who art in heaven* (Mt 6:9).

In our desire for him all other things should grow cheap in our eyes; the things among which we were born are not meant to be our destiny, because it is on his account that we have been reborn. Let them be for our use as we need them, not for our affections to cling to them. Treat them like a tavern for a traveler, not like a mansion for a landowner. Stop for refreshment, and then go on your way. You're on a journey, think about whom you're going to, because great indeed is the one who came to you. By departing from this life[6] you make way for someone else coming along; that's the rule with taverns; you go, so that someone else may take your place. But if you want to reach the safest of all places, don't let God depart from you, seeing that we say to him, *You have led me along the paths of your justice, for the sake of your name* (Ps 23:3), not for the sake of my merits.

3. So the journey of mortality is one thing, the journey of piety another. The journey of mortality is common to all who get born, the journey of piety is not common to all. I mean, all who have ever been born walk along that road; only those who have been born again along this one. To the first belongs being born, growing up, growing old, dying. It's for all this that we need board and lodging. Let our expenses be simply what is enough for this journey. Why weigh yourself down? Why carry so much on a short road, stuff that doesn't help you reach the end of it, but that becomes in fact an even heavier burden for you at the road's end? It's a wretched enough matter, what you apparently want to happen to you; you load yourself up, you carry a vast amount of baggage, money weighs you down along this road, and after this road ends, you are weighed down by avarice. Avarice, you see, is an uncleanness of the heart. You can take nothing that you've loved from this world; what you do take is the vice of having loved it. If you persist in loving the world, the one who made the world won't find you clean.[7]

So keep a moderate amount of money for temporal uses, treat it as journey money, with the end in view stated in the text: *A measure of money without love is sufficient for present needs* (Heb 13:5).[8] Notice above all what he put first: *Without love*, he says; put your hand in the purse in such a way that you release your heart from it. Because if you are prepared to have your heart tied up with love of money, you're involving yourself in many pains; and then where are the words, *You though, man of God, flee from these things* (1 Tm 6:11)? You see, he didn't say, "Leave and forsake," but *Flee from*, as from an enemy. You were trying to flee with gold; flee from gold instead. Let your heart flee from it, and your use of it need have no worries. Do without greed, don't do without concern for others. There's something you can do with gold, if you're its master, not its slave. If you're the master of gold, you can do good with it; if you're its slave, it can do evil with you. If you're the master of gold, the person clothed by you praises the Lord. If you're the slave of gold, the person despoiled and stripped by you blasphemes God. Now it's cupidity that enslaves you, charity that sets you free. You'll be the slave of that one, if you don't flee from her. *You though, man of God, flee from these things*. In this matter, if you don't want to be a slave, be a runaway.[9]

4. You've heard what you should run away from; you also have here what you should pursue. You are not, after all, running away aimlessly, or so letting go of something that you don't get hold of something else. So, *pursue justice, faith, godliness, charity* (1 Tm 6:11). Let these things make you rich. These riches are inside; thieves can't get at them, unless a bad will gives them their chance. Make your interior strong-room secure, that is, your conscience. These riches can't be taken from you by any robber, or any enemy, however powerful or influential, or by any hostile incursion of barbarians, not even, finally, by any

shipwreck; if you emerge from that with everything lost, you emerge from it with everything really intact. I mean to say, that man wasn't really stripped of everything, though outwardly he seemed to have nothing, the man who said, *The Lord has given, the Lord has taken away; as it pleased the Lord, so has it come about; may the name of the Lord be blessed* (Job 1:21).

This abundance is praiseworthy, these riches vast. Stripped of gold, abounding in God; stripped of all transitory means, abounding in the will of his Lord. Why go looking for gold with such laborious travels? Love these riches instead, and you are filled with them right now. Their source is not closed if your heart is open. The heart is opened by the key of faith; it both opens and cleans up the place you put it in.[10] Don't think of yourself as too cramped and narrow; your riches, your God, when he comes in, will himself widen and enlarge you.

A difference between being rich and wanting to be rich

5. So then, *without love a measure of money is sufficient for present needs* (Heb 13:5). Why for present needs? Because *we brought nothing into this world, nor can we take anything out of it* (1 Tm 6:7); that's why for present needs, not for future ones. But what is it that misleads people into the calculations of avarice? "Supposing I live a long time?" Can't the one who gives you life give you the means of passing your life? In any case, there's your income; why also try to amass a treasure, a big deposit? There's some income from business, income from the workshop, income from sales; let that suffice, don't store up a treasure; or where you put your treasure, your heart may stay there too, and you will hear in vain the command "Lift up your hearts," and make a false reply.[11] I mean, when you answer that most holy command, and subscribe to it with your voice, isn't your heart inside accusing you of lying? Although your heart is weighed down and oppressed, doesn't it say to you within, "You're placing me under the ground, why are you lying?" So now, doesn't it say to you, "I'm there where your treasure is; so you're lying." Or perhaps he's lying, the one who said, *Where your treasure is, there will your heart be also* (Mt 6:21)?

You say, "It won't be there."

Truth says, "It will be there."

"But it won't be there, because I don't love the treasure."

"Prove it with deeds. You don't love it, but you're rich. You're certainly paying attention, and making the right distinction for yourself; distinguishing from the person who's rich the one who wants to be rich. There's a great deal of difference, after all, between being rich and wanting to be rich. It's a very just distinction, it cannot be denied; in the first case, means, in the second, greed."

Avarice is indeed insatiable

6. I mean, yes, the apostle himself didn't say "Those who are rich," but *Those who want to become rich*, who want to become, *fall into temptation and a snare,*

and many desires, and harmful ones too (1 Tm 6:9); by wanting to become, not by actually being, rich. That's why he said *desires*. Desires, after all, mean that you want to attain to what you haven't yet got, because you never desire what you already have. Avarice is indeed insatiable; and even with people who already have much one can still talk about desire, not for the thing they possess, but for the one they want to possess. He owns this farm, he desires to get possession of another which he doesn't own. But when he's also got that one, he will start desiring another; he won't, however, be desiring what he's already acquired, but what he hasn't yet acquired.

So by wanting to be rich he's all steamed up with desire, he has a raging thirst, and like someone suffering from dropsy, the more he drinks, the thirstier he gets. There's an amazing similarity with this disease of the body; it's exactly the case that the avaricious person has dropsy of the heart. You see, the disease of dropsy means that the body is full of fluid, and is indeed endangered by fluid, and yet never has enough fluid. In the same way a dropsical heart means the more you have, the more you need. When you had less, you wanted less, you could enjoy yourself with fewer things, you were thrilled with small sums in your coffers. But because you have now been filled, it means you have also been stretched, you've become grossly opulent, legacies coming in daily; you go on drinking, and go on being thirsty. "If I can get this, I'll be able to do that. Now I can't do very much, because I haven't got very much." In fact, when you get this, what you have more of is wishing; it's your needs that have increased, not your power to act.

Only the rich of God are the true rich

7. "But," he says, "I don't love what I've got, in order to be able to lift up my heart." I fully agree; if you don't love it, your heart can be lifted up. Why, after all, should a heart that's free not be lifted up? But let's just see if you don't love; tell yourself honestly, in answer to your own questions, not my accusations.

"Certainly I don't love," he says. "It's true, I'm rich; but because I already am, though it's not my wish to be and so to fall *into temptation and a snare, and many foolish and harmful desires, which plunge a person into ruin and perdition* (1 Tm 6:9); a really horrible evil, dangerous and destructive. I'm already rich," he says; "it's not that I want to be."

"You're already rich?"

"I am," he says.

"You don't want to be?"

"No," he says.

"If you weren't, would you still not want to be?"

"I wouldn't want to be," he says.

"So then, because you already are so, and the word of God has come across you rich outwardly, made you rich inwardly, take to heart what was said to the rich."[12]

You see, what was said in these words, *We brought nothing into this world, and what is more we can take nothing out of it; having board and lodging, let us be content with these. For those who wish to become rich fall into temptation,* etc.; *those who wish to become rich,* he says, as though addressing the poor. Have these words of the apostle encountered you as a poor person? Say them, and you're rich. Say them in your heart and from the heart: "I brought nothing into this world, and what's more I cannot take anything out of it. Having board and lodging, with these I am content. For if I wish to become rich, I will fall into temptation and a snare." Say it, and remain as you were found. Don't involve yourself in many pains, or when you want to extricate yourself, you may be torn to ribbons.

But were you encountered by the apostle's words as a rich person? There are other words too which we should quote. People who have been found already rich mustn't imagine nothing has been said to them. To the same Timothy the apostle says—but he's saying it to a poor man; Timothy, you see, was poor, like Paul. So what is he going to say on this subject to Timothy, a poor man, that will concern those who have been encountered already rich? Let me tell you what: *Command,* he says, *the rich of this world*—because there are also the rich of God; and only the rich of God are the true rich, such as Paul himself was, who said, *For I have learned in whatever circumstances I am, to find it enough for me* (Phil 4:11). Give me one of the rich of this world who can say that: *I have learned in whatever circumstances I am, to find it enough for me;* not enough, though, for the avaricious.

So then: *Command,* he says, *the rich of this world.* What am I to tell them? "Don't wish to be rich?" But they already are rich; let them listen to what's said to them, to the chief point: *not to be haughty* (1 Tm 6:17). This is what having riches and loving them much results in. A nest is constructed for pride, where it can be fed and grow; and what makes it worse, it doesn't eventually fly away; it stays. So, before anything else, *not to be haughty.* To understand, to appreciate the fact, to think about the fact that they are mortal, exactly the same as the poor are mortal. The earth received both sorts naked,[13] death awaits both, fevers have no respect for either. The poor catch them, bedded on the ground, while the rich can't frighten them off, when they come, by their beds chased in silver.

So, *Command the rich of this world not to be haughty.* They should acknowledge that the poor are their peers; poor people are also people; different clothes, but the same skin; and if a rich person on dying is buried in perfumes and spices, it doesn't mean he won't rot, but only that it will happen later. He rots more slowly; does it mean he won't rot at all? But let's suppose they don't both rot; still they are both lacking in sensation. *Command the rich of this world not to be haughty.* Let them avoid being haughty, and they will truly be such as they wish to appear; they will possess their riches without love, they won't be possessed by them.

We use things out of necessity, we enjoy them for fun

8. But see what follows: *Not to be haughty, nor to place their hopes in the uncertainty of riches.* You love gold; make certain, if you can, that you are not afraid of losing it. You've amassed a fortune; give yourself, if you can, security. *Nor to place their hopes in the uncertainty of riches.* They come, they go; just now they were there, now they're lost, now you're afraid of losing them. So don't place your hopes in the uncertainty of riches.

He's taken your hopes from there. Where has he fixed them? *But in the living God.* That's where to fix your hopes, where to cast the anchor of your heart,[14] so that the storms of the world won't tear you from there and wreck you. *But in the living God, who bestows all things on us abundantly for our enjoyment* (1 Tm 6:17). If all things, how much more himself? And indeed for our enjoyment he will himself be all things. Because I don't think that *who has given us all things abundantly for our enjoyment* refers to anything else but himself. Using things, after all, appears to be one thing, enjoying them another.[15] I mean we use things out of necessity, we enjoy them for fun. So he has given us these temporal things to use, himself to enjoy. So if it's himself he gives, why does it say *all things,* unless because of what's written, *That God may be all in all* (1 Cor 15:28)? So set your heart there for enjoyment, so that it may be a heart lifted up. Untie yourself from here, but moor yourself there; it's dangerous for you in these stormy conditions to remain without a mooring.

Lift up your heart, don't have it down on the ground

9. *Not to place their hopes in the uncertainty of riches;* not however nowhere, *but in the living God, who bestows all things on us abundantly for our enjoyment* (1 Tm 6:17). What can be all things as much as the one who made all things? I mean, all these things wouldn't have been made by him unless he had known them. Will anyone have the nerve to say, "God made this thing which he didn't know"? He made what he knew. So he had it before he made it. But he had all these things in wonderful ways, not as he made them, temporal and transitory, but as a craftsman makes things; he has inwardly what he makes outwardly. So there, in God's knowledge, all things are excellent, immortal, unfailing, permanent, and God himself is *all in all* (1 Cor 15:28); it is for his saints, though, for his just ones that he will be all in all. So he suffices us, and he alone suffices us, of whom someone said, *Show us the Father and it suffices us;* but *Am I with you all this time,* came the answer, *and you do not know me? Whoever has seen me has also seen the Father* (Jn 14:8-9). God, Father, Son and Holy Spirit, is all things. Quite rightly does he alone suffice.

If we must be avaricious, let us love him. If we desire wealth, let us desire him. He alone will be able to satisfy us, about whom it says, *Who satisfies your desire with good things* (Ps 103:5). Is this not enough for the sinner? Such a great good as this, is this alone not enough for the sinner?[16] By wanting to have more, he lost all things, because *the root of all evil is avarice* (1 Tm 6:10). Rightly does God through the prophet reproach the sinful soul that goes whoring away from him, and say, *"You thought, if you withdrew from me, you would have more* (Is 57:8 LXX). But like that younger son, why, you have ended up feeding pigs; why, you have lost all things; why, you have remained in want, and left it very late before you grew tired and came back.[17] Now at least realize that what the Father gave you, he could keep for you more safely. *You thought, if you withdrew from me, you would have more."*

O sinful soul, filled with harlotries, turned foul and faded, turned unclean, and still loved like that! So go back to the beautiful one, in order to return to beauty; go back and say to him who alone suffices you, *You have destroyed everyone who goes whoring away from you.* So what suffices, but that which comes next? *But for me it is good to cling to God* (Ps 73:27-28). So lift your heart up, don't leave it down on the ground, nor in those beggarly treasures, nor in a place to rot. In Adam too the root of all evils was avarice. You see, he wanted more than he had received, because God had not been enough for him.

We give earth, and we receive heaven

10. So what are you going to do with what you've got, rich man? Listen. Already you are avoiding being haughty; fine. You aren't placing your hopes in the uncertainty of riches, but you are hoping *in the living God, who bestows all things on us abundantly for our enjoyment* (1 Tm 6:17); splendid. So don't drag your feet about what follows: *let them be rich in good works.* Let us see that, and then we may believe what we can't see also.

You were saying, "I do have gold, but I don't love it." But your not loving it is your own business, inside you; if I've deserved well of you at all, prove it to me too; you're not hiding it from your God; prove it also to your brother. "How," you say, "shall I prove it?" From what follows: *Let them be rich in good works, always ready to give.* Be rich to this end, that you are always ready to give. The poor person, you see, wants to give and can't; he has difficulties, you have the facilities. *Let them be ready to give, let them share.* Do they lose anything? *Let them store up for themselves a good capital base for the future* (1 Tm 6:18-19).

And in case we should love even for the next world gold and silver and estates, and all the things that seem so fine in the property of human beings, and desire such things there when we are told: "Emigrate to there, deposit your treasure there"; he warns us against such materialistic thoughts, and says, *that they may grasp the true life* (1 Tm 6:19); not gold, which remains on earth, not amenities that rot and decay, not transitory goods, but the true life. So how are we to emigrate, when all this won't cross over to there, and we won't have there what we transfer from here? In a kind of way the Lord our God wants us to be traders, he makes deals with us; we give what there's plenty of here, we receive what there's plenty of there. It's the way many business people make deals of exchange; they give something in one place, and receive something else in the place they go to. For example, he says to his friend: "Accept gold from me here, and in Africa give me oil." He transfers something, and yet he doesn't transfer it. He had already transferred what he's given, but this isn't what he has received. He receives what he desires.

This sort of exchange, my brothers and sisters, is like our trading transaction. What do we give, and what do we receive? We give here what we can't take with us, even if we wanted to; so why should we lose it? Let's give here what's less, in order that what is much more may be found by us there. We give earth, and we receive heaven; we give temporal things, and receive eternal things; we give things that go rotten, and we receive things that are immortal; in a nutshell, we give what God has given us, and we receive God. So let's not drag our feet over this exchange of goods, over this inexpressibly profitable kind of trading. Let's profit from being here, profit from having been born, profit from our wandering exile here. Don't let's return home destitute.

You're holding God's bond

11. Don't let the moth of evil thoughts get into the closet of your heart. You mustn't say, "I won't give, in case I don't have anything tomorrow." Don't give too much thought to the future—or rather give a great deal of thought to the future, but to the distant future. *Let them store up for themselves*, he says, *a good capital base for the future, that they may grasp the true life* (1 Tm 6:19). And not even in the way the apostle mentioned, *so that it means relief of others, but difficulty for you; but each of you from what you have* (2 Cor 8:13). Only don't love it. Keep it, hoard it, rely on accumulated capital; all that is placing your hopes in uncertainties. How many people have gone to sleep rich, got up poor!

You see, it's because of such thoughts that after saying, *Without love, a measure of money is sufficient for present needs* (Heb 13:5)—because of those evil thoughts that say, "If I haven't got savings deposited, who will give me anything, when I start being in want?" And again, "I've plenty to live on, quite enough to live on; but what if I have to go to law? What will I meet such expenses with?" However much you manage to count up and insure against all the bad things that can happen to the human race, often enough a single disaster upsets all your calculations and lists,[18] and not only do all your insurance policies go for nothing, but you will find nothing left in your hands. So against this maggoty kind of thought, against this destructive moth God placed something in his scriptures, rather as various strongly scented things[19] are commonly put among clothes to prevent them getting moth-eaten. What's this? You were making sure of not lacking the means to cope with this and that, and making a list of many possible disasters; weren't you afraid of one single huge one?

Pay attention to what comes next: *Without love, a measure of money is sufficient for present needs*, because he himself said, "*I will not forsake you, I will not desert you*" (Heb 13:5; Dt 31:6.8; Jos 1:5). You were afraid of I don't know what evils, for that reason you were saving up money; count me as your guarantor." That's what God says to you. It isn't a man, not your equal or you yourself, but God who says to you, *I will not forsake you, I will not desert you*. If a man made such a promise, you would trust him; God makes it, and you hesitate? He made the promise, put it in writing, made out the bond; you needn't worry at all. Read what you've got in your hand, you're holding God's bond; as your debtor you hold the one whom you have asked to cancel your debts.[20] Amen.

NOTES

1. This date, more precisely May-June 397, is proposed by Perler and Lambot, who also say the sermon was preached in Carthage. Others put it later, between 410 and 412.

2. School of Christ, in the sense that we talk of the school of some philosopher or other. Augustine is still very much in the tradition, which goes back to Justin Martyr in the mid-second century, that regarded Christianity as the one wholly true philosophy.

3. Augustine conflates this verse with the conclusion of 2 Tm 2:22. Perhaps they were already conflated in his text.

4. He is being gratuitously offensive to the philosophers here; their moralists rated justice and faith, in the sense of fidelity, as highly as any Christian preacher. The only thing they would have omitted from this sentence is the opening address and the last phrase. But he does go on to explain himself a little.

5. The most notable example was Diogenes, the founder of the school of the Cynics, who lived in a tub.

6. *Vita*; an alternative reading is *via*, by departing from this way. But Augustine would never suggest that departing from the way is the normal or right thing to do. This sermon exists in two editions, which differ from each other in innumerable points of detail. I only draw attention to them where I depart from the reading given in the latest edition.

7. An easily remembered pun in the Latin, on *mundus*, world, and *mundus*, clean, neat or tidy.

8. He certainly construes this text rather willfully, as he could easily have ascertained had he consulted the Greek; the single word *aphilarguros* in that language, meaning "not-money-loving," is translated in the Latin by *sine amore pecuniae*. But Augustine takes the genitive *pecuniae* with the following noun, *modus*. This is even clearer later on in the sermon, where he rearranges the words in the order *sine amore modus pecuniae*. It is only in the Latin that *without love* is put first.

9. He has to say "in this matter," because he could not allow himself to be understood as encouraging slaves to run away from their masters—for which the penalty in any case could be exceedingly savage.

10. See Acts 15:9.

11. The reply, "We have lifted them up to the Lord." In the Latin it is *Sursum corda* answered by *Habemus ad Dominum*.

12. In his characteristically teasing way he delays saying what this is for a whole paragraph and more.

13. When they were born.

14. See Heb 6:19.

15. A theme developed at length in *Teaching Christianity*; a very stark principle of Augustinian ethics.

16. He is thinking of Adam, the archetypal sinner, as will become clear at the end of the section.

17. See Lk 15:14-19.

18. Meaning all your insurance policies against all the eventualities you have thought about.

19. Horse chestnuts, I remember my mother preferring to moth-balls.

20. In the Lord's Prayer, Mt 6:12.

SERMON 178

ON THE WORDS OF THE APOSTLE, TITUS 1:9: *THAT HE* [THE BISHOP] *MAY BE STRONG TO ENCOURAGE HIS PEOPLE IN SOUND DOCTRINE, AND TO CONFUTE THOSE WHO CONTRADICT IT;* AGAINST THE PLUNDERERS OF OTHER PEOPLE'S GOODS

Date: after 396[1]

A bishop must be strong in sound doctrine

1. When the blessed apostle's letter about appointing bishops was read, it undoubtedly reminded me that I should take a look at myself; but it also reminded you that you shouldn't judge me; especially because we all heard the last sentence of the reading just now from the passage of the gospel: *Do not make personal judgments, but judge with a just judgment* (Jn 7:24). And so you should never pass judgment on another person's character,[2] if you don't pass judgment on your own. The blessed apostle says somewhere, *I do not box as though beating the air; but I chastise my body and reduce it to slavery, lest perchance while preaching to others, I myself should be found to be disqualified* (1 Cor 9:26-27). His anxiety has terrified us; I mean, what will the lamb do, when the ram trembles?

So among the many things which the apostle wrote about what a bishop should be like, we also heard this one point upon which it must be enough to talk and reflect for the time being. I mean, if we tried to discuss every single point and reflect on it as it deserves, my powers would not be up to the necessary talking, nor would yours to the necessary listening. So what is it I want to say, if the one who has terrified me will help me? Among other things, he said a bishop must be strong in sound doctrine, in order to be able to confute those who contradict it. It's a very big task, a heavy burden, a steep slope. But *I will hope*, it says, *in God, since it is he who will deliver me from the snare of the hunters, and from the harsh word* (Ps 91:2-3). You see, there's nothing which makes a person who is God's steward more reluctant to argue with those who contradict, than fear of harsh words.

289

The plunderer of other people's property
must be rotten with sores

2. First of all, then, I will explain to you, as far as the Lord enables me to, what is meant by arguing with those who contradict. There's more than one way of understanding who are meant by those who contradict. Those who contradict us in words, you see, are really very few indeed; but plenty who do so by the bad way they live. When will a Christian ever have the nerve to say to me that it is a good thing to plunder other people's things, seeing that he won't even dare to say that it is good to keep a very tight grip on one's own? I mean, take that rich man, whose lands had prospered, and who was delighted to have hit on the plan of pulling down his old barns and putting up new and roomier ones, so that he could fill them, and say to his soul, *Soul, you have many good things to last a long time; rejoice, have fun, take your fill* (Lk 12:16-19); so was this rich man after other people's property? He was making arrangements to gather his own crops, planning where to put them, not thinking about gathering them from some neighbor's fields, by upsetting the boundary, or robbing a poor man, or cheating a simple fellow, but only about gathering them from his own. Listen to what this man heard, who just kept a very tight grip on what was his own; and from that work out what those who plunder other people may expect.

So while he was thinking what a very far-sighted plan he had worked out, about pulling down his old cramped barns, and building new, more capacious ones, and about gathering and storing all his crops, not about hankering after and grabbing someone else's; God said to him, "*Fool*; just where you think you're clever, precisely there, fool. *Fool*," he said, "*this very night they are requiring your soul from you; these things you have got ready, whose will they be?* (Lk 12:20)—if you keep them, they won't be yours; if you distribute them, they will be. "Why," he asks, "store up what you are going to leave behind?"

There you have someone rebuked as a fool for the bad practice of hoarding. If the man who hoards what is his own is a fool, I leave you to find the right name for one who makes off with what belongs to others. If the hoarder of his own goods is lousy, the plunderer of other people's must be rotten with sores. But not like that man, covered with sores, who used to lie at the rich man's gate, and whose sores were licked by the dogs.[3] It was only his body, after all, that was rotten with sores; but it's the plunderer's heart.

Out of heartless stinginess the rich man had failed to give

3. Someone may perhaps answer and say, "It wasn't a very big punishment for that man to whom God said *Fool*." God's saying *Fool* is not like a man's saying it. Such a word from God against anyone is a judgment. I mean to say, do you suppose God is going to give the kingdom of heaven to fools? And if he's not going to give them the kingdom of heaven, what's left for them but the punishment of gehenna? You think that's just my guess; let's see it stated openly and clearly. After all, that other rich man, before whose gate lay the poorest of the poor covered with sores, he wasn't said either to be a plunderer of other

people's property. *There was a certain rich man*, it says, *who used to wear purple and fine linen, and feast sumptuously every day* (Lk 16:19). He said he was rich; he didn't say, "A swindler"; he didn't say, "An oppressor of the poor"; he didn't say, "A plunderer of other people's property, or a receiver, or an informer";[4] he didn't say "A despoiler of orphans"; he didn't say "A persecutor of widows"; he didn't say any of these things; just *There was a certain rich man*. What's so special about that? He was rich, rich with what belonged to him. Who had he taken anything from? Or perhaps he would do that sort of thing, and the Lord would keep quiet about him, and be a respecter of persons to the point of concealing his crimes, the one who says to us *Do not make personal judgments* (Jn 7:24); is that it?

So if you want to hear what that rich man's crime was, look no further than what you hear from Truth: *He was rich. He used to wear purple and fine linen, and feast sumptuously every day*. So what was his offense? The man lying at his gate covered with sores, and given no help. This, you see, is openly said about him, that he was callously hardhearted. After all, beloved, if that poor man lying at his gate had received enough bread from the rich man, would it have said about him that *he longed to be filled with the crumbs that fell from the rich man's table* (Lk 16:21)? It was solely because of this inhumanity which let him ignore the poor man lying at his gate, and do nothing to feed him suitably, that he died and was buried; and when he was in torment in the infernal regions, he lifted up his eyes, and saw the poor man in Abraham's bosom. And why should I spend any longer on it? He desired a drop, though he hadn't given a crumb; it was by a just sentence that he didn't receive, since out of heartless stinginess he had failed to give. So if that's the punishment of the stingy, what must be the punishment of plunderers?

Wishing to give alms with stolen property

4. But the plunderer of other people's property says to me, "I'm not like that rich man. I provide 'agape meals,'[5] I send food to those chained up in prison, I clothe the naked, I welcome strangers." Do you really imagine you're giving? Stop grabbing, and then you have really given. The person you've given something to rejoices; the one you've snatched something from is crying; which of these two is the Lord going to listen to? You say to the one you've given something to, "You should thank me for what you've received." But the other person says to you from the other side, "I'm wringing my hands for what you've taken from me; and anyway, you've taken practically everything, and given him the merest fraction."

So even if you had given the needy the whole of what you took off that other person, not even so does God like such works. God says to you, "Fool, I commanded you to give, but not from what belongs to someone else. If you have property, give from what is yours. If you have nothing to give from what is yours, you would do better not to give anything to anyone than to despoil other people."[6]

The Lord Christ is going to say, when he takes his seat at his great assize and separates some to the right and others to the left, he's going to say to those who do good, *Come, blessed of my Father, receive the kingdom*; to the unprofitable ones, however, who have done nothing good for the poor, *Go into everlasting fire*. And what's he going to say to the good? *For I was hungry, and you gave me to eat*, etc. And they will answer him. *Lord, when did we see you hungry?* And he will tell them, *When you did it for one of the least of mine, you did it for me*. So understand, you fool you, wishing to give alms with stolen property, that when you feed a Christian, you're feeding Christ; when you strip a Christian, you're stripping Christ. Just notice what he said to those on the left: *Go into everlasting fire*. Why? *For I was hungry, and you did not give me to eat; I was naked, and you did not clothe me* (Mt 25:31-46). Go. Where to? *Into everlasting fire*; straightaway, go. Why? *I was naked, and you did not clothe me*. So if the person to whom Christ is going to say *I was naked and you did not clothe me*, is going into eternal fire, what place in the eternal fire, do you think, will that person have, to whom he is going to say, "I was clothed, and you stripped me"?

Do not rob a pagan

5. Here perhaps, to get out of hearing such words, and Christ saying to you, "I was clothed, and you stripped me," you're going to change your tune and consider stripping a pagan and clothing a Christian. Here too Christ will answer you, indeed he will answer you right now through the mouth of his servant and his minister of sorts;[7] Christ will answer you and say, "Here also, spare me damage to my interests. When you, a Christian, you see, strip a pagan bare, you prevent him becoming a Christian."

Even here too, perhaps, you'll still have an answer: "Oh, I'm not inflicting punishment out of hatred, but rather out of a love of discipline; the reason I'm stripping the pagan bare is by this harsh and salutary discipline to make him a Christian." I would listen to you and believe you, if what you have taken from him as a pagan, you gave back to him as a Christian.[8]

Restrain yourselves from grabbing what doesn't belong to you

6. I have been speaking against the single vice of robbery,[9] which is everywhere making a mess of human affairs; I've been speaking, and nobody is contradicting me. Who, after all, would have the nerve to speak in contradiction of the most manifest truth? So I'm not doing what the apostle urged me to, I'm not confuting those who contradict; I'm addressing obedient people, instructing people who applaud, not arguing against people who contradict.

Fine; but they do contradict, not with their tongues but their lives. I warn, he robs; I teach, he robs; I command, he robs; I argue, he robs. How can you say he's not contradicting? So let me say what I think should be sufficient on this subject. Restrain yourselves, brothers; restrain yourselves, my sons, from this habit of grabbing what doesn't belong to you. And you others, who groan and moan under the hands of grabbers, refrain from the greedy desire to grab. Someone else is powerful and influential, and grabs things; you are sighing and sobbing in the hands of the grabber. It's because you can't grab, that's why you don't. Just have the means, and then I will praise you for taming your greed.

Findings must be restored

7. *Blessed*, says holy scripture, *is the person who has not gone after gold; who was able to transgress and did not do so; who was able to do evil, and did not do it* (Sir 31:8.10). You're saying, though, "I have never denied it, when something belonged to someone else."[10] Because, perhaps, nobody has entrusted you with anything; or perhaps they have, but have done so in the presence of witnesses. Tell me, have you given back something deposited with you, when you received it all alone with the other person, and only God was between you? If you did give it back then, if when the depositor was dead, you gave it back to his son who knew nothing about it; then I will praise you, because you have not gone after gold; because you were able to transgress and did not do so; because you were able to do evil and did not do it. Or if you found on the road, where no one saw you, someone else's purse full of money, and gave it back without delay to the person it belonged to.

Come now, brothers and sisters, return into yourselves, take a look at yourselves, question yourselves, and give yourselves true answers, and judge yourselves without respect of persons, but make a just judgment of yourselves. Look here, you're a Christian, you come regularly to church, you hear the word of God, you are moved to raptures by the readings from God's word. You praise the preacher to the skies; what I'm looking for is a doer; you, I repeat, praise the speaker; I in turn am looking for a doer.

You're a Christian, you come regularly to church, you love God's word, and enjoy listening to it. So here you are, this is the point I'm putting to you; examine yourself on it, weigh yourself against it, take your seat on the bench of your mind about it, and set yourself before yourself, and try yourself; and if you find you are a bit crooked, straighten yourself out and correct yourself. So here's the point I'm putting to you: God says in his law that findings must be restored;[11] God says in his law, which he gave to his first people, for whom Christ had not yet died, that anything found which belongs to someone else must be given back; if for example you find someone else's purse of money on the road, you must give it back. But you don't know who to? Ignorance won't make excuses, if avarice hasn't got the upper hand.

An example of restitution

8. I've something to tell your graces, because these things are God's gifts; and there are those in the people of God who don't listen to God's word to any purpose; I'll tell you what an extremely poor man did, when I was resident in Milan; he was so poor that he was doorkeeper for a teacher of grammar;[12] but

certainly a Christian, while the other was a pagan teacher; the one at the door a better person than the one in the master's chair. He found a purse, containing, if my memory doesn't deceive me, almost two hundred dollars.[13] Remembering the law, he put a notice up publicly. He knew, you see, that it had to be restored to its owner, but he didn't know who that was. He put up a public notice: "Let the person who has lost some money come to such-and-such a place and ask for so-and-so." The owner, who was rushing round everywhere, wringing his hands, saw and read the notice, and came to the man. And in case he should be trying to get hold of another person's property, he asked for indications, questioned him about the quality of the purse, about the seal, also about the number of coins. And when he had answered satisfactorily, he gave back what he had found.

The other man, of course, was overjoyed, and wishing to repay him, offered him twenty dollars, as a tenth of the sum recovered. But he wouldn't take it. He offered him at least ten; he wouldn't take it. He asked him at the very least to accept five; he refused. So in a huff the man threw down the purse: "I haven't lost anything," he said; "if you won't accept anything from me, then I haven't lost anything either." What a contest, my brothers and sisters, what a contest, what a fight, what a clash of wills! The world a theater, God the spectator. Eventually he gave in and accepted what he was offered; he gave it all away immediately to the poor, didn't leave a single dollar in his own house.

Be honest finders

9. So now what? If I have acted at all upon your feelings, if God's word has settled in you, if it's found a resting place among you, do this, my brothers and sisters. You mustn't think you will suffer a loss if you do it; you will make a big profit if you do what I'm telling you. "I've lost twenty dollars, I've lost two hundred, five hundred." What have you lost? They had vanished from your house, someone else had lost them, not you. The earth is common to us all, you are in the same house, you are both travelers in this world, you've entered the same tavern of this life.[14] He put it down, he forgot it; it fell out of his pocket, you found it somewhere else. Who found it? You, a Christian. Who found it? You, who have heard the law, a Christian who have heard the law. Who found it? You, who applauded loudly when you heard it, you have found it. So if you were applauding sincerely, give back what you have found. So if you haven't given back what you found, you bore witness against yourself when you applauded.

Be honest finders, and then find fault to your heart's content with iniquitous plunderers. Because anything you've found and not given back, you have in fact plundered. As far as you could, you've done it. It was because you couldn't do more that you didn't do more. If you deny it belongs to someone else, you'd grab it if you could. It's fear that stops you grabbing it; you aren't doing good, just being afraid of something bad.

God questions the heart, not the hand

10. What's so special about being afraid of something bad? It's very special, not doing something bad; it's very special, loving the good. I mean, even the brigand is afraid of bad things; and also when he lacks the power he doesn't do it; but he's still a brigand.[15] God, you see, questions the heart, not the hand. A wolf comes to the sheepfold, looks for ways of getting in, of slaughtering, of devouring; the shepherds are alert, the dogs bark; it can't do anything, can't drag away, can't kill; but all the same it comes a wolf, it goes away a wolf. Just because it didn't take a sheep, does that mean it came a wolf, and went away a sheep? The wolf comes growling, it goes away howling; it's still a wolf all the same, both growling and howling.

So question yourself, whoever you are, wishing to sit in judgment; and see if you don't do wrong, even when you can do it and escape human punishment. In that case you fear God; nobody's there except you and the person you can do wrong to, and God who can see you both. Think, be afraid in that case too. It's little enough, what I've said, "Think, be afraid of evil in that case too." In that case, love the good. Because even if you refrain from doing wrong out of fear of hell, you are not yet perfect. I make bold to say, that if you refrain from doing wrong out of fear of hell, you indeed have faith, because you believe that God's judgment is coming; I'm very glad about your faith, but I'm afraid about the badness of your character. What's this I've said? That if you refrain from doing wrong out of fear of hell, it means you are not doing good out of a love of justice.

Fan this spark of good love in yourselves

11. It's one thing to fear punishment, another to love justice. You ought to have a chaste love; a love by which you desire to see, not heaven and earth, not the liquid plains of the sea,[16] not frivolous shows, not the flash and sparkle of gems; but desire to see your God, to love your God, because it says, *Dearly beloved, we are God's children, and it has not yet appeared what we shall be; but we know that when he appears we shall be like him, since we shall see him as he is* (1 Jn 3:2). There's the vision for you, for the sake of which you should do good; there's what you should refrain from doing evil for.

You see, if you are longing to see your God, if during this exile, this wandering, you are sighing for love of him; why, then the Lord your God is testing you, as if he were to say to you: "Look, do what you like, satisfy all your greedy desires, extend the scope of your wickedness, give free rein to self-indulgence, consider as lawful whatever happens to please you; I won't punish you for any of this, I won't cast you into hell; I will just deny you the sight of my face." If that has horrified you, then you have really loved. If your heart shuddered at what has just been said, that your God will deny you the sight of his face, it means you accounted not seeing your God to be a terrible punishment; it means you have loved freely.

So if my sermon has found in your hearts just a spark of such spontaneous love of God, nurse it carefully. Tell yourselves urgently to increase it by prayer, humility, the pain of repentance, the love of justice, good works, sincere sighs, a praiseworthy way of life, loyal friendship. Fan this spark of good love in yourselves; nourish it in yourselves. When it grows, and bursts into flame with a glorious, satisfying blaze, then it burns up the straw of all the greedy desires of the flesh.

NOTES

1. The date suggested by the scholars merely means after Augustine became bishop of Hippo Regius, which is obvious enough. From the confident tone of the sermon I would infer that he had been bishop for some time; so I myself would date it after 400 at the earliest. And again the tone leaves me in no doubt that he was preaching to his own flock in one of the churches of Hippo.

2. Reading *Personam itaque nemo accipiat alienam*, instead of the text's . . . *accipit* . . . , which makes a straight indicative sentence out of it; one, surely, that is for the most part untrue!

3. See Lk 16:20.

4. A common way of "legally" laying hands on other people's property was by informing against them.

5. *Agapes*, the Greek word for charity, also used in early Christian literature for the community meals in the course of which the eucharist was celebrated (see Jude 13; also 2 Pt 2:13 in one reading; and 1 Cor 11:17-26). Long before Augustine's time these community meals had been detached from the eucharist proper, and held after it. By his time this was probably only an occasional affair, and perhaps the name was now given to meals laid on by wealthier Christians for the poorer members of the community.

6. On the face of it, Augustine would not have approved of Robin Hood as a model of social behavior. But then Robin Hood would have claimed that he was only doing his bit to rectify social injustices by a forceful redistribution of property; whereas the people whose hypocrisy Augustine was excoriating were for the most part well-to-do citizens who were not in the least scrupulous about how they made their money, and who went in for merely token charity.

7. Augustine himself.

8. There is a certain rather sour irony here. What Augustine's hypocritical plunderers say here, is almost exactly what he would later say himself in justification of the crippling fines and confis-cations that would be imposed by imperial edicts on obstinate Donatists; the purpose of these laws, he would say, was by this harsh and salutary discipline to make them Catholics.

9. Mostly "legalized" robbery—daylight robbery, as we say.

10. The case he's dealing with now is that of not repaying loans, or not returning pledges that have been deposited with you.

11. See Dt 22:3; no question of "finder's keepers."

12. Himself hardly a wealthy man; a man running a small private school all on his own, apart from his doorkeeper.

13. *Solidi*, for which the literal equivalent would be shillings. Above I have just translated it "money."

14. He is not putting his illustration very clearly. But what it seems to be is something like this: A has entrusted to B for safekeeping $20, $200, $500. B says (dishonestly?) "I've lost it." Augustine says to him, "No you haven't; it's disappeared from your house, but it's A who's lost it." Then comes this slight sidetrack about all being in the same boat together. Then he goes on, with the case changing a little, to suggest that A dropped it in B's house and B found it. All rather confused; but with him acting the dialogue in the pulpit it may have been clearer to his audience.

15. As well as his fear of bad things (punishment if he's caught), it is also his lack of power that deters him sometimes from acts of brigandage.

16. I suspect a quotation from a classical author (Horace, perhaps?), but am too ignorant of the classics to be able to trace it.

SERMON 179

ON THE WORDS OF THE APOSTLE JAMES 1:19. 22: *BUT LET EACH OF YOU BE QUICK TO HEAR, BUT SLOW TO SPEAK* AND ON THESE OTHERS IN THE SAME PLACE: *BUT BE DOERS OF THE WORD, AND NOT HEARERS ONLY*

Date: before 409[1]

> *It's a futile preacher outwardly of God's word,*
> *who isn't also inwardly a listener*

1. The blessed apostle James is summoning us to be earnest hearers of the word of God, when he says, *But be doers of the word, and not hearers only, deceiving yourselves* (Jas 1:22). It isn't, you see, the one whose word it is, nor the one through whom the word is uttered, but your own selves that you deceive. So on the strength of this utterance flowing from the wellspring of truth, through the absolutely truthful mouth of the apostle, I too make bold to add my own exhortation to you; and while I'm exhorting you, to take a look at myself. After all, it's a futile preacher outwardly of God's word, who isn't also inwardly a listener. Nor are we, who have to preach the word of God to his various peoples,[2] such strangers to common humanity and faithful reflection, that we are unaware of our own danger when we do so. However, he gives us the reassurance that while we are put in danger by our ministry, we are aided by your prayers.

Because to show you, brothers and sisters, how much safer a place you are standing in than we are, I need only quote another saying of this same apostle: *But let each of you be quick to hear, but slow to speak* (Jas 1:19). And so first let me speak about this duty and task of ours, because of this saying in which we are urged to be quicker to listen and slower to speak; and then, when I have made my excuses for this duty of ours which has us speaking so often, I will come to the point which I first put before you.

> *When I hear, that's when I rejoice*

2. It is our duty to exhort you not to be hearers only of the word, but also doers. So because we speak to you so often, wouldn't anyone, who disregards our obligations, pass judgment on us when he reads, *But let every person be quick to hear but slow to speak* (Jas 1:19)? Well there you are,[3] your eagerness

never permits us to observe this recommendation. So you ought to be praying, to be supporting me whom you are compelling to be in danger.

And yet, my brothers and sisters, let me tell you something I would like you to believe, because you can't see it in my heart. Here I am, speaking to you so assiduously, at the bidding of my lord and brother, your bishop, and at your insistence; and yet I tell you that what gives me really solid satisfaction is listening. I repeat, the time my satisfaction, my joy, is really solid and unalloyed is when I am listening, not when I'm preaching. Then, you see, I can enjoy myself without a qualm. That pleasure has no side to it; where there is only the solid rock of truth, there's no need to fear the precipice of pride. And to show you that that's how it is, listen to what it says here: *To my hearing you will give exultation and gladness.* When I hear, that's when I rejoice. Then he went on to add, *The bones that have been humbled will exult* (Ps 51:8).

So when we are listening, we are humble; but when we are preaching, even if we aren't hurtling down the steep slope of pride, we are certainly at least having to put the brakes on. Even if I don't get a swollen head, I'm in real danger of getting one. But when I'm listening, I can enjoy it without anyone to cheat me of it, I can take pleasure in it without anyone noticing me.[4] Such joy was also known by that friend of the bridegroom, who said, *The one who has the bride is the bridegroom; but the bridegroom's friend stands, and listens to him.* And that precisely is why he stands, because he listens to him. Because even the first man stood by listening to God, and fell by listening to the serpent. So, *the bridegroom's friend stands and listens to him; and with joy,* he says, *he rejoices because of the bridegroom's voice* (Jn 3:29). Not because of his own voice, but because of the bridegroom's. And yet, while he heard the bridegroom's voice inwardly, he did not fail to relay it to the people outwardly.

Mary was listening to the word of Christ

3. This is the part that Mary also chose for herself, who sat at the Lord's feet and listened at leisure to his word, while her sister was serving them and distracted with all the serving. John the Baptist was standing, she was sitting; yet she in her heart was standing, and he in his humility was sitting. Standing, you see, signifies perseverance; sitting, humility.[5] And to show you that standing signifies perseverance, the devil is said not to have had this perseverance; it's said about him, *He was a murderer from the beginning, and did not stand in the truth* (Jn 8:44). Again that sitting signifies humility is shown by that psalm, where it is reminding us about repentance, and says, *Arise after you have sat down, you who eat the bread of sorrow* (Ps 127:2). What's the meaning of *Arise after you have sat down? Whoever humbles himself shall be exalted* (Lk 14:11).

What a good thing, though, it is to listen, the Lord himself attests, when he speaks about Mary who was sitting at his feet and listening to his word. When her sister, you see, distracted with the serving, complained that she had been deserted by her own sister, what she heard from the Lord she had appealed to was: *Martha, Martha, you are busy with many things; for all that, one thing is needed. Mary has chosen the better part, which shall not be taken away from her* (Lk 10:41-42). Was it something bad, then, that Martha was doing? Can any of us find suitable words to express what a wonderfully good thing it is to offer hospitality to the saints? If to any saints at all, how much more to the head and chief members, Christ and the apostles? Don't all of you who practice this excellent virtue of hospitality, when you hear what Martha was doing, don't you all say to yourselves, "O blessed, O lucky woman, to have the honor of receiving the Lord; whose guests turned out to be the apostles, walking about in the flesh!" And you mustn't lose heart either, just because you can't do what Martha did, welcome Christ into your house with his apostles; he himself reassures you: *When you did it for one of these least of mine, you did it for me* (Mt 25:40).

So it's a great work, a really great work, which the apostle enjoins on us when he says, *contributing to the needs of the saints, practicing hospitality* (Rom 12:13). He also praises it in the letter to the Hebrews, when he says, *This way some people have entertained angels unawares* (Heb 13:2). So it's a great service, a great gift. And yet *Mary has chosen the better part*; because while her sister was worrying and slogging away, and taking care of all sorts of things, she was unoccupied, sitting down, listening.

Martha's part passes away,
but the reward given for it does not pass away

4. The Lord, however, showed us what made that the better part. Immediately after saying *Mary has chosen the better part*; as though we were to query this, wishing to know what made it better, he added, *which shall not be taken away from her* (Lk 10:42). What are we to make of this, my brothers and sisters? If the reason the part she chose is better, is that it shall not be taken away from her, then undoubtedly Martha chose the part which will be taken away from her. Plainly, it will be taken away from all people who minister to the bodily needs of the saints; what they do will be taken away from them. After all, they are not always going to be ministering to the saints. I mean, what do they minister to, but infirmity? What do they minister to, but mortality? Who do they minister to, but the hungry and the thirsty? All these things will have ceased to be, when this perishable thing has put on imperishability, and this mortal thing has put on immortality.[6] When the need has disappeared, there will be no ministering to the need.

The hard work will be taken away, but the reward will be paid. Who will there be then to serve food to, when no one is hungry? Or drink, when nobody's thirsty? Or lodging, when nobody's a stranger? So in order to be in a position to pay the reward for this work, the Lord agreed to be in need, together with his disciples. He too was hungry and thirsty, not because he was compelled to be, but because he agreed to be. Yes, it was a good thing that the one through whom all things were made[7] should be hungry; this after all would be a piece of good fortune for whoever might feed him. And when anybody fed the Lord, what was being given, who was it being given by, what was it being given from, who was it being given to?

What was being given? Food was being given to bread. Who was it being given by? Obviously, by those who wished to receive more. What was it being given from? Not from what was their very own, surely? I mean, what did they have that they had not received?[8] To whom was it being given? Wasn't it to the one who had created both what he was receiving and the person he was receiving it from? Yes, this is a great service, a great work, a great gift. And yet *Mary has chosen the better part, which shall not be taken away from her.* So Martha's part passes away; but, as I said, the reward given for it does not pass away.

Mary was eating the one she was listening to

5. Mary's part, though, does not pass away. Notice how it doesn't pass away. What was Mary enjoying while she was listening? What was she eating, what was she drinking? Do you know what she was eating, what she was drinking? Let's ask the Lord, who keeps such a splendid table for his own people, let's ask him. *Blessed,* he says, *are those who are hungry and thirsty for justice, because they shall be satisfied* (Mt 5:6). It was from this wellspring, from this storehouse of justice, that Mary, seated at the Lord's feet, was in her hunger receiving some crumbs. You see, the Lord was giving her then as much as she was able to take. But the whole amount, such as he was going to give at his table of the future, not even the disciples, not even the very apostles, were able to take in at the time when he said to them, *I still have many things to say to you; but you are unable to hear them now* (Jn 16:12).

So what, as I was saying, was Mary enjoying? What was she eating, what was she drinking so avidly with the mouth of her heart? Justice, truth. She was enjoying truth, listening to truth, avid for truth, longing for truth. In her hunger she was eating truth, drinking it in her thirst. She was being refreshed, and what she was being fed from was not diminishing. What was Mary enjoying, what was she eating? I'm lingering on the point, because I'm enjoying it too. I make bold to say that she was eating the one she was listening to. I mean, if she was eating truth, didn't he say himself, *I am the truth* (Jn 14:6)? And what more yet can I say? He was being eaten, because he was bread: *I,* he said, *am the bread who came down from heaven* (Jn 6:41). This is the bread which nourishes and never diminishes.[9]

What Mary chose was growing, not passing along and away

6. And so, would your graces please think hard. Look, we're talking about ministering to the saints, preparing food, serving drink, washing feet, making beds, welcoming under a roof; isn't all this going to pass away? But has anyone the nerve to say that we are now being fed on truth, but won't be fed on it when we attain to immortality? If we are now being fed on crumbs, won't we then have a full table? It was about that spiritual food, you see, that the Lord was talking, when he praised the centurion's faith and said, *Amen, I tell you, I have not found such great faith in Israel. And therefore I tell you, that many shall*

come from the east and the west, and shall sit at table with Abraham and Isaac and Jacob in the kingdom of heaven (Mt 8:10-11). Far be it from us to think of that food on the table of that kingdom, as if it were the same sort as that about which the apostle says, *Victuals for the belly, and the belly for victuals; but God will eliminate both it and them* (1 Cor 6:13). Why will he eliminate them? Because there won't be any hunger there. What will be eaten there won't ever come to an end.

This, after all, is the reward he is promising his saints when he says, *Amen I tell you, that he will make them sit down; and he will pass along and wait upon them* (Lk 12:37). What can *he will make them sit down* mean, but he will make them rest, make them take their ease? And what about *he shall pass along* (or he will pass[10]) *and wait upon them*? After this passing along of his he will wait upon them. Here, you see, Christ made a passing along, or a passing over. We will come to him where he has passed over to; there he is no longer passing over. You see, "Pasch" in the Hebrew language means Passover.[11] The Lord indicated this, or rather the evangelist, where he said about the Lord, *But when the hour had come for him to pass over from this world to the Father* (Jn 13:1).

So what Mary chose was growing, not passing along and away. The human heart's delight, you see, in the light of truth, in the wealth of wisdom, the delight of a human heart, a faithful heart, a holy heart—no pleasure can be found to compare with it in any respect at all, not even to be called less than this. I mean, if you call anything less, it can imply that by growing it will become equal. I don't want to say "less"; I'm not making any comparison, it's of a different kind altogether, it's quite, quite different. Why is it, after all, that you are all paying attention, all listening, all excited, and when something true is said you are delighted? What have you seen, what have you grasped? What color has appeared before your eyes, what form, what shape, what figure, what lines and limbs, what beauty of body? None of these things. And yet you love it. I mean, when would you have applauded like that, if you didn't love it? When would you have loved it, if you hadn't seen anything? And so, though I am not showing you any form of a body, any lines, color, beautiful movements, though I'm showing you nothing, you all the same are seeing, loving, applauding. If this delight in the truth is lovely now, it will be much lovelier then. *Mary has chosen the better part, which shall not be taken away from her* (Lk 10:42).

Inwardly, where nobody can see us, we are all hearers

7. I have shown your dearest graces,[12] to the best of my ability, as far as the Lord has been kind enough to help me, how much safer a place you are standing in by listening than I am by preaching. You, in this way, are doing, after all, what we are all going to be doing then. I mean, there won't then be any teacher of the word, but only the Word as teacher. So we come now to the consequence, which it is up to you to put into practice, up to us to remind you about. You, after all, are hearers of the word, we its preachers. Inwardly though, where nobody can see us, we are all hearers; inwardly in the heart, in the mind, where

he is teaching you, who prompts you to applaud. I, you see, am speaking outwardly, he is arousing you inwardly. So we are all hearers inwardly, and all of us, both outwardly and inwardly in the sight of God, ought to be doers.

How can we be doers inwardly? *Because whoever looks at a woman to lust after her, has already committed adultery with her in his heart* (Mt 5:28). He can even be an adulterer where no human eye can see, but God can certainly punish. So who is the doer inwardly? The one who does not look lustfully. Who is the doer outwardly? *Break your bread to the hungry* (Is 58:7). When you do that, your neighbor too can see it; but what spirit you do it in, only God can see. So, my dear brothers and sisters, *be doers of the word, and not hearers only, deceiving yourselves* (Jas 1:22), not God, not the one who's preaching. I, after all, or anyone else who preaches the word to you, can't see your hearts; what you are doing inside, in your thoughts, we can't see. Man cannot do it, but God is looking, since the human heart cannot be concealed from him. He can see with what eagerness you listen, what you think, what you grasp, how much you profit from what he supplies you with, how urgently you pray, how you beg God for what you haven't got, how you thank him for what you have; he knows all this, because he is going to demand his due. We bishops can invest the Lord's money in you; the rent-collector is coming, who said, *Wicked servant, you should have given my money to the bankers, and I, when I came, could have collected it with interest* (Mt 25:26-27).

To hear and to do is to build upon rock

8. So, my brothers and sisters, don't deceive yourselves, just because you come eagerly to hear the word, if you fail to do what you hear. Just think; if it's lovely to hear, how much more so to do. If you don't hear it at all, if you neglect the matter of hearing, then you are building nothing. If you hear and don't do, then you're building a ruin. On this matter Christ the Lord gave us an extremely apt comparison: *Whoever hears*, he said, *these words of mine and does them, I will compare him to a sensible man who builds his house upon rock. The rain poured down, the rivers came up, the winds blew, and struck that house, and it did not fall.* Why didn't it fall? *For it was founded upon rock.* So to hear and to do is to build upon rock. Because merely to hear is to build. *But whoever*, he says, *hears these words of mine and does not do them, I will compare him to a foolish man who builds.* He too builds. What does he build? Here you are; *he builds his house*; but because he doesn't do what he hears, even by hearing *he builds upon sand.* So the one who hears and doesn't do, builds on sand; the one who hears and does, on rock; the one who doesn't hear at all doesn't build either on sand or on rock. But notice what follows: *The rain poured down, the rivers came up, the winds blew, and they struck at that house and it fell; and its ruin was complete* (Mt 7:24-27). What a sad, sad sight!

9. So someone says, "What's the point of my hearing what I'm not going to do? Because by hearing," he goes on, "and not doing, I will be building a ruin. Isn't it safer to hear nothing?" That's an alternative, to be sure, that the Lord declined to touch on in the comparison he put forward. But he gave us a clue to the answer. In this world, you see, rain, winds, rivers are never still. You're not building on rock, so that they can come, but not throw you down? You're not building on sand, in case when they come they should tumble your house down? So because you are hearing nothing, you will be left just like that, without any roof at all. The rain comes, the rivers come; does that mean you're safe, because you are carried away naked, stripped of everything? So consider carefully just what part you have chosen for yourself. You won't find security, as you imagine, by not hearing. You will of necessity be overwhelmed, carried off, drowned.

So if it's a bad thing to build on sand, a bad thing to build nothing at all; the only good thing left is to build on rock. So it's bad not to hear; it's bad to hear and not do; the only thing left is to hear and to do. So, *be doers of the word, and not hearers only, deceiving yourselves* (Jas 1:22).

10. After such an exhortation, I'm afraid that instead of uplifting you with the word, I may crush you with desperation. Possibly, you see, there's someone in this packed congregation, one person perhaps, or two, or even several, who is inclined to pass judgment on me and say, "I would like to know if this guy who's speaking to me does all the things that he hears himself or says to others." My answer to him is, *But to me it is a very small matter to be judged by you or any human court* (1 Cor 4:3); since I too am able to know, partly at least, what I am; what I may be tomorrow I don't know. But to you, whoever you are that are bothered in this way, the Lord has given an assurance about me. You see, if I do what I say or what I hear, *be imitators of me, as I in my turn am of Christ* (1 Cor 4:16). But if I say and don't do, listen to the Lord: *What they say, do; but what they do, don't do* (Mt 23:3).

So if you have a good opinion of me, you can praise me; if a poor opinion you can accuse me; but you can't excuse yourself. I mean to say, how are you going to excuse yourself if you hurl an accusation against an evil preacher of the truth, who tells you God's word and does his own evil works; when your Lord, your redeemer, who shed his blood as your price, who enrolls you in his militia, and makes a brother out of his slave, when he never stops warning you and saying, *What they say, do; but what they do, don't do? For they say,* he goes on, *and do not do.* They say good things, do bad things; you, then, listen to the good things, and don't do the bad things.

Here you will answer, "How can I hear good things from a bad man? *Do they gather grapes from thorns?* (Mt 7:16)."[13]

NOTES

1. Another suggestion for the date is before 405. The sermon was clearly preached in another bishop's diocese (see section 2). Carthage was, of course, the city he most often preached in outside his own diocese. But the extra warmth with which he addresses the congregation at the beginning of section 7 makes me wonder if he was not perhaps preaching in his home town of Thagaste, where his lifelong friend Alypius was the bishop.

2. *Verbum Dei populis*. The genitive *Dei* can be construed with either *verbum* or *populis*. I have in fact construed it with both. The flavor of the plural *populis* I try to convey by saying "his various peoples"; meaning members of all the different local Churches, of Hippo, Thagaste, Carthage, etc.

3. *Ecce*; I infer some loud expression of dissent from such a judgment on the part of the congregation.

4. The preacher is in danger of getting a swollen head precisely when he is acclaimed as a good preacher; when he's noticed and applauded, and thereby "cheated" of pure enjoyment, because his pleasure begins to be tainted with self-satisfaction.

5. This is a very widely spread cultural symbolism. It could probably be said that only in the European tradition is standing in someone's presence a sign of respect and humility. In Africa, in Melanesia, as in ancient Israel, one humbles oneself by sitting down on the ground in the presence of greatness and authority. See, for example, 2 Sam 7:18. So the European custom of standing for the reading of the gospel to show respect slightly misfires in these other cultures. On the other hand, to stand throughout the service, as they seem to have done in the ancient Church, would be a sign of perseverance, of dogged steadfastness in the faith.

6. See 1 Cor 15:53.

7. See Jn 1:3.

8. See 1 Cor 4:7.

9. *Reficit, nec deficit.*

10. He uses two forms of the future tense of *transeo: transiet* in his first quotation, *transibit* in the second. Both appear to have been acceptable usage, though the former only occurs in the so-called silver age of Latin literature. Perhaps it struck Augustine as slightly colloquial.

11. Latin kept the Hebrew (or rather, Aramaic) word *pascha*, where English has substituted Passover for the Jewish festival, Easter for the Christian one.

12. It sounds funny in English, but then it was certainly unusual in Augustine's Latin: *dulcissimae caritati vestrae*. It's this touch of unusual warmth that suggests the congregation were for the most part known to him personally, and that therefore it was more probably in his birthplace, the small town of Thagaste, that he was preaching than the huge city of Carthage.

13. It is impossible to imagine Augustine ending on this note—unless he was suddenly taken ill. But the stenographer would certainly have noted that. So the ending has presumably got lost. Apparently the scribe of the manuscript from which the Maurist text was taken copied out, at this point, the last portion of Sermon 49, sections 8-11, instead of the proper ending. The poor man's computer must have been playing him up.

What Augustine presumably went on to say, as he has said elsewhere, was that sometimes vines in the hedges are entangled with thorn bushes; the good words come from the true vine, God, whose words they really are; but the bad actions come from the bad tree, the thorn. See Sermons 46, 22; 137, 13.

SERMON 179A

ON THE LETTER OF JAMES 2:10, WHERE IT SAYS: *WHOEVER KEEPS THE WHOLE LAW, BUT OFFENDS IN A SINGLE POINT, HAS BECOME GUILTY OF THEM ALL*

Date: before 410[1]

Mercy and pardon

1. It was a terrifying reading that our ears heard before the psalm; that *whoever keeps the whole law, but offends in a single point, has become guilty of them all* (Jas 2:10). So who wouldn't cry out in such peril, *Have mercy on us, Lord, have mercy on us* (Ps 123:3)?[2] If his mercy has not been withdrawn from us, you see, we will be able to remind ourselves of the danger more urgently, and also the more urgently to commend ourselves to him. *Do not enter into judgment with your servant*, someone or other says, a saint, certainly, but still a human being; *Do not enter into judgment with your servant, since in your sight shall nobody living be justified* (Ps 143:2). So he didn't want to be brought to judgment. But *judgment without mercy for the one who does not show mercy* (Jas 2:13).

As against this, let us work out another statement, and see where we should place our hopes. If, you see, *judgment without mercy for the one who does not show mercy*, then without a doubt there is judgment with mercy for the one who does show mercy. This statement, that there is *judgment without mercy for the one who does not show mercy*, was uttered by the apostle James, from whose letter that terrifying reading was chanted. The contrary one, however, which I made myself, that there is judgment with mercy for the one who does show mercy, was expressed by the Lord, when he said, *Blessed are the merciful, since they shall obtain mercy* (Mt 5:7). So there is hope in God's mercy, if our misery is not so barren as to yield no work of mercy. What do you want from the Lord? Mercy. *Give, and it shall be given to you.* What do you want from the Lord? Pardon. *Forgive, and you will be forgiven* (Lk 6:38.37).

The difficulty of the verse

2. However, people usually want to know how we should take *Whoever keeps the whole law, but offends in a single point, has become guilty of them all* (Jas

306

2:10). We must be on our guard, you see, and take care not to conclude that a thief can be compared with a murderer or an adulterer. That would be a dangerous, a grievous mistake; there's a great difference between theft and murder. But then the objection is levelled against us: "So it's certain that *whoever keeps the whole law, but offends in a single point, has become guilty of them all.*" He keeps himself from murder, keeps himself from adultery, keeps from bearing false witness, keeps from idolatry, keeps from any sort of detestable sacrilege.[3] But he has stolen; will he now be branded as a murderer and an adulterer and a false witness and an idolater and as guilty of sacrilege, because he has committed theft?

So it's not certain that if you offend in one single point, you have become guilty of them all. To explain this, the same apostle, whose letter it is, went on to add: *For the one who said, You shall not commit adultery, also said, You shall not kill. But if you do not kill, while you do commit adultery, you have become a transgressor of the law.* After he had placed this danger before their very eyes, and they had all started trembling, he added by way of a kind of comfort, *So speak and so act, as though you were on the point of being judged by the law of liberty. For there is judgment without mercy for the one who does not show mercy* (Jas 2:11-13).

So whether we are able to unravel this knotty question, or whether perhaps our efforts will be defeated by the difficulty of it, and I am either unable even to think suitably what I should say, or else at least to say what I am able to think, it is up to you to be keenly involved in works of mercy. This is plain enough, obvious enough, it doesn't call for someone to explain it, but for someone to hear and do it. All the same, I will try somehow or other to clear up that problem; may your prayers help us with God. It's the time, of course, at the moment for listening, not for praying;[4] but if you are expecting to receive from God what I am going to say, then you are already praying.

One charity fulfills everything

3. The law contains many commandments; and in fact the particular law which is called the decalogue has ten commandments. But the ten commandments are so to say general laws, to which all the countless other ones may be referred. However, to show how the other commandments, which seem to be innumerable, may be reduced to this small number of ten, would mean an infinite amount of discussion. What we can at least demonstrate now, to the extent that the Lord helps us to, is that just as the other commandments are all referred to these ten, which I said would be an enormous labor to discuss, so these ten can be referred to two.

The ten, of course, are these: About worshiping the one God, not worshiping any other, there is one commandment there; *You shall not make yourself an idol, nor the likeness of anything, neither of the things in heaven above, nor of the things on earth beneath* (Ex 20:4). *The Lord your God is one Lord* (Dt 6:4). The second commandment is, *You shall not take in vain the name of the Lord your*

God (Ex 20:7). The third commandment is, *Observe the day of the sabbath* (Dt 5:12). These commandments refer to God.

To teach a Christian anything about the observance of the sabbath would seem to be rather superfluous. On the contrary, not only is it not superfluous, but it is in fact basic, bed-rock doctrine; because it is a shadow of things to come.[5] The people, you see, are forbidden to perform servile works on the sabbath. Now are we, I ask you, not forbidden to perform servile works? Listen to the Lord: *Everyone who commits sin is the slave of sin* (Jn 8:34). And yet to hope to receive from God this very thing, of not committing sin, that is to celebrate the sabbath; that's why it is written, *God rested on the seventh day from all his works* (Gn 2:2). God rested: God causes you to rest. For God himself to rest, well when did he tire himself out working, seeing that he created all things with a word?[6]

So these three refer to God; the seven others refer to man. *Honor father and mother; you shall not commit adultery; you shall not kill; you shall not bear false witness; you shall not steal; you shall not covet your neighbor's wife; you shall not covet your neighbor's property* (Ex 20:12-17). If you love God, you neither worship any other, nor take his name in vain, and you keep the sabbath for him, so that he may rest in you, when he causes you to rest. While if you love your neighbor, you both honor your parents, and don't commit adultery, and don't kill, and don't harm anybody with false witness, and don't steal from anybody, and don't covet anyone's wife, and don't covet anyone's property. And in this way, *You shall love the Lord your God with your whole heart, and with your whole soul, and with your whole mind*; and *You shall love your neighbor as yourself. In these two commandments is fulfilled the whole law, and the prophets* (Mt 22:37.39-40).

Listen also to the apostle: *The fullness of the law*, he says, *is charity* (Rom 13:10). He didn't send you off to carry out many things, not even ten, not even two; one charity fulfills everything. However, this charity is twofold: toward God, and toward your neighbor. Toward God, how much? With the whole. The whole what? I mean, not the whole ear, and nose, and hand, and foot. He can be loved with the whole of what? With the whole heart, with the whole soul, with the whole mind; with the whole of what is alive in you, you shall love the fountain of life.[7] So if I have to love God with the whole of what is alive in me, what will I leave myself to love my neighbor with? You see, when you were instructed about loving your neighbor, you weren't told "with the whole heart, and the whole soul, and the whole mind," but *as yourself*. God with the whole of you, because he is better than you are; your neighbor as yourself, because he is the same as you are yourself.

Two commandments and three things to be loved

4. So there are two commandments; and yet three things to be loved. Two commandments given: love God and love your neighbor; and yet I see three things to be loved. After all, it wouldn't say *and your neighbor as yourself*, unless you were also to love yourself. So if there are three things to be loved,

why are there only two commandments? Why? Here's the answer. God didn't consider you had to be admonished to love yourself; there are no people, after all, who don't love themselves. But because there are many who suffer the loss of themselves by loving themselves badly, by being told to love God with the whole of yourself, you were also given a rule there on how you should love yourself. Do you want to love yourself? Love God with the whole of yourself; there, you see, you will find yourself, or else in yourself you might lose yourself. If you love yourself in yourself, you are bound to fall away even from yourself, and go looking for many things besides yourself.[8]

Which is why the apostle traced all evil back to that one source, where he says, *For people will be loving themselves.* There you are, you've chosen to love yourself. Let's see if you even manage to remain in yourself. It's not true, you can't remain there; fallen away from God, you've also fallen away from yourself. There, after all, is where the firmament is; that's where you should have stuck fast, that's where you should have made yourself a fortress and a house of refuge. Now, though, you have slackened off the connecting rope of your love, or you've even cut it between him and you;[9] you can't even remain in yourself. Listen, anyway, to the apostle himself: After saying *For people will be in love with themselves,* he immediately added, *lovers of money* (2 Tm 3:2).

Didn't I say that you weren't going to remain even in yourself? Are you money? Just look, you've even become lost to yourself, once you have withdrawn from God. What's left for you, but to squander the inheritance of your mind, living recklessly with harlots, that is to say with lusts and various greedy desires, and to be compelled by want to feed pigs? That is, because unclean avarice has taken possession of you, unclean demons are to be fed from what you have. But that son, after enduring extremes of want, and being worn down by hunger, *returned to himself and said.* He returned to himself because he had been lost to himself, and in himself he found himself in great need; he looked for gratification everywhere, and found it nowhere. He returned to himself, and what did he say? *I will arise and go.* Go where? *To my father* (Lk 15:17-18). He had already returned to himself, but he was still lying there; "*I will arise and go*; I won't lie here, I won't remain any longer."

So a rule has been laid down for you, how you should love yourself; love one who is better than you, and you have already loved yourself. But I mean one better by nature, not by will. After all, many people can be found who are better than you by will, but only God is so by nature; creator, establisher, maker, himself made by none.[10] Fix yourself firmly there. Come to your senses some time or other, and say, *But for me.* But for you, what? *To attach myself to God is good.* Why so? Notice what he had said just before: *You have lost everyone who goes whoring away from you* (Ps 73:28.27). So because he has lost everyone who goes whoring away from him, you have found yourself; *but for me to attach myself to God is good,* that is, not to go whoring away from God, not to remove myself from God. Do you wish to see what is being promised you in this connection? *But whoever attaches himself to God is one spirit* (1 Cor 6:17).

So this is your love, or love of yourself, that is, the love you love yourself with: to love God. Now I can also entrust your neighbor to you, whom you are to love as yourself; because I can see that you have begun to love yourself. I mean, if you loved gold and possessed gold, and loved your neighbor as yourself, in loving him you would be dividing what you possessed, and making him a sharer in your gold. But by this division you would each have less. So why not possess the one, in whom you will experience no diminution of property with your co-heir? However many people you can persuade, however many you can invite, summon, compel to love God, he is wholly there for all of them, and wholly there for each of them.

Charity is the root of all good works

5. So love God, and love your neighbor as yourself. I mean, I can see that you love yourself, because you love God. Charity is the root of all good works. Just as *greed*, after all, *is the root of all evil* (1 Tm 6:10), so charity is the root of all good things. *So the fullness of the law is charity* (Rom 13:10). So I can say straightaway: whoever offends against charity, has become guilty of every-thing. I mean, if you offend against the very root, what part of the tree do you leave unoffended?

So what are we to do? Whoever offends against charity, has become guilty of everything; it's absolutely true. But the thief offends against charity in one degree, the adulterer in another, the murderer in another, the person guilty of sacrilege in another, the blasphemer in another. They all offend against the same charity, because where there is full and perfect charity, there cannot be any sin at all. But charity is something that grows in us, in order some time or other to reach perfection; such perfection that there is nothing further to be added. When it is so perfect that there is nothing further it can grow toward, nothing further to be heaped on it, then there will be no sins. But when will this be, if not when death is swallowed up in victory? Then, you see, they will say, because there will be absolutely no sin at all, *Where, death, is your striving? Where, death, is your sting?* Where is it? Why, look, it just isn't there at all. Why, look, you aren't being stung any more, you aren't being laid low. *Where, death, is your sting?* And what does that mean, Where is your sting? Listen to his explanation: *Now the sting of death is sin* (1 Cor 15:54-56).

So, brothers and sisters, anyone who commits minor sins is guilty of all of them; and whoever commits some greater criminal act of a sin is guilty of all of them. But this person is more guilty, that one less; and yet they are both guilty of everything. So the only thing to be considered in the different kinds of sin is the matter of greater and smaller, more and less.[11] He's committed a theft; if he had charity, he wouldn't commit theft; because, *You shall not commit adultery*, says the apostle, *you shall not commit murder, you shall not steal, you shall not covet, and any other commandment there may be, it is all summed up in this word: you shall love your neighbor as yourself. Love of neighbor does not work evil. Now the fullness of the law is charity* (Rom 13:9-10). So both the one who commits a theft is guilty of everything, because he has damaged charity, and the one who commits adultery is guilty of everything, because he has damaged charity. I mean, how can he not have violated all the commandments, if he has damaged the root? But that one has damaged it less, this one has damaged it more.

Your iniquity has indeed been demolished,
but your infirmity remains

6. Yet even the one who has done less damage must not be slack. *For judgment without mercy for the one who does not show mercy* (Jas 2:13). The faithful were forgiven all their sins when they were baptized; nothing at all was left over, which that consecration did not at that time eliminate and extinguish. It's true; who doubts it? But if you had then departed from this body, innocence would have continued to stay with you, as it had begun; however, because you are still living here, your iniquity has indeed been demolished, but your infirmity remains.

Through various tiny, fine little chinks and cracks in this infirmity and sort of fragility of humanity, water seeps in from the sea and flows together into the bilges. He hasn't gone as far as murder; he has avoided being shipwrecked by a huge wave.[12] But don't you know that neglected bilges can sink boats? So the sacrament of baptism washes everything clean, and is given for the sake both of the bigger waves and any little trickles seeping in. But because this ship, which is sailing far over the sea, is so fragile, and is being tossed about by temptations as by storms, and because it is unavoidable that some smaller sins should seep in, another remedy has been given us, because we couldn't be given another sacrament of baptism.[13]

Baptism is a once only sacrament; this other remedy is for every day; what I mentioned a short while ago: *Judgment without mercy to the one who does not show mercy* (Jas 2:13). *Give, and it will be given you; forgive, and you will be forgiven* (Lk 6:38.37). And after a certain fashion you are cleansed every day from daily light and minor sins through your prayers, if you say from the heart, if you say truthfully, if you say in faith, *Forgive us our debts, as we too forgive our debtors* (Mt 6:12).

You are being cured in the Church

7. If you don't forgive your adversary, you become your own adversary yourself. Do you want to see how much difference there is? For example, he's harmed you by taking your money; you cheat yourself by not earning pardon. In any event you are going to say, "He was extremely brutal; he was after my blood." He was after the blood of your flesh; you yourself were after the death of your soul. "I won't forgive him," you say. "He's done me such harm, he's crossed me and opposed me so much." You're treating yourself much worse.

"I won't forgive him."

"I beg you, pardon him, forgive him."

"But he isn't begging me."

"You do his begging for him."

"No, I certainly will not forgive him."

You want to pick a quarrel, and you don't realize whom you should pick it with. You love quarreling; fine, come back to yourself, be angry and do not sin.[14] Be angry with yourself, in order not to sin. Be savage with yourself, punish yourself.

You have something inside which you should be slapping, and you're sleeping.[15] You observe your neighbor outside as someone to quarrel with, your partner, your companion, your joint owner. What you don't observe, don't see, is that other thing, that other law in your members, fighting back against the law of your mind, and taking you prisoner to the law of sin which is in your members. "But he's plundered me!" You're being dragged away prisoner, and you're angry with someone for plundering you!

Have you recognized yourself, have you seen where you really are? You've recognized your capturer,[16] show yourself a fighter, look for a redeemer. Just as that man himself, after saying *taking me prisoner to the law of sin which is in my members*, went on to add, *Unhappy man that I am, who will deliver me from the body of this death? The grace of God, through Jesus Christ our Lord* (Rom 7:23-25). But can you call upon grace if you don't see the punishment that's coming to you? So understand clearly, see where you are being dragged off to.

"But I take delight in justice."[17]

I know you do; after all, you take delight in the law of God according to the inner self.[18] But you can see another law in your members. You take delight in the law of God; there's another law in your members; live by it and you'll die by it. Robbers have left you half-dead on the road; but you've been found lying there by the passing and kindly Samaritan. Wine and oil have been poured into you, you have received the sacrament of the Only-begotten Son; you have been lifted onto his mule, you have believed that Christ became flesh;[19] you have been brought to the inn, you are being cured in the Church.

We all have one king; may we all reach the one kingdom

8. That's where and why I'm speaking; this is what I too, what all of us are doing; we are performing the duties of the innkeeper.[20] He was told, *If you spend any more, I will pay you back when I return* (Lk 10:35). If only we spent at least as much as we have received! But however much we spend, brothers and sisters, it's the Lord's money. We are your fellow servants; we live on what we feed you with. Nobody should give us the credit for the benefits bestowed; we will be bad servants if we don't do it. But if we do do it, we shouldn't arrogate any credit to ourselves, because we aren't doing it with our own property. Let us all love him, all esteem him, and for his sake all love and esteem one another. We all have one king; may we all reach the one kingdom.

NOTES

1. Augustine rather neatly solves the problem posed by this uncompromising statement by reducing the law, the whole law of Moses, to the ten commandments, and then reducing these to the twin commandment of love. But one may be left at the end, wondering whether he did really solve it after all. The sermon is as likely to have been preached in Hippo Regius as anywhere else.

2. This was probably the psalm.

3. He would have had in mind such acts as consulting astrologers, or seeking the help of sorcerers.

4. The proper time for praying formally would come with the prayer of the faithful, and above all with the Our Father.

5. See Heb 10:1. From this and other texts it seems clear that the Church in Augustine's day—at least the African Church—had no laws or customs about literal sabbath day observance; they had not as yet applied the Old Testament sabbath law to the Lord's day; the sabbath still meant Saturday. So Augustine always treats the commandment about keeping the sabbath as purely symbolic and prophetic.

6. See Ps 148:5.

7. See Ps 36:9.

8. See *The Trinity* XII,14-16.

9. It seems to be a kind of mountaineering metaphor. If you stop loving God, to whom you are roped at the top of the rock, you are cutting the rope that supports you; you can't support yourself.

10. If you had asked Augustine whether angels are better by nature than we are, he would have said "Yes," with a shrug; meaning that their natural superiority is not very important, since they are creatures just as much as we are—and some have fallen away as demons, to become worse than we are (so far) by will.

11. I doubt if the majority of moral philosophers and theologians would agree with him here.

12. *Evasit naufragus fluctum. Naufragus* is normally a second declension noun (or adjective), meaning a shipwrecked person. So on the face of it this phrase means "being shipwrecked, he has avoided the huge wave." That doesn't seem to me to fit the picture here. So I have assumed that Augustine is treating *naufragus* as a fourth declension noun, here in the genitive singular, meaning "shipwreck"; an alternative form of *naufragium*.

13. Nowadays we would here automatically say "the sacrament of penance." But penance in those days was a very different discipline from what it is now, and concerned only with the graver sins. The second remedy Augustine always thinks of in this connection is prayer and almsgiving.

14. See Ps 4:4.

15. . . . *quod domes, et dormis*; more precisely, ". . . which you should be taming, and you're sleeping."

16. Yourself, your other, sinful, self.

17. Still thinking of justice against the adversary, whom you refuse to forgive.

18. See Rom 7:22.

19. The Samaritan is Christ, of course, as always in patristic exegesis. But here he is Christ in his divinity, the Only-begotten Son. His humanity, his flesh, is represented by the Samaritan's beast (I presume it was a mule; the original is not so specific).

20. By "we" he may mean only himself and the clergy (or other bishops if they were present). But I get the impression that he is bringing the whole congregation into the role of innkeeper; by being forgiving toward one another and by performing other works of mercy.

SERMON 180

ON THE WORDS OF THE APOSTLE JAMES 5:12: *ABOVE ALL DO NOT SWEAR*, ETC.

Date: 414-415[1]

Do not swear

1. The first reading which was chanted to us today from the apostle James, has been presented to us for discussion, and has to some extent been imposed on us. It has certainly made you alert, admonishing you above all not to swear. This is a difficult question. Is there anyone not caught by this sin, if swearing is a sin? I mean, that forswearing, or perjury, is a sin, and a great sin, nobody can doubt. But the apostle whose reading we are dealing with did not say, "*Above all, my brothers*, do not forswear," but *do not swear*. A similar admonition was also given earlier in the gospel by the Lord Jesus Christ himself: *You have heard*, he said, *that it was said to the ancients, You shall not forswear yourself. But I tell you, Do not swear, neither by heaven, because it is God's throne; nor by earth, because it is his footstool; and you shall not swear either by your head, because it is not in your power to make one hair of it white or black. But let your word be: Yes, yes; No, no. If there is anything over and above, it comes from what is evil* (Mt 5:33-37).

The reading from the apostle we have mentioned fits this admonition of the Lord's perfectly, so that it seems that God commanded nothing else but this, because the one who said this is none other than the one who said through the apostle, *Above all, my brothers*, says he, *do not swear, neither by heaven nor by earth, nor any other kind of oath at all. But let your word be: Yes, yes; No, no* (Jas 5:12). The only thing he added was *Above all*; thereby he made us very alert, and only increased the difficulty of the question.

The only thing that makes a guilty tongue is a guilty mind

2. We find, you see, that the saints have sworn, that the first to have sworn is the Lord himself, in whom there is no sin whatsoever. *The Lord has sworn, and will not repent: You are a priest for ever, according to the order of Melchizedek* (Ps 110:4). He promised the Son an eternal priesthood with an oath. You also have *By myself I swear it, says the Lord* (Gn 22:16). As a man swears

314

by God, so God by himself. So isn't it a sin to swear? It's hard to say so; and since we have said that God has sworn, how blasphemous it seems to say so! God swears, and he has no sin; so it is not a sin to swear, but it's a sin, rather, to forswear oneself.

Someone may say, perhaps, that we shouldn't bring in the Lord God as an example of swearing oaths. He's God, after all, and perhaps he alone is competent to swear since he cannot perjure himself. People, you see, swear falsely, either when they are being deceitful or being deceived. I mean, you either think something's true when it's false, and swear to it rashly; or you know or think it's false, and yet swear it's true, and still swear a criminal oath, regardless. These two sorts of perjury, though, which I have mentioned are very different. Suppose this person swears, who thinks what he's swearing to is true, and yet it is in fact false. He isn't deliberately perjuring himself; he's just mistaken, he regards as true what is in fact false; he doesn't knowingly interpose an oath for something false. Now give me another person who knows it's false and says it's true, and swears as though what he knows to be false were true. Can you see what a detestable monster this is, properly to be eliminated from human society? I mean who would like this sort of thing to be done? All people detest such things.

Take another person; he thinks it's false, and swears to it as if it were true—and it so happens it is true. For example, to help you understand: "Did it rain in that place?" you ask someone, and he thinks it didn't, but it suits his purpose to say "Yes, it did." But he thinks it didn't. You say to him, "Did it really rain?" "Yes, really," and he swears it did; and in fact it did rain there, but he doesn't know it, and thinks it didn't; he's a perjurer. What makes the difference is how the word comes forth from the mind. The only thing that makes a guilty tongue is a guilty mind.

But is there anybody who is never mistaken, even though nobody has ever wanted to be mistaken? Is there anybody who is not sometimes caught out in a mistake? And yet swearing doesn't disappear from people's mouths, it's a commonplace; often there are more oaths than words. If you were to count up how often you swear throughout the day, how often you inflict wounds on yourself, how often you strike and run yourself through with the sword of your tongue, could you find anywhere in yourself that remains unhurt? So because perjury is a grave sin, scripture has given you a simple formula: Don't swear.

Swearing is a narrow ledge, perjury a precipice

3. What am I, a man, to say to you? Swear the truth? There you are, you swear the truth, you're not sinning; if you swear the truth, you aren't committing a sin. But you're a human being set in the midst of trials and temptations, wrapped round in flesh, trampling earth under earth, while the body that decays is weighing down the soul, and the earthly habitation depresses the mind thinking many things;[2] among these many uncertain, flickering thoughts of yours, human conjectures, human mistakes, when does something untrue not creep into your mind, placed as you are in the region of falsehood?[3]

So do you wish to keep far away from perjury, from forswearing yourself? Give up swearing. You see, if you swear, you can sometimes swear the truth; but if you don't swear at all, you can never swear a lie. So let God swear, since he can swear safely, and nothing deceives him, nothing escapes him, who is totally incapable of deceiving, because he cannot either be deceived. When he swears, after all, he calls himself as a witness. Just as you, when you swear, call God as a witness, so he, when he swears, calls himself as a witness. You, when you call him as a witness, perhaps to a lie of yours, are taking in vain the name of the Lord your God.[4]

So in order not to swear to a lie, don't swear at all. Swearing is a narrow ledge, perjury a precipice.If you swear, you're near the edge; if you don't swear, you're far away from it. You sin, and gravely, if you swear to what is false; you don't sin, if you swear the truth; but then you don't sin either, if you don't swear at all. But if you don't swear and don't sin, you are a long way away from sin; while if you do swear the truth, you don't sin, but you are near to sin. Suppose you are walking in some place, where there is plenty of space on your right, and you don't face any narrow paths; on your left the ground falls away in a cliff. Where do you prefer to walk? Along the borderline, on the edge of the cliff, or far away from it? Far away from it, I rather think. So too, if you swear, you're walking on the borderline; and you're walking on shaky, because human, feet. If you stumble, down you go. If you slip, down you go. And what's waiting for you at the bottom? The penalty of perjury. So you were wishing to swear the truth? Listen to God's advice: don't swear at all.

Swear to the truth or don't swear at all

4. If swearing were a sin. it wouldn't say in the old law, *You shall not forswear yourself; but you shall render to the Lord your oath.*[5] We would not, I mean, be commanded to do what is a sin. But your God says to you, "If you swear, I won't condemn you; if you swear the truth, I won't condemn you. But do you imagine I will condemn you if you don't swear at all? There are two things," he says, "which I never condemn: swearing a true oath and not swearing any oath. But I do condemn swearing a false oath." A false oath is deadly, a true oath is dangerous, swearing no oath at all is safe.

Yes, I know it's a difficult question, and I confess to your graces that I've always avoided it. But now, when this same reading has been recited on a Sunday, with the obligation of preaching a sermon, I really believed I was divinely commanded[6] to deal with it. This is what God wanted me to talk about; this is what he wanted you to hear. I beg you not to shrug the matter aside, I beg you to give me the steady attention of your minds, to alter the fickle habits of your tongues. It's certainly not pointless, not without meaning, that while I have always wanted, as I said, to avoid this question, the necessity of dealing with it has been thrust on me, in order also to be thrust upon your graces.

The apostle Paul also swore

5. To show you that swearing to the truth is not a sin, we find that the apostle Paul also swore: *I die daily by your glory, brothers, which I have in Christ Jesus our Lord* (1 Cor 15:31). "By your glory" is an oath. He didn't say "I die by your glory," as though meaning your glory is making me die; as you might say, "He died by poison, he died by the sword, he died by a wild beast, he died by an enemy's hand"; that is, with an enemy causing his death, a sword causing it, poison causing it, and so on. That's not how he meant *by your glory*. The Greek text removes all ambiguity. We look in the Greek letter, and we find there an unambiguous oath: *Ne ten humeteran kauchesin*. When a Greek says *Ne ton Theon*, he's swearing. You hear Greeks every day, and those of you who know Greek—when he says *Ne ton Theon*, you know *Ne ton Theon* is an oath: "by God." So nobody should doubt that the apostle was swearing when he said *By your glory, brothers*—and in case we should think he was swearing by human glory—*which I have in Christ Jesus our Lord*.

Somewhere else there's an absolutely certain and explicit oath: *I call God to witness upon my life*. The apostle says, *I call God to witness upon my life, that it is to spare you that I have not yet come to Corinth* (2 Cor 1:23). And in another place to the Galatians, *But as to what I am writing to you, before God I am not lying* (Gal 1:20).

Using an oath

6. Pay attention, please, and take note; and if what I'm saying doesn't strike you as all that plausible, because of the trickiness of the question, it's still useful if it reaches to your innermost feelings. Look here, the apostle swore. Don't let those people deceive you, who wish to make I don't know what distinctions between oaths, or rather wish not to understand correctly, and say that it isn't an oath when you say, "God knows"; "God is my witness"; "I call to God upon my life that I'm telling the truth." "He called upon God," he says; "he made God a witness; did he swear?" People who say this only want to call upon God as a witness when they lie. Is it really the case, though, whoever you are of a crooked and twisted mind, that if you say "By God," you're swearing, while if you say "As God is my witness," you aren't swearing? Well, what does "By God mean," but "God is my witness"? Or what's "As God is my witness" if not "By God"?

Great harm comes to you, when you deceive your neighbor
and present God to him as a witness

7. Now what is swearing, really, but handing over a right to God, when you swear by God; handing over a right to your health, when you swear by your health; handing over a right to your children, when you swear by your children?[7] But what right or duty do we owe to our health, our children, our God, but that of love, of truth, and not of falsehood? Now it is supremely a real oath when one swears by God; because even when you say "By my health," you are binding

your health to God; when you say "By my children," you are pledging your children to God, so that whatever comes out of your mouth may alight upon their heads; if truth, the truth; if falsehood, falsehood.

So when any of you in swearing an oath name your children, or your head, or your health, you are binding whatever you name to God. How much more so when you forswear yourself by God himself! You're afraid to swear falsely by your son, and you're not afraid to swear falsely by your God? Perhaps this is what you are saying to yourself: "I'm afraid to swear falsely by my son, in case he dies. But what harm can happen to God, who cannot die, even if someone swears a false oath by him?" You're right to say that no harm can come to God when you swear falsely by God. But great harm comes to you, when you deceive your neighbor and present God to him as a witness.

If you did something with your son as a witness, and said to a friend or a neighbor or anybody at all, "I didn't do it," and touched the head of your son, who witnessed your doing it, and said, "By this boy's salvation, I swear I didn't do it"; perhaps your son would cry out, trembling under his father's hand, dreading though, not his father's, but God's hand, "Don't, Father; don't hold my salvation cheap; you've invoked the name of God upon me, I saw you, you did it, don't perjure yourself; yes, I have you as my begetter, but I am more afraid of the one who is both your and my creator."

The life of the body is the soul; the life of the soul is God

8. But because God doesn't say to you, when you swear by him, "I myself saw you; don't swear; you did it"; but you're afraid this man may kill you, so you kill yourself first;[8] so because he doesn't say "I myself saw you," do you imagine he didn't see you? And what about his words, *I kept quiet, I kept quiet; shall I keep quiet always?* (Is 42:14). And in any case, he frequently does say "I saw you," but in a different kind of way, when he punishes perjury.[9] But he doesn't punish all cases of it; that's why people are encouraged to follow the bad example.

"I know; he swore me a false oath, and he's still alive."

"He swore you a false oath and is still alive?"

"He swore falsely and is still alive; that man swore falsely."

"You're mistaken. If you had the eyes to see this person's death; if you too were not mistaken about what dying and not dying really is, you would see this person's death."

And now pay attention to scripture;[10] and there you will find the person you thought was alive lying dead. Because he's walking on his feet, touching things with his hands, because he sees with his eyes and hears with his ears, and makes use of the other various functions of different parts of his body, you think he's alive. He is alive, but only his body; his soul, though, is dead, what's best in him is dead. The dwelling is alive, the occupant dead. "How," you will ask, "can his soul be dead, since his body's alive; since the body wouldn't be alive unless it were being animated by the soul?" So how can the soul, by which the body lives, be dead? Listen, then, and learn; the human body is God's creature, and the human soul is God's creature. God gives life to the flesh through the soul, and again he gives life to the soul through himself, not through the soul itself. So the life of the body is the soul; the life of the soul is God. The body dies when the soul departs; so the soul dies if God departs. The soul departs, when the body is struck with a sword; and do you imagine that God doesn't depart, when the soul stabs itself with perjury?

Do you want to see that the person you are talking about really is dead? Read scripture: *The mouth that lies kills the soul* (Wis 1:11). You, though, would consider God to be present as avenger, if the man who deceived you with a false oath were to expire on the spot. If he expired before your eyes, it's his flesh that expired. What does that mean, his flesh expired? It cast out the spirit by which it was being animated.[11] That is, it expired when the spirit was excluded, by which the flesh lived. He forswore himself; he excluded the spirit by which his soul lived. He expired, but you don't know it; he expired, but you don't see it. You see the flesh lying there without the soul; you can't see the soul reduced to wretchedness without God.

So believe, apply the eyes of faith. No perjurer goes unpunished. Not a single one; they all carry their punishment with them. If they suffered tortures of the flesh on their beds, they would have been punished;[12] he suffers the torments of his conscience in the inner chamber of his heart, and he is said to go unpunished? And yet what is it you're saying? "He's alive, he's enjoying himself, he's having a high old time, the man who swore a lie to me; what's the point of referring me to invisible factors?" Well, because God himself, by whom he swore, is also invisible. He swore by one who is invisible; he is smitten with a punishment that is invisible. "But he's alive," you say, "and kicking; just somehow or other bubbling and boiling over with loose living." If that's the case, that he's bubbling over with loose living, boiling over with loose living, then these are the maggots in a dead soul. In any case, every sensible person who observes perjurers being wildly extravagant, since he has a healthy sense of smell in his heart, turns away, doesn't want to see, doesn't want to hear. What is it makes this healthy attitude turn away, but the stench of a dead soul?

Above all be on the watch

9. Listen then, my brothers and sisters, for a little while longer; let me conclude the sermon by fixing in your minds a salutary concern: *Above all, do not swear* (Jas 5:12). Why *above all*? If perjury is a grave misdeed, but no blame attaches to swearing the truth, why *above all, do not swear*? I mean, he ought to have said, "Above all, do not perjure yourselves." *Above all*, he said, *do not swear*. Swearing, after all then, is worse than stealing? Swearing is worse than committing adultery? I'm not talking about swearing falsely; I'm talking about swearing. Swearing is worse than killing a person? Perish the thought! Killing people, committing adultery, stealing, they're sins; swearing is not a sin; but swearing to something false is a sin.

So why *above all*? This expression he uses, *above all*, has put us on our guard against our tongues. He says *above all*, to give this the first claim on your attention, to put you on the watch against the habit of swearing creeping up on you. It's as though he has placed you in a look-out post over against yourself; *above all* has lifted you up above other things, to where you can observe yourself from. You see, he considers you swearing, "By God, by Christ, I'm going to kill him"; and this how often every day, how often every hour! You can't open your mouth except to swear like that. You would rather he didn't say to you *above all*, in order to make you very determined against the habit, in order to get you inspecting all your words, keeping the most diligent watch over all the movements of your tongue, being on your guard against this bad habit of yours, in order to restrict it? Listen: *Above all*. You were asleep, I'm poking you in the ribs: *Above all*; I'm applying thorns. What does *Above all* mean? Above all be on the watch; above all be alert.

Augustine's habit of swearing

10. I too have sworn heedlessly and all the time, I have had this most repulsive and death-dealing habit. I'm telling your graces; from the moment I began to serve God,[13] and saw what evil there is in forswearing oneself, I grew very afraid indeed, and out of fear I applied the brakes to this old, old habit. When the brakes are put on, it's restricted; when it's restricted it grows weaker; as it grows weaker it dies away, and the bad habit is succeeded by a good one. For all that, I'm not telling you that I don't swear. I mean, if I do say that, I'm lying. As far as I am concerned, I do swear; but as I see it, only when obliged to by great necessity. When I see that I won't be believed unless I do so, and that it's not in the interests of the person who doesn't believe me not to believe me, then after carefully weighing this reason, balancing this consideration, with great trepidation I say, "Before God," or "As God is my witness," or "Christ knows that that is what I have in mind."

And I can see that this is more, that is to say it is over and above *Yes, yes; No, no;* but anything over and above comes from what is evil;[14] even if not from what is evil in the person swearing, from what is evil in the person who won't believe. In any case, he doesn't say "If he does over and above, he is evil"; and, "Let there be in your mouth Yes, yes; No, no; if anyone does over and above, he is evil; but *Let there be in your mouth Yes, yes; No, no; but what is over and above comes from what is evil.* But ask whose, or in whom."

But for all that, this dreadful human habit works quite differently.[15] Even when you are believed, you swear; even when nobody is requiring it of you, you swear; and when people are rather shocked, you swear; you never stop swearing; you hardly manage to keep healthy by not forswearing yourself. Unless perhaps you imagine, brothers and sisters, that even if the apostle Paul had known the Galatians would believe him, he would still have added an oath, and said, *As for what I am writing to you, behold, before God, that I am not lying* (Gal 1:20). He could see people there who believed him, and he could also see others who didn't.

So don't say, "I don't swear," if it happens to be demanded of you; what you're doing does indeed come from what is evil, but it's the evil of the person who's demanding it. Because as far as you are concerned, you have no other means of clearing yourself, you can't find any other way of concluding the business that is pressing. But an oath when it is demanded of you is one thing, an oath freely offered another; and in the case of one freely offered, one thing when it's offered to someone who doesn't believe you otherwise, another when it's waved in the face of someone who does believe you in any case.

Prune swearing away from your tongues

11. So keep your tongue in check, and this habit, as far as you can; not like some people, when they're told, "Are you telling the truth? I don't believe you. You didn't do it? I don't believe you; let God judge; swear to me."[16] And as for the one who requires the oath, it makes all the difference if he doesn't know that the other is going to swear falsely, or if he does. If he doesn't know, and the reason he says "Swear to me" is that he wants to be given assurance; then I cannot quite say it isn't a sin, but yet it's a human temptation.[17] If, however, he knows he's done it, is aware he did it, saw him do it, and still compels him to swear, he's a murderer. The other man, you see, destroys himself by his perjury; but this one both directs the hand of the slayer and presses it home.

When, though, some scoundrel of a thief hears, "Swear, if you didn't take it, swear if you didn't do it," from a person who doesn't know whether he did do it, and he then answers, "A Christian isn't allowed to swear; when an oath is demanded of him, he isn't allowed to swear; I'm a Christian, I'm not allowed to"; catch such a fellow out; turn away from him, change the subject from the business you were talking about; bring other matters into the conversation, and you'll soon find him swearing a thousand times, the man who refused to swear once.

So then, get yourselves out of this daily, constant, pointless habit of swearing when nobody's obliging you to, nobody's doubting your word; prune it away from your tongues; circumcise it from your mouths.

A stronger habit calls for stronger determination

12. "But it's a custom," they usually say. They usually say, but I don't say. That's the point of *Above all.* Why *Above all*? Be careful about this before other things, pay more attention to this than to other matters. A stronger habit calls for stronger determination; it isn't a trifling habit. If you were doing something with your hand, you could easily order your hand not to do it; if you had to go somewhere on foot, and sloth was delaying you, you could bestir yourself to get up and go. The tongue moves very easily, it's in a moist, well-lubricated place, it slithers and slides around very easily. The quicker and nimbler it is to move, the more resolute must be your opposition to it.

You will tame it, if you keep awake; you will keep awake if you are afraid, if you reflect that you are a Christian. Because swearing is so infected with evil, that those who worship stones are afraid of swearing falsely by their stones; and are you not afraid of the God who is present, the living God, God who knows, God who abides, God who takes vengeance on those who despise him? That man closes the temple on a stone, and goes home; he has shut the temple on his god, and yet when he is told, "Swear by Jupiter," he is afraid of the eyes of his god as if he were present.[18]

God punishes you deceiving

13. And look, I'm telling your graces, that even the person who swears falsely by a stone is a perjurer. Why do I say this? Because many people are mistaken on this point, and think that because what they are swearing by is nothing, they aren't implicated in the crime of perjury. Undoubtedly you're a perjurer, because you are swearing falsely by what you consider holy. "But I don't consider it holy." The person you are swearing to thinks it's holy. After all, when you swear, you aren't swearing to yourself, or to the stone idol; you're swearing to your neighbor. You're swearing to a human being in front of a stone; but isn't it also in front of God? The stone can't hear you speaking; but God does punish you deceiving.

Put a stop to swearing

14. So above all, my brothers and sisters, I beseech you, don't let it be that God has compelled me to say all this for nothing. It's in his presence, you see, that I say what I said earlier, that I have often avoided this question. I was afraid that by warning and instructing I would make the people who weren't going to listen all the more guilty. But today I was more afraid of refusing to speak what I was ordered to speak. But it's as if all my toil and sweat would bear a little fruit, if all those who have been applauding me would cry out against themselves, not to swear falsely against themselves; if so many people who have been listening to me so intently would be as intent against their habit, and would admonish themselves today, when they get home, when they fall into the habit again by a slip of the tongue; if neighbor would admonish neighbor: "This is what we heard today, this is the obligation we were laid under."

Don't let it be done today, certainly not with the sermon so recent. I can speak from experience; don't let it be done today, tomorrow it becomes slacker. If it isn't done tomorrow either, the one who's watching out has less trouble; the new habit of the previous day, you see, helps out. On the third day the disease I am struggling over dies away; and I will rejoice over your fruit, because you will bear an abundant crop of great good if you rid yourselves of so great an evil.

Turning to the Lord, etc.

NOTES

1. I see no reason to doubt that the sermon was preached in Hippo Regius. The reference in section 5 to hearing Greek spoken every day suggests a seaport, either Hippo or Carthage. We may remind ourselves that Augustine's predecessor as bishop of Hippo, Valerius, was a Greek. From section 4 we learn he was preaching on a Sunday.

The sermon could be regarded as one in which he is arguing with the Quakers on the subject of swearing; and while not agreeing with their absolute prohibition of it, still showing considerable sympathy for their stance.

2. See Wis 9:15. The earth under which the earth is trampled is of course the flesh, the body, which was fashioned from earth, Gn 2:7.

3. There is a certain Platonist flavor to this sentence; the region of falsehood echoing the world of appearances, of opinion, of seeming, in which no real truth is to be found—that being reserved for the world of ideas, of unchanging forms.

4. See Ex 20:7.

5. The first half of the text is from Lv 5:11, but the second, quoted in Mt 5:33, is not actually part of the written law, but presumably a gloss of the scribes, part of what Jews call *halakah*. However, with respect to the closely related concept of vow, we do have such a text as Ps 50:14: *Pay your vows to the Most High.*

6. Reading *imperatum* with some manuscripts, instead of *inspiratum*, inspired, with the text. I don't think Augustine would here be claiming divine inspiration; a divine command suits the context much better.

7. He is saying that *jurare*, swearing, is the same as *jus reddere*, which I translate as handing over a right. He is perfectly correct; the connection in Latin between *jurare* and *jus* is plain; the idea common to both is that of binding. The difficulty in English is how to translate *jus*; we have no such connecting link between "swear," "oath," and "right" or "obligation"; because *jus* can equally well mean duty or obligation. The handing over of a right to God is well expressed in the Hebrew formula, "May God do such-and-such to me, and more also, if I do not . . ."

Swearing by my health could equally well be translated "by my salvation."

8. You are swearing you didn't do whatever it is, because you are afraid, if you admit it, that your angry accuser may kill you—if you have been poaching for example, or making advances to his wife. So you kill yourself first by perjuring yourself.

9. When self-imposed curses like "May God do such-and-such to me, and more also" come home to roost.

10. You will have to wait until the next paragraph before you are told which text of scripture.

11. To expire is to breathe out the breath, the spirit. The connection in Latin between *exspiro* and *spiritus* is immediately apparent.

12. He actually says "a torturer of the flesh," which conjures up a rather grotesque picture; perhaps he intended it. But I interpret him as meaning the torments of some painful disease.

13. He doesn't exactly mean from the moment of his conversion, but from the moment he began to live the religious life in a small community in his home town of Thagaste on his return to Africa from Milan in 388.

14. See Mt 5:37.

15. Differently from the way in which the reformed Augustine sometimes swears an oath.

16. These people are left hanging in the air, until they are plucked down out of it at the beginning of the next paragraph in the shape of the thief who refuses to swear on the grounds that Christians are not allowed to. So Augustine is here qualifying the "as far as you can" of the first sentence; sometimes you cannot avoid swearing, when it is demanded of you.

17. See 1 Cor 10:13.

18. An involved *a fortiori* argument, that was no doubt more significant to his hearers than it may be for modern readers.

SERMON 181

ON THE WORDS OF THE FIRST LETTER OF JOHN 1:8-9: *IF WE SAY THAT WE HAVE NO SIN, WE DECEIVE OURSELVES, AND THE TRUTH IS NOT IN US,* ETC; AGAINST THE PELAGIANS

Date: 416[1]

Nobody can live here without sin

1. The most blessed apostle John, in his sound and truthful writing, says among other things, *If we say that we have no sin, we deceive ourselves, and the truth is not in us. But if we confess our sins, he is faithful and just, so as to forgive us our sins, and cleanse us of all iniquity* (1 Jn 1:8-9). With these words the blessed John has taught us, or rather the Lord Jesus himself speaking through John, that nobody in this flesh, in this perishable body, on this earth, in this ill-favored age, in this life full of trials and temptations, nobody can live here without sin. It's an absolute statement, and doesn't require explanation: *If we say that we have no sin.* Who is there, after all, who doesn't have any sin? As scripture says, *Not even the infant whose life has lasted one day on the earth* (Jb 14:4 LXX). Such a baby hasn't committed sin, but has contracted it from its parents.

So in no way can anybody say he never had any sin. But the believer came by faith to *the bath of regeneration* (Tit 3:5), and all sins were forgiven him; he now lives under grace, he lives in faith, he has become a member of Christ, he has become a temple of God. And yet, somehow or other, he has become a member of Christ and temple of God in such a way, that if he says he has no sin he is deceiving himself, and the truth is not in him; quite simply, he's lying, if he says, "I am just."

The errors of the Pelagians

2. But there are some inflated bladders, full of the hot air of self-importance, not vast in bulk, but swollen with the disease of pride, who have the nerve to say that people can be found without sin. So they say that the just have absolutely no sin in this life. Now it's the Pelagian heretics, who are the same as the Celestians, that say this. And when you answer them, "What's this you're

324

saying? So a person can live here without sin, and not have any sin at all, neither in deed, nor in word, nor in thought?"; they reply from that wind of pride they are so full of—a wind I wish to God they would finish with, breathe out and keep quiet, become humble, that is to say, and not self-satisfied—they reply, as I was saying, "Certainly, these holy people, God's faithful, cannot have any sin at all, neither in deed, nor in word, nor in thought." And when you say, "Who are these just people, who are without sin?" they answer and say, "The whole Church."

"I would have been astonished if I could find one, two, three, ten, as many as Abraham was asking for. Abraham, I mean, came down from fifty to ten;[2] whereas you, Mr. Heretic, answer and tell me the whole Church. How can you prove this?"

"I can prove it," you say.

"Prove it, please do. I mean, you would bring me great joy, if you could teach me that absolutely the whole Church, in each and every one of its faithful, had no sin."

"I can prove it," you say.

"Tell me how."

"The apostle says so."

"What does the apostle say?"

"*Christ*, he says, *loved the Church*."

"I hear you, and I recognize the apostle's words: *Cleansing her with the bath of water by the word, that he might present to himself a glorious Church, not having stain or wrinkle, or any such thing* (Eph 5:25-27). We have heard mighty thunders from the cloud. The apostle, you see, is God's cloud. These words have pealed, and made us tremble.

You're members of the Church, and you have stains and wrinkles

3. "But tell us, before we inquire how the apostle meant these words; tell us, I say, whether you yourselves are just or not."

"We are just," they reply.

"So you don't have any sin? Every day and every night, all day long and all night long, you do nothing bad, say nothing bad, think nothing bad?" They daren't say "Nothing"; but what answer do they give?

"We indeed are sinners; but we are talking about the saints, not about ourselves."

"What I'm asking you is this: are you Christians? I'm not asking, are you just? Are you Christians?" They daren't deny it:

"We're Christians," they say.

"So are you believers? Have you been baptized?"

"We've been baptized," they say.

"Were all your sins forgiven?"

"They were," they say.

"So how can you be sinners?"

That's enough for me to repulse you with. You're Christians, you've been baptized, you're believers, you're members of the Church, and you have stains and wrinkles? So how is the Church at this time without stain and wrinkle, since you are its stains and wrinkles? Or if you only want that to be the Church which is without stain and wrinkle, cut yourselves off from its membership with your wrinkles and stains, cut yourselves off from its body. But why should I go on telling them to separate from the Church, when they've already done this? After all, they're heretics, they are already outside; with all their cleanliness they have remained outside. Come back and listen; listen and believe.[3]

God does not accept your lying humility

4. Perhaps you're going to say, in your swollen, puffed-up hearts, "Could we actually say that we are just? Of course we had to say, for the sake of humility, that we are sinners." So for the sake of humility you tell a lie? You're just, you're without sin; but out of humility you say you're a sinner. How can I accept your evidence as a Christian in someone else's case, when I've caught you giving false evidence against yourself? You're just, you're without sin, and you say you have sin. So you're bearing false witness against yourself.

God does not accept your lying humility. Examine your life, take a look at your conscience. So you're just, but you cannot do other than say you are a sinner? Listen to John; he will repeat to you what he also said so truly earlier on: *If we say*, he says, *that we have no sin, we deceive ourselves and the truth is not in us* (1 Jn 1:8). You don't have any sin, and you say that you do have sin; the truth is not in you. Because John did not say "*If we say we have no sin*, humility is not in us"; but he said, *we deceive ourselves and the truth is not in us*. So we are lying if we say that we have no sin. If John was afraid of lying, are you not afraid of lying, by saying you're a sinner when in fact you're just? So how can I accept you as a witness in anyone else's case, when you lie in your own case? You make the saints guilty, when you give false evidence against yourself.[4] What are you going to do to someone else, if you smear yourself? How can anyone else avoid your false accusations, when you make your own self guilty with your lying tongue?

By lying you were turned into what you had been avoiding

5. Again I'll interrogate you another way: Are you a just person, or a sinner? You answer, "A sinner." You're lying, because you don't say with your lips what you believe yourself to be in your heart. So even if you weren't a sinner, you begin to be one as soon as you lie. What you're saying, you see, is, "It's for the sake of humility that we say we are sinners; because God can see that we are just." So since you tell a lie for the sake of humility, if you weren't a sinner before you lied, by lying you were turned into what you had been avoiding. The truth is not in you, unless you say you are a sinner in such a way that you also actually know you are. What truth means is that you should say what you actually are. After all, how can there be any humility where falsehood is reigning?

6. Finally, let's leave aside John's words: here we are in the body of the Church, which you say has no stain or wrinkle or any such thing, and is without sin; here's the hour of prayer coming, the whole Church is going to pray, and you indeed are outside. Come to the Lord's prayer, come to the weigh-in, come and say: *Our Father, who are in heaven.* Carry on: *hallowed be your name. Your kingdom come. Your will be done, as in heaven, also on earth. Give us today our daily bread.* Carry on, and say, *Forgive us our debts.* Answer, Mr. Heretic, what are your debts? Did you perhaps receive a loan of money from God? "No," he says.

So I'm not questioning you any further about that; because the Lord himself is going to explain what the debts are which we are asking to be released from. So let's say what comes next: *As we also forgive our debtors.* Let the Lord explain this: *For if you forgive people their sins* —so your debts are sins—*your Father too will forgive you your sins.* So come back, Mr. Heretic, to the prayer, if you have grown deaf to the true import of the faith. *Forgive us our debts*; do you say it, or don't you? If you don't, then even should you be present in the body, you are still outside the Church.

This, you see, is the Church's prayer; it's the voice coming from the Lord's own magisterial chair. It was he who said, *Pray like this* (Mt 6:9-14); he said to the disciples *Pray like this.* He said it to the disciples, said it to the apostles, said it to us, whatever sort of little lambs we are; he said to the rams of the flock, *Pray like this.* Notice who said it, and to whom he said it: Truth to the disciples, the Shepherd of shepherds to the rams: *Pray like this: Forgive us our debts, as we too forgive our debtors.* The king was speaking to his soldiers, the master to his slaves, Christ to his apostles. Truth was speaking to men, the Most High to the humble: "I know what's going on in you; I am weighing you up, I'm reading you off from my scales, I can undoubtedly say what's going on in you; I, you see, know this much better than you do. Say, *Forgive us our debts, as we too forgive our debtors.*

7. I'm asking you, just man, holy man, man without stain and wrinkle; I'm asking you, I say: Is this the prayer of the Church, of the faithful, or of the catechumens? It's clear, of course, that it's the prayer of those who have been born again, that is of the baptized;[5] finally, and this is what really counts, it's the prayer of the children; I mean, if it's not the children's prayer, how can one have the face to say, *Our Father, who is in heaven*? Where are you, O just and holy ones? Are you among the members of this Church, or aren't you? You were there, but now you're there no longer.

And if only, now they have cut themselves off, they would listen to reason and believe! So if the whole Church says, *Forgive us our debts*, anyone who doesn't say this is disqualified. And we too, indeed, when we say *our debts*, until we receive what we are asking for, are disqualified, because we are sinners.

But we do what you don't do, that is we confess our sins, and so are cleansed; provided, of course, we do what we say: *as we forgive our debtors.*

So where are you now, Pelagian or Celestian heretic? Here we have the whole Church saying *Forgive us our debts*; so it has stains and wrinkles. But by confession the wrinkle is smoothed out, by confession the stain washed off. The Church stands in prayer,[6] to be cleansed by confession; and as long as it lives here, it stands like that. And whenever people depart from the body, all the debts they had, which were of the sort to be forgiven, are forgiven, because they are also forgiven by daily prayer.[7] And then they depart cleansed, and the Church is stored up in the Lord's treasury as pure gold; and in this way the Church enters the Lord's treasury without stain and wrinkle.

And if it's without stain and wrinkle there, what has to be prayed for here? To be granted pardon. The one who grants pardon wipes out the stain; the one who forgives smooths out the wrinkle. And where is our wrinkle smoothed out? As on the tenter or stretcher of the great fuller, on the cross of Christ.[8] It was on that cross, you see, that is on that tenter, that he shed his blood for us. And you, the faithful, know what testimony you bear to the blood you have received; you certainly say, after all, "Amen."[9] You know what blood it is that was shed for many for the forgiveness of sins. There you have how the Church is turned out without stain and wrinkle, well cleansed, as it were, and stretched out on the tenter of the cross.

But this is certainly something that can be effected here. The Lord is presenting himself with a glorious Church, not having stain or wrinkle; he is effecting this here too; he presents the result there. You see, he is doing all this so that we may not have any stain or wrinkle. The one who is doing this is very great, he takes very good care, he's a most skilled craftsman. He stretches us on the wood and smooths away our wrinkles, after washing away our stains. He himself, though he came without stain and without wrinkle, was stretched on the tenter; but for our sakes, not his own, in order to make us without stain and wrinkle. So let us ask him to go on doing it, and after he has done it to bring us to his storerooms and lay us up there, where there will be no press.[10]

When we forgive, we are also forgiven

8. So you, then, who were talking,[11] are you without stain and wrinkle? What are you doing here in the Church, which says, *Forgive us our debts*? It confesses it has debts, which can be remitted. If people don't confess, it doesn't mean they don't have them; it does mean they are not remitted. Confession heals us, and also a careful life, a humble life, prayer with faith, contrition of heart, unfeigned tears flowing from the depths of the heart, that we may be forgiven the sins without which we cannot be. Confession, I repeat, heals us, as the apostle John says: *If we confess our sins, he is faithful and just, so as to forgive us our sins, and cleanse us from all iniquity* (1 Jn 1:8).

It does not, however, mean, because I say we cannot be here without sin, that we ought to commit murders, or adulteries, or other deadly sins, which slay at a stroke. Such things are not committed by Christians of good faith and good hope; but only the sort which may be wiped off by the brush of daily prayer. Let us humbly and devoutly say every day, Forgive us our debts; but provided we do what follows: *as we too forgive our debtors.* This contract with God is a true contract and fixed condition. You're human, and you have a debtor, and you're also a debtor yourself. You approach God, who has debtors and isn't a debtor, to request to have your debts written off. But this is what he says to you: "I don't have any debts, you do; after all, you are in debt to me. But your brother is also in debt to you. You're my debtor, and you also have your own. You're my debtor, because you have sinned against me; your brother is in your debt, because he has sinned against you. What you do with your debtor, I also do with mine; that is, if you forgive, I forgive; if you insist on payment, I insist on payment. You insist on it against yourself, if you don't forgive the other."

So none of us should say we are without sin; but that doesn't mean we should love sin. We must hate him,[12] brothers and sisters; even if we aren't without sins, all the same we must hate them; and above all we must abstain from grave crimes; we should also refrain, as far as we can, from lighter sins. "I," says heaven knows who, "don't have any sins." He's deceiving himself, and the truth is not in him. Let us go on and on praying that God will forgive; but let us do what it says, let's also forgive our own debtors ourselves. When we forgive, we are also forgiven. We can say this every day, and we can do it every day, and it can happen in us every day. We cannot be here without sin, but we shall depart from here without sin.

NOTES

1. This is a very aggressive sermon against the Pelagians, and not at all fairly argued; one of Augustine's less pleasant sermons, in fact. My instinct would be to locate it in Carthage rather than Hippo Regius. He also calls the Pelagians Celestians, from Pelagius' African disciple Celestius.

2. See Gn 18:24-32. I don't know if Augustine was immediately aware that he was implying an equation between the Church and Sodom.

3. I cannot avoid the suspicion that he is to some extent mixing up the Pelagians with his old adversaries the Donatists. These did indeed claim to be a Church of the saints, to be at least without grave sin, sin in the strictest sense. But I don't think this was ever a claim of the Pelagians, who didn't in fact form a Church at all. What they said was, that it was entirely up to them, up to any human being, whether they sinned or not, purely a matter of free will, free choice. If they, or anyone, chose to be without sin, they could be. And of course, they would say, any self-respecting Christians should choose so to be, and could be if they would. And if they sinned, they could again, of their own accord, without any need of divine grace, repent.

4. What I think he began by meaning, is that since I can't believe what you say about yourself (that you're a sinner, though you consider yourself to be just), then I can't believe what you say about the saints, that they are entirely without sin. But the following sentences show that what he ends up by meaning is—you calumniate yourself; you are bound to calumniate everyone else. In his ill-temper with the Pelagians he is being too clever by half, and again inconsequentially unfair.

5. Because it is prayed during the Mass, just before communion, from which the catechumens had earlier been excluded.

6. Standing, not kneeling, was the normal posture of prayer.

7. He is distinguishing the lesser sins we cannot avoid in this life from the graver sins, for which it is not sufficient to recite the Lord's prayer, however sincerely, but for which a more formal absolution is required.

8. I suppose most of us are totally ignorant of what fulling cloth involves. The craft only survives in our minds in the dehydrated metaphor "on tenterhooks." That's why I keep the unusual word "tenter." Augustine goes on to tell us all we need to know (for the moment) about the process: it involves stretching.

9. At Mass, after the words of institution, as becomes clear from the next sentence. See Mt 26:28.

10. There seems to be quite a mixture of metaphors here, storerooms, treasuries, presses (presumably wine or oil presses), clean garments. But I suppose the press could mean, even in those days, a clothespress.

11. Well, it was Augustine who was setting up the talker. This is an instance of what I have called the rather unpleasant unfairness of tone of this whole sermon.

12. Reading *eum* with all the manuscripts instead of *ea*, them, with the Italian editors. A striking personification of sin. In the previous sentence it was in the singular; but it is neuter, so he should have said *id*, "it." *Eum*, masculine, can here only be "him."

SERMON 182

ON THE WORDS OF THE FIRST LETTER OF JOHN 4:1-3: *DEARLY BELOVED, DO NOT BELIEVE EVERY SPIRIT; BUT TEST THE SPIRITS, WHETHER THEY ARE FROM GOD;* AGAINST THE MANICHEES

Date: 417[1]

Not to believe every spirit

1. When the apostle John was being read, we heard the Holy Spirit speaking through him and saying, *Dearly beloved, do not believe every spirit, but test the spirits, whether they are from God* (1 Jn 4:1). I repeat, because it is very necessary for me to repeat, and as far as God helps me, to drum this forcefully into your minds: *Dearly beloved, do not believe every spirit, but test the spirits, whether they are from God. Because many false prophets have come out into this world.*

The Holy Spirit has commanded us not to believe every spirit, and has told us the reason why he has commanded this. What is this reason? *Because many false prophets,* he says, *have come out into this world.* So any people who ignore these commands, and think every spirit is to be believed, are bound to get mixed up with false prophets, and what's much worse, to speak ill of true prophets.

Turn your ears away from those who deny that Jesus Christ has come in the flesh

2. At this point, now that you have been put on your guard by this instruction, you're going to say to me, "I've heard, I get the point, I am eager to comply, because I certainly don't want to get mixed up with false prophets. Who would want to, I mean to say; want to be taken in by liars? Obviously, a false prophet is a lying prophet. Give me religious people, they don't want to deceive; give me godless, sacrilegious people, they want to deceive, they don't want to be deceived. So since the good don't want to deceive, while neither the good nor the bad want to be deceived, is there anybody who would want to get mixed up with false prophets?"

I'm speaking the part of the person who's consulting me; but obviously, nobody willingly gets mixed up with a false prophet. He goes on: "I've heard

331

John's instruction, or rather the instruction of the Lord through John, *Do not believe every spirit.* I accept that, I want to follow it. He goes on to say, *But test the spirits, whether they are from God* (1 Jn 4:1). How can I test them? I would like to test them, if I could avoid going wrong. Clearly, unless I can tell which spirits are from God, I am bound to get mixed up with spirits which are not from God, and so be seduced by false prophets. What am I to do? How am I to tell the difference? Oh, if only Saint John, as well as telling us, *Do not believe every spirit, but test the spirits, whether they are from God*, would be good enough to tell us how the spirits which are from God are to be tested!"

Don't worry; listen to this point too. *This is how the spirit from God is to be recognized.* This is certainly what you were expecting to hear, so that you could test the spirits which are from God. *This is how the spirit from God is to be recognized.* John said it, not me; it follows in the reading I'm dealing with. First, you see, he made us rather anxious, and careful not to believe every spirit, but to test the spirits which are from God, for the good reason that many false prophets have come out into this world. Then straightaway he saw what we would be eager to know; he met our expectation, he cast his eye on our silent thoughts. Thanks be to God, who was ready to tell us this too through John.

This is how the spirit from God is to be recognized. Come now, listen; listen, understand, tell the difference, stick to the truth, stand up to falsehood. *This is how the spirit from God is to be recognized.*

"How, please, how? This is what I was longing to hear."

Every spirit which confesses that Jesus Christ has come in the flesh is from God; and every spirit which does not confess that Jesus Christ has come in the flesh is not from God (1 Jn 4:3). So meanwhile,[2] dearly beloved, turn your ears away from every debater, preacher, writer, whisperer who denies that Jesus Christ has come in the flesh. So turn the Manichees away from your houses, your ears, your hearts. The Manichees, you see, deny quite openly that Christ has come in the flesh.[3] So their spirits are not from God.

Let the error die, the person live

3. Here I can see what way the wolf would like to slink in by; I can recognize it, and to the best of my ability I will show you how to ward it off. It's here, in what I've said, or rather what I have recalled the apostle saying: that *every spirit which denies that Jesus Christ has come in the flesh, is not from God.* The Manichee lies in wait at this word, and says to me: "There you are; the spirit which denies that Jesus Christ has come in the flesh, is not from God; so where is it from, then? If it's not from God," he says, "where is it from? Can it be there at all, I mean, unless it's from somewhere else? So if," he says, "it's not from God, and is from somewhere else, you can see here the two natures."[4]

We've located the wolf; let's spread out the nets, let's hunt him, capture him, and once he's caught, slay him. Certainly, let's slay him; let the error die, the person live. There you are: in what I've just said; "Let us capture and slay him; let the error die, the person live"; there you have the solution to the problem.

But call to mind what I proposed, or if you've forgotten the question, you won't understand the solution. *Every spirit which does not confess that Jesus Christ has come in the flesh, is not from God.*

And straightaway the Manichee says, "And where is it from? If it's not from God, it's from somewhere else. If it's from somewhere else, I have established that there are two natures." Hold onto this question, and then turn your minds back to my words, when I said, "Let us capture and slay him; let the error die, the person live." The error is not from God, the person is from God. Come back to the question: *Every spirit which does not confess that Jesus Christ has come in the flesh, is not from God.* I, though, also say: *All things were made through him* (Jn 1:3); *Let every spirit praise the Lord* (Ps 150:6). But if every spirit is not from God, how can the spirit which is not from God praise the Lord? Let absolutely every spirit praise the Lord. I can see each side of the question; as I understand it, one spirit is ill; let the fault be cured, the nature set free. The fault is not a nature, but the enemy of nature. Cure what is making you ill, let what you offer praise with remain. Medicine harries faults, not nature. *Every spirit which does not confess that Jesus Christ has come in the flesh is not from God.* Insofar as it does not confess that Christ has come in the flesh, to that extent it is not from God; because this error which does not confess that Christ has come in the flesh is not from God.

Brothers and sisters, why is it that we are born again? If we were born well, why is it we are born again? It means that the nature which had been spoiled is being restored; the nature which had fallen is being lifted up; the nature which was lying there deformed, is being reformed by grace. Only the creator, you see, Father, Son, and Holy Spirit, three in one, one in three; only that nature, unchangeable, invariable, liable neither to regress nor progress, neither falls lower to become less, nor rises higher to become more; perfect, eternal, altogether unchangeable is that nature alone. As for creation, it is good, but totally unequal to the creator. You are wishing to adhere to the devil's desertion, if you claim to put on a par with the founder his foundation.[5]

The soul is not God

4. Let the soul acknowledge its condition; it isn't God.[6] When the soul thinks it's God, it offends God; it finds in him a bringer, not of salvation, but of condemnation. Because when God condemns bad souls, he doesn't condemn himself; if, though, the soul is the same as what God is, he does condemn himself. Let us give real honor, brothers and sisters, to our God, to whom we cry out, *Deliver us from evil* (Mt 6:13).

And if he should whisper to you, to present you with a temptation even in the Lord's prayer, and say to you, "What's this you've cried out, *Deliver us from evil*? Is there really not such a thing as evil?"[7] answer him like this:

"I am evil, and if he delivers me from evil, from being evil I will become good. Let him deliver me from myself, in case I should get mixed up with you."

Say this to the Manichee: "If God delivers me from myself, I won't get mixed up with you; because if God delivers me from me as evil, I will be good; if I am good, I will be wise; if I am wise, I won't go wrong; if I don't go wrong, it won't be possible for me to be deceived by you. So let God deliver me from myself, and I won't get mixed up with you.

"You see, the fault is mine, that I should go wrong and believe you, because my soul is filled with illusions.[8] I am not my own light; if I were, I would never have gone wrong. That's why I am not part of God, because the substance of God, the nature of God, cannot go wrong. But I go wrong; I mean, you really admit this yourself; you say you're wise; you're trying to deliver me from error. So how can I go wrong, if I'm God's nature? Be ashamed of yourself, give honor to God. I say that you're still going very wrong; but anyway, as you yourself admit, you had gone wrong previously.[9] So had the nature of God gone wrong? Had the nature of God descended to impurity? Was the nature of God committing adultery? Was the nature of God going in for unlawful debauchery? Was the nature of God blind and not knowing where he was going? Was the nature of God being overwhelmed under outrageous and shameful deeds? Be ashamed of yourself, give honor to God."

We are in need of enlightment, we are not the light

5. You cannot be your own light; you can't, you simply can't. *That was the true light.* It was said in comparison with John the Baptist. *That was the true light.* Wasn't John also a lamp? *He was a burning and shining lamp* (Jn 5:35). The Lord said so. Isn't a lamp, then, light? But there was a *true light.* A lamp can be lit, and it can be put out; the true light can impart light, it can't be put out. So *that was the true light, which enlightens every person coming into this world* (Jn 1:9). We are in need of enlightenment, we are not the light. Wake up, cry out with me, *The Lord is my enlightenment* (Ps 27:1).

So what's that you're saying? So aren't there evil things in existence? There are, but they can change, and they will become good; because these evil things are evil by defect, not by nature. What's the meaning of *Deliver us from evil*? Couldn't we and can't we say these words instead: "Deliver us from darkness"?[10] From what darkness? From ourselves, if there are any remnants of darkness in us, until we are totally turned into light, having nothing in us that might stand in the way of charity, that might be repugnant to truth, that might be subject to infirmity, that might fade away by reason of mortality. See what this totality will be, when it will be: *This perishable thing will put on imperishability, and this mortal thing will put on immortality. Then will the word come to pass that is written: Death shall be swallowed up in victory. Where, death, is your striving? Where, death, is your sting? Now the sting of death is sin* (1 Cor 15:53-56). Where is evil?

Every human evil is error and weakness

6. What, at the present moment, are the evils of humanity? Error and weakness. Either you don't know what to do, and you go wrong, you fall into error;

or else you know what should be done, and you are overpowered by weakness. So every human evil is error and weakness. Against error cry out, *The Lord is my enlightenment*; against weakness add: *and my salvation* (Ps 27:1). Believe, become good; you are at the moment bad, you will become good. Don't divide things up; nature is to be healed in you, not cut in two.[11] Do you want to know what you are? Darkness. Why darkness? A person who can say, "God can be spoiled," could anything be deeper than darkness like that?

Believe, acknowledge that Christ has come in the flesh, that he received what he was not, and did not lose what he was; that he changed man into himself, wasn't himself changed into man.[12] Acknowledge this, and you yourself from being bad will become good, from being darkness will become light. Or am I lying, and is there no way I can convince you? You accept the apostle—if you're not just pretending to accept him.[13] You read the apostle, and you are deceived, and you deceive. Why are you deceived? Because you go wrong about yourself by what is your own badness.[14] But if you believe and shake off your error, you will hear from the apostle, *For you were once darkness, but now light*. He added *light*; but where? *In the Lord* (Eph 5:8). So darkness in you, light in the Lord. Because you can't light yourself up, by approaching you are enlightened, by drawing away you are darkened; because you yourself are not your own light, you are enlightened from elsewhere. *Approach him, and be enlightened* (Ps 34:5).

Repulse those who deny that Christ has come in the flesh

7. I know, dearly beloved, that from this reading of Saint John I have lingered at some length over one point; and I can see that I mustn't tire you any further, or try to fill you up beyond capacity; and I've also got to think about my own weakness. Because these words of Saint John still have their many obscurities. Meanwhile, repulse those who deny that Christ has come in the flesh. It's clear, after all, that they are not from God. Insofar as they go wrong, insofar as they sin, insofar as they blaspheme, they are not from God; only let them be cured, and they will be from God, because by nature they were from God. However much I have argued on the point, just pay attention to the scriptures. Don't believe those who deny that Christ has come in the flesh.

But of course, you're going to say to me, "So is anyone who does say that Christ has come in the flesh from God? Are we to listen to the Donatists, because they confess that Christ has come in the flesh? Are we to listen to the Arians, because they confess that Christ has come in the flesh? Are we to listen to the Eunomians,[15] because they confess that Christ has come in the flesh? Are we to listen to the Photinians,[16] because they confess that Christ has come in the flesh? I mean to say, if all the spirits that confess that Christ has come in the flesh are from God, how many lying, deceptive, crazy heresies there are, that all the same confess that Christ has come in the flesh!" So what are we to say? How are we to solve this problem? However it is to be solved, it can't be solved today. Consider me to be in your debt. But pray to God both for me and for yourselves as our help.

Turning to the Lord, etc.

NOTES

1. This is rather a late date for a sermon against the Manichees; but they continued to be quite a force to be reckoned with throughout Augustine's life, and he may have recently come across some of their propaganda. At the end he talks of owing his congregation another sermon on, or against, other kinds of heretics; a debt he pays back in Sermon 183. I doubt if he would employ this language of owing a sermon in his own Church of Hippo Regius, where preaching was his regular duty. So my guess would be that this sermon was preached in Carthage. But it could have been any fairly large city, where one would expect to find a great variety of religious belief.

2. "Meanwhile," because, as we shall see at the end of the sermon, this rule of thumb for discerning the spirits will not be entirely sufficient; but it's good enough to deal with the Manichees, or any other "spirits" which deny the doctrine of the incarnation.

3. Basically, because they regarded the flesh, like all matter, as substantively evil.

4. The two natures of Manichee doctrine being the substantive nature of good: the good God, spiritual being, souls, which are particles of the good God; and the substantive nature of evil: the bad God, the God of the Old Testament, creator of the material world, as also the material world created by him. Manicheanism was an offshoot of the ancient Persian dualist religion, of the god of light, Ormuzd, and the god of darkness, Ahriman.

5. The Manichees did this to the extent that they regarded the good God and his works as being equally balanced with the evil god and his works. But the language of creator and creation is strictly Judeo-Christian language, and doesn't really fit the Manichean scheme of things.

6. The Manichees would say that the soul, the spiritual element in us, is a part of God, or an emanation from God. That is why I have just said that creation language does not really apply to them.

7. For the Manichees evil is a substance; it is in fact matter, the material world.

8. See Ps 38:7.

9. Simply by being human, a composite of spirit and body. The Manichee, according to his own views, had "gone wrong," in that the spirit had been captured by evil matter, and got mixed up with it. The whole religious effort of the Manichees was directed to rescuing souls, particles of the God of light, by their various disciplines and rituals, from the evil material world.

10. Darkness, a specifically Manichee term.

11. The Manichees assert two natures in us, one good, the soul; the other evil, the body. And for them the object of religion is to deliver the good nature from the bad one. Augustine, along with almost the whole of Christian antiquity, with its Platonist worldview, did indeed have a moderately dualist idea of the human entity, as we have noticed time and again. But he resolutely resisted the temptation to say that we are, or have, two natures; even more the Manichee determination to regard one of these component elements, the flesh or the body, as evil.

12. The first part of this last clause, that he changed man into himself, must not be strictly applied to the incarnation. Christ's humanity was not changed into divinity. But the effect of the incarnation on humanity as a whole, on us as identified with and incorporated into the man Christ Jesus, who is one person with the divine Word, has been to divinize us, to make us partakers of the divine nature (2 Pt 1:4); and in this sense he changed man into himself.

13. The Manichees rejected the Old Testament, like so many of the Gnostics before them, but accepted the authority of at least some of the New Testament.

14. Reading *Errando malo tuo de te ipso*, instead of the text's . . . *malo tuo te ipso*, which would mean, "by the badness which you are yourself." This hardly fits his whole argument against them, if one takes it strictly. But they can be rhetorically identified with their own badness, just as they, or we, are identified first with darkness and then with light.

15. Extreme Arians.

16. Their error was rather to deny the divinity of Christ; a more unitarian position than that even of the Eunomians, who attributed, as it were, a lesser divinity, or a different sort of divinity, to the Son.

SERMON 183

AGAIN ON THE WORDS OF THE FIRST LETTER OF JOHN 4:2: *EVERY SPIRIT WHICH CONFESSES THAT JESUS CHRIST HAS COME IN THE FLESH, IS FROM GOD*

Date: 417[1]

The various errors

1. The expectant desire of your graces demands the repayment of my debt. I am sure you remember what I promised, relying on the Lord's help, about the reading from Saint John. So when you heard the reader, I believe you thought I should repay my debt. As the sermon looked like going on rather long,[2] we put off dealing with a big question; how we should rightly understand what is said in his letter by the blessed John, the Evangelist, not the Baptist: *Every spirit which confesses that Jesus Christ has come in the flesh, is from God* (1 Jn 4:2). I mean, we can see many heresies confessing that Christ has come in the flesh, and yet we can't say that they are from God. The Manichee denies that Christ has come in the flesh. There's no need to labor the point, or to persuade you any further that this error is not from God.

But the Arian confesses that Christ has come in the flesh, and the Eunomian, the Sabellian, the Photinian. How can we find witnesses to refute and convince these people? How can anyone count how many such pests there are?[3] But for the time being let us deal with the ones that are better known. To many people, I'm sure, the ones I've named are unknown, and this ignorance is much safer. What we certainly all know, the Donatist confesses that Christ has come in the flesh; and yet heaven preserve us from saying this error is from God. To speak of more recent heretics, the Pelagian confesses that Christ has come in the flesh; yet quite certainly this error is not from God.

They do not confess that Christ has come in the flesh

2. Accordingly, dearly beloved, let us consider the matter carefully, since we cannot doubt the truth of the statement, *Every spirit which confesses that Jesus Christ has come in the flesh is from God*; so it has to be proved against these people that they don't confess that Christ has come in the flesh. Because if we grant them such a confession, we will be admitting that they are from God. How,

in that case, can we ban or deter you from their errors, or defend you against them with the shield of truth? May the Lord assist us, because your eager expectation is a kind of prayer for me, to prove against these people that they do not confess that Christ has come in the flesh.

The Arian question

3. The Arian hears, and proclaims, the child-bearing of the virgin Mary. So does he confess that Christ has come in the flesh? No. How can we prove it? If the Lord assists your understanding, with the greatest of ease. What are we demanding? Whether he confesses that Jesus Christ has come in the flesh. How can someone confess that Jesus Christ has come in the flesh, when he denies Christ himself? Who, after all, is Christ? Let us question the blessed Peter. You heard just now, when the gospel was read, when the Lord Jesus Christ himself had asked who people said he, the Son of man was, how the disciples answered with the opinions of others and said, *Some John the Baptist, others Elijah, others Jeremiah, or one of the prophets.* Those who confessed, or confess, such things, don't know Jesus Christ as more than a man. But if they don't know Jesus Christ as more than a man, quite simply they don't know Jesus Christ. I mean, if he's only a man, and nothing further, he isn't the real Jesus Christ. *You therefore*, he says, *who do you say that I am?* Peter answered, one for them all, because representing unity in all, *You are the Christ, the Son of the living God* (Mt 16:14-16).

Lowliness replies about truth, and truth about lowliness

4. There you have a true confession, a full confession.[4] You must join both things together, you see, what Christ says about himself and what Peter says about Christ. What does Christ say about himself? *Who do people say that I am, the Son of man?* What does Peter say about Christ? *You are the Christ, the Son of the living God* (Mt 16:13.16). Join them both, and Christ has come in the flesh. Christ says about himself what is the lesser part, Peter says about Christ what is the greater part. Lowliness replies about truth, and truth about lowliness; that is, lowliness about the truth of God, and truth about the lowliness of man.[5] *"Who do people say that I am*, he says, *the Son of man?* I am telling you what I have been made for your sakes; you, Peter, tell us who made you."

So anyone who confesses that Jesus Christ has come in the flesh, is actually confessing that the Son of God has come in the flesh. Now let the Arian tell us whether he confesses that Christ has come in the flesh. If he confesses that the Son of God has come in the flesh, then he confesses that Christ has come in the flesh. If he denies that Christ is the Son of God, then he doesn't know Christ; he's mixing him up with someone else, he isn't really naming him. What, after all, is the Son of God? Just as we were inquiring what Christ is, and we heard that he is the Son of God; so let us inquire what the Son of God is. Here's the Son of God for you: *In the beginning was the Word, and the Word was with*

God, and the Word was God. This was in the beginning with God (Jn 1:1-2). In the beginning was the Word. What do you say, Mr. Arian? *In the beginning,* as Genesis says, *God made heaven and earth* (Gn 1:1). You, though, say, "In the beginning God made the Word." You say the Word was made, you call the Word a creature. You, therefore, say, "In the beginning God made the Word." But the evangelist says, *In the beginning was the Word.* And that's why *in the beginning God made heaven and earth*; it's because the Word was. *All things were made through him* (Jn 1:3). You say he was made. If you say he was made, you are denying he is the Son.

The form of a servant was added, not the form of God subtracted

5. You see, we are looking for the Son by nature, not by grace; the only Son, the Only-begotten, not an adopted son. That's the sort of Son we are looking for, such a true Son, that *while he was in the form of God*—they're the apostle's words, let me remind the less well instructed among you, in case you should suppose they are mine—we are looking for that Son *who while he was in the form of God*, as the apostle says, *did not reckon it robbery to be equal to God.* Not robbery, because it was his nature. It was his nature, it wasn't an act of robbery. *He did not reckon it robbery to be equal to God.* It wasn't robbery for him, it was nature; that's what he was from eternity, that's how he was coeternal with his begetter, that's how he was equal to the Father, that's how he was.

He emptied himself, so we could confess that Jesus Christ has come in the flesh. *He emptied himself.* How? By losing what he was, or by taking on what he was not? Let the apostle carry on, let us listen: *He emptied himself, taking the form of a servant* (Phil 2:6-7). That's how he emptied himself, taking the form of a servant, not losing the form of God. The form of a servant was added, not the form of God subtracted. That is to confess that Christ has come in the flesh. The Arian, though, doesn't confess that Christ is equal, doesn't confess that he is the Son. If he doesn't confess he is the Son, he doesn't confess Christ. If he doesn't confess Christ, how can he confess that Christ has come in the flesh?

The Eunomian

6. It's the same too with the Eunomian, his fellow, his companion, not very different. We're told, you see, that the Arians confessed that the Son is at least like the Father; even if they said he isn't equal, but he's like him. This man says, not even like him. So this one too denies Christ. If the true Christ, after all, is equal to the Father and like him, it follows that whoever denies he's equal is denying Christ; whoever denies he is like him is denying Christ. So whoever denies he is equal and like him, is denying that Christ has come in the flesh.

I'm asking, you see: "Has Christ come in the flesh?"

He answers, "He has"; and we are supposing he confesses this.

I question him: "Which Christ has come in the flesh? One equal to the Father or unequal?"

He answers, "Unequal."

"So you're saying that one unequal to the Father has come in the flesh; you're denying that Christ has come in the flesh, because Christ is equal to the Father."

The Sabellian

7. Listen to the Sabellian. "The one who is the Father is also the Son." That's what he says, that's where his sting is, that's where he spreads his poison from. "He," he says, "is the Father. When he wants to be, he's the Son; when he wants to be, he's the Father."

"This isn't the Christ. You too are on the wrong track, if this is the Christ who you say has come in the flesh. Because this is not, in fact, the Christ, you are denying that Christ has come in the flesh."

Photinus

8. What do you say, Photinus? Photinus says, "Christ is only a man, he isn't God." You are confessing the form of a servant, denying the form of God. And Christ in the form of God is equal to the Father, in the form of a servant is sharing our lot. You too deny that Christ has come in the flesh.

The Donatist

9. What about the Donatist? Most Donatists confess the same as we do about the Son, that the Son is equal to the Father, and of the same substance; some of them, however, confess indeed that he is of the same substance, but deny that he is equal.[6] What need is there to discuss those who deny that he is equal? I mean, if they deny he is equal, they are denying the Son. If they are denying the Son, they are denying Christ. If they are denying Christ, how can they confess that Christ has come in the flesh?

Christ is denied by deeds

10. Over those of them who confess what we do ourselves, that the only-begotten Son is equal to the Father, of the same substance, coeternal with the eternal, there is a rather more intricate discussion. But all the same, they are Donatists. Let's try saying to them, "You confess it in words, you deny it by your deeds." You can deny things, you see, by your deeds. Not everyone who denies something does so by word. Clearly there are people who deny by their deeds. Let's question the apostle: *All things*, he says, *are pure to the pure; but to the impure and unbelievers nothing is pure, but their minds and consciences are defiled. For they confess that they know God, but deny him by their deeds* (Tit 1:15-16).

What is denying by your deeds? Being proud and making schisms; making your boast not in God, but in man. That's how Christ is denied by deeds; Christ, of course, loves unity. Finally, here is how they too deny Christ, to speak more plainly. The one we call Christ is the one of whom John the Baptist said *He that has the bride is the bridegroom* (Jn 3:29). It's a good marriage, a holy wedlock, the bridegroom Christ, the bride the Church. From the bridegroom we get to know the bride. Let the bridegroom himself tell us what bride he has; let him tell us, in case perhaps we should make a ghastly mistake, and being invited to the wedding, should disturb the exchange of holy vows;[7] let him tell us, let him first show us himself as the bridegroom.

Christ is the bridegroom of the Church
spread throughout the whole wide world

11. After his resurrection he said to his disciples, *Did you not know that it was necessary for all things to be fulfilled which are written about me in the law of Moses, and the prophets, and the psalms?* Then the evangelist carries on and says, *Then he opened their minds to understand the scriptures, and said to them, that thus it was necessary for the Christ to suffer, and to rise again from the dead on the third day* (Lk 24:44-46). There you are; the bridegroom, whom Peter confessed, that is the Son of the living God, had necessarily to suffer and on the third day rise again. And it happened; they saw it fulfilled, they had the head to hold onto, they were seeking the body. What's the head? Christ himself; he suffered, the third day he rose again; he's the head of the Church. What's the body? The Church itself.

So the disciples could see the head, they couldn't see the body. So, as they couldn't see the body, let the head teach them. "Tell us, Lord Jesus, tell us, holy bridegroom, instruct us about your body, about your bride, about your beloved, about your dove,[8] whom you have endowed with your blood, tell us."

It was necessary for the Christ to suffer, and rise again from the dead on the third day.

"There we have the bridegroom; tell us about the bride, fill up the matrimonial tablets."[9]

Hear about the bride; *And for there to be preached*, he says; that's how it goes on you see. *It was necessary for the Christ to suffer, and rise again from the dead on the third day, and for there to be preached in his name repentance and forgiveness of sins throughout all nations.*

Where are you hiding yourself?[10] *Throughout all nations, beginning from Jerusalem* (Lk 24:46-47). And that's how it happened. We can read the promise, we can see the fulfillment. That's where my light is; where is your darkness? So Christ is the bridegroom of this Church, which is being proclaimed to all the nations, and is burgeoning and growing as far as the ends of the earth, beginning from Jerusalem; it's of this Church that Christ is the bridegroom. What do *you* say? Of whom is Christ the bridegroom? Of the party of Donatus? Not he, not he; not he, my good man; or rather, my bad man, not he. We've come to the wedding, let's read the documents, don't let's wrangle. So if you say Christ is the bridegroom of the party of Donatus, I read the documents, and I find that Christ is the bridegroom of the Church spread throughout the whole wide world.

If you say he is the other thing, and he isn't the other thing, then you are denying that Christ has come in the flesh.

The Pelagian

12. There remains the Pelagian; not that it's the only heresy left, but out of the ones I mentioned a short while ago. As I said before, who could possibly count how many of these pests there are? "What do you say, Mr. Pelagian?" Listen to what he says; he seems to confess that Christ has come in the flesh, but examine him carefully, and he's found to deny it. Christ, you see, came in the flesh, which would be the likeness of the flesh of sin, but would not actually be the flesh of sin. They are the apostle's words: *God sent his Son in the likeness of the flesh of sin* (Rom 8:3). Not in the likeness of the flesh, as though his flesh wasn't flesh; but *in the likeness of the flesh of sin*, because it was flesh, but was not the flesh of sin.

Now this Pelagian tries to equate all the other flesh of every infant with the flesh of Christ. It's not like that, dearly beloved. The likeness of the flesh of sin in Christ would not be emphasized as being so important, unless all other flesh were the flesh of sin. So what use is it, your saying Christ has come in the flesh, and trying to equate him with the flesh of all infants? To you also I say what I said to the Donatist: Not he; that isn't him.

Look, I can see mother Church bearing witness with her breasts. Mothers come hurrying with their little children, they press them on the Savior to be saved, not on Pelagius to be damned. Any woman who's a mother, hurrying along in her loving concern with her little son, says, "Let him be baptized, so he may be saved."

Pelagius retorts, "What do you mean, be saved? There's nothing in him to be saved; he has no defect or fault, he hasn't contracted anything from the transmission of condemnation."

If he's equal to Christ, why does he come looking for Christ? Look, I'm telling you: the bridegroom, the Son of God who came in the flesh, is the savior both of the big and the little, both of adults and of infants, and that is who Christ is. But you say that Christ is the savior of adults, not of little ones; well, that isn't him. If it isn't him, you too are denying that Christ has come in the flesh.

Join an upright life to right faith, so that you may confess
that Christ has come in the flesh

13. And if we were to discuss all heresies, we would find they all deny Christ has come in the flesh. All heretics deny that Christ has come in the flesh. Why be surprised if the pagans deny that Christ has come in the flesh? Why be surprised if the Jews deny that Christ has come in the flesh? Why be surprised if the Manichees quite openly deny that Christ has come in the flesh? But I must tell your graces that all bad Catholics too confess in words that Christ has come in the flesh; but by their deeds they deny it. So don't be too smug, so to say, and

self-assured about the faith. Join an upright life to right faith, so that you may confess that Christ has come in the flesh, both by speaking the truth in words and by living a good life in deeds. Because if you confess it in words and deny it by deeds—the faith of such bad people is practically the same as the faith of demons.

Listen to me, dearly beloved, listen to me, or this sweat of mine may bear witness against you; listen to me. When the apostle James was talking about faith and works against those who thought their faith was enough, and didn't want to have good works, he said, *You believe that God is one; you do well; the demons too believe, and tremble* (Jas 2:19). Will the demons, do you suppose, be delivered from eternal fire, just because they believe and tremble? Look, there's what you heard just now in the gospel, what Peter said: *You are the Christ, the Son of the living God* (Mt 16:16); read, and you'll find the demons said, *We know who you are, the Son of God.* Peter, though, is praised, the demon put down. One voice, different deeds. What distinguishes these two confessions from each other? Love is praised, fear condemned. I mean, the demons didn't say this out of love, *You are the Son of God.* They said this out of fear, not love. Finally, in their confession they said, *What is there between us and you?* (Mk 1:24-25). But Peter said, *I am with you to the death* (Lk 22:33).

Peter's faith is the rock

14. But take Peter too, my brothers and sisters; from where did he get it that he could say out of love, *You are the Christ, the Son of the living God*? Where did he get it from? Really from his own resources? Perish the thought! It's just as well that this same passage of the gospel shows both things, what Peter got from God's, what from his own resources. You've got them both there; read; there's nothing you should be waiting to hear from me. I'll just remind you of the gospel: *You are the Christ, the Son of the living God.* And the Lord to him: *Blessed are you, Simon Bar-Jona.* Why? Blessed from your own resources? No. *Because flesh and blood has not revealed it to you*; that, after all, is what you are. *Flesh and blood has not revealed it to you, but my Father who is in heaven* (Mt 16:16-17). And he goes on to say more things which it would take too long to mention.

Shortly afterward, after these words of his in which he approved of Peter's faith and showed that it was the rock,[11] he began there and then to show his disciples that it would be necessary for him to come to Jerusalem, and suffer many things, and be rejected by the elders and the scribes and the priests, and be killed, and on the third day rise again. Then Peter, out of his own resources, was terrified, horrified at the thought of Christ's death, the sick man terrified of his own medicine. *Far be it from you, Lord*, he said; *do yourself a favor; this must not happen.*

And what about, *I have power to lay down my life, and I have power to take it up again* (Jn 10:18)? Have you forgotten, Peter? Have you forgotten *Greater love has no one than that one should lay down one's life for one's friends* (Jn

15:13)? You have forgotten. That forgetfulness came from what was his own; trepidation, horror, and fear of death, all from what was Peter's; or rather from what was Simon's, not Peter's. And the Lord: *Get back, Satan. Blessed are you, Simon Bar-Jona. Get back, Satan. Blessed are you, Simon Bar-Jona*; but that's from God. *Get back, Satan*; where's that from? Recollect why he was blessed. I have already said: *because flesh and blood did not reveal it to you, but my Father who is in heaven.* Why Satan? Let the Lord say why: *For you do not savor the things that are of God, but the things that are of men* (Mt 16:21-23).

Confess that Christ has come in the flesh,
both by believing and by living good lives

15. Hope in the Lord, and join good deeds to true faith. Confess that Christ has come in the flesh, both by believing and by living good lives, and hold on to both as received from him, and hope for both to be increased and perfected by him. For cursed is everyone who places his hope in man.[12] And it is good for any of us, that whoever boasts, should boast in the Lord.[13]

Turning to the Lord God the Father almighty, from a pure heart, as far as our littleness is able, let us give him the most sincere and true thanks; praying his singular gentleness with our whole hearts, that he would be pleased at his good pleasure to hearken to our prayers; that he would also drive the enemy away from our actions and thoughts with his great power; that he would increase our faith, guide our minds, grant us spiritual thoughts, and bring us to share in his own bliss; through Jesus Christ his Son. Amen.[14]

NOTES

1. See the previous sermon, note 1. This Sermon 183 was probably preached a week later; evidently not on the following day.

2. It was in fact one of his shorter sermons.

3. This, to our ears, rather gratuitous insult, is partly prompted by a chance for the kind of rhyming word-play he so loves. The two sentences run: *Quid istis convincendis quaerimus testes? Quis tot numerat pestes?*

4. As Augustine frequently points out, "confession" is used in two senses: confession of sins and confession of praise or of faith. In this sermon it is confession in the latter sense only that we are concerned with.

5. Christ as divine is truth. Man, whether Peter or Christ as human, is lowliness. Augustine accepts without question the traditional and tidy, but in fact mistaken, explanation of the titles Son of man and Son of God for Jesus as signifying respectively his humanity and his divinity. In fact, it would have been psychologically almost impossible, the revelation of "my Father" notwithstanding, for Peter at this stage to have recognized and expressed the divine nature or personality of Jesus. For him the title "Son of God" was simply reiterating in other words the title "the Christ." See for a source of the title in this sense Ps 2:7.

6. I have not come across any other reference in Augustine's works to this brand of Donatists.

7. I suppose by making a fuss when the guests are told, "If any here present do know of any reason why these two should not be joined together in holy matrimony, let them speak now or forever hold their peace." It is unlikely, of course, that that was quite the formula in Augustine's day; but weddings, no doubt, were sometimes rather roughly disrupted by disapproving relatives.

8. He is echoing the Song of Songs; for example, 2:14.

9. The marriage contract, which was read out at Roman weddings.

10. He is addressing the Donatist.

11. Notice, Augustine takes Peter's faith, not Peter himself, to be the rock on which the Church is to be built.

12. See Jer 17:5.

13. See 1 Cor 1:31.

14. For another place where this closing formula is used, see Sermon 15A, final note.

Augustine's proof in this sermon that only good Catholics really confess that Christ has come in the flesh, and his running through the list of those who don't: first heretics of various kinds, then Jews and pagans, reminds me in a back to front kind of way of Vatican II's Constitution on the Church, *Lumen Gentium*, chapter 2, sections 14-16, which discusses how all the different varieties of humanity, from Catholics, through other Christians bodies, to Jews, Moslems, other religions, and even atheists, are (or can be) somehow connected to the Church of God. Two very different approaches to the same problem. Are they mutually contradictory? Readers of both must decide for themselves.

CHRONOLOGICAL TABLE

Abbreviations of Names

(B)	Anne Marie La Bonnardière	(M)	Christine Mohrmann
(Ba)	Tarcisius van Bavel	(Maur)	Maurists
(Be)	Bonifatius Fischer (Beuron)	(Me)	Frits van der Meer
(D)	Michel Denis	(Mo)	Paul Monceau
(DB)	Donatien De Bruyne	(Mor)	Germain Morin
(Ét)	Raymond Étaix	(P)	Othmar Perler
(F)	Georges Folliet	(Po)	Suzanne Poque
(K)	Adalbert Kunzelmann	(V)	Pierre-Patrick Verbraken
(L)	Cyrille Lambot	(W)	André Wilmart

Abbreviations of Works

CCL	Corpus Christianorum, Series Latina (Turnhout-Paris, 1953ff.)
CSEL	Corpus Scriptorum Ecclesiasticorum Latinorum (Vienna, 1866ff.)
MA	*Miscellanea Agostiniana* (2 vols.; Rome, 1930-31). The first volume is *Sermones post Maurinos reperti,* ed. G. Morin
NBA	Nuova Biblioteca Agostiniana (Rome: Città Nuova Editrice)
PL	Patrologia Latina, ed. J.-P. Migne (Paris, 1878-90)
PLS	Patrologiae Latinae Supplementum, ed. A. Hamann (Paris, 1957ff.)
PW	*Paulys Realencyklopädie der klassischen Altertumswissenschaft,* new ed. by G. Wissowa et al. (Stuttgart, 1893ff.).
RB	*Revue Bénédictine* (Maredsous, 1884ff.).
SC	Sources Chrétiennes
SPM	Stromata Patristica et Mediaevalia 1 (= C. Lambot, *S. Aurelii Augustini Sermones selecti duodeviginti*) (Utrecht, 1950).

Short Titles of Frequently Cited Works

Borgomeo	*L'Eglise* P. Borgomeo, *L'Eglise de ce temps dans la prédication de saint Augustin* (Paris, 1972)
Mohrmann	*Etudes* C. Mohrmann, *Etudes sur le latin des chrétiens* I (Rome, 1958); II (Rome, 1961)
Mohrmann	*Sondersprache* C. Mohrmann, *Die altchristliche Sondersprache in den Sermones des hl. Augustinus* I. *Einfuhrung, Lexikologie, Wortbildung* (Latinitas Christianorum Primaeva 3; Nijmegen, 1932)
Pontet	*L'exégèse* M. Pontet, *L'exégèse de saint Augustin prédicateur* (Théologie 7; Paris, 1946)
Poque	*Augustin d'Hippone* S. Poque (ed.), *Augustin d'Hippone. Sermons pour la Paque* (SC 116; Paris, 1966)
Verbraken	*Etudes* P.-P. Verbraken, *Etudes critiques sur les sermons authentiques de saint Augustin* (Instrumenta Patristica 12; Steenbrugge-The Hague, 1976)

347

Nr.	Theme	Date	Edition
148	Acts 5:4	Sunday, Octave of Easter after 409 (L); from 412 (Po)	PL 38:799-800
149	Acts 10; Mt 5:16—6:4	c. 400 (Po) 412 (K, Be) Easter season (B)	PL 38:800-807
150	Acts 17:17-34	413-414	PL 38:807-814
151	Rom 7:15-25	September-October 418 (K, L) 419 (B, P)	PL 38:814-819
152	Rom 7:15—8:4	October 418 (K, L) 419 (B, P)	PL 38:819-825
153	Rom 7:5-13	October 13, 418 (K, L) October 419 (B)	PL 38:825-832
154	Rom 7:14-25	October 14, 418 (K, L) 419 (B)	PL 38:832-840
154/A	Rom 7:15 ff.	417 (K, Be)	Morin 4 MA 1:601-605 PLS 2:667-670
155	Rom 8:1-11	October 15, 417 (Maur) October 15, 418 (K, L) October 15, 419 (B, P)	PL 38:840-849
156	Rom 8:12-17	October 17, 417 (Maur) 418 (K, L, Be) 419 (B, P)	PL 38:849-859
157	Rom 8:24-25		PL 38:859-862
158	Rom 8:30-31	after 409 (Ro) 417 (B) 418 (K)	PL 38:862-867
159	Rom 8:30-31; Jas 1:2-4	before 409 (Ro) c. 418 (K, B, Be)	PL 38:867-872
160	1 Cor 1:31	c. June 24, 397 (L, P) 412-416 or 397 (Be)	PL 38:872-877
161	1 Cor 6:9-19		PL 38:877-884
162	1 Cor 6:9-18		PL 38, 885-889
162/A	1 Cor 12:31 ff.	401 (Mor) 404 (K, B, L, Be)	Denis 19 MA 1:98-111
162/B	2 Cor 5:20		PL 39:1709-1710
163	Gal 5:16-17	417	PL 38:889-895
163/A	Gal 5:16-17	one Sunday c. 416	Morin 10 MA 1:624-626 PLS 2,676-678
163/B	Gal 6:1-10	September 8, 410	Frangipane 5 MA 1:212-219
164	Gal 6:2-5	411	PL 38:895-902
164/A	Gal 6:9-10	during priestly ordination	Lambot 28 RB 66 (1956) 156-158
165	Eph 3:13-18; Rom 9:11	417	PL 38:902-907
166	Eph 4:25; Ps 115:11	Sunday, octave of Easter 410?	PL 38:907-909 SPM 1:61-63
167	Eph 5:15-16	410-412 (K, Be)	PL 38:909-911
167/A	Eph 6:12		PL 39:1733-1734
168	Eph 6:23	just before 416 (K, B, Be)	PL 38:911-915

Nr.	Theme	Date	Edition
169	Phil 3:3-16	416 (K, B, Be)	PL 38:915-926
170	Phil 3:3-15: Jn 6:39	c. 417	PL 38:926-933
171	Phil 4:4-6		PL 38:933-935
172	1 Thes 4:13	commemorating the dead (B)	PL 38:935-937
173	1 Thes 4:13	commemorating the dead c. 418 (B)	PL 38:937-939
174	1 Tm 1:15; Lk 19:1-10	one Sunday 411 or 413	PL 38:939-945
175	1 Tm 1:15-16	412 (K, Be)	PL 38:945-949
176	1 Tm 1:15-16 Lk 17:2-19	414 (K, Be)	PL 38:949-953
176/A	1 Tm 3:2		PL 39:1734
177	1 Tm 6:7-19	410-412 c. May 22/ June 24, 397 (L, P)	PL 38:953-960 SPM 1:64-73
178	Ti 1:9	after 396 (K, Be)	PL 38:960-966
179	Jas 1:19-22	before 405 (B) before 409 (Ro)	PL 38:966-972
179/A	Jas 2:10	before 410 (K, Be)	Wilmart 2 MA 1:673-680 PLS 2:708-715
180	Jas 5:12	414-415	PL 38:972-979
181	1 Jn 1:8-9	416-417	PL 38:979-984
182	1 Jn 4:1-3	after 416	PL 38:984-988
183	1 Jn 4:2	after 416 417 or 419? (B)	PL 38:988-994

For a complete Chronological Table refer to Section III, Volume I, pages 138-163.

INDEX OF SCRIPTURE

(The numbers after the scriptural reference refer to the particular sermon and its section)

Old Testament

Genesis

1:1	183, 4
2:2	179A, 3
2:17	152, 5
3:4-5	153, 11
3:5	163, 8
3:6	151, 5
3:7	151, 5
17:12	169, 3
22:16	180, 2
22:18	168, 1

Exodus

2:11	160, 3
3:14	156, 6
8:19	155, 3
20:4	179A, 3
20:7	179A, 3
20:12-17	179, 3
20:16	170, 5
20:17	152, 5; 169, 8; 170, 2
20:19	155, 6
31:18	155, 6
33:20	170, 9

Leviticus

12:3	169, 3

Deuteronomy

5:12	179A, 3
6:4	179A, 3
31:6.8	177, 11
32:39	169, 10

Joshua

1:5	177, 11
5:2	169, 3

1 Samuel

17:45	153, 11

Job

1:21	177, 4
7:1	163B, 4
14:4 LXX	181, 1

Psalms

1:2	149, 4; 153, 10
3:3	158, 9
5:3	169, 17
6:2-3	163, 7
8:5; 144:3	163, 12
10:3	153, 6; 163B, 5
13:3	159, 4
14:1	162, 1
16:5	156, 17
17:15	158, 7
18:1	150, 9
18:36	169, 15
18:43-44	158, 5
19:1.3-4	163, 5
19:3-4	171, 5
19:4.3	162A, 11
19:9	161, 9
23:3	177, 2
24:1	149, 3
24:10	160, 3
25:9	157, 2
26:2	159, 1
27:1	182, 5, 6
27:4	169, 16, 17
27:9	156, 11
27:14	157, 1; 170, 9
30:11-12	163, 3
32:4	175, 4
34:2	155, 4
34:5	176, 5; 182, 6
34:8	159, 4
34:15-16	161, 2

350

Daniel

13:35   156, 15

Hosea

13:14   151, 2, 3; 155, 2

Joel

2:32   169, 11

Habakkuk

2:4   158, 4

New Testament

Matthew

1:21   174, 8
5:6   179, 5
5:7   179A, 1
5:11-12   163B, 6
5:16   149, 11, 12, 14
5:17   155, 8
5:28   179, 7
5:33-37   180, 1
5:40   167, 4
5:43   149, 16
5:45   156, 2; 164A, 3, 4
6:1   149, 14
6:1.4   149, 11
6:3   149, 15
6:4   149, 12
6:9   156, 15; 170, 6; 177, 2
6:9-14   181, 6
6:12   155, 9; 163, 9; 163B, 3; 179A, 6
6:13   152, 2; 182, 4
6:21   177, 5
6:24   162, 3; 171, 1
7:7   159, 9; 163B, 2
7:11   159, 9
7:16   179, 10
7:23   154, 11
7:24-27   179, 8
8:10-11   179, 6
8:29   162A, 4
9:12   174, 8
10:16   175, 8
10:22   164, 8
10:27   159, 8
10:28   156, 8; 161, 5, 8
10:39   159, 8
11:9   154A, 5; 163B, 2
11:28   164, 4, 6
11:29   164, 6, 7
11:30   157, 2; 164, 7
12:28   155, 3
13:11-12   165, 4
15:23-24   154A, 5
15:26-28   154A, 5

16:13.16   183, 4
16:14-16   183, 3
16:15-17   168, 2
16:16   183, 13
16:16-17   158, 6; 162A, 4; 183, 14
16:17   158, 6
16:19   149, 7
16:21-23   183, 14
17:24-27   155, 7
19:16-17   150, 10
20:15   168, 4
20:22   160, 5
22:34   173, 1
22:37-40   149, 18
22:37.39-40   179A, 3
22:41   173, 1
23:3   179, 10
24:12   165, 4
24:13   165, 4
25:1-8   163B, 6
25:26-27   179, 7
25:31-46   178, 4
25:35-45   162A, 5
25:40   179, 3
26:39   160, 5

Mark

1:24   168, 2
1:25   158, 6
1:24-25   183, 13
2:11   155, 12
2:16   175, 3
2:17   156, 2; 169, 11; 176, 2
3:11   168, 2
10:14   174, 9
11:9   154A, 5

Luke

1:6   169, 6
1:35   153, 14
2:29-30   163, 4
3:6   153, 8
6:21   175, 2
6:27   164A, 2, 4
6:38.37   179A, 1, 6
8:4   159, 4
10:24   163, 4
10:27.29   171, 2
10:35   179A, 7
10:38-42   169, 17
10:41-42   179, 3
10:42   179, 4, 6
11:9   163B, 2
11:20   155, 3
11:26   155, 13
12:4-5   161, 8
12:16-19   178, 2
12:20   178, 2
12:37   179, 6
13:16   162B, 1
14:11   179, 3

INDEX

(prepared by Joseph Sprug)